Accounting Information Systems

Basic Concepts and Current Issues

Accounting Information Systems

Basic Concepts and Current Issues   *Third Edition*

Robert L. Hurt
California State Polytechnic University, Pomona

The McGraw·Hill Companies

McGraw-Hill
Irwin

ACCOUNTING INFORMATION SYSTEMS: BASIC CONCEPTS AND CURRENT ISSUES,
THIRD EDITION

2 3 4 5 6 7 8 9 0 QVR/LEH 1 0 9 8 7 6 5 4 3 2

ISBN 978-0-07-802533-4
MHID 0-07-802533-8

Vice President & Editor-in-Chief: *Brent Gordon*
Vice President of Specialized Publishing: *Janice M. Roerig-Blong*
Publisher: *Tim Vertovec*
Sponsoring Editor: *Daryl Bruflodt*
Marketing Coordinator: *Colleen P. Havens*
Project Manager: *Melissa M. Leick*
Design Coordinator: *Brenda A. Rolwes*
Cover Designer: *Studio Montage, St. Louis, Missouri*
Cover Image Credit: *© Getty Images / Stockbyte RF*
Buyer: *Nicole Baumgartner*
Media Project Manager: *Balaji Sundararaman*
Compositor: *Laserwords Private Limited*
Typeface: *10/12 TimesLTStd-Roman*
Printer: *Quad/Graphics*

Library of Congress Cataloging-in-Publication Data

Hurt, Robert L.
    Accounting information systems: basic concepts and current issues / Robert L. Hurt.—3rd ed.
      p. cm.
    ISBN 978-0-07-802533-4 (alk. paper)
      1. Accounting—Data processing. 2. Information storage and retrieval systems—Accounting.   I. Title.
HF5679.H865 2013
657.0285—dc23
                                                     2011039785

Preface

To the Instructor

Greetings, colleagues . . .

Thank you for your interest in the third edition of this book—and a special thank you to those of you who have used it in your classes since the first edition. I appreciate the constructive comments many of you have offered via e-mail, reviews, and phone conversations; I've incorporated many of them in this new edition, resulting in a strong AIS text that offers you plenty of flexibility to tailor the course to your own preferences and needs.

With each edition, I've made changes to the organization and table of contents of the book. I know that can present a challenge to folks who have used the earlier editions, but I believe the changes I've made each time have enhanced both the content and organization of the text. I'm quite content with those elements of this edition and foresee no future changes to the organization or table of contents of the book.

The book retains its conversational style, as well as its applied orientation, while continuing to offer the fundamentals of AIS in a cohesive way that students will appreciate. I think this edition, more so than the previous two, captures the interdisciplinary nature of AIS. You'll notice an entirely new chapter titled "Management Concepts" in Part One; that chapter combines material from the previous editions (enterprise risk management and business process management) with new material (expectancy theory). To keep the size of the text (and therefore its cost to students) reasonable, I've combined material on professionalism, ethics, and career planning into a single chapter in Part Five. Many of you have said covering all the chapters is a challenge in a single term, so I hope that change will assist you in that regard.

I'm also particularly excited about three other features of this new edition. First, starting in Chapter 9, each chapter includes an exercise that requires students to revisit prior material; I believe this feature will discourage them from doing a "within course memory dump." Second, I've created an AIS blog that, while independent of the text, is closely related to it. I hope the blog will accomplish two goals: (1) give us a better way to dialogue about AIS and the text and (2) allow me to provide updates and additional material in a much more reliable way. Finally, I'm very delighted to say that the publisher has restored the computerized test bank in the third edition. I've rewritten the test bank completely, while still retaining its essential features from the first two editions. Each chapter's test bank includes 50 multiple choice questions, 10 problems, and 5 short answer questions. Each question is tagged with the related learning objective, a difficulty level, and the appropriate level of Bloom's taxonomy to assist in your assessment efforts.

As always, I welcome your comments, constructive criticisms, suggestions for improvement, and other feedback.

Bob Hurt
(RLHurt@csupomona.edu)

About the Author

Dr. Robert L. Hurt *California State Polytechnic University, Pomona*
Robert L. Hurt is Professor of Accounting in the College of Business Administration at California State Polytechnic University Pomona, where he teaches Accounting Information Systems, Forensic Accounting, and Government Accounting. Dr. Hurt received his Ph.D. in Management with a concentration in information science from Claremont Graduate University. He also holds an M.S. in Business Administration (concentration in business education) from Cal Poly Pomona and a B.S. in Business Administration (concentration in accounting) from Southeast Missouri State University.

Hallmarks of Dr. Hurt's classroom approach include utilizing active learning, developing students' critical thinking skills, and incorporating information technology to enhance the teaching/learning environment. Dr. Hurt's courses are also competency based to help students focus their efforts on important skills.

Dr. Hurt is published in the *Journal of Accounting Case Research, Strategic Finance, NACADA Journal,* and *Journal of Education for Business.* Bob is active with the Association of Certified Fraud Examiners and the National Academic Advising Association.

Acknowledgments

We could not produce a textbook of the quality and scope of *Accounting Information Systems: Basic Concepts and Current Issues* without the help of a great number of people.

The efforts of many people are needed to develop and improve a text. Among these people are the reviewers who point out areas of concern and areas of strength and make recommendations for change. The following professors provided feedback that was enormously helpful in preparing the third edition of *Accounting Information Systems: Basic Concepts and Current Issues.*

Tanya Benford
Florida Gulf Coast University
Mark Best
The University of Kansas School of Business
Dr. Passard C. Dean
Saint Leo University
Dr. Marina Grau
Houston Community College
Andrew Griffith
Iona College
James E. Groff
University of Texas–San Antonio
Lois S. Mahoney
Eastern Michigan University
Ann O'Brien
University of Wisconsin–Madison
Robert L. Osborne
Ohio Dominican University

Michael Prindle
Simpson College
Vasant Raval
College of Business Administration–Creighton University
Michael Ridenour
Pennsylvania State University–Fayette Campus
Jason L. Smith
University of Nevada–Las Vegas
Dan Stone
University of Kentucky
Eileen Z. Taylor
North Carolina State University
James F. Waegelein
Emporia State University
Linda Wallace
Virginia Tech

I am grateful for the outstanding support from McGraw-Hill. In particular I would like to thank Tim Vertovec, Publisher; Daryl Bruflodt, Sponsoring Editor; Janice Hansen, Editorial Assistant; Jennifer Lewis, Director of Marketing and Sales; Colleen Havens, Marketing Campaign Coordinator; Melissa Leick, Project Manager; Brenda A. Rolwes, Design Coordinator; and Balaji Sundararaman, Media Project Manager. All contributed significantly to the project, and I appreciate their efforts.

Walkthrough

What's New in This Edition!

Features

- *Text organization*. The third edition is once again organized in five parts, but the material within each part has been shifted.
- *New chapter*. The third edition includes an entirely new chapter titled "Management Concepts." It discusses enterprise risk management, business process management, and expectancy theory, giving the third edition an interdisciplinary lens for considering AIS topics.
- *Flowcharting*. The chapter on flowcharting has been updated and revised to make the process more understandable for students. I am deeply indebted to Dr. Kathy Hurtt of Baylor University for helping me focus my thinking on this important topic. (And, in case you were wondering, she's not related to me.)
- *Business process chapters reorganized*. The three chapters on business processes have been reorganized to reflect more closely the generic AIS structure discussed in Chapter 1.
- *Prior material application*. Starting in Chapter 9, every chapter includes this problem type. These problems help students apply fundamentals from previous chapters, such as the generic structure of AIS and systems development life cycle, to later topics in the course.
- *Multiple choice questions*. Every chapter now includes two sets of multiple choice questions. The first, titled "Multiple Choice Review," appears early in the end-of-chapter materials; answers to the multiple choice review questions can be found near the end of the text. The second set, "Multiple Choice Questions," focuses on higher-order thinking.
- Every chapter has an updated "AIS in the Business World," along with many new problems.

AIS blog

I've created an AIS blog that, while independent of the text, is related to it. Many of the exercises in the third edition refer to the blog; its URL is bobhurtais.blogspot.com.

Computerized test bank

After an absence from the second edition, a computerized test bank is once again available.

Overall Features

Readability

The writing style has been highly praised. Students easily comprehend chapter concepts because of the conversational tone. The author has made every effort to ensure that the writing style remains engaging, lively, and consistent.

Philosophy

The text emphasizes the art of AIS over its "science." It helps students begin to develop their professional judgment as accountants, rather than encouraging them to memorize examples and solutions.

Structure

The text puts the most important, fundamental topics first, followed by applications in transaction cycles. Nice-to-know topics are included and can be covered or not at the instructor's discretion.

Content

The text incorporates modeling techniques and information technology, but at a level appropriate for accountants rather than CIS majors/professionals. The second edition discusses and applies the systems development life cycle, tying it clearly and directly to accounting. While remaining true to its accounting roots, the text moves beyond a strict accounting orientation; it integrates information technology, behavioral issues, management concerns, quantitative reasoning, and ideas from business law and ethics. Thus, students will have a clear grasp of how AIS concepts impact business practice, regardless of the organizational contexts where they pursue their careers.

Chapter Features

Real-World Examples

Each chapter opens with an illustrative vignette about an AIS issue/concept—in most chapters, those vignettes are based on actual organizations. Thus, students develop a clearer understanding of how AIS works in the "real world."

Chapter **Thirteen**

Acquisition/Payment Process

AIS in the Business World

Home Depot

My brother used to work for a Home Depot Distribution Center (www.homedepot.com). The basic job of a distribution center (DC) is to coordinate inventory between suppliers and retail Home Depot stores. The corporate office orders merchandise from various suppliers and arranges for its shipment to a DC based on location and merchandise type. When it arrives at the DC, the merchandise is unloaded and processed by the receiving department; bar codes tell where the merchandise should be shelved within the DC, which is the size of several football fields.

Orders come in from the retail stores to the DC on a daily basis. DC inventory workers use handheld devices to locate the required merchandise; the DC's information system lists the merchandise for each order in a specific sequence to minimize travel time throughout the DC. Once all the related goods for an order have been "picked" from the shelves, the same inventory worker stages them. Shipping clerks then load the staged merchandise on trucks, which deliver it to the retail stores. Neither the trucks that bring the merchandise to the DC nor the trucks that carry the merchandise away from it are owned by Home Depot. Rather, they contract with independent carriers for that purpose.

From Home Depot's point of view, those steps are associated with our topic for this chapter: the acquisition/payment process. Note that the acquisition/payment process is the flip side of the sales/collection process we discussed in the last chapter.

Discussion Questions

1. Which activities in Porter's value chain are associated with the acquisition/payment process?
2. What are the steps involved in the acquisition/payment process?
3. How are the five generic parts of the AIS discussed in Chapter 1 applied/exemplified within the context of the acquisition/payment process?

229

Reflection and Critical Thinking

Each chapter presents basic ideas and then encourages students to reflect on those ideas. "Reflection and Self-Assessment" activities throughout each chapter will help students think critically about the material. In addition, each chapter now includes a "critical thinking" application that gets students started down that path.

Reflection and Self-Assessment	6.1

What type of flowchart would be most appropriate in each of the following situations?

1. Steps in a Visual Basic program for producing financial statements.
2. Steps associated with purchasing inventory.
3. Relationships between a central server and desktop computers.
4. Path of a sales invoice through an information system.
5. Origination, processing, and termination of a payroll check.
6. Local area network configuration.
7. Employee evaluation process.

End-of-Chapter Activities

The homework material remains a strength of the text. The shear number of questions, problems, and Internet assignments will test and therefore expand the students' knowledge of chapter concepts. Further, many chapters include questions and problems that refer back to earlier material in the text and earlier courses in the accounting curriculum to discourage students from doing a "memory wipe" once they've studied a particular topic.

End-of-
Chapter
Activities

1. *Reading review questions.*
   a. What is a flowchart? Describe four different kinds of flowcharts and explain which are most often used in an accounting information system.
   b. Summarize the rules and conventions commonly observed in the preparation of flowcharts.
   c. List and explain the meaning and use of 10 common flowcharting symbols. What sources would you consult for learning about additional symbols not on your list?
   d. How are flowcharts used in working with accounting information systems?
   e. Respond to the questions for this chapter's "AIS in the Business World."

2. *Reading review problem.* The Sarbanes-Oxley Act of 2002 (SOX) was a reaction to the corporate accounting scandals of the late 20th century. In discussing some of the positive results of SOX, Harrington stated:

   Companies can find additional uses for Sarbanes-Oxley documentation as a tool for audit committees, a way to enhance employee decisions based on cross-function process information and a means of increasing efficiencies by eliminating duplicate controls. Alltel Corporation (www.alltel.com) documented 100 company processes within the scope of [SOX]. Alltel's internal audit team reports to the company's audit committee. Its process documentation includes six flowcharts per process, supported by memos and narratives. The audit committee can use this information to support its decisions.

   She concluded her article with these summary comments:

   CPAs can use the documentation to provide audit committees with more detailed information, to empower all employees to consider cross-functional processes and to lead the entire company in using section-404-type documentation. Since there is no way to avoid the cost, companies might just as well find ways to spread the expenditures over this greater array of benefits.

   So, flowcharts aren't just something you study in AIS class. In fact, in a survey conducted by Bradford, Richtermeyer, and Roberts, nearly half of the respondents reported using flowcharts to document accounting information systems.

   Sources: Cynthia Harrington, "The Value Proposition," *Journal of Accountancy* (September 2005), pp. 77–81; Marianne Bradford, Sandra B. Richtermeyer, and Douglas F. Roberts, "System Diagramming Techniques: An Analysis of Methods Used in Accounting Education and Practice," *Journal of Information Systems* (Spring 2007), pp. 173–212.

   a. Which type(s) of flowcharts discussed in the chapter would be relevant in this case? Explain your response.
   b. SOX imposes serious requirements regarding internal control on publicly-traded corporations. Those requirements include the CEO and CFO personally reviewing the company's internal control system, identifying weaknesses and known cases of fraud. Suppose you were creating a systems flowchart depicting a typical SOX process; identify three or four symbols you would expect to use in that flowchart, and explain how you would use them.

3. Multiple choice review questions. Please select the best answer for each question.
   1. Which of the following best describes a systems flowchart?
      a. Shows the flow of documents through an information system.
      b. Shows the logic used to create a program.
      c. Shows the "big picture" view.
      d. Shows how hardware elements are configured in a system.
   2. Which of the following statements about "white space" in a flowchart is most true?
      a. White space prohibits the use of color in flowcharts.
      b. At least 50 percent of the page should be devoted to white space.

Supplements

For the Instructor

Instructor's Online Learning Center (www.mhhe.com/hurt3e) includes:

Instructor's Resource and Solutions Manual includes the solutions to all the discussion questions, end-of-chapter questions and problems, and reflection and self-assessment questions.

Test Bank includes a substantial number of questions in each chapter offering a large pool of material to choose from when creating a test.

EZTest Computerized Test Bank can be used to create different versions of the same test, change the answer order, edit and add questions, and conduct online testing.

PowerPoint Presentations deliver a complete set of slides covering many of the key concepts presented in each chapter.

For the Student

PowerPoint Presentations (www.mhhe.com/hurt3e) are available on the Student Center of the text's Online Learning Center. These presentations accompany each chapter of the text and contain the same slides that are available to the instructor.

Technology

Online Learning Center

www.mhhe.com/hurt3e

For instructors, the book's Web site contains, the Instructor's Solutions Manual, Power-Point slides, Test Bank, EZTest software, Text and Supplement Updates, and links to professional resources.

The student section of the site features online chapter quizzing activities, including a multiple-choice quiz to accompany each chapter of text. PowerPoint presentations are also available to download. The author has listed several important links relating to text and professional material.

Message from the Author

To the Student

Welcome to the study of accounting information systems (AIS) and the third edition of this book! You've embarked on the first stage of a lifelong education about accounting; AIS touches every area of professional practice, so what you learn in this class will be relevant to you whether your career takes you into public accounting, the corporate world, governmental and not-for-profit accounting, or some other area of practice.

I heard from several students who used the previous editions of the book, and I've incorporated many of their suggestions and ideas in this new edition. I've also retained the features from prior editions they found most useful. Here's a list of some of the guiding principles I had in mind as I prepared this new edition for you:

- At its core, AIS is about critical thinking and judgment—it's not fundamentally about journal entries and information technology, although both those and other traditional accounting topics are important in AIS. I've included several activities to help you develop your professional judgment and critical thinking skills because I think the best way to develop those skills is to practice them; I encourage you to "think out loud" with both your fellow scholars and your professors.

- In AIS, many problems have more than one acceptable solution. But don't take that to mean that every solution is acceptable! In other words, a problem might have several "right" answers—but some answers are clearly "wrong."

- For many accounting students, reading an accounting textbook ranks at about the same place as having a root canal at the dentist's office. As in the previous editions, I've tried to use a lively, conversational tone that will make reading this text easier for you.

- You want to know that what you learn in school has clear, direct relevance to your career. So, I've used plenty of examples from the literature, my own professional experience, and the professional experience of friends and colleagues with that goal in mind.

AIS will likely be very different than your other accounting courses, in both its content and approach. I think I've written a text that will facilitate your learning and professional development; I hope you'll take the time to provide me feedback about this new edition. Please drop me an e-mail (RLHurt@csupomona.edu) to let me know how I can improve the book in the future. While I cannot promise a response to every single e-mail, I'll do my best to acknowledge your questions/comments and incorporate them in subsequent editions of the text.

Dr. Bob Hurt, C.F.E.

Brief Contents

Contents

Part One

AIS Fundamentals

The ideas in these chapters are fundamental to the study of accounting information systems, regardless of approach or philosophy. They define the nature of accounting information systems, review the accounting cycle, analyze various schools of ethical thought and provide a firm foundation in internal controls. They also begin developing the idea that accounting information systems (AIS) is a multidisciplinary field by examining relevant concepts from both management and information systems. While these chapters present the topics at a basic level, the material is reinforced and applied in various contexts throughout the rest of the text.

Chapter One

Role and Purpose of Accounting Information Systems

AIS in the Business World

Richie's Diner

Virtually every Sunday morning, my brother and I go out for breakfast. Our usual "haunt" is Richie's Diner in Rancho Cucamonga, California. You can learn more about them at www.richiesdiner.com/. We're always seated with one of our two favorite servers (Nicole or Yolanda), whom we've known for several years. Richie's has a fairly standard process for serving food that goes something like this:

1. Seat customers.
2. Give each customer a menu.
3. Take the customer's drink order.
4. Take the customer's food order.
5. Prepare the food.
6. Deliver the food to the table.
7. Present the bill at the end of the meal.
8. Collect payment.

Servers record drink and food orders on paper; the kitchen uses those orders to prepare the food. Servers use copies of the orders to prepare the bill. Customers are supposed to pay at the cash register, but many give their credit card or cash to the server for processing.

The purpose of this text is to help you understand how companies like Richie's account for their various transactions—not just the debits and credits, but the documents, tools, and controls they use that ultimately produce general-purpose financial statements and other reports. Each chapter opens with a short vignette like this one, followed by some discussion questions to stimulate your thinking.

Discussion Questions

1. What are the essential elements of an accounting information system?
2. How do examples of those elements change for different businesses?
3. Does the presence or absence of computers and other forms of information technology determine whether or not a business has an accounting information system?

We'll explore various kinds of audits and their relationship to the AIS in Chapter 17.

Welcome to the study of accounting information systems (AIS)! AIS is a critically important area of study for future accountants. It ties together what accounting students often see as separate, unrelated areas of accounting: financial, managerial, tax, and governmental. Additionally, AIS brings in considerations from management, finance, and information systems. Finally, a deep, fundamental comprehension of accounting information systems is a great help in the study of auditing.

You'll often hear the phrase "single, correct, deterministic responses" throughout this text— that's another way of saying there is "one right answer."

Many accounting students are drawn to the discipline because of its perceived objectivity; they like solving problems that have "right answers." And your prior study of accounting may have focused on such problems. But, in practice, such problems are few and far between. And even when they exist, you won't be able to look up the right answer in a textbook or solutions manual. Problems and issues in accounting information systems seldom have single, correct, deterministic responses. So, to get you ready to confront and respond to those kinds of problems in practice, I'm including many of them in this textbook. One of this book's main purposes is to help you develop professional judgment and confidence in your ability to analyze **unstructured problems**.

Examples of structured questions with deterministic responses include the following: How much cash is in the bank at a given point in time? What are the three parts of a balance sheet? Unstructured, nondeterministic questions, on the other hand, require critical thinking. They include questions like this: What documentation tool should I use to design an AIS and/or to describe a business process? What internal controls should be implemented for a business process?

You'll find a paragraph like this one at the beginning of every chapter in the book. The enumerated items are often referred to as "learning objectives" or "expected student outcomes."

When you've finished studying this chapter, and completing the activities at its conclusion, you should be able to:

1. Define "accounting information systems."
2. Discuss why AIS is an important area of study for future accountants.
3. Compare and contrast AIS with other areas of study in accounting.
4. Explain the structure of most accounting information systems.
5. Locate and evaluate information sources on accounting information systems.
6. Describe the structure and content of the remainder of this text.

Different university accounting curricula place the AIS course differently. In some schools, AIS is the first course accounting majors take after the introductory sequence. In other programs, AIS is near the end of the required sequence. And you'll find some schools allow students discretion in the timing of AIS study. In my university, students study AIS early in their accounting education—within one or two terms of completing their introductory sequence. But this book can be used in any of the three frameworks mentioned above.

As you can probably tell already, I tend to write in a conversational tone—as if I'm talking to you. I've found students appreciate such an approach, and that it motivates them to read the text more systematically and regularly. If something in the text seems unclear, or could be stated differently to enhance your understanding, I encourage you to contact me with your thoughts. My e-mail is RLHurt@csupomona.edu. While I can't promise a response to every e-mail I receive, I can promise every one will receive serious consideration in future editions of the text. You're also welcome to try calling my office if there's something you'd like to discuss in "real time." Please visit my Web page (www.csupomona .edu/~rlhurt) for my office phone and office hours.

DEFINITION AND IMPORTANCE OF AIS

You've probably heard of the FASB by this time in your accounting education. It develops the rules we use to prepare financial statements. You can learn more about them at their Web site (www.fasb.org).

An **accounting information system** is a set of interrelated activities, documents, and technologies designed to collect data, process it, and report information to a diverse group of internal and external decision makers in organizations. A well-designed AIS can significantly enhance decision making in organizations in several ways, including responding to many elements of the Financial Accounting Standards Board Conceptual Framework.

FASB developed the **conceptual framework** in the late 1970s as a guide for the development of future accounting principles. While the jury is still out on whether the conceptual framework has fulfilled that purpose, it is a fundamental part of accounting practice. You also can be fairly confident that you'll see questions on the conceptual framework on most accounting professional exams (CPA, CMA, and the like).

Detailed study of the conceptual framework often comprises the first part of intermediate accounting, so we won't go into great detail on it here. Basically, the conceptual framework looks like the one shown in Figure 1.1. The framework has three levels. The first, at the top of the triangle, explains what accounting is trying to do: provide information for decisions. The second level presents two sets of ideas: What information does accounting provide (elements of financial statements), and what characteristics should the information have to make it useful for decisions (qualitative characteristics)? The third level of the framework highlights some ideas that pervade accounting and the design of accounting information systems (assumptions, principles, and constraints).

Reflection and Self-Assessment   1.1

Which terms in the conceptual framework do you recognize from your previous accounting courses? Which ones are unfamiliar? Do some research and define or give examples of at least three of the latter.

A well-designed accounting information system relates to the conceptual framework by

- *Capturing data on the elements of financial statements.* No matter what form they take or information technologies they use, accounting information systems document changes in assets, liabilities, equity, revenues, expenses, gains, and losses. Many continue to use a traditional debit/credit format for doing so, although some scholars in the area have suggested that debits and credits may have less relevance in the future.
- *Transforming those data into relevant and reliable information.* Well-designed accounting information systems also can gather data beyond the elements of financial statements. Items like sales by geographic area, customer characteristics and transaction histories, demand for inventory items, and vendor quality ratings can improve decision making by enhancing the elements of relevance: predictive value, feedback value, and timeliness. Additionally, internal controls in the accounting information system promote reliability (verifiability, neutrality, and representational faithfulness), as you'll see in later chapters.
- *Recognizing and adapting to the cost–benefit constraint.* Accounting information systems are all about choices and trade-offs: What data should I capture? What information technologies should I use to process them? What information should I report? Looking at the conceptual framework diagram in Figure 1.1, you'll see "cost-effectiveness" as one of the

FIGURE 1.1   An Overview and Summary of the FASB Conceptual Framework

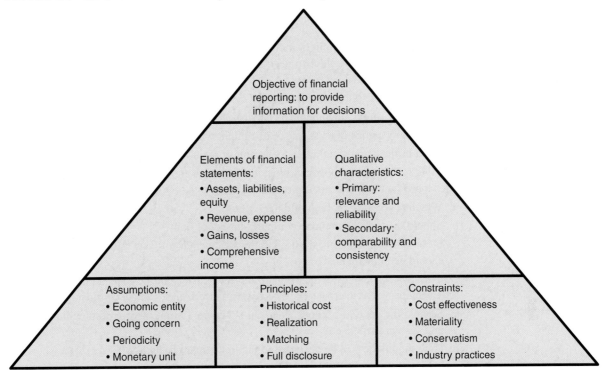

constraints on accounting information. Cost-effectiveness reminds us that we can't design the world's perfect accounting information system. Even in the best organizations with the most effective systems, you'll find managers who want more data or different data, who question the system's integrity, and/or who want business processes to be structured differently. As a designer, implementer, and interpreter of accounting information systems, always keep in mind that the benefit of having data, processes, and information must outweigh the costs of obtaining or implementing them. Those costs and benefits might be economic, behavioral, psychological, or financial, but they should always be considered.

Next, let's think about the structure of a "typical" accounting information system.

AIS STRUCTURE

I often refer to "organizations" rather than "companies" or "businesses." That's because every organization needs an AIS, but not all organizations are "businesses."

An accounting information system is a set of interrelated activities, documents, and technologies designed to collect data, process them, and report information to a diverse group of internal and external decision makers in organizations. Most accounting information systems comprise five parts, as shown in Figure 1.2.

FIGURE 1.2
Generic AIS
Structure

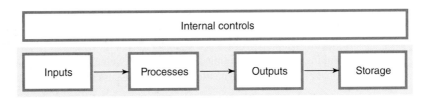

Each part of the **AIS structure** plays a vital role in its overall efficiency and effectiveness. And each part is filled with the kinds of design choices and cost–benefit trade-offs mentioned earlier. Consider the questions below to illustrate them:

1. *Inputs.* Inputs to an AIS might include documents such as sales invoices and purchase orders. Accountants would also need to ask questions like these to design and/or audit the system:

   a. What kinds of source documents will system users need?

   b. Should the source documents be paper-based, electronic, or both?

   c. How many copies of each source document will be required?

   d. What information should the documents contain?

2. *Processes.* Processing tools can include computers and satellites. Here are some other questions you might ask about processing tools:

   a. Which processing tools should the AIS use?

   b. Should the tools be manual, computer-based, or both?

   c. If computer-based tools are used in the AIS, which software and hardware packages should be implemented?

3. *Outputs.* System outputs for most organizations would include the general-purpose financial statements as well as internal reports such as variance analyses. Other considerations include

   a. Beyond the general-purpose financial statements, what other reports will managers and system users need?

   b. How should the AIS be designed to facilitate their production?

4. *Storage.* Data in an accounting information system could be stored in paper form, electronically, or a mix of both. If the data are stored electronically, they are often broken down into three broad file types. Master files typically contain data about "things," such as inventory, customers, and vendors. Transaction files usually focus on "activities," such as earning revenue and incurring expenses. Junction files link other files together, as you'll see later in the text. Relevant questions about storage include

   a. How should data be stored? On paper? Electronically? Both?

   b. Where should data be stored? Locally? Remotely? Both?

   c. How long should data be stored?

   d. Under what conditions can/should data be destroyed?

5. *Internal controls.* We'll explore internal controls in much greater depth later in the text. Most organizations employ internal controls such as daily backup of data and separation of duties (custody, authority, and recordkeeping) to maintain control over specific assets. Other questions might be

   a. What controls are necessary to promote information integrity in the AIS?

   b. What behavioral effects are the controls likely to have?

   c. Are the controls cost-effective?

The preceding questions don't have clear-cut, easy, simplistic answers. They do have "common" or "usual" answers, and that's part of what you'll learn throughout this course. But the rest of what you'll learn may be even more important. You'll learn how to make choices and judgments within the context of accounting information systems—choices and judgments that may not be perfect but that you'll be able to explain, along with their costs and benefits. Additionally, you'll be able to critique and evaluate the choices made by others. At first blush, that kind of thinking may seem daunting. Try to set aside your anxiety so you can think critically. Recognize that even seasoned professionals have to discuss and debate ideas to solve problems.

How do you feel about starting a course that doesn't have clear-cut, easy, simplistic answers? What study tools and techniques could you use to develop your ability to respond to open-ended questions?

So, to move you forward toward that goal, let's examine places (other than this book) where you can find information about AIS, as well as some guidelines for evaluating that information.

AIS INFORMATION SOURCES AND INFORMATION LITERACY CONCEPTS

If you're like some of my students, you may have heard about information literacy in a philosophy or English class. So, you may be wondering why we're talking about it in AIS. Here's the connection: Accounting information systems is a rapidly changing field; with the possible exception of forensic accounting and fraud examination, it may be the newest field of study for accounting students. And, to a greater degree than with other areas of accounting, practitioners and professors alike take different approaches to it. So, throughout the course, you'll often be called upon to do research as part of answering questions/responding to problems/preparing projects.

When your professor assigns a research or current article project, where is the first place you look? If you're like most accounting students, you answered, "the Internet." And, since AIS is such a "hot topic" in today's business world, you're bound to find tons of

Society is full of urban legends that may or may not be true. For example, some people believe the Earth is flat. Others believe that the first U.S. landing on the moon was nothing more than a hoax. Choose one of those urban legends or some other you prefer. Find an information source that attempts to assess its validity, and comment on the believability of the source.

According to Dictionary.com, "validity" refers to something that is well grounded or something that is binding. Although validity doesn't appear formally in the conceptual framework, it is definitely implied—particularly by the qualitative characteristics of accounting information.

information on it there. But you're probably not surprised to learn that not all information on the Internet is valid, trustworthy, or reliable. In other words, you can't necessarily believe everything you read on the Internet. You should evaluate information critically for yourself, rather than believe everything you read on the Internet.

Basically, information about accounting information systems on the Internet falls into three main groups: sponsored information, popular/practitioner information, and scholarly information. Let's consider the identifiers of each group as objectively as possible, then talk about how to evaluate information you find on the Internet (and, indeed, in other places).

Sponsored/commercial information means that someone has paid a fee or given other consideration to have their information put on the Internet. The main purpose of sponsored/commercial information is to sell products and services. Often, Internet users can access this information free of charge, which may give it the appearance of being objective. Sponsored information sites aren't necessarily 100 percent biased, but they may limit the information they disseminate or the choices available to Internet users. Again, the point isn't to reject all sponsored information sites "out of hand" for research and information purposes; the point is to evaluate them critically using guidelines we'll look at in a few paragraphs. www.investopedia.com is an example of sponsored/commercial information. So, for example, if you were looking for information on a particular piece of software, you might be looking at sponsored/commercial information. Suppose you were investigating various general ledger software packages, such as QuickBooks and Peachtree. You'd expect to get a lot of information from the companies that publish the software, although that information might paint a more optimistic, positive picture than a third-party review.

Popular/practitioner information has gone through a review process prior to publication. It may recount the experiences of a specific company or group of companies, offer suggestions to managers, or present new ideas or ways of thinking. Because popular/practitioner information has passed through a review process prior to publication, it's usually more trustworthy and objective than sponsored information on the Internet. But you should always ask yourself about the author's motivation and the context of the information. For example, if an article talks about the successful implementation of an enterprise resource planning system, consider (among other things) whether the author works for the ERP vendor, the size and industry of the organization, and the resources (human, technological, and monetary) devoted to the project. Consider the Web site for the *Journal of Accountancy* (www.aicpa.org/pubs/jofa/joahome.htm) in this category. If you were responding to a problem about how things happen in practice, such as how companies deal with internal control issues in an e-business environment, you'd probably consult popular/practitioner information.

Scholarly information also has gone through a review process prior to publication. As a future accountant, you may only rarely access scholarly information on AIS. Generally, scholarly information contains a clear research question, a review of related literature, a thorough description of the methods used to answer the question, and the results and conclusions of the research project. This additional detail is necessary so that readers can more easily evaluate the results and conclusions in light of the methodology; the review of related literature helps carve out the "value added" by an individual article in light of what other authors have discovered/written about a topic. *Business Ethics Quarterly* (www.pdcnet.org/beq.html) is a scholarly publication focused on various aspects of business ethics. A lot of scholarly information may be difficult for you to understand; it's often written by people with advanced degrees, for people with advanced degrees. However, if written clearly and simply, you may benefit from reading the results and/or conclusions of a scholarly research study—particularly if you're looking for "hard evidence" on a topic (such as how people from different cultures respond to ethics issues).

Evaluating information reliability on the Internet comes under the broad heading of "information literacy" or "information competence." For ease of discussion, I'll use the term **information competence** (IC) here, but you're likely to hear both terms in conversation about this topic. IC is much, much broader than the evaluation of information reliability, but we'll limit our discussion here to that aspect of it. According to the California State University's Work Group on Information Competence (Curzon, 1995), it is "the ability to find, evaluate, use, and communicate information in all of its various formats."

Why is information competence important in the study of accounting information systems? AIS is full of emerging concepts, ideas, and issues. Answers to the problems you'll

---

Depending on the kinds of assignments your instructor gives you this term, you may find yourself doing a lot of research for this class. The point of this section of the chapter is to give you tools to evaluate the information you find during your research— to think about it critically, rather than assuming it's all "true" on its face.

If you'd like to learn more about information competence in general and assess the degree to which you have it, I encourage you to visit the American Association of School Librarians' Web site on the topic: www.ala.org/ala/aasl/aaslproftools/informationpower/informationliteracy.htm.

Your university library probably has numerous materials on information literacy as well; most librarians are well versed in the topic and eager to share their knowledge with students.

confront in this class are not always found in textbooks but may require significant research. Evaluating the validity of sources you encounter in that research is a critical skill for reaching reliable conclusions and finding genuinely valuable information.

You'll also find a lot of resources about this important topic at www .calstate.edu/LS/ Tutorials.shtml.

Many sources can assist you in evaluating information, but I've found the checklist developed by the University of Maryland's University College (UMUC) to be especially helpful. You can find the checklist at http://umuc.edu/library/guides/evaluate.html. The UMUC site presents five evaluation criteria, each with several specific questions you can use in your research. The five criteria are

1. *Authority.* Can you tell who created the information? The purpose of its creation? Can you contact the author or creating organization, or otherwise establish their credentials? For example, authors published in *Strategic Finance* (the monthly publication of the Institute of Management Accountants) are required to provide background and contact information as part of their articles. Reading that information carefully can help you make decisions about authority as you evaluate information for AIS course projects.

2. *Accuracy.* Does the site/article/source tell you where the information came from? Does it contain any obvious errors of fact or misleading graphs, charts, or statistics? Consider, for instance, information presented in a graph. Differences can be exaggerated simply by changing the graph's scaling. Consider Figure 1.3 as an illustration of this point. Notice how the differences appear more pronounced in graph (a) than in graph (b), although the only difference between the two graphs is the scaling on the vertical axis.

3. *Objectivity.* Does the information contain advertising? Is it available freely? By this time in your accounting education, you have probably heard of the Sarbanes-Oxley Act of 2002. We'll explore the details of SOX later in the text, but consider www.soxlaw.com in terms of this information criterion. Figure 1.4 gives you a partial screen shot of the Web site. Although I've found the information there objective and valuable in learning

FIGURE 1.3

Data Displays

FIGURE 1.4
Sarbanes-Oxley Information Web Site, www.soxlaw.com

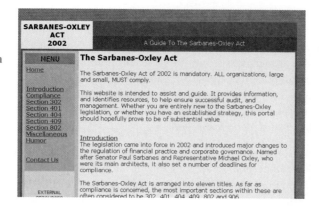

about SOX, notice the "Contact Us" link on the left side. Clicking that link reveals the name of the consulting firm that compiled the information, offering its services to help companies comply with SOX.

4. *Currency.* Can you tell when the source was created/written? When was the last time it was updated? Does the page contain any "dead links"? Later in the text, we'll explore how to create databases of accounting information; one of the important concepts in that area is data normalization. Data normalization refers to the set of rules designers use to ensure that databases are as effective and as efficient as possible. You'll find the rules of data normalization nicely summarized at www.datamodel.org/NormalizationRules.html. As I prepared this chapter for the first edition, the Web site showed its last update as June 13, 2005. Is that current enough? In this case, it probably is—the rules of data normalization have been well established for quite some time.

5. *Coverage.* Is the source still under construction? Does it cover the subject with sufficient depth? In some sense, all Web sites are always "under construction." In most cases, they have to be updated periodically to stay current and relevant. But if a page is perpetually "under construction," you should consider whether it would be a valuable, trusted source for research and problem solving.

I encourage you to point your Web browser to the University of Maryland Web site and see the full list of questions and other guidelines there; as a reminder, you'll find it at http://umuc.edu/library/guides/evaluate.html.

Reflection and Self-Assessment   1.4

Use your university's library to find an article reasonably related to accounting. Evaluate the article based on the five criteria listed previously, or some other set your instructor prefers.

Again: how is the information you just read related to your study of accounting information systems? It's related in at least two important ways: (1) it gives you some guidance about the kinds of information you may need to consult in doing research and responding to problems throughout the text and (2) it gives you a set of criteria you can use to evaluate that information, rather than treating all information you find as the full and absolute "truth."

CRITICAL THINKING

By this time in your university education, you've probably heard at least one professor talk about the need to "think critically." But what exactly does that mean? Dictionary.com defines critical thinking as "the mental process of actively and skillfully conceptualizing, applying, analyzing, synthesizing, and evaluating information to reach an answer or conclusion." And the Critical Thinking Community (www.criticalthinking.org) says that someone who thinks critically does five things:

- Raises vital questions and problems, formulating them clearly and precisely.
- Gathers and assesses relevant information, using abstract ideas to interpret it effectively.
- Comes to well-reasoned conclusions and solutions, testing them against relevant criteria and standards.
- Thinks openmindedly [*sic*] within alternative systems of thought, recognizing and assessing, as needs be, their assumptions, implications, and practical consequences.
- Communicates effectively with others in figuring out solutions to complex problems.

Every area of accounting requires critical thinking; every day, accountants make judgments and respond to questions that may have more than one acceptable answer. Throughout this book, I'll often ask you to think critically so you can develop the skills you'll need to succeed in our profession. To help you toward that goal, each chapter in the text will contain a section like this one. I hope that studying them will help you develop your critical-thinking skills.

For this chapter, I'd like to focus on the "statement evaluation" exercises you'll find throughout the text. In each of them, I'll give you 10 statements; your job will be to determine if each one is (a) always true, (b) sometimes true, or (c) never true. For those that are "sometimes true," you'll need to provide an explanation; your instructor may include similar exercises on quizzes and exams.

Consider the following statements, which talk about the role of computers in accounting information systems:

1. Computers can be an important processing tool in the AIS.
2. Computers are always an important processing tool in the AIS.
3. Computers are important processing tools in the AIS.

At first blush, without thinking critically, all three statements may seem alike to you—but they're not. Each statement has a unique phrase that differentiates it from the others: "can be," "are always," and "are."

The first statement (Computers can be an important processing tool in the AIS) is always true. When you see the phrase "can be," think of it as meaning "have the potential to be." It's always true that computers have the potential to be an important processing tool—even though they are not used in every AIS.

The second statement (Computers are always an important processing tool in the AIS) is never true. The phrase "are always" means that there are no exceptions. Here's a parallel example: People with blonde hair always have blue eyes. While it's true that people with blonde hair often have blue eyes, the two don't always go together; some people with blonde hair, for example, have green eyes. Similarly, some accounting information systems employ computers as processing tools—but some don't. So it is never true that computers are always an important processing tool in the AIS.

The third statement (Computers are important processing tools in the AIS) is sometimes true. In other words, in some accounting information systems, computers are important processing tools; but in other systems, they are not.

Take a look at the statement evaluation exercise at the end of this chapter. Statement (a) (Data in an accounting information system are stored electronically, such as on a disk) is sometimes true. Statement (b) ("Truth" is one of the qualitative characteristics identified by the FASB conceptual framework) is never true. Statement (c) (The FASB conceptual framework identifies eight elements of financial statements) is always true.

I often tell my students that accounting really isn't about numbers at all; it's really about the use of language. And becoming a critical thinker means, in part, that you're able to use language accurately and precisely. The statement evaluation exercise at the end of each chapter will be challenging for you at first, I'm sure. But, as you practice thinking critically, the exercise will make more sense. If you ever find yourself "stumped" by one of those statements, don't hesitate to drop me an e-mail (RLHurt@csupomona.edu) and let me know; I'll do my best to clarify and point you in the right direction.

TEXT STRUCTURE AND CONTENT

This book is structured in five parts:

AIS fundamentals. In this section, we'll look at topics that form the foundation of most AIS courses. Here in Chapter 1, we examined the basic nature of accounting information systems; we also looked at information literacy and critical thinking. Chapter 2 reviews the accounting cycle and talks about how human judgment and information technology are involved in its activities. Chapter 3 introduces you to internal control. The last two chapters in Part One emphasize the multidisciplinary nature of AIS. Chapter 4 looks at three important management-related topics and their relationship to AIS: enterprise risk management, business process management, and behavioral issues. Chapter 5 introduces you to a similar set of ideas related to information systems: the systems development life cycle, the capability maturity model, and software selection. The topics from all five chapters reappear later in the text, where they are applied in various contexts.

Documentation techniques. Whether you're designing a completely new accounting information system, making changes to an existing system, or auditing a system, documentation techniques are important. In these three chapters, we'll look at three common ways accountants create models of accounting information systems: flowcharts (Chapter 6), data flow diagrams (Chapter 7), and REA models (Chapter 8). In Chapters 7 and 8, we'll also explore database design. Later chapters on business processes will give you the chance to apply the skills you acquire in systems documentation in more specific contexts.

Information technology in the AIS. The three chapters in the third part of the book look at ways various forms of information technology are used. Chapter 9 discusses one of the most important IT developments in the last decade: XBRL. XBRL is used to tag accounting-related data so it can be interpreted by a wide variety of software and hardware combinations. In Chapter 10, we'll take a look at e-business and enterprise resource planning systems. Chapter 11 provides an overview of an area my students find especially interesting: computer crime and IT security.

Business processes. The chapters in this part of the book take a look at various business processes that cut across organizations: sales/collection (Chapter 12), acquisition/payment (Chapter 13), and other business processes (Chapter 14). We'll take many of the ideas from previous sections and apply them within the context of those business processes: internal control, systems documentation, the SDLC, risk management, business process management, behavioral issues, and information technology.

Other topics in AIS. I've included three chapters in the last part of the text: decision-making models and knowledge management (Chapter 15), professionalism, ethics, and career planning (Chapter 16), and auditing and evaluating the AIS (Chapter 17). I've included these topics, which are not often part of other AIS texts, for several reasons: (a) they are areas my own students have been interested in, (b) they provide an opportunity to apply some fundamental topics (internal control, database design, information technology) in new areas, (c) they connect accounting with other areas of business (such as management), and (d) they connect AIS with other areas of accounting (such as auditing).

As a new feature for this edition, I've also created an AIS blog you'll want to visit. You'll find it at bobhurtais.blogspot.com. In addition to providing another way for us to communicate, you'll also find more detailed discussion of the topics from the text (such as critical thinking), comprehensive case studies, and a host of other materials. As always, I encourage you to communicate with me, either on your own or through your professor, about aspects of the book that are working well for you and those that could use some improvement.

Summary

Each chapter in the text ends with a brief summary of its major points, structured in terms of the learning objectives at the beginning of the chapter.

1. *Define "accounting information systems."* An accounting information system (AIS) is a collection of interrelated parts, some of which may incorporate information technology. Its purpose is to collect data, process it into information, and report the information so it can be used by internal and external decision makers.

2. *Discuss why AIS is an important area of study for future accountants.* AIS is important because it cuts across traditional functional lines in accounting. It provides the "big picture" and allows students to develop their critical-thinking and problem-solving skills.

3. *Compare and contrast AIS with other areas of study in accounting.* AIS is like other areas of accounting in that it includes consideration of financial statements and internal reports. It is different, though, from other parts of accounting. AIS typically includes more open-ended problems that do not have deterministic responses. It also cuts across traditional accounting subdivisions (financial, managerial, and the like) and incorporates material from disciplines outside accounting (such as management and information systems).

4. *Explain the structure of most accounting information systems.* Most AIS incorporate five main parts. Inputs are used to collect data and get them into the system; they include source documents such as checks and invoices. Processing tools transform the data into information; processing tools can be manual or automated. Outputs provide some of the information decision makers need in organizations. Typical outputs of an AIS include the general-purpose financial statements. Internal controls are the policies and procedures established in an AIS to promote information integrity and safeguard assets. And storage refers to the methods for keeping data secure and available.

5. *Locate and evaluate information sources on accounting information systems.* Information on AIS can be found in both traditional and online sources. The chapter grouped information sources into three parts: sponsored/commercial, popular/practitioner, and scholarly. All information, regardless of source, should be evaluated for validity. One useful checklist for information evaluation is provided by the University of Maryland: authority, accuracy, objectivity, currency, and coverage. The ability to find, evaluate, and use information appropriately is often referred to as information competence.

6. *Describe the structure and content of the remainder of this text.* The text is structured in five main parts: (1) AIS fundamentals, (2) systems documentation techniques, (3) information technology in the AIS, (4) business processes and (5) other topics in AIS.

So, as you can see, you're in for a fascinating, highly relevant, diverse study this term in your AIS course. I hope you'll approach your study with enthusiasm and commitment, knowing that what you learn this term will serve you very well in your career as a professional accountant.

Key Terms

These terms are defined in the glossary at the end of the text, as well as in the chapter.

accounting information system, *4*

AIS structure, *6*

conceptual framework, *4*

information competence, *8*

popular/practitioner information, *8*

scholarly information, *8*

sponsored/commercial information, *7*

unstructured problems, *3*

Chapter Reference

Curzon, S. 1995. *Information Competence in the CSU.* www.calstate.edu/LS/Archive/info_comp_report.shtml (May 25, 2005).

End-of-Chapter Activities

1. *Reading review questions.* These questions will help you assess your understanding of the text readings. If you've studied the chapter thoroughly, you should be able to answer them without reference to the text itself. Although these questions appear first, you may find them easier to answer after completing the rest of the end-of-chapter assignments. I urge you to answer them in your own words, rather than with quotations from the text itself.

   a. What is an accounting information system?

   b. Describe the purpose of the FASB conceptual framework. Discuss how it relates to your study of accounting information systems.

   c. List and discuss the five parts of a generic accounting information system.

   d. Compare and contrast sponsored information, practitioner/public information, and scholarly information.

   e. Identify five broad criteria you can use to evaluate information on the Internet and in other sources.

   f. In a manner specified by your instructor (e.g., individually or with a group, as a written paper or as an oral presentation), prepare an original response to one or more of the questions for this chapter's "AIS in the Business World."

2. *Multiple choice review questions.* You'll find five questions like these in every chapter. They're "low-context" multiple choice questions, which means you should be able to answer them based on a careful reading of the text. You'll find the answers to these questions at the end of the book.

1. Which of the following is not essential to the definition of an accounting information system?
   a. Software
   b. Documents
   c. Decision makers
   d. Financial data

2. The FASB conceptual framework links accounting information systems with what other area of accounting?
   a. Taxation
   b. Auditing
   c. Cost accounting
   d. Financial accounting

3. Most accounting information systems comprise _____ parts.
   a. Two
   b. Four
   c. Five
   d. Some other number

4. Terms like "master file" and "transaction file" are most commonly associated with which generic element of the AIS?
   a. Inputs
   b. Storage
   c. Outputs
   d. Internal controls

5. Which types of information have typically gone through a review process prior to publication?
   a. Sponsored and popular
   b. Sponsored and scholarly
   c. Popular and scholarly
   d. Sponsored, popular, and scholarly

3. *Reading review problem.* When I grew up in St. Louis, Missouri, my mom would often take me and my brothers to Dairy Queen if we'd been especially well behaved. (I'll leave it to you to wonder how often that happened!) But, when I moved to southern California in 1983, I found that Dairy Queen stores were few and far between. So, you can probably imagine how happy I was to find one only a few miles from my home. As a boy, my only interest in visiting was the ice cream; I still enjoy the ice cream today, but I also think about how their accounting information system works whenever I visit.

Dairy Queen is a franchised operation; their Web site (www.dairyqueen.com) outlines five steps to owning a franchise. They are

   i. Complete a form to request information from the corporate office.
   ii. Start the application process.
   iii. Have the application reviewed; if approved, select a site for the store.
   iv. Begin construction and participate in a management training program.
   v. Open the new store.

The whole process, according to the Web site, takes less than a year in most cases. As you'll learn in this chapter, most accounting information systems have five parts: inputs, processes, outputs, storage, and internal controls.

    a. Does Dairy Queen need an accounting information system? Why, or why not?

    b. Suggest one example of each generic AIS element within the context of Dairy Queen.

    c. How might this case be incorporated in other accounting courses, such as financial accounting, cost accounting, and taxation?

4. *Making choices and exercising judgment.* As you read in the chapter, AIS is all about making choices and evaluating their costs and benefits. These questions and exercises are designed to help you develop those skills. When I give exercises like these to my own students, they frequently say, "So does this mean there's no right or wrong answer?" You may be thinking the same thing, so I'll tell you what I tell them: The point isn't whether your answer is "right" or "wrong," or even if such answers exist. The point here is for you to make choices and create answers you can defend in the face of other alternatives.

    a. RKH Company is a small consulting service based just outside Los Angeles. It has two partners, Sebastian and Viola, and average monthly sales revenue of $25,000. At any one time, Sebastian and Viola have up to three consulting engagements running simultaneously. Monthly expenses include office rent, supplies, utilities, professional magazine subscriptions, and automobile expenses. What form(s) of information technology, if any, should Sebastian and Viola use in their accounting information system? Explain the costs and benefits of your recommendation.

    b. Most accounting information systems in use today employ principles of debit and credit for recording transactions. What are the costs and benefits of using the debit/credit system for transaction recording? If the system is destined to fade into disuse, what do you think will replace it?

5. *Field exercises.* These exercises will require you to go out "into the field" to interview an accountant, observe a business process, do library research, or collect other kinds of data. Your instructor may ask you to complete one or more field exercises with a group of students; they also could be used as the basis for a major course writing assignment or presentation.

    a. Interview an accountant or other financial professional in an organization of your choice. Ask what information technologies (if any) are used in the accounting information system and about the costs and benefits of their use. If time permits, also ask for examples of internal controls in the organization. Don't forget to write a thank-you note or e-mail after your interview.

    b. Visit a movie theater, retail store, fast-food outlet, or other business organization near your home or campus. Carefully observe the process of making sales and collecting payments. What processes and tools does the organization use to keep its cash safe?

    c. Visit a local office supply store and ask to see the business documents section. Find examples of at least two documents from the following list: purchase requisition, purchase order, sales invoice, check, remittance advice, and customer statement. Either through a conversation with a store employee, individual research, and/or your own deductive powers and experience, discuss the purpose and use of the documents. List the information on the documents and explain how each information item helps achieve the document's purpose.

    d. Talk to one of your university's librarians about information competence / information literacy. Find out, from a librarian's perspective, why it's important. Identify two resources available on your campus to help you learn more about information competence.

6. *Information types.* Using the three classifications discussed in the chapter, determine whether each of the following is sponsored, practitioner, or scholarly in nature.

    a. *Accounting, Behavior and Organizations*

    b. *Harvard Business Review*

    c. *Journal of Accountancy*

    d. *Management Accounting Quarterly*

    e. *MIS Quarterly*

    f. *Strategic Finance*

    g. *Fraud Magazine*

    h. **www.findaccountingsoftware.com**

    i. **www.findarticles.com**

    j. **www.erpsolutions.net**

7. Other than those listed in Question 5, find one or two examples (each) of sponsored, practitioner, and scholarly Web sites, journals, or other periodicals. Be prepared to explain your choices and their classifications.

8. Look up the following references online or in your school's library. Using the criteria and specific questions from the UMUC Web site referenced in the chapter, evaluate and discuss the quality of each reference. (*Note:* To do a thorough evaluation of these references, you *must* get the list of questions from the UMUC Web site. You won't be able to rely on my summary in the chapter to do your best work.)

   "Xelltec Reports Laptop Security Microchip." *Wireless News*, 25 February 2011.

   Bollinger, M. "Implementing Internal Controls." *Strategic Finance*, January 2011.

   Cascone, J., et al. "Equipped to Sustain." *Internal Auditor*, December 2010.

   Johansmeyer, T. "Top 4 Small Business Accounting Software for 2008." *CPA Magazine*, November 2008.

   Weisman, A., and M. Brodsky. "Fighting Fraud with Both Fists." *The CPA Journal*, January 2011.

9. *Terminology.* Each chapter also includes an exercise like this one. Not only will completing them help you master each chapter's vocabulary; you also may find questions like this one on your class exams and accounting professional exams. Please match each item on the left with the most appropriate item on the right.

1. *Business Ethics Quarterly* **e**	a. A constraint of the conceptual framework
2. Comparability and consistency **c**	b. A principle of the conceptual framework
3. Currency **g**	c. Accounting information's secondary qualitative
4. Deterministic **f**	characteristics
5. Going concern **d**	d. An assumption of the conceptual framework
6. *Journal of Accountancy* **h**	e. An example of scholarly information
7. Matching **b**	f. Another name for problems with single correct
8. Materiality **a**	answers
9. Objective of financial reporting **j**	g. Concerns whether information is up-to-date
10. Relevance and reliability **i**	h. Example of practitioner information
	i. Primary qualitative characteristics of accounting
	information
	j. To provide information for decision making

10. *Multiple choice questions (high context).* The multiple choice questions presented in Question 2 above are "low context." You should be able to answer them simply by a careful reading of the chapter. These questions, on the other hand, are "high context." They will require critical thinking and reasoning on your part.

    1. Which of the following is an example of an internal control in the accounting information system?

       (a) Bank reconciliation

       b. Sales order

       c. Balance sheet

       d. Steps in the accounting cycle

2. Which of the following is most closely related to the "middle level" of the FASB conceptual framework depicted in Figure 1.1?

   a. Preparing an operating budget

   b. Expensing the cost of a wastebasket

   c. Reporting investments at their fair market value

   d. Providing information for decisions

3. All of the following are facts about accounting information systems except:

   a. They should all involve some form of internal control.

   b. They always incorporate information technology.

   c. They usually provide general-purpose financial statements as outputs.

   d. They can involve three types of storage files.

4. Which of the following best pairs a generic element of the AIS with a specific example of that element?

   a. Input, balance sheet

   b. Internal control, general ledger software

   c. Internal control, balance sheet

   d. Input, general ledger software

5. Which of the following statements shows the strongest level of information competence?

   a. Never using Wikipedia to do research

   b. Consulting the AICPA Web site for information on fraud examination

   c. Investigating an author's professional background

   d. Using only scholarly information as the basis for a paper

11. *Statement evaluation.* As you learned in the chapter, designing and implementing accounting information systems requires judgment and critical thinking. Each chapter will include an exercise like this one to help you develop those skills. Several statements related to the material in the chapter are listed below; your job is to explain whether each statement is (i) always true, (ii) sometimes true, or (iii) never true. If you answer (ii), explain when the statement is true.

   a. Data in an accounting information system are stored electronically, such as on a disk.

   b. "Truth" is one of the qualitative characteristics identified by the FASB conceptual framework.

   c. The FASB conceptual framework identifies eight elements of financial statements.

   d. Information you find on the Internet is reliable.

   e. Cost-effectiveness is an important criterion in the design of accounting information systems.

   f. A Web site that is "under construction" may have a problem with adequate coverage according to the UMUC information criteria.

   g. Both internal and external parties can use information provided by the accounting information system.

   h. Most companies have two different accounting information systems: one for internal use and one for external use.

   i. In an AIS, source documents are paper-based.

   j. Problems and questions in accounting information systems are open-ended; they do not have "right" or "wrong" answers.

12. *Blog exercises.* Point your Web browser to the text's new blog: bobhurtais.blogspot .com. Read the post titled Critical Thinking (dated 27 February 2011). Generate one question at each level of Bloom's taxonomy for learning objective 4 in this chapter: "Explain the structure of most accounting information systems."

Chapter **Two**

Transaction Processing in the AIS

AIS in the Business World

City of Denver

Like business organizations, many local governments sell goods and services. Unlike business organizations, however, local governments follow the principles of fund accounting in processing their transactions and preparing their financial statements. Most disseminate their financial information using a Comprehensive Annual Financial Report (CAFR). You can find the CAFR for the City and County of Denver at www .denvergov.org.

One service that many city governments sell is parking. If you've ever gone to a restaurant, club, or office in a major downtown area, you probably resigned yourself to the fact that you would have to pay to park. Some city governments, such as Denver, operate municipal golf courses to bring in additional money. Transactions where cities sell goods and services to parties external to the government are accounted for in enterprise funds, one of the two types of proprietary funds in the government accounting information system. Enterprise funds follow the principles of accrual accounting, making their transaction processing strikingly similar to business.

Because their accounting information systems follow the principles of fund accounting, many cities use hierarchical coding for their chart of accounts. Doing so makes preparing fund-basis and government-wide financial statements more efficient.

Discussion Questions

1. What are the three major types of funds found in most local government accounting information systems?
2. Find Denver's CAFR for the year ended December 31, 2009. Examine the section for proprietary funds and respond to the following questions:
   a. What are the two broad categories of proprietary funds?
   b. Within each category, how many funds does Denver have? What are they?
3. What is "hierarchical coding" with respect to a chart of accounts? How would hierarchical coding be useful for the City of Denver?

As I mentioned in Chapter 1, you may be studying accounting information systems near the start or near the finish of your formal accounting education. If you're taking this course before intermediate accounting, you'll likely want to devote significant attention to this chapter, which talks about the steps in the accounting cycle. If you're studying AIS after completing one or more courses in intermediate accounting, your instructor may use this chapter as a review, or skip it altogether.

When you've finished studying this chapter, and completing the activities at its conclusion, you should be able to:

1. Differentiate *accounting* and *bookkeeping.*
2. List, discuss, and complete, in order, the steps in the accounting cycle.
3. Identify common internal controls associated with the accounting cycle.
4. Describe common chart of accounts coding systems.
5. Explain how human judgment and information technology affect the accounting cycle.

Understanding the steps in the accounting cycle is important in the study of AIS. Without grasping the "big picture" of transaction processing, you'll be at a significant disadvantage when we begin talking in later chapters about documentation, internal controls, business processes, and current trends in AIS.

ACCOUNTING AND BOOKKEEPING

Many students and business professionals confuse bookkeeping with **accounting.** Before the advent of information technology, most accountants spent considerable time on bookkeeping tasks. Thankfully, we have tools available to us today that allow us to focus on more interesting and important areas, such as using accounting information for competitive advantage and management decision making.

You can find more information about AAA on its Web site: http://aaahq.org/index.cfm.

The American Accounting Association (AAA) is a group of accounting educators with members all over the world. A committee of the AAA developed the following definition of accounting:

> Accounting is the process of identifying, measuring, and communicating economic information to permit informed judgments and decisions by users of the information.

Note that the definition has three principal elements: identifying, measuring, and communicating.

Implied within the AAA's definition is the **bookkeeping** process: that part of accounting devoted to identifying and measuring the economic information. So you may be able to see why bookkeeping often is confused with accounting. A solid understanding of bookkeeping is essential for any practicing accountant, but knowing the rules and procedures of bookkeeping is by no means sufficient to guarantee success in the accounting profession! Several years ago, a student told me that, upon graduation, she wanted a job where she could "sit in a room and make journal entries all day." I said: "First, you'll need to visit the Physics Department and ask them to invent a time machine. Jobs like that haven't existed in accounting for at least the last two decades."

As an undergraduate accounting student at Southeast Missouri State University (www .semo.edu), I had a friend named Gary. Gary, like me, started his higher education as an accounting major. But, after only one semester (and before taking his first accounting course), Gary changed his major to computer science. When I asked him why, his reply was simple: by the time we graduate, all accountants are going to be replaced by computers. That was in 1977 and the accounting profession is still alive and well. Gary was clearly confusing accounting with bookkeeping. Most bookkeeping today is handled via information technology; accountants can then take the summarized information and complete the remaining tasks in the AAA definition: communicating, facilitating informed judgments, and making decisions.

Next, we'll look at the steps in the accounting cycle—the process of identifying and measuring economic events that leads to communication and decision making.

ACCOUNTING CYCLE

The **accounting cycle** comprises 10 steps (Spiceland, Sepe, and Tomassini, 2001, p. 60):

1. Obtain information about external transactions from source documents.
2. Analyze transactions.
3. Record the transactions in a journal.
4. Post from the journal to the general ledger accounts.
5. Prepare an unadjusted trial balance.
6. Record adjusting entries and post to the general ledger accounts.
7. Prepare an adjusted trial balance.
8. Prepare financial statements.
9. Close the temporary accounts to retained earnings (at year-end only).
10. Prepare a post-closing trial balance (at year-end only).

Some descriptions of the accounting cycle include an 11th step: prepare reversing entries. But the cycle isn't our primary focus here, so we'll omit it. You'll learn about reversing entries in intermediate accounting.

Notice how the ten steps relate to the five elements of the AIS we talked about in Chapter 1. Obtaining information from source documents is an input. Steps 2 through 7 of the accounting cycle relate to processes, as well as steps 9 and 10. Step 8 focuses on one type of output from the AIS: the general purpose financial statements.

Transactions come in two basic types in most accounting information systems: external and internal. **External transactions,** appropriately enough, are those that involve exchanges of goods and services with other individuals and business entities—suppliers, shareholders, government agencies, employees, and the like. **Internal transactions** include adjusting entries, closing entries, and reversing entries. Accountants become aware of external transactions, in most cases, through the use of **source documents.** Source documents can be paper or electronic; their use helps retain some level of objectivity in the accounting information system; recall that objectivity is part of the FASB conceptual framework we discussed in Chapter 1. They can include purchase orders, remittance advices, and invoices, for example. Common internal controls associated with source documents include:

- *Sequential numbering.* For example, the checks in your checkbook are numbered sequentially. Thus, you would know if a check had been used out of sequence, which may indicate an internal control breach.
- *Physical security.* Keeping important source documents physically secure is also important. For example, a company should not keep its blank checks in an easily accessible location; rather, they should be secured (such as in a locked filing cabinet) to prevent unauthorized use.
- *Transaction limits.* A new purchasing agent, for example, might not be authorized to issue purchase orders over a certain amount. Requiring a second signature or supervisory approval can cut down on errors and potential misuse of assets.

Source documents themselves would be a cumbersome way to capture transaction information, so accountants distill the essential information from them and use the principles of transaction analysis to enter them into the accounting information system. Transaction analysis involves five steps:

- Identify the accounts affected by the transaction.
- Identify the effect of the transaction on each account (i.e., increase or decrease).
- Determine the element of financial statements represented by each account. The FASB conceptual framework identifies eight elements of financial statements. We'll confine our discussion here to the five most common: assets, liabilities, equity, revenues, and expenses. The five elements are related through the expanded accounting equation:

$$\text{Assets} = \text{Liabilites} + \text{Equity} + \text{Revenue} - \text{Expense}$$

- Based on the **principles of debit and credit,** determine which kind of entry is required for each account. *Debit* is accounting shorthand for the left side of an account; *credit* is accounting shorthand for the right side. Because the terms *debit* and *credit* have other meanings in general usage, many students have difficulty remembering the principles of debit and credit in an accounting context. But the rules are actually quite straightforward if you relate them back to the equation. On the left side of the equation, the "plus" is on the left, so assets increase with debits and decrease with credits. On the right side of the equation, the "plus" is on the right. Liabilities, equity, and revenue, then, increase with credits and decrease with debits. Because expenses have a minus sign in front of them, the rules are reversed again: expenses increase with debits and decrease with credits.
- Verify that, for each transaction, the total debits equal the total credits. The equality of debits and credits is at the heart of a double-entry accounting system. Without it, we revert to a single-entry system similar to your checkbook. Single-entry systems have no internal checks and balances; they also fail to provide all the meaningful information of double-entry systems. Ensuring that debits and credits are equal is a form of internal control; even if a bookkeeper makes errors in account names and/or amounts, the errors can be corrected if the entries balance.

After they've been analyzed, transactions are recorded in a journal. The journal may be paper-based or computerized; it is often referred to as the "book of original entry," since it

FIGURE 2.1   General Journal Illustration

	DATE	ACCOUNT TITLE	DOC. NO.	POST. REF.	DEBIT	CREDIT	
		GENERAL JOURNAL				PAGE	
1							1
2							2
3							3
4							4
5							5
6							6
7							7
8							8
9							9

You may have heard of "special journals" in your previous study of accounting. Sales journals, for example, have a special structure that facilitates the recording of sales on account only. Very few organizations still use special journals, however, so they are not a major topic of discussion here.

is the first place a transaction is formally recorded in the accounting information system. The most common form of journal is the general journal, illustrated in Figure 2.1. Recall from our discussion of the five elements of an AIS in Chapter 1 that journal entries are commonly stored in transaction files.

In a general journal, debits are recorded first. Credits are indented slightly, as shown below:

9/27/04	Equipment	$80,000	
	Cash		$ 8,000
	Notes payable		72,000

In the preceding transaction, the company purchased equipment with a 10 percent down payment and notes payable for the rest. If a transaction is particularly complex, accountants often will write a short description of it in the journal for clarification.

Reflection and Self-Assessment   2.4

Think of two events that would be important to a business organization that would *not* be recorded in the accounting information system. Explain why they would not be recorded; refer to the FASB conceptual framework as needed to justify your responses.

Then, record each of the following transactions in general journal format:

1. DMN Corporation issued 10,000 shares of $1 par capital stock for $15 per share.

2. Purchased inventory on account, $30,000.

3. Sold inventory with a cost of $6,000 on account for $9,000.

4. Paid current period's salaries, $12,000.

5. Paid creditors on account, $4,000.

6. Received cash from clients on account, $6,000.

In most computerized AIS, a transaction that has been posted to the general ledger cannot be changed or deleted. To promote good internal control, posted transactions can only be corrected with an additional journal entry.

The journal, then, is a chronological listing of all the organization's recordable transactions. But, to produce financial statements and other reports, data in the AIS need to be organized according to the account(s) they affect. The process of posting from the journal to the ledger reorganizes the transactions in that way. Posting by hand takes a lot of time and opens up the AIS to all sorts of errors: transposing numbers, recording in the wrong account, recording on the wrong side, and/or omitting part of a transaction are only a few. In most modern accounting information systems, posting is handled via information technology. While IT doesn't eliminate the possibility of incorrect transaction recording, it does cut down on the time and types of errors noted above.

Preparing a trial balance is the next step in the accounting cycle. A trial balance is a listing of all the accounts in an organization's general ledger, with their balances, that demonstrates the equality of debits and credits in the ledger. Note that the trial balance does not warrant that the AIS is error-free. If, for example, a transaction is posted to the wrong account, but on the correct side, the trial balance will still be in balance. Table 2.1 shows a trial balance.

Once again, information technology is used in most accounting information systems to prepare a trial balance. And a trial balance can serve as an additional form of internal control, ensuring that the ledger accounts balance before preparing the financial statements.

Reflection and Self-Assessment   2.5

Use the trial balance in Table 2.1 and the journal entries you prepared in Reflection and Self-Assessment 2.4 to prepare a new trial balance for DMN Corporation.

TABLE 2.1
Trial Balance

DMN CORPORATION Trial Balance September 30, 2011		
	Debit	**Credit**
Cash	$15,800	
Accounts receivable	5,200	
Inventory	4,800	
Equipment	5,000	
Accumulated depreciation		$ 1,400
Accounts payable		2,000
Notes payable		800
Bonds payable		6,000
Capital stock		12,000
Additional paid-in capital		7,400
Retained earnings		2,500
Sales		13,800
Cost of goods sold	6,300	
Advertising expense	5,000	
Depreciation expense	2,800	
Supplies expense	1,000	
Totals	$45,900	$45,900

TABLE 2.2   Adjusting Entries

1 Income stmt / 1 B/S

Type	Description	Example	General Format of Adjustment
Accrued revenues	An organization provides service to its customers before collecting cash	Unbilled client fees	Debit an asset Credit a revenue
Accrued expenses	An organization receives service before paying cash	Unpaid employee wages	Debit an expense Credit a liability
Deferred revenues	An organization receives cash before providing services to clients	Insurance premiums	Debit a liability Credit a revenue
Prepaid expenses	An organization uses up assets that have previously been paid for	Supplies	Debit an expense Credit an asset
Uncollectible accounts	Estimates of amounts clients will be unable or unwilling to pay	Bad debts	Debit an expense Credit a contra-asset
Depreciation	Periodic allocation of an asset's cost to the periods that benefit from its use	Equipment	Debit an expense Credit a contra-asset

The basic idea behind the matching concept is simple: it costs money to make money. But, although simple, the matching concept is profoundly important in accounting. It gives us the theoretical basis for things like depreciation and pension accounting.

The sixth step in the accounting cycle requires accountants to record adjusting entries and post them to the general ledger accounts. In this context, adjusting entries refer to internal journal entries made to account for timing differences in the flow of cash and the recognition of accrual-basis revenues and expenses. Adjusting entries are required by the matching concept in the FASB conceptual framework. Six types of **adjusting entries** are common in most accounting information systems as shown in Table 2.2.

Notice that each adjusting entry requires one account for the income statement and one account for the balance sheet. "Cash" is not involved in any of the preceding types of adjustments. The specific account titles will change depending upon the exact item being adjusted.

Reflection and Self-Assessment   2.6

Describe a specific transaction for each adjustment type noted above. For example, an accrued revenue description might say: "DMN Corporation had unbilled client fees of $2,000." Then, explain how the adjustment would be recorded in the accounting information system. For example, debit Accounts Receivable and credit Sales.

After adjusting entries are journalized and posted, it's a good idea to prepare an adjusted trial balance. The purpose and nature of an adjusted trial balance are the same as for an ordinary trial balance; the only difference is the timing of its preparation. An adjusted trial balance reflects the status of the ledger accounts after the adjusting entries have been posted.

The accounting cycle continues with the preparation of the **general-purpose financial statements.** They are four in number and include

- The *income statement,* which summarizes the results of business operations on the accrual basis for a specified period of time. The income statement reports revenues, expenses, gains, and losses from the accounting information system.
- The *statement of changes in shareholders' equity* reports changes in capital stock and retained earnings accounts for the same period of time as the income statement. Net income increases retained earnings; net losses and declaration of dividends decrease retained earnings. Capital stock can increase or decrease for a variety of reasons, the most common of which is issuance of new shares.
- The *balance sheet* shows the financial position of an organization at a specific point in time. It contains assets (listed in order of their liquidity), liabilities (listed with the most current due dates first), and equity (which comes from the statement of changes in shareholders' equity). Naturally, the assets must equal the liabilities plus equity on the balance sheet.
- The *statement of cash flows* is the relative newcomer to the general-purpose financial statements. Developed in the late 1980s by the Financial Accounting Standards Board, the statement of cash flows reports inflows and outflows of cash for a specified period of time. Cash flows on the statement fall into three categories: operating, investing, and financing. Accountants can choose between the direct and indirect methods of calculating operating cash flows.

You can access the financial statements of publicly traded companies online via EDGAR. EDGAR is administered by the Securities and Exchange Commission; its URL is www.sec .gov/edgar.shtml .

You'll probably have an entire course in auditing as part of your accounting program; we'll also discuss auditing in the last chapter of this text. Audits are important forms of internal control. Internal audits can help promote organizational efficiency and encourage compliance with management directives; external audits ensure that financial statements are prepared in accordance with generally accepted accounting principles.

Reflection and Self-Assessment   2.7

Use EDGAR or some other source to access the financial statements of Martha Stewart Living Omnimedia Inc.

What is your assessment of the corporation's financial position and performance based on the statements?

Revenues
Expenses
Dividends

After preparing financial statements, the accounting information system must be readied for the next fiscal period's entries. That objective is accomplished via closing entries. Balances from temporary (nominal) accounts on the income statement are transferred into retained earnings (a real, permanent account in the equity section of the balance sheet). Finally, then, the accounting information system produces a post-closing trial balance. Similar in form to the other trial balances discussed above, the post-closing trial balance differs in content. Because all the nominal accounts have been closed, the post-closing trial balance contains only balance sheet accounts. See the illustration in Table 2.3 for an example.

Most accounting information systems fall into one of two types: view-driven systems or event-driven systems. View-driven systems are the more traditional; they are focused on providing a particular "view" of the data and information—the view provided by the general purpose financial statements. The steps in the accounting cycle are primarily focused on collecting data and reporting information in view-driven systems.

TABLE 2.3
Post-closing Trial Balance

DMN CORPORATION Post-closing Trial Balance September 30, 2011		
	Debit	**Credit**
Cash	$15,800	
Accounts receivable	5,200	
Inventory	4,800	
Equipment	5,000	
Accumulated depreciation		$ 1,400
Accounts payable		2,000
Notes payable		800
Bonds payable		6,000
Capital stock		12,000
Additional paid-in capital		7,400
Retained earnings		1,200
Totals	$30,800	$30,800

We'll talk about event-driven systems later in the text. Event-driven systems are a fairly recent development in the business world; they focus on capturing more comprehensive information about business events. A view-driven system would be concerned about which accounts and amounts to debit and credit; an event-driven system would capture those data and other details, such as sizes and colors of merchandise ordered. Event-driven systems use relational database technology to provide various ways of viewing the data—it's possible to get the general purpose financial statements from an event-driven system, but it's also possible to get a much greater variety of reports as well.

You may be able to imagine how much time accountants spent simply completing the steps in the cycle before the advent of information technology. Later in the chapter, we'll take a look at how IT has facilitated the accounting cycle, as well as ways in which human judgment is still paramount in its 10 steps.

CODING SYSTEMS

In both manual and automated accounting information systems, each account typically has both a name and a number; account numbers facilitate transaction recording and posting, particularly when the AIS relies heavily on automation. In most cases, you'll walk into an organization with an established chart of accounts; however, at some point in your career, you may need to create a chart from scratch. At a minimum, you'll need to be able to understand your company's and/or clients' charts of accounts. In this section, we'll look at some of the systems used in practice to establish and modify charts of accounts.

Williamson (2006) lists five important reasons for maintaining a clear, logical chart of accounts:

- efficiency of data capture, entry and analysis . . .
- frequency of use and familiarity . . .
- consistency and understanding of use within the organization . . .
- saving on computer processing time and storage . . .
- similar items can be related by means of a coding system, whereas a verbal description could be very inefficient . . .

In addition, Williamson identified several common coding systems often used in organizations; while they are not exhaustive, they do provide a comprehensive overview. So, let's look at four of them briefly.

- *Sequential coding,* as the name implies, simply numbers items in sequence. Think of the checks in your checkbook when you think of sequential coding. In automated accounting information systems, transactions might be assigned sequential numbers by a computer as a method of internal control.

- *Block coding* is quite common in a chart of accounts. Numbers are assigned in blocks; each block is reserved for a particular kind of account. For example, all current asset accounts might start with "1," while equity accounts might start with "5." Thus, you can tell what kind of account you're dealing with simply by looking at its first digit.

- *Hierarchical codes* are a more sophisticated form of block coding. In hierarchical coding, each digit/block of digits conveys important information to people who know the code. The Harvard Law School uses hierarchical coding in its chart of accounts (www .law.harvard.edu/about/administration/financial/accounts.html). Its codes are organized in seven parts, with each part communicating specific information. Many enterprise resource planning systems, such as PeopleSoft, use hierarchical coding. Hierarchical coding is also very common in government AIS. They use a system called "fund accounting."

- *Mnemonic codes,* by their nature, help people remember the meaning of the code. At my university, as at most universities, course prefixes are mnemonic. ACC is the code for courses in the accounting department, while CIS stands for computer information systems. In an accounting information system, product and customer codes might be mnemonic in nature. Keep in mind that data about products and customers are commonly stored in master files, as noted in Chapter 1's discussion of the elements of the AIS.

See Table 2.4 for examples of account coding.

While many organizations develop their own unique chart of accounts, some use a standardized chart of accounts. Thorp (1991) talked about the "European Uniform Chart of Accounts" as a way of facilitating information exchange between and within organizations. For example, a company with five geographic locations might use a uniform chart of accounts to make preparing financial statements easier.

TABLE 2.4   Chart of Accounts Coding

Coding System	Example	Format
Sequential	Purchase order numbers	101, 102, 103
Block	Uniform system of accounts for restaurants	Current assets: 101, 105, 109 Plant assets: 202, 206, 208 Current liabilities: 301, 303, 305
Hierarchical	State university	101-11-08-81 101: Big City campus 11: academic affairs division 08: college of business 81: accounting department
Mnemonic	Inventory items	DVR: digital video recorder FSTV: flat-screen television

HUMAN JUDGMENT AND INFORMATION TECHNOLOGY

Susan Wolcott, of Wolcott Lynch Associates, has developed a methodology for enhancing critical thinking and judgment skills. Called the "Steps for Better Thinking," you can find more information about it at www .wolcottlynch.com. We'll be exploring SBT in more depth in the chapter on decision-making models and knowledge management.

Principles-based accounting is an alternative to the current rules-based approach. For more information, do a library search on principles-based accounting. You also may consult Howard Stock, "SEC Urges Principles-Based Accounting," *Investor Relations Business,* August 4, 2003, p. 1.

Accounting has been a "system" since the 14th century; using information technology tools to assist in the collection, processing, and dissemination of accounting information is a relatively recent phenomenon in the profession. And, while IT has had a profound impact, it has only increased the need for and opportunity to exercise human judgment.

Human judgment comes into play in the AIS in at least the following ways:

- *Designing source documents.* We'll consider issues of forms design in greater detail in future chapters. But, for now, be aware that source documents should be clear and easy to read, omit unnecessary information, and provide plenty of space for filling in required data. Sequential numbering, such as in your checkbook, is also important for strong internal control.

- *Recognizing recordable transactions.* Not every document in an AIS indicates a recordable transaction; further, not every recordable transaction is represented by a source document. Therefore, accountants must exercise professional judgment in recognizing recordable transactions.

- *Estimating amounts and interpreting accounting rules.* Many journal entries, particularly adjusting entries, require the use of estimates. For example, accountants must estimate the useful economic life and salvage value of fixed assets to calculate depreciation. Further, FASB pronouncements and other authoritative accounting documents require significant interpretation. As principles-based accounting standards, such as International Financial Reporting Standards (IFRS), become the norm, interpretation will become even more important.

At the same time, **information technology** has cut down on the tedium associated with many steps in the accounting cycle. Transactions can be posted automatically or with the touch of a button; the same applies to closing the accounts at the end of the period. Reports, including the general-purpose financial statements, can easily be generated with the "touch of a button" as well. We'll explore information technology issues in greater depth in Part Three of the book.

CRITICAL THINKING

I'd like to explore two topics with you in this chapter's critical thinking section: recognizing transactions that should be recorded in the AIS and creating a coding system for a chart of accounts.

As you read earlier in the chapter, human judgment is important in several areas of the accounting cycle—one of which is recognizing transactions that should (and should not) be recorded. Consider the three items that follow, along with their explanations:

1. *FNF Corporation sold merchandise with a cost of $800 to customers on account for $1,000.* This transaction should be recorded in the AIS; goods were exchanged between two willing parties, and the evidence of it is clear and objective. Assuming the use of a perpetual inventory system, this transaction would be recorded as follows: debit Accounts Receivable, $1,000; debit Cost of Goods Sold, $800, credit Sales, $1,000; credit Inventory, $800.

2. *During 20x3, FNF Corporation purchased temporary investments with a cost of $10,000. The market value of those investments at the end of 20x3 was $12,000; FNF classified them as trading securities.* Of course, the initial purchase of the investments should be recorded in the AIS. But the increase in market value also should be recorded.

According to FASB No. 115, trading securities should be reported at their fair value. At first, this idea may seem to violate the objectivity principle of the FASB conceptual framework. The key here, though, is that the market value of the investments is readily determinable by looking at the financial press. An accountant couldn't simply decide to increase the market value based on his/her own judgment; but, if the market value of the investments can be looked up, then the investments must be increased. The $2,000 difference would be referred to as an *unrealized gain,* which means that it hasn't been "economically experienced" by FNF. To experience (realize) the gain, FNF would have to sell the investments.

3. *FNF purchased the land for its headquarters 10 years ago at a cost of $65,000. In 20x3, a real estate investor offered to purchase the land for $165,000.* In this case, the $100,000 would not be recorded in the AIS unless FNF actually sold the land. The fact that they've had an offer to buy it isn't objective enough; in addition, the land is not held as an investment—it's used for their headquarters. So, unlike item 2, the increase in market value would not result in an "unrealized gain" for FNF.

So, as you can tell, recognizing which transactions to record in an AIS requires critical thinking and a solid understanding of accounting principles.

When it comes to designing a chart of accounts, critical thinking is important. Whatever coding system an organization uses (sequential, block, hierarchical, mnemonic), it must be easily understood and rational. Consider the example below, which used a random number generator to assign account numbers in an AIS:

Poorly Designed Chart of Accounts	
252	Cash
256	Accounts receivable
311	Accounts payable
698	Wages payable
461	Capital stock
507	Retained earnings
824	Sales
617	Interest earned
633	Cost of goods sold
924	Depreciation expense

There's no "rhyme or reason" to that chart of accounts; you would practically have to memorize each number and account name individually. On the other hand, the chart of accounts could be made much more understandable with a block-coding system:

Block Coded Chart of Accounts	
101	Cash
103	Accounts receivable
301	Accounts payable
305	Wages payable
402	Capital stock
406	Retained earnings
501	Sales
701	Interest earned
633	Cost of goods sold
635	Depreciation expense

In the block-coded chart, current assets begin with "1," while current liabilities begin with "3." Equity accounts start with "4." Operating revenue (such as sales) is differentiated from nonoperating revenue (such as interest earned) easily with block coding.

Consider these additional account titles and suggested numbers that would conform to the block-coding system:

105	Inventory
201	Land
203	Equipment
213	Accumulated depreciation—equipment
405	Treasury stock
801	Interest expense

Inventory, as a current asset, has a number starting with "1." Because current assets start with "1" and current liabilities with "3," what kinds of accounts should start with "2"? Long-term assets, such as land and equipment. Notice the numbering similarity between equipment (203) and its related accumulated depreciation account (213). As an equity account, treasury stock has a number that starts with "4." Interest expense starts with an "8" because it would normally be considered a nonoperating expense.

Is block coding the only way to organize a chart of accounts? Definitely not. Is it the best way? In some cases, sure—but not every time. And you could come up with completely different numbers even using a block-coding system. The important idea is being able to explain the coding system to others so that they can use it effectively.

Summary

This chapter has presented a review of the steps in the accounting cycle. Here is the usual summary based on the chapter's learning objectives:

1. *Differentiate accounting and bookkeeping.* Bookkeeping is the part of accounting concerned with recording transactions in the AIS. Accounting goes far beyond that, concerning itself with identifying those transactions and communicating information for decision making.

2. *List, discuss, and complete, in order, the steps in the accounting cycle.* The chapter examined 10 steps in the accounting cycle:

   a. Obtain information about external transactions from source documents.
   b. Analyze transactions.
   c. Record the transactions in a journal.
   d. Post from the journal to the general ledger accounts.
   e. Prepare an unadjusted trial balance.
   f. Record adjusting entries and post to the general ledger accounts.
   g. Prepare an adjusted trial balance.
   h. Prepare financial statements.
   i. Close the temporary accounts to retained earnings (at year-end only).
   j. Prepare a post-closing trial balance (at year-end only).

3. *Identify common internal controls associated with the accounting cycle.* Internal controls include sequentially numbered documents, physical security, transaction limits, equality of debits and credits, trial balances, and audits.

4. *Describe common chart of accounts coding systems.* The chapter discusses four common systems: sequential, block, hierarchical, and mnemonic.

5. *Explain how human judgment and information technology affect the accounting cycle.* Accountants exercise their judgment in deciding which transactions are recordable in the accounting information system. Information technology can be used for a variety of tasks in the cycle: recording transactions, posting them to the ledger, preparing trial balances and financial statements, and closing the accounts.

Accounting education has typically emphasized transaction processing throughout the undergraduate curriculum; understanding this topic is important in your education as an accountant. We'll use it as a foundational topic, exploring more advanced issues throughout the rest of the text.

Key Terms

accounting, *20*
accounting cycle, *21*
adjusting entries, *25*
bookkeeping, *20*
external transactions, *21*

general-purpose financial statements, *26*
human judgment, *29*
information technology, *29*
internal transactions, *21*

principles of debit and credit, *22*
source documents, *21*

Chapter References

Spiceland, J. D., J. F. Sepe, and L. A. Tomassini. 2001. *Intermediate Accounting.* Updated 2nd ed. New York: Irwin/McGraw-Hill.

Thorp, J. A. 1991. "European Uniform Chart of Accounts." *Management Accounting,* July/August, pp. 20–23.

Williamson, D. 2006. "Coding Systems for Accountants: An Introduction." www.duncanwil.co.uk (June 20, 2006).

End-of-Chapter Activities

1. *Reading review questions.*

   a. In your own words, explain the similarities and differences between accounting and bookkeeping.

   b. What systems do accountants use to create and modify a chart of accounts?

   c. What internal controls are common in the accounting cycle?

   d. How is human judgment involved in the accounting cycle?

   e. How has information technology been employed in the accounting cycle?

   f. List and discuss the six common types of adjusting entries found in most accounting information systems.

   g. Explain the purpose and structure of each general-purpose financial statement.

   h. Respond to the questions for the chapter's "AIS in the Business World."

2. *Multiple choice review questions.* Please indicate the best answer for each question.

   1. Which of the following best explains the relationship between bookkeeping and accounting?
      a. Bookkeeping is one activity involved in accounting.
      b. Accounting is one activity involved in bookkeeping.
      c. Bookkeeping and accounting are two terms for the same thing.
      d. Bookkeeping never involves human judgment, while accounting always does.

   2. How many trial balances are commonly prepared as part of the 10 steps in the accounting cycle?
      a. One
      b. Two

    c. Three

    d. More than three

3. Which of the following is the best example of an accrued revenue?

    a. Interest earned but not received on a note receivable

    b. Interest received but not earned on a note receivable

    c. Sales on account

    d. Purchases on account

4. All of the following chart of accounts coding systems typically use numbers except:

    a. Block.

    b. Hierarchical.

    c. Mnemonic.

    d. Sequential.

5. Human judgment can be involved in the AIS via:

    a. Designing source documents.

    b. Recognizing recordable transactions.

    c. Estimating amounts.

    d. All of the above.

3. *Reading review problem.* According to its Web site (**www.rkr.csupomona.edu**), "The Restaurant at Kellogg Ranch (RKR) is a student-operated restaurant, serving both lunch and dinner. The restaurant is part of the Hospitality Management curriculum at The Collins College of Hospitality Management at Cal Poly Pomona."

RKR's chart of accounts is block coded. For example, assets related to food and beverage operations all have four-digit account numbers that begin with "1." Expenses for nonsalable items (such as cleaning supplies for the kitchen) have four-digit account numbers that begin with "7."

RKR's transaction processing software, developed and created by Lawrence Browning, is called DataTrap; it runs as an add-on to Excel. DataTrap organizes RKR's accounting and operating data into several worksheets within a single Excel file. Some of those worksheets include net sales, counts of lunch and dinner items, credits for lunch and dinner items, waste, crew meals for both lunch and dinner, and inventory. RKR uses those data to complete a weekly income statement summary sheet that reports both financial data (such as revenue from lunch, revenue from dinner, breakage expenses, supplies expense) and nonfinancial data (such as the number of guests for lunch and dinner, food cost as a percentage of food revenue).

RKR's transaction processing is complicated a bit by its relationship to the University. It must periodically transmit its financial data to the Cal Poly Pomona Foundation (**http://foundation.csupomona.edu/**), but the Foundation uses the principles of not-for-profit accounting, not the traditional accrual accounting businesses use. In effect, that reporting arrangement requires RKR to maintain two sets of accounting records: one for internal purposes, which is used for student assignments and management decision making, and one for use by the Foundation as part of its financial relationship with the University.

a. Is transaction processing more closely related to accounting or bookkeeping? Explain your response.

b. What does it mean to say RKR's chart of accounts is "block coded"? What other coding systems are available, and when might they be most appropriately used?

c. How should RKR maintain strong internal control over its transaction processing activities?

d. Suggest three to five transactions RKR would need to record on a routine basis. Indicate which accounts would be debited and credited for each transaction.

4. *Making choices and exercising judgment.*

   a. Which of the following would be recordable transactions in an accounting information system? For each item that would not be a recordable transaction, explain why not.

      i. Purchasing land with a down payment and a note payable.

      ii. Verifying an increase in the market value of land.

      iii. Establishing an exclusive relationship with a raw material supplier.

      iv. Estimating the amount of warranty expense for the next accounting period.

      v. Negotiating with an employees union for wage increases.

   b. How will principles-based accounting influence the design of accounting information systems? The steps in the accounting cycle?

   c. Use EDGAR to obtain the 10-K reports for Barnes & Noble dated 1 April 2009 and 2 April 2008. Compare their financial statements and comment on which company is stronger.

5. *Field exercises.*

   a. Point your Web browser to **www.download.com**. Investigate BS1 Accounting and 3S Accounting—two general ledger packages that can help companies with the steps in the accounting cycle. Identify and describe at least two modules in each system; explain the types of accounting transactions the modules are designed to record.

   b. Point your Web browser to **www.law.harvard.edu/administration/financial/coa**. Describe Harvard Law School's chart of accounts coding system.

   c. Contact an accounting professional at a local organization such as your university, a bank, or a retail store. Find out how he/she employs human judgment and information technology in completing the steps of the accounting cycle.

6. *Journal entries.* Record each of the following transactions in general journal format.

   a. Issued 50,000 shares of $1 par capital stock for $35 each.

   b. Billed customers for services provided, $10,000.

   c. Purchased supplies on account, $3,000.

   d. Paid monthly utility bill, $1,500.

   e. Verified 20 percent increase in market price of stock.

   f. Paid wages for the current month, $6,000.

   g. Purchased equipment with a list price of $50,000 by making a 20 percent down payment and financing the remainder with a six-month, 12 percent note payable.

   h. Collected cash from customers, $5,000.

   i. Paid vendors, $1,400.

   j. Recorded one month's accrued interest on note payable.

7. *Adjusting entries.* The unadjusted trial balance for GLP Corporation appears on the next page.

   End-of-period analysis revealed the following:

   a. The market value of equipment had decreased by 30 percent of its original cost. Depreciation for the quarter totaled $1,000.

   b. The note payable was signed on August 1, 20x4. Its interest rate was 10 percent, and no interest had been recorded since the signing.

   c. Unpaid employee wages at September 30 totaled $1,000.

   d. Deferred fees represented a consulting contract signed at the beginning of September. The contract's duration is three months, and the work is spread evenly throughout the contract period.

   e. Supplies on hand totaled $150.

   f. The market value of capital stock had increased by 15 percent.

   g. Actual bad debt write-offs during September were $300; 1 percent of sales will likely become uncollectible in the coming period.

GLP CORPORATION
Trial Balance
September 30, 20x4

	Debit	Credit
Cash	$ 6,000	
Accounts receivable	2,500	
Allowance for bad debts		$ 200
Inventory	4,500	
Supplies	800	
Equipment	15,000	
Accumulated depreciation—equipment		10,000
Accounts payable		1,200
Notes payable		6,000
Deferred fees		900
Capital stock		7,000
Additional paid-in capital		8,000
Retained earnings		11,000
Sales		16,000
Cost of goods sold	13,500	
Advertising expense	5,000	
Wages expense	12,000	
Miscellaneous expense	1,000	
Totals	$60,300	$60,300

Prepare the required adjusting entries based on the preceding information. Then, prepare an adjusted trial balance.

8. *Financial statements.* Use the adjusted trial balance from Problem 6 to prepare an income statement for the quarter ended September 30, 20x4, and a balance sheet as of September 30, 20x4, for GLP Corporation.

9. *Coding systems.* Which type of coding system is indicated in each of the following independent situations? Be prepared to explain your reasoning.

    a. Airport codes (LAX, OGG)
    b. Automatically assigned transaction numbers in a cash register
    c. Consecutively numbered purchase orders (101, 102, 103, and so on)
    d. Dewey Decimal System (used to classify library books)
    e. Invoice numbers
    f. National Association of Home Builders chart of accounts (look this one up on the Internet)
    g. Standard chart of accounts included with QuickBooks
    h. Telephone numbers
    i. Universal Product Codes (UPCs)
    j. ZIP codes (91768, 63135)

10. *Terminology.* Please match each item on the right with the most appropriate item on the left.

1. Accrued revenue	a. Book of original entry
2. Credit	b. Cash is received before service is provided
3. Debit	c. Decreases to revenue
4. Deferred revenue	d. Increases to liabilities
5. Human judgment	e. Purchase orders, invoices, and receipts
6. Information technology	f. Service is provided before cash is received
7. Journal	g. Simplifies the bookkeeping process
8. Posting	h. Transferring information from the journal to the ledger
9. Source document	i. Used to recognize recordable transactions
10. Trial balance	j. Verifies the equality of debits and credits in the ledger

11. *Multiple choice questions.*

1. BRN Corporation has two divisions: California and Nevada. Both divisions have the same basic chart of accounts, which numbers current assets in the 100s, plant assets in the 200s, and so on. BRN differentiates them with an appended "C" or "N" after the account number. From BRN's point of view, the chart of accounts coding system would best be described as:

   a. Block.
   b. Hierarchical.
   c. Mnemonic.
   d. Sequential.

2. Consider the data from Question 1. From the divisions' point of view, the chart of accounts coding system would best be described as:

   a. Block.
   b. Hierarchical.
   c. Mnemonic.
   d. Sequential.

3. Which of the following is a characteristic of all adjusting entries?

   a. They are written in the journal, but not posted to the ledger.
   b. They always involve an entry to Cash or Retained Earnings.
   c. They always include one nominal account and one permanent account.
   d. They always involve estimates.

4. Consider the trial balance of DMN Corporation shown in Table 2.1. Based on that trial balance alone, which of the following income statement items would total $7,500?

   a. Revenue
   b. Gross profit
   c. Net income
   d. Net loss

5. Consider the trial balance of DMN Corporation shown in Table 2.1. Based on that trial balance alone, DMN's income statement would report:

   a. Net income of $7,500.
   b. Net loss of $7,500.
   c. Net income of $1,300.
   d. Net loss of $1,300.

12. *Statement evaluation.* Determine whether each of the following statements is (i) always true, (ii) sometimes true, or (iii) never true. For those that are (ii) sometimes true, explain when the statement is true.

    a. Bookkeeping and accounting are two ways of referring to the same thing.

    b. If a transaction increases a liability, it will also increase an expense.

    c. The accounting cycle involves human judgment.

    d. A company's chart of accounts should use block coding.

    e. Information technology has eliminated the need for human judgment in the accounting cycle.

    f. An "accrual" refers to a situation where a company provides service before receiving cash.

    g. An adjusting entry for depreciation recognizes an asset's loss in market value over time.

    h. Adjusting entries involve one balance sheet account and one income statement account, but never cash.

    i. In automated accounting information systems, block coding facilitates closing entries.

    j. The complete accounting cycle incorporates three different forms of a trial balance.

13. *International Financial Reporting Standards (IFRS).* Do an Internet search for information on IFRS. Visit at least two Web sites, including the International Accounting Standards Board, and respond to the following questions about IFRS:

    a. Compare and contrast the IFRS framework with the FASB conceptual framework discussed in Chapter 1. List three similarities and three differences between the two.

    b. Choose two countries that have adopted IFRS. If an organization had operations in both countries, how would you communicate that fact in their chart of accounts?

Chapter **Three**

Internal Controls

AIS in the Business World

Enron

By this time in your accounting education, you are likely at least somewhat familiar with the Enron fraud. Although it came to light nearly a decade ago, the issues and lessons raised by the scandal for both business in general and accounting specifically are as timely today as they were in 2002. Pitt (2006) offered the following comments just as Enron executives Ken Lay and Jeff Skilling were about to be tried for their role in the fraud (**emphasis added**):

> The principal deficiencies that led to Enron's demise are easy enough to catalog. They include, in no special order: **a serious lack of meaningful internal controls;** directors who didn't really understand their functions or how to perform them; rampant conflicts of interest between senior managers and the shareholders of Enron; off-balance-sheet obscuring of significant liabilities; impenetrable accounting chicanery, designed to make the company look profitable; and a culture of lawlessness and unaccountability.

The consequences of Enron and the other frauds of the late 20th century resulted in the most sweeping legislation impacting the accounting profession since the 1930s: the Sarbanes-Oxley Act of 2002.

Discussion Questions

1. What is internal control? What are its purposes?
2. Why is internal control a fundamental part of accounting information systems?
3. How did the Sarbanes-Oxley Act attempt to address the issue of internal control?

Source: H. L. Pitt, "Trials and Tribulations of Enron and S-Ox," *Forbes*, 23 January 2006. Retrieved 2 January 2011 from www.forbes.com.

Internal controls have been at the heart of accounting information systems practically since AIS emerged as a separate field of study for accounting students. A lack of sound internal controls can have serious consequences for a company—particularly with the advent of Sarbanes-Oxley and the Public Companies Accounting Oversight Board. In this chapter, we'll lay a foundation in the study of internal control; later chapters will apply the basic ideas you learn here to specific contexts within your study of accounting information systems.

When you complete your study of this chapter, you should be able to:

1. Define *internal control* and explain its importance in the accounting information system.
2. Explain the basic purposes of internal control and its relationship to risk.
3. Describe and give examples of various kinds of risk exposures.
4. Prepare a simple risk/control matrix.
5. Summarize and explain the importance of COSO's "Internal Control—Integrated Framework."
6. Critique existing internal control systems and design effective internal controls.

A solid understanding of internal controls is important in any area of accounting. If you're considering a career in auditing, you need to be able to assess internal controls as part of an audit. If you're thinking about a career in corporate or not-for-profit accounting, you may have to design internal controls to comply with Sarbanes-Oxley.

INTERNAL CONTROL DEFINITION AND IMPORTANCE

You can find COSO's Web site at www.coso .org. Click the "publications" link for executive summaries of the reports discussed here.

So what is internal control? In *Internal Control—Integrated Framework* (1985), the Committee of Sponsoring Organizations of the Treadway Commission (COSO) defined **internal control** as "a process, effected by an entity's board of directors, management and other personnel, designed to provide reasonable assurance regarding the achievement of objectives in the following categories: effectiveness and efficiency of operations, reliability of financial reporting and compliance with applicable laws and regulations." Notice these important elements of the COSO definition:

- *Internal control is a process.* Popular wisdom states that 20 percent of employees in most organizations will not defraud the company under any circumstances; 60 percent of employees will defraud the company if it's easy; and the remaining 20 percent will go out of their way to defraud the company. Because internal control is a process, it is subject to process improvement; single correct answers to control problems seldom exist. Accountants must use judgment and experience in designing and implementing internal controls; the controls must be periodically reviewed to ensure their continued effectiveness.

- *Internal control necessarily involves people in the organization.* The COSO definition lays the responsibility for internal control squarely at the feet of management and the board of directors. Internal controls, therefore, require discussion during design, implementation, and evaluation. They impact human behavior, and control systems designers, as far as possible, must anticipate their behavioral effects. As a new feature in this edition of the text, we'll look at some important concepts from management, including behavioral issues in AIS, in Chapter 4.

- *Internal controls are designed to provide reasonable assurance.* Dictionary.com defines reasonable as "governed by or being in accordance with reason or sound thinking; being within the bounds of common sense; not excessive or extreme." So, internal controls should not, and probably cannot, be designed to provide absolute assurance of anything. Going back to our prior discussion of the conceptual framework of accounting, internal controls are subject to a cost–benefit constraint. Their cost must be outweighed by their benefit if they are to be meaningful.

- *Internal controls provide reasonable assurance in a few common areas, such as operations, financial reporting, and human behavior.* When I talk to students and business professionals about internal control, I identify four purposes: safeguarding assets, ensuring financial statement reliability, promoting operational efficiency, and encouraging compliance with management's directives. In short, internal controls are there to help ensure that no one steals from the company and everyone follows the rules.

Why are internal controls important? One answer certainly lies with the purposes of internal control (as shown in Table 3.1). Most managers, stockholders, employees, and other organizational stakeholders want a company to operate as effectively and efficiently as possible, to have financial statements that are reliable, and to make sure their assets are safe. Apart from those issues, though, internal control is also legally mandated by several important pieces of legislation.

You can find out more about the FCPA on its Web site: www.usdoj .gov/criminal/fraud/ fcpa.html.

The **Foreign Corrupt Practices Act (FCPA)** was passed by the U.S. Congress in 1977. U.S. businesses had begun expanding internationally in the mid-1970s. And, in some foreign countries, bribery is an acceptable way of doing business. In fact, an SEC investigation in the 1970s showed that over 400 U.S. companies had paid bribes to foreign officials for a variety of reasons. Although bribery is an acceptable business practice in some countries, it is not in the United States. So, the FCPA was enacted to stop those practices by U.S. businesses and to restore some confidence in U.S. business practices around the world. The FCPA requires corporations covered by its provisions to maintain an adequate system of internal accounting controls. The act also states, "no person shall knowingly circumvent or knowingly fail to implement a system of internal accounting controls or knowingly falsify any book, record, or account." The legislation also mentions the concept of reasonable assurance, defining it as "such level of detail and degree of assurance as would satisfy prudent officials in the conduct of their own affairs." Companies failing to comply with the Foreign Corrupt Practices Act can be subject to both fines and imprisonment.

Details of SOX are available all over the Internet. One site I've found useful is www .soxlaw.com. It is a proprietary site, but the information is accurate and easy to read.

In response to the corporate scandals of the late 20th century, Congress passed the **Sarbanes-Oxley Act of 2002.** Sarbanes-Oxley (SOX for short) is the most sweeping accounting-related legislation business professionals have seen since the FCPA. It is a broad-reaching act that significantly changed the way U.S. companies do business, as well as impacting the roles of top management, the board of directors,

TABLE 3.1 **Purposes of Internal Control**

Safeguarding assets
Ensuring financial statement reliability
Promoting operational efficiency
Encouraging compliance with management's directives

independent auditors, and audit committees. Provisions of SOX related to internal controls include

- Management and the external auditors must assess the company's internal controls on an annual basis.
- Management has certain required disclosures when reporting to the SEC. They include acknowledgment that management is personally and organizationally responsible for the design and implementation of internal controls, particularly as they relate to reasonable assurance of reliable financial statements. Management also must disclose any internal control changes since the last reporting cycle, if those changes are likely to have a noticeable effect on internal controls over financial reporting. Finally, management must certify that they have informed the auditors and the board of director's audit committee of any significant problems or weaknesses in internal control.
- Management must personally sign the required certifications and reports related to the preceding items. The signature cannot be delegated, even via power of attorney.

Many of the SOX requirements related to internal control are found in section 404 of the act. In practice, people often refer to conducting/having a "404 audit."

So, internal controls are very important for organizations of all types. As an accounting professional, you may be involved in the design, implementation, or evaluation of internal controls as an external (independent) auditor, internal auditor, controller, or consultant.

Reflection and Self-Assessment   3.1

Compare the content and purpose of the FCPA and SOX. What similarities and differences do you notice? If a nonaccountant asked you how you know that financial statements are fair and reliable, what would you say?

To design effective internal controls, accountants and managers should consider the risks associated with doing business. By identifying risks, we can develop controls to mitigate them successfully.

RISKS

Risk is a part of everyday life—both personally and professionally. The question is, are businesses taking risks unnecessarily, to the point that they cannot operate effectively or rely on their accounting systems to produce reliable information?

Most business professionals, including accountants, find it easier to think about risk if they have some organizational structure for doing so. An organizational structure for knowledge, like types of risk, is sometimes referred to as a *taxonomy.*

Think about risks you have taken today. For example, you risked that your car wouldn't start when you came to school. You may have taken a risk in leaving your house, residence hall, or apartment later than usual. List six additional risks you've taken today and organize them in some way that makes sense to you.

FIGURE 3.1   Brown's Risk Taxonomy

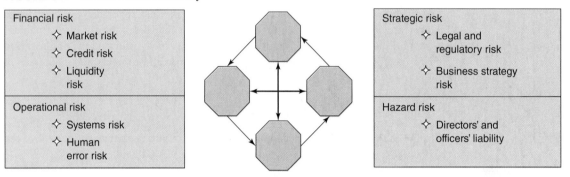

Financial risk
   ◇ Market risk
   ◇ Credit risk
   ◇ Liquidity risk

Operational risk
   ◇ Systems risk
   ◇ Human error risk

Strategic risk
   ◇ Legal and regulatory risk
   ◇ Business strategy risk

Hazard risk
   ◇ Directors' and officers' liability

Brown (2001) takes a very practical view toward the management of risk. He identified four categories of risk and suggested eight specific risks within the four categories, as shown in Figure 3.1. Here are some definitions and examples of the elements of **Brown's taxonomy of risk:**

1. *Financial risks* are related to monetary activities. The worldwide financial crisis that started in 2007 had elements of all three forms of financial risk.

   a. *Market risk* refers to changes in a company's stock prices, investment values, and interest rates. For example, if an organization fails to diversify its financial investments adequately, it runs the risk of a significant decrease in value that will impact financial statements.

   b. *Credit risk* is associated with customers' unwillingness or inability to pay amounts owed to the organization. For example, you may have seen department store employees outside of stores during the holiday season. They want you to fill out an application for a credit card, which is virtually guaranteed to get you at least a small amount of credit. While granting credit without a solid investigation will probably boost sales in the short run, the company runs the risk of nonpayment.

   c. *Liquidity risk* involves the possibility that a company will not have sufficient cash and near-cash assets available to meet its short-term obligations. If an organization has no budget or spending plan for its cash and near-cash assets, it is exposed to this risk.

2. *Operational risks* concern the people, assets, and technologies used to create value for the organization's customers.

   a. *Systems risk* relates directly to information technology (IT). As organizations become increasingly dependent on computers and related IT to deliver goods and services to customers, they risk the possibility that IT resources will fail at a critical moment.

   b. *Human error risk* recognizes the possibility that people in the organization may make mistakes. Those mistakes might result in asset misappropriation or theft, divulgence of trade secrets, legal action from breaking laws, or other consequences. For example, a manager might create a hostile work environment for an employee, leading to a sexual harassment lawsuit.

3. *Strategic risks,* according to Brown (2001, p. 44), "relate to the entity's decision-making process at the senior management and board of directors level."

    a. *Legal and regulatory risk* is concerned with the chance that those parties might break laws that result in financial, legal, or operational sanctions. For example, if the CEO and/or the CFO knowingly falsify the reports required by SOX, they may be subject to governmental penalties.

    b. *Business strategy risk* comprises poor decision making related to a company's basis for competing in its markets. You may remember the era of Web-based grocery stores in the United States. Firms such as WebGrocer are now out of business, at least in part because they did not adequately consider the risk associated with trying to develop a new market for a previously nonexistent service.

4. *Hazard risk,* in Brown's taxonomy, has a single category: *directors' and officers' liability.* Organizations in which directors and officers are accused of mismanagement by shareholders, government agencies, employees, or other stakeholders bear this risk in a very direct way. Many corporate officers of companies like Enron, WorldCom, and HealthSouth have spent or are spending time in prison as a result of the corporate scandals of the late 20th century.

Brown's taxonomy of risk is not the only one available for risk assessment. For example, Hollander, Denna, and Cherrington (2000) suggest five categories of risk, some of which overlap with Brown's four categories. The Hollander categories include strategic risk, decision risk, operating risk, financial risk, and information risk. If you completed Reflection and Self-Assessment 3.2, you created your own taxonomy of risk. The point here is not which taxonomy is better or the best; your goal should be to work with a comprehensive taxonomy that makes sense to you in identifying risks associated with the design and implementation of accounting information systems.

Reflection and Self-Assessment   3.3

The Institute of Internal Auditors (www.theiia.org) publishes a monthly newsletter called "Tone at the Top." Look up an article from the February 2002 edition titled "The Lessons that Lie Beneath." List three ways the information in the article relates to the material you just read on risk assessment and internal control.

By using a taxonomy to identify risks, accountants, managers, and other organizational stakeholders are in a much better position to establish internal controls that will ameliorate (lessen the impact of) those risks.

COSO'S INTERNAL CONTROL INTEGRATED FRAMEWORK

The Committee of Sponsoring Organizations of the Treadway Commission (**COSO** for short) comprises the Institute of Management Accountants, the American Institute of Certified Public Accountants, the American Accounting Association, the Institute of Internal

FIGURE 3.2

Components of the COSO Internal Control Framework

Sep of duties
custody
Recording
Reconciliation
Authorization

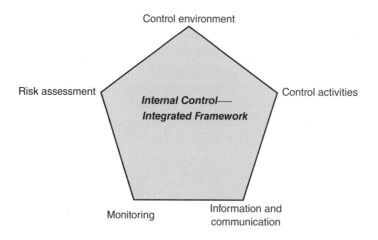

Auditors, and the Financial Executives Institute. COSO's first publication, **Internal Control—Integrated Framework,** suggested five interrelated components for achieving effective internal control: control environment, risk assessment, control activities, information and communication, and monitoring. (See Figure 3.2.) Although each component has its own definition and explanation, the five truly form an *integrated framework* in the best sense of the term. Managers and accountants cannot afford to pay attention to a subset of the five components; they must be considered simultaneously to achieve the internal control objectives discussed earlier in this chapter.

The *control environment* refers to the tone at the top of the organization. It reminds accountants and managers that, without the clear, demonstrated commitment of upper management and opinion leaders in the organization, internal control will not be taken seriously elsewhere in the hierarchy. To develop and sustain a strong control environment, managers and other influential people in the organization should

ISACA (Information Systems Audit and Control Association, www.isaca.org) developed another control framework, often referred to as COBIT (Control Objectives for Information and Related Technology). We'll explore COBIT in more depth in our discussion of computer crime later in the text.

1. Be committed to integrity and ethical behavior.
2. Demonstrate a commitment to competence in carrying out their duties and responsibilities.
3. Actively seek the participation of the board of directors and its audit committee in decisions related to internal control.
4. Maintain a consistent, appropriate management philosophy and operating style.
5. Structure the organization for efficiency, effectiveness, and reasonable internal control.
6. Assign authority and responsibility with integrity and the best interests of the organization in mind.
7. Develop and enforce human resource policies and practices that encourage all employees to maintain a sound internal control system.

Risk assessment is the second component of the integrated framework. It involves using a taxonomy, business experience, research, and dialogue to identify the risks associated with operations. By identifying risks, we can design appropriate, cost-effective internal controls to provide reasonable assurance of safeguarding assets, ensuring financial statement reliability, promoting operational efficiency, and encouraging compliance with management's directives.

The *control activities* refer to the actual internal controls implemented on the basis of the risk assessment. Control activities also can be organized into a number of taxonomies, one of which is based on their purpose and function. *Preventive controls* such as requiring two signatures on checks over $1,000 help prevent errors and irregularities from happening. *Detective controls* such as airport metal detectors help stakeholders determine when an error or irregularity has occurred. Finally, *corrective controls,* which include things like anger management courses or punishments for subverting internal controls, focus on fixing a problem, error, or irregularity after it has occurred.

A single control may serve more than one purpose in the preceding taxonomy. For example, seeing an employee lose his/her job because of consistent cash shortages that cannot be explained serves as a corrective control for one employee, but may serve as a preventive control for a co-worker. Likewise, airport metal detectors could be classified in all three categories. They help prevent dangerous items from being brought on board airplanes; they also detect such substances before they are actually brought on board. Subsequent searches and legal action help correct the problem.

The presence of information technology in an accounting information system requires a different level or set of controls, referred to as information processing controls. *General controls* apply to an entire information system or significant "chunks" of the system. They include items such as backing up data files regularly and installing virus detection and removal software. *Application controls* are associated with a specific IT application such as the accounting information system. For example, most general ledger software packages such as QuickBooks and Peachtree do not allow users to make journal entries where the debits and credits are unequal.

Reflection and Self-Assessment   3.4

Consider the internal controls listed below. For each one, explain: (a) the risk it addresses, (b) the risk category from Brown's taxonomy, (c) the broad purpose of internal control it achieves, and (d) the nature of the control (preventive, detective, corrective).

1. Reconciling a bank statement.
2. Requiring that all purchase requisitions are coordinated through a central purchasing department.
3. Encouraging employees to attend annual seminars on ethical behavior in the workplace and related topics.
4. Tearing ticket stubs in half at a movie theater when a patron enters.
5. Collecting cash at one window and delivering the order in a different window at a fast food establishment.

Information and communication is the fourth component of COSO's integrated framework. For an internal control system to function effectively, its purpose, methods, and results must be communicated throughout the organization. Employees at all levels should understand the risk exposures they face and the controls employed to mitigate those exposures. They should be able to articulate how their position "fits into" the overall organizational structure and how the work they do every day contributes to fulfilling the objectives of sound internal control: safeguarding assets, ensuring financial statement reliability, promoting operational efficiency, and encouraging compliance with management's directives. Communicating information throughout the organization is a daunting task, particularly in large, decentralized, geographically dispersed organizations. Newsletters, seminars, individual or small group conferences, and focus groups can be used effectively to fulfill this important element of the integrated framework.

Finally, managers must determine the quality of internal control performance, a process known as *monitoring*. As noted previously, SOX mandates internal control monitoring and personal certification by the CEO and CFO of the organization. Companies' objectives and business processes change over time, so the monitoring function is an important part of maintaining good internal control. Monitoring systems can be automated, but many involve human interaction. For example, a company could monitor the number of customer compliments and complaints it receives. Managers, accountants, and/or internal auditors could keep records of the number and estimated dollar cost of internal control breaches. The accounting information system, if properly designed, also can produce reports of internal control costs by category or by type of risk. In a perfect world, internal control monitoring is seen as a formative process, not a summative one. In other words, the results of monitoring should be used to guide employee behavior, as opposed to being used to "whack employees over the head" for small violations of internal control policies.

In 2006, COSO published *Internal Control over Financial Reporting—Guidance for Smaller Public Companies.* When SOX was passed in 2002, many companies complained about its implementation cost—particularly smaller companies. That COSO document recognizes that smaller organizations face some unique challenges with respect to internal control, including (COSO, 2006)

- *Resources.* Obtaining sufficient resources to achieve adequate segregation of duties.
- *Management Domination.* Management's ability to dominate activities and significant opportunities for improper management override of processes. This could result in the appearance that business performance goals have been met, when in fact, they have not.
- *Board Expertise.* Recruiting individuals with requisite financial reporting and other expertise to serve effectively on the board of directors and audit committee.
- *Financial Competence.* Recruiting and retaining personnel with sufficient experience and skill in accounting and financial reporting.
- *Running the Business.* Taking critical management attention away from running the business in order to provide sufficient focus on accounting and financial reporting.
- *Information Technology.* Controlling information technology and maintaining appropriate general and application controls over computer information systems with limited technical resources.

The 2006 document lists and discusses 20 basic principles to help smaller organizations achieve strong, effective internal control.

Next, we'll turn our attention to a discussion of some common internal control procedures.

Reflection and Self-Assessment 3.5

Explain why COSO's Internal Control Integrated Framework is important to you as an accounting professional. Also check out the COSO Web site (www.coso.org).

What additional internal control publications has COSO issued?

INTERNAL CONTROL EXAMPLES

Internal control systems are as unique and different as the organizations and managers that utilize them. But some internal controls are so common that they merit a closer look. While the list below does not represent the "universe" of internal controls, it does give you an introduction to some you're likely to encounter in practice. (The items are listed in alphabetical order so you can refer to them easily later.)

1. *Adequate documentation.* Understanding how things are supposed to happen in an accounting information system is an important first step in designing and assessing internal controls. Process documentation, often in the form of flowcharts (Chapter 6) and/or data flow diagrams (Chapter 7), can help you critique internal controls and determine if they are functioning effectively.

2. *Background checks.* People are the heart of most organizations today. Particularly for employees in sensitive positions, such as those that deal with large amounts of money, background checks are essential. For example, they may reveal financial difficulties or criminal convictions that may create pressure to breach internal controls.

3. *Backup of computer files.* If done regularly, backing up computer files takes only a few minutes—a small inconvenience compared to the alternative of recreating files from scratch. Daily backups ensure that no more than one day's work is lost in the event of a systems failure.

4. *Backup of power supplies.* A few years ago, California was subject to power blackouts when the state's electrical grid was overloaded. During that time, backup power supplies were commonly employed as an internal control. While a computer cannot run indefinitely on a backup power supply, the backup supply can give the user time to save any open files, ensuring they are not lost.

5. *Bank reconciliation.* You probably learned how to reconcile a bank statement in your introductory accounting course. The basic purpose of a bank reconciliation is to account for timing differences between the account holder's records and the bank's records of a cash account. Reconciling the bank statement at least monthly can be helpful in spotting out-of-sequence checks, fraudulent signatures, and errors in the information system.

6. *Batch control totals.* When an accounting information system is processing a group (batch) of documents, users can calculate various control totals to promote data integrity. For example, you could add up the invoice numbers for a group of sales invoices. Would the total have any meaning in the AIS? Probably not. But, as the invoices move through the AIS, the total should remain the same.

7. *Data encryption.* In today's world of wireless networks, data encryption is critically important. Without it, hackers and other computer criminals can easily access, change, and/or steal data, compromising data integrity and privacy throughout the accounting information system.

8. *Document matching.* Whether electronic or paper-based, document matching helps ensure that vendor invoices are only paid when merchandise has been properly ordered and invoiced. The purchasing department would send a copy of all purchase orders to the accounting department; the receiving department would likewise send a copy of the receiving report. Then, when the vendor mails the invoice, an accountant will match the three documents before initiating payment. In practice, we often use the term "three-way match" to describe such an arrangement.

9. *Edit checks.* You've seen edit checks in operation if you've ever purchased books or airline tickets online. The information system "echoes" the data you've entered back to

you before it completes final processing. That process allows you to edit the data for any errors or other changes.

10. *Firewalls.* Along with data encryption, a firewall is an important element of AIS security—particularly in a wireless environment. Firewalls are also useful in wired environments. They can prevent unauthorized intrusions into an accounting information system and warn users when such intrusions are detected.

11. *Insurance and bonding.* While insurance and bonding cannot prevent internal control breaches, they can help organizations correct any financial losses they experience as a result. If you've ever hired contractors to work in your home, they were probably bonded. Companies often bond key employees as a safeguard against error and/or fraud.

12. *Internal audits.* We'll look more closely at audits, including internal audits, in the last chapter of the text; your university may even offer a course in internal auditing. Internal audits can reveal indications of fraud, waste, and inefficiency, thus strengthening internal control. You can also learn more about internal auditing from the Web site of the Institute of Internal Auditors (www.theiia.org).

13. *Limit checks.* An accounting information system can incorporate various kinds of limit checks; for example, if a manager is authorized for purchases less than $1,000, a limit check can ensure that the manager doesn't violate the limit for a specific transaction. Most general ledger packages limit transaction dates to the current year; they don't allow users to pre- or post-date transactions.

14. *Lockbox systems.* Lockbox systems help promote strong internal control over cash. Rather than remitting payment directly to an organization, customers send their payment to a lockbox. An independent company, for a fee, monitors the lockbox and deposits cash receipts daily in the bank. (See Figure 3.3 for an illustration of how a lockbox system works.)

15. *Physical security.* Internal control doesn't have to be extraordinarily sophisticated. Simple actions such as locking doors and securing computers and related equipment can go a long way in safeguarding assets.

16. *Preformatted data entry screens.* Remember that one of the purposes of internal control is promoting operating efficiency. Using preformatted data entry screens for things like customer orders and cash disbursement processing greatly improves data entry efficiency. Check out Figure 3.4 for an illustration of a preformatted data entry screen. If your AIS instructor incorporates material on relational databases in your course, you may learn how to design such a screen—usually referred to as a "form."

17. *Prenumbered documents.* Checks, purchase orders, sales invoices, and other documents should be prenumbered to promote strong internal control. If an accounting

FIGURE 3.3
Typical Lockbox System

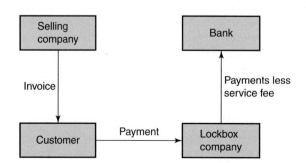

FIGURE 3.4
Preformatted Data Entry Screen www .giveanything.com

information system is automated, the numbers may be assigned using an "auto numbering" function. A seriously out-of-sequence document (such as a check numbered in the 400s when others are in the 100s) can be a warning sign for internal control breaches and/or fraud.

18. *Restrictive endorsement and daily deposits of checks received.* You endorse checks when you deposit them in your bank account; you may use a "blank endorsement," which means your signature alone. Here's the problem: blank endorsements weaken internal control. An unethical person with a fake ID can easily cash such a check at the bank. Restrictive endorsements give the bank more specific instructions that limit the uses of the endorsed check; the most common is "for deposit only," often with an account number included. In addition, all cash receipts (coin, currency, and checks) should be deposited daily in the bank to keep them secure.

19. *Segregation of duties.* Although all of the controls in this list are important, segregation of duties may be the most important of all. Basically, segregation of duties means that, to the extent possible, three different people should each take on one responsibility with respect to a specific asset: authorization for use, physical custody, and recordkeeping. Consider cash, for example: physical custody rests with the bank, while authorization for use is vested with signatories on the account. Recordkeeping refers to both journal entries and bank reconciliations. So, for example, someone authorized to sign checks should not reconcile the bank statement. The same duties (authorization, custody, and recordkeeping) should be separated for other assets, such as inventory, plant assets, and supplies.

20. *User training.* Finally, let's consider user training. All the internal control processes in the world are virtually worthless if people don't know how to apply them. Thus, employees should receive periodic training/reminders about appropriate internal control procedures, their rationales, and the reasons they exist.

Remember: the controls we've just considered are not the sum total of available choices. They are a good beginning, but you should think creatively when designing and critiquing internal control systems—both in class and in practice. Let's conclude this chapter by looking at some ways to apply the ideas of risk management and internal control in various organizational settings.

INTERNAL CONTROL APPLICATIONS

This section of the chapter presents four vignettes illustrating various internal control strengths and weaknesses. Although the names of the individuals and companies involved have been disguised, they represent actual internal control issues in actual organizations.

Vignette #1: Internal Control over Cash

Alphabet Soup Consulting employs a staff of 50 consultants and is managed by a three-person board of directors: Robbie (president), Vicki (vice president), and Richard (treasurer). The company's bylaws specify that checks over $500 require the signatures of two directors to be valid. However, if an invoice over $500 is due and Robbie or Vicki cannot be reached, Richard frequently writes two (or more) smaller checks to cover the total amount. For example, if an invoice totals $900, Richard might write three checks for $300 each or two checks for $450 each. Richard feels justified in his actions because of increased efficiency.

Clearly, Richard's actions constitute a breach of internal controls. Recall the four basic purposes of internal control, and you'll realize that Richard is not fulfilling two of them: safeguarding assets and ensuring compliance with management directives. By implication, he also is interfering with financial statement reliability. To keep Richard from circumventing controls, Alphabet Soup Consulting could take a number of actions, including (1) restricting Richard's access to checks; (2) asking an independent third party, such as the firm's CPA, to handle check writing and bill paying; or (3) removing Richard as a signatory on the account. Each of those controls has a cost, as shown in the table below:

Control	Type	Cost
Restricting Richard's access to checks	Preventive	Decreased efficiency
Asking an independent third party to handle check writing and bill paying	Corrective	Increased monetary cost; time delays in paying bills
Removing Richard as a signatory on the account	Preventive	Extra burden on Robbie and Vicki

So what really happened in this situation? Vicki and Robbie continued to allow Richard to circumvent the company's controls. Richard had no external controls over his spending of the company's money, and Alphabet Soup Consulting eventually went out of business due to poor liquidity.

Vignette #2: Embezzling

Gary and Dan were psychologists in private practice. They employed Christina as a receptionist, and a local CPA firm to handle many (but not all) financial matters. Christina opened the mail, collected cash payments from clients, and wrote checks for Gary's or Dan's signature each month. Each month, the practice would get a bank statement in the mail; Christina was supposed to pass on the bank statement to the CPA firm for reconciliation. Unfortunately, Christina got into a personal financial dilemma. Having access to the company's checks and knowing what Gary's and Dan's signatures looked like, she began forging checks written to her husband. The checks were stored in boxes in an unlocked filing cabinet; Christina would take checks to forge from the bottom of the box so they would not be missed until much later. Additionally, although she had regularly been forwarding the bank statements to the CPA firm, the CPAs had not reconciled them for at least six months. One Saturday, Gary came into the office and noticed the bank statement sitting on Christina's desk. Thinking to save himself and his partner some money, he decided to reconcile the bank statement on his own rather than sending it to the CPA firm. He noticed the out-of-sequence checks with signatures that resembled his and Dan's but were not exactly "right." Christina had embezzled a total of $250,000 before Gary and Dan caught onto her scheme.

The preceding vignette illustrates several important internal controls for cash: sequential numbering of checks (preventive), separation of duties (check writing, check signing, and reconciliation—both preventive and detective), and sequentially numbered documents (preventive). But the system broke down when the CPAs did not do their job by balancing the checkbook monthly (a detective control). In addition, the checks were kept in an unlocked filing cabinet; the company would have achieved stronger internal control by locking up the blank checks more securely (a preventive control).

So what happened? Gary and Dan confronted Christina about her embezzlement. At first, she denied it, but later she confessed when confronted with the evidence. Gary and Dan fired her and she was prosecuted for embezzlement; the bank restored the embezzled funds into Gary and Dan's account, and they hired a new CPA firm.

Vignette #3: Information Technology

The College of Business at Southern State University has over 200 faculty and four information technology staff members. The college's e-mail is maintained on a central server; each administrator, staff member, and professor can check his/her e-mail from any computer in the world that has Internet access. When a new hire comes to work for the college, his/her e-mail password is the same as the e-mail user name. For example, if Dr. J. M. Ortiz is hired as a professor, both his user name and initial e-mail password are *jmortiz*. A small group of students figured out that connection and started hacking into faculty members' e-mail accounts for illicit purposes. David, the lead information technology staff member, therefore introduced several new policies related to e-mail security:

- *Random creation of initial passwords.* Rather than establishing the initial password as the user name, David's staff now uses a password generator to create new passwords for new hires.
- *Mandatory password changes every six months.* New passwords must contain at least six characters. The six characters must contain at least two of the following: capital letters, lowercase letters, or numbers. The passwords cannot be recycled for a period of two years. So, for example, if someone establishes a password of PhdCma1977 for six months, that password cannot be used again for two years after the six-month period ends.
- *Daily file backup.* David and his staff back up the files from the e-mail server every day.
- *Virus, spyware, and spam protection.* The e-mail server, as well as other information technology assets, is equipped with extensive software to prevent, detect, and correct those problems.

The college has experienced no significant internal control problems with information technology since those policies were instituted.

Vignette #4: Inventory

John is the purchasing manager for The Village Bookstore in Claremont, California. He monitors inventory, prepares purchase orders to send to book publishers, and receives the books when they arrive at the store. The bookstore uses a perpetual inventory system, in which inventory records in the accounting information system are updated with every purchase and sale. For example, when books are purchased, the accountant debits inventory and credits accounts payable; when books are sold, the accountant debits cost of goods sold and credits inventory. John also handles merchandise returns when books arrive in unacceptable condition. Since Village uses a perpetual inventory system, John sees no need for periodic counts of inventory—he views them as a waste of time, since the accounting information system is always up-to-date.

Possibly the biggest internal control problem for The Village Bookstore is separation of duties. To safeguard assets and ensure financial statement reliability, three important duties should be borne by different people in most organizations: (1) physical custody of an asset, (2) recordkeeping for the asset, and (3) authorization to use the asset. In this example, John has both physical custody of inventory and authorization for its use. By vesting both those important responsibilities in a single person, it becomes far too easy for John to steal books and tell the accountant they were returned to, or never received from, the publisher. In addition, although the company uses a perpetual inventory system, they still need an annual inventory to promote financial statement reliability.

Thankfully, John was a trustworthy employee. Although he had multiple opportunities to defraud The Village Bookstore, he never did so. An external consultant from a local accounting firm pointed out the bookstore's internal control weaknesses and the company corrected them before they experienced significant financial losses.

CRITICAL THINKING

Almost any business transaction has certain associated risks; those risks can be addressed, in many cases, by developing and implementing a few internal controls.

I was walking around my campus a few days ago and noticed the number of students carrying MP3 players of various sorts; I got my first MP3 player in 2007, and I really don't know how I lived without one for so long! As you may be aware, there are two basic ways to add content (music, movies, TV shows, and such) to an MP3 player: uploading from your personal library and downloading from the Internet. Let's think about the risks involved in downloading music from the Internet and identify some associated internal controls; once you've studied this section, you might want to complete a similar analysis for "uploading from your personal library."

To make the discussion a bit more concise and easy to read, I'm going to organize it in a simple "risk/control matrix" (see Table 3.2). Like so many AIS topics, there's no "one right way" to design a risk/control matrix. So I encourage you not to memorize the format of the matrix; try to stay focused on its content.

This analysis doesn't present all the risks associated with downloading music from the Internet for your MP3 player; I'm giving you a few as examples to show you a good way of thinking about the design of internal controls. I've usually found it most productive to think first about "what could go wrong" with a transaction; that is, what are its associated risks. Then, I think about how I want to handle that risk—what the COSO ERM framework

TABLE 3.2   Risk/Control Matrix for MP3 Downloads

Risk	Risk Category (Brown)	Internal Control	Internal Control Purpose	Comments
Downloading material you don't like	Human error	Listen to a song excerpt.	Preventive	Most music libraries allow you to listen to a short clip before buying a song.
	Human error	Review a song's details, such as the artist and year.	Preventive	Most songs have related data available: it's just a matter of referring to it.
Song doesn't download correctly	Systems	Get it from another source.	Corrective	You could buy a CD with the song and download it from there. Or you could look at some other online service.
Computer firewall blocks the download	Systems	Set up firewall to allow downloads from that site.	Preventive/ corrective	If you set up the firewall in advance, this control is preventive. If it happens "after the fact," it's corrective.
No room for new music on the MP3 player	Systems	Monitor amount of space available on MP3 player.	Detective	Most MP3 players give you a graphic display of the amount of space used and the amount of space available.
	Systems	Buy an MP3 player with more capacity.	Corrective	Of course, you'd have to consider the cost of a new player.
Credit card used for payment isn't accepted	Credit/liquidity	Only use "gift cards" to pay for music.	Preventive	Your ability to download music, then, would depend on having a gift card available.
	Credit/liquidity	Dedicate one credit card to nothing but this kind of transaction.	Preventive/detective	Unless you download a *lot* of music, it's unlikely the card will reach its credit limit too quickly. Also, using one card for nothing but music downloads would help you detect fraudulent activity.

would call a "risk response." And, when I've decided how I want to respond to a risk, I think about ways to enact the response. For example, I don't want to try to download a song to my MP3 player only to discover that I don't have room for it. So, that's a risk I want to try to detect before it happens. I normally do that, as the risk/control matrix points out, by keeping tabs on how much space I have available.

Notice that a specific risk can have more than one associated internal control; it's not a "one-to-one correspondence." Keep in mind, though, that internal controls aren't free—they take time, money, and energy to develop and implement. As we've discussed before, you must always strive to balance the cost of a control with the benefit you receive from it.

Summary

Here is the usual chapter summary, structured according to the learning objectives:

1. *Define* internal control *and explain its importance in the accounting information system.* Internal control refers to the ways an organization keeps its assets safe and ensures that everyone follows estabished organizational procedures. Without solid internal control in the AIS, an organization can open itself up to fraud. Weak internal controls also necessitate more extensive auditing procedures.

2. *Explain the basic purposes of internal control.* Internal control has four basic purposes: (*a*) to safeguard assets, (*b*) to ensure financial statement reliability, (*c*) to promote operational efficiency, and (*d*) to encourage compliance with management's general and specific directives.

3. *Describe and give examples of various kinds of risk exposures.* Taxonomies for classifying and describing organizational risks are numerous in the literature and in practice. Brown advanced a four-part structure: financial risk, operational risk, strategic risk, and hazard risk. Financial risks include not having sufficient cash on hand to meet short-term obligations. Operational risks concern (among other things) the possibility that people will make mistakes. Strategic risks include entering a market not aligned with organizational strategy. Hazard risks relate to fraud and errors committed by the board of directors and/or company management.

4. *Prepare a simple risk/control matrix.* Table 3.1 in this chapter's "Critical Thinking" section illustrates a simple risk/control matrix.

5. *Summarize and explain the importance of COSO's Internal Control—Integrated Framework.* The framework has five parts: control environment, risk assessment, control activities, monitoring, and information and communication. It gives managers comprehensive guidance on risk management and internal control.

6. *Critique existing internal control systems and design effective internal controls.* This process starts with a comprehensive risk assessment. Managers must then consider various responses to risk, as well as the cost–benefit relationship of various internal controls. As with most issues we study in accounting information systems, the design, implementation, and evaluation of internal controls is at least as much "art" as "science." The question most managers face in most organizations is not Which internal controls are the "right" ones? but Which internal controls can I implement in a cost-effective way to provide reasonable assurance of information integrity, asset safety, and procedural compliance?

As you consider the end-of-chapter materials that follow, try not to "second guess" me or your AIS instructor; try, instead, to put yourself in each situation and come up with the most original solutions you can.

Key Terms	Brown's taxonomy of risk, *42* internal control, *39* Sarbanes-Oxley Act

Key Terms

Brown's taxonomy of risk, *42*
COSO, *43*
Foreign Corrupt Practices
Act, *40*

internal control, *39*
*Internal Control—Integrated
Framework, 44*

Sarbanes-Oxley Act
of 2002, *40*

**Chapter
References**

Brown, B. 2001. "Step-by-Step Enterprise Risk Management." *Risk Management,* September,
pp. 43–49.
Committee of Sponsoring Organizations of the Treadway Commission. 1985. *Internal Control—
Integrated Framework.* New York: Committee of Sponsoring Organizations of the Treadway
Commission.
Committee of Sponsoring Organizations of the Treadway Commission. 2006. *Internal Control
over Financial Reporting—Guidance for Smaller Public Companies.* New York: Committee of
Sponsoring Organizations of the Treadway Commission.
Hollander, A. S., E. L. Denna, and J. O. Cherrington. 2000. *Accounting, Information Technology,
and Business Solutions.* 2nd ed. New York: Irwin/McGraw-Hill.

**End-of-
Chapter
Activities**

1. *Reading review questions.*
   a. What is internal control? Why is internal control important in organizations?
   b. What are the four basic purposes of internal control? Give an example of each one.
   c. List and discuss four broad categories of organizational risk exposures. For each broad
      category, suggest two examples.
   d. What is COSO? Why is the work of COSO important in internal control?
   e. Prepare a response to the questions for this chapter's "AIS in the Business World."

2. *Multiple choice review questions.* Please select the best answer for each question.
   1. Which of the following legally requires management to assess a company's internal con-
      trols annually?
      a. Foreign Corrupt Practices Act
      b. Brown's risk taxonomy
      c. COSO *Internal Control* framework
      d. Sarbanes-Oxley Act
   2. Which of the following is a type of financial risk according to Brown's taxonomy?
      a. Credit risk
      b. Systems risk
      c. Legal and regulatory risk
      d. Business strategy risk
   3. In the COSO *Internal Control* framework, the "tone at the top" is most closely related to:
      a. Monitoring.
      b. Control environment.
      c. Control activities.
      d. Information and communication.
   4. To develop and sustain a strong control environment, managers and others should:
      a. Be committed to integrity and ethical behavior.
      b. Demonstrate a commitment to competence in carrying out their duties and responsibilities.
      c. Maintain a consistent, appropriate management philosophy.
      d. All of the above.
   5. All of the following are basic purposes of internal control except:
      a. Eliminating fraud.
      b. Ensuring reliable financial statements.

    c. Promoting operating efficiency.

    d. Safeguarding assets.

3. *Reading review problem.* Consider the following story from the December 10, 2008, edition of the *Las Vegas Review-Journal*:

> Authorities unsealed the indictments of 15 people involved in a Eurasian gang on Tuesday, revealing an organized crime ring that raked in about $1.5 million through stolen credit cards and identity theft in the Las Vegas Valley. The suspects are facing federal charges including trafficking and possession of counterfeit devices, identity theft, production and use of counterfeit devices and fraud. [A U.S. attorney] said some of the suspects were involved in "skimming," an act by which a person can obtain credit card information by running the card through a handheld counterfeiting device. The gang members would have people working in restaurants, bars and smoke shops who would scan a customer's credit card on a legitimate machine and then swipe it again with a counterfeiting device.

If you've ever been the victim of that kind of crime, or known someone who was, you know that it can take quite a while to repair the damages.
Source: Lawrence Mower, "ID Theft Operation Outlined," Las Vegas Review Journal, December 10, 2008, p. 2B.

Suppose the *Las Vegas Review-Journal* contacted you for some feedback on the article. Prepare a response to the following questions:

    a. What is internal control?

    b. What type(s) of risk are indicated by this situation?

    c. What internal controls would you recommend to address the risks?

4. *Making choices and exercising judgment.*

    a. Consider the four vignettes presented in the last section of the chapter. For each one, suggest one additional internal control procedure. Discuss whether the procedure you suggest is preventive, detective, or corrective; also identify the type of risk it is designed to control based on the risk categories discussed in the chapter.

    b. Hassan and Ashok are employed by one of the Big Four CPA firms. Both have recently earned their CPA licenses, however, and are considering starting their own practice. Using Brown's risk taxonomy, identify and describe at least five risks Hassan and Ashok must be aware of if they start their own business. For each risk you identify, suggest one or more internal controls that could ameliorate it.

5. *Field exercises.*

    a. Through observation and/or interview, collect information about internal control over inventory from a local retail establishment such as a bookstore, coffee shop, or discount store. How does the information you collected about processes, procedures, and documents align with the information presented in the chapter?

    b. Read the articles listed below about actual internal control breaches. In each case, suggest at least two internal controls the company needs to institute.

        i. "Big Banks Face Fines on Role of Servicers," *The Wall Street Journal Online*, 16 February 2011.

        ii. G. Heslop and L. Kapp, "An Institutional Response to Fraud, Scandal and Embarrassment—The Dallas Independent School District Procurement Card Case," *Journal of Leadership, Accountability and Ethics*, December 2010.

        iii. B. Leonard, "When HR Goes Bad," *HR Magazine*, January 2011.

    c. The chapter presented a simple risk/control matrix. Read the articles listed below and summarize their main points with respect to the same topic.

        i. R. Egerdahl, "A Risk Matrix Approach to Data Processing Facility Audits," *Internal Auditor*, June 1995.

        ii. J. Roth and D. Espersen, "The Matrix Revisited," *Internal Auditor*, August 2004.

d. Point your Web browser to the COSO Web site (www.coso.org). Find the executive summary for *Internal Control over Financial Reporting—Guidance for Smaller Public Companies*. List the 20 principles the document offers as guidance.

6. Internal control has four basic purposes: safeguarding assets, ensuring financial statement reliability, promoting operational efficiency, and encouraging compliance with management's directives. Consider each of the internal control procedures described below. For each procedure, indicate which purpose(s) of internal control it is designed to address.

   a. Conducting surprise cash counts.

   b. Creating a policy manual.

   c. Creating separate departments for purchasing inventory and receiving inventory.

   d. Deleting an employee's computer account when the employee retires or is fired.

   e. Employing internal auditors.

   f. Installing virus cleaning software on all computers.

   g. Locking filing cabinets with sensitive documents.

   h. Performing background checks on employees.

   i. Reconciling the bank statement monthly.

   j. Requiring all management employees to take annual vacations.

7. Visit the Web site of the Wild Cat Zoo in southern California (www.cathouse-fcc.org). Classify each of the following risks using Brown's taxonomy. Also suggest one or more internal controls to address each risk. For each internal control you suggest, specify which broad purpose(s) of internal control it satisfies, as well as whether it is preventive/detective/corrective in nature. Explain your responses.

   a. The zoo fails to attract a sufficient number of visitors.

   b. One or more animals get sick.

   c. The zoo's Web site becomes unavailable due to a computer virus.

   d. Promotional and educational literature contain errors of fact about the animals and the zoo's operating hours.

   e. One of the animals escapes because a keeper fails to lock its cage securely.

   f. An employee falsifies his/her credentials to obtain a position as a veterinarian.

   g. The zoo's admission prices are prohibitively high for school groups.

   h. The zoo loses its 501(c)(3) status with the Internal Revenue Service.

   i. The gift shop runs out of a popular souvenir item.

   j. A disgruntled former volunteer attempts to set a fire at the zoo.

8. Do a Google search for the Fortune 100 companies. Choose two of the companies from the list and prepare a risk/control matrix similar to the one illustrated in the chapter. Include five to seven risks for each company you choose. (You'll find an example for Walmart Stores on my blog.)

9. (CMA adapted, December 1992) In each of the following independent situations, identify internal control deficiencies and make suggestions regarding their correction/improvement.

   a. Many employees of a firm that manufactures small tools pocket some of these tools for their personal use. Since the quantities taken by any one employee were immaterial, the individual employees did not consider the act as fraudulent or detrimental to the company. As the company grew larger, an internal auditor was hired. The auditor charted the gross profit percentages for particular tools and discovered higher gross profit rates for tools related to industrial use than for personal use. Subsequent investigation uncovered the fraudulent acts.

   b. A company controller set up a fictitious subsidiary office to which he shipped inventories and then approved the invoice for payment. The inventories were sold and the proceeds deposited to the controller's personal bank account. Internal auditors suspected fraud when auditing the plant's real estate assets. They traced plant real estate descriptions to the assets owned and leased and could not find a title or lease for the location of this particular subsidiary.

c. The manager of a large department was able to embezzle funds from his employer by carrying employees on the payroll beyond actual termination dates. The manager carried each terminated employee for only one pay period beyond the termination date so the employee would not easily detect the additional amount included on the W-2 reporting of wages to the Internal Revenue Service. The paymaster regularly delivered all checks to the department manager, who then deposited the fraudulent checks to a personal checking account. An internal auditor discovered the fraud from a routine tracing of sample entries in the payroll register to the employees' files in the personnel office. The sample included one employee's pay record whose personnel file showed the termination date prior to the pay period audited. The auditor investigated further and discovered other such fraudulent checks.

10. (CMA adapted, June 1994) MailMed Inc. (MMI), a pharmaceutical firm, provides discounted prescription drugs through direct mail. MMI has a small systems staff that designs and writes MMI's customized software. Until recently, MMI's transaction data were transmitted to a third party for processing on their hardware.

MMI has experienced significant sales growth as the cost of prescription drugs has increased and medical insurance companies have been tightening reimbursements in order to restrain premium cost increases. As a result of these increased sales, MMI has purchased its own computer hardware. The computer center is installed on the ground floor of its two-story headquarters building. It is behind large plate-glass windows so that the state-of-the-art computer center can be displayed as a measure of the company's success, attracting customer and investor attention. The computer area is equipped with high-tech fire suppression equipment and backup power supplies.

MMI has hired a small computer operations staff to operate the computer center. To handle the current level of business, the operations staff is on a two-shift schedule, five days per week. MMI's systems and programming staff, now located in the same building, have access to the computer center and can test new programs and program changes when the operations staff are not available. As the systems and programming staff are small and the work demands have increased, systems and programming documentation are developed only when time is available. Periodically, MMI backs up its programs and data files, storing them at an off-site location.

Unfortunately, due to several days of heavy rains, MMI's building recently experienced serious flooding, which reached several feet into the first floor level and affected the on-site hardware, data, and programs.

Based on the preceding narrative, describe at least two specific computer weaknesses for MMI. For each weakness you identify, suggest a way to compensate for it.

11. (CMA adapted, June 1994) Richards Furniture Company is a 15-store chain, concentrated in the southwest, that sells living room and bedroom furniture. Each store has a full-time manager and an assistant manager, who are paid on a salary basis. The cashiers and sales personnel typically work part-time and are paid an hourly wage plus a commission based on sales volume. The company uses cash registers with four-part sales invoices to record each transaction; the invoices are used regardless of the payment type (cash, check, credit card).

On the sales floor, the salesperson manually records his/her employee number and the transaction, totals the sales invoice, calculates any appropriate discount and the sales tax, and calculates the grand total. The salesperson then gives the sales invoice to the cashier, retaining one copy in the sales book.

The cashier reviews the invoice and inputs the sale into the cash register. The cash register automatically assigns a consecutive number to each transaction. The cashier is also responsible for obtaining credit authorization approval on credit card sales and approving sales paid by check. The cashier gives one copy of the invoice to the customer and retains the second copy as the store copy. Returns are handled in exactly the reverse manner with the cashier issuing a return slip when necessary.

At the end of each day, the cashier sequentially orders the sales invoices and provides cash register totals for cash, credit card, and check sales, as well as cash and credit card returns. These totals are reconciled by the assistant manager to the cash register tapes, the total of the consecutively numbered sales invoices, and the return slips. The assistant manager prepares a daily reconciled report for the store manager's review.

Cash sales, check sales, and credit card sales are reviewed by the manager, who then prepares the daily bank deposit. The manager physically deposits these at the bank and files the validated deposit slip. At the end of the month, the manager performs the bank reconciliation. The cash register tapes, sales invoices, return slips, and reconciled report are then forwarded daily to the central Data Entry Department at corporate headquarters for processing. The Data Entry Department returns a weekly Sales and Commission Activity Report to the manager for review.

Please respond to the following questions about Richards Furniture Company's operations based on the preceding narrative:

a. What risks does Richards face?

b. If you were an unethical customer and/or employee of Richards, how could you defraud the company given their current procedures?

c. What internal control strengths does the company possess? What risks are those strengths designed to address?

d. How could internal control be improved at Richards?

12. (CMA adapted, June 1993) PriceRight Electronics Inc. (PEI) is a wholesale discount supplier of a wide variety of electronic instruments and parts to regional retailers. PEI commenced operations a year ago, and its records processing has been on a manual basis except for stand-alone automated inventory and accounts receivable systems. The driving force of PEI's business is its deep-discount, short-term delivery reputation that allows retailers to order materials several times during the month to minimize in-store inventories. PEI's management has decided to continue automating its operations, but, because of cash flow considerations, this needs to be accomplished on a step-by-step basis.

It was decided that the next function to be automated should be sales order processing to enhance quick response to customer needs. PEI's systems consultants suggested and implemented an off-the-shelf software package that was modified to fit PEI's current mode of operations. At the same time, the consultants recommended and installed a computerized database of customer credit standings to permit automatic credit limit checks as the lingering recessionary climate has resulted in an increase in slow paying or delinquent accounts. The new systems modules are described below:

Marketing. Sales orders are received by telephone, fax, mail, or e-mail and entered into the sales order system by marketing personnel. The orders are automatically compared to the customer database for determination of credit limits. If credit limits are met, the system generates multiple copies of the sales order.

Credit. On a daily basis, the credit manager reviews new customer applications for creditworthiness, establishes credit limits, and enters them into the customer database. The credit manager also reviews the calendar month-end accounts receivable aging report to identify slow-paying or delinquent accounts for potential revisions to or discontinuance of credit. In addition, the credit manager issues credit memos for merchandise returns based on requests from customers and forwards copies of credit memos to Accounting for appropriate accounts receivable handling.

Warehousing. Warehouse personnel update the inventory master file for purchases and disbursements, confirm availability of materials to fill sales orders, and establish back-orders for sales orders that cannot be completed from stock on hand. Warehouse personnel assemble and forward materials with corresponding sales orders to Shipping and Receiving. They also update the inventory master file for merchandise returns that are received by Shipping and Receiving.

Shipping and Receiving. Shipping and Receiving accepts materials and sales orders from Warehousing, packs and ships the order with a copy of the sales order as a packing slip, and forwards a copy of the sales order to Billing. Merchandise returns received from customers are unpacked, sorted, inspected, and sent to Warehousing.

Accounting. The Accounting Department comprises three functions relevant to this narrative: Billing, Accounts Receivable, and General Accounting. Billing prices all sales orders received, which takes approximately five days after order shipment. To spread the work effort throughout the month, customers are segregated and placed in 30-day billing cycles. There are six billing cycles for which invoices are rendered during the month. Monthly statements, prepared by Billing, are sent to customers during the cycle billing period. Outstanding carry-forward balances reported by Accounts Receivable and credit memos prepared based on credit requests received from the credit manager are included on the monthly statement. Billing also prepares sales and credit memo journals for each cycle.

Copies of invoices and credit memos are forwarded to Accounts Receivable for entry into the accounts receivable system by customer account. An aging report is prepared at the end of each billing cycle and forwarded to the credit manager.

The accounts receivable journal reflecting total charges and credits processed through the accounts receivable system for each cycle is forwarded to General Accounting. General Accounting compares this information to the sales and credit memo journals and posts the changes to the general ledger.

Based on the preceding narrative:

a. Identify at least two internal control strengths of PEI's system. Indicate why each is a strength.

b. Identify at least three internal control weaknesses in PEI's system. Explain the nature of each weakness and recommend a way to address it.

13. *Terminology.* Please match each item on the right with the best item on the left.

1. Business strategy risk	a. 1977 legislation
2. Foreign Corrupt Practices Act	b. 2002 legislation
3. General controls	c. Apply to a broad range of IT applications
4. Legal and regulatory	d. Internal control example
5. Liquidity	e. A group that offers advice about internal control and enterprise risk management
6. Reasonable assurance	f. Organizational risk example
7. Sarbanes-Oxley Act	g. Poor decision making related to market competition
8. Separation of duties	h. Strategic risk category
9. Systems	i. Type of financial risk
10. COSO	j. What internal controls provide

14. *Multiple choice questions.*

1. Which of the following best explains the relationship between "monitoring" and "information and communication" as the terms are used in the COSO *Internal Control* framework?

a. Monitoring must be done by an individual, while information and communication must be done by a group.

    b. Information and communication must be done by an individual, while monitoring must be done by a group.

    (c.) Monitoring involves ongoing changes to an organization's internal control plan; information and communication focuses on letting stakeholders know about current internal controls.

    d. Information and communication involves ongoing changes to an organization's internal control plan; monitoring focuses on letting stakeholders know about current internal controls.

2. Which of the following best pairs a specific risk exposure with a category from Brown's taxonomy?

    (a.) Company sanctions for violation for the Foreign Corrupt Practices Act, legal and regulatory risk

    b. Failure to follow proper imprest systems procedures for petty cash, systems risk

    c. Failing to give employees proper credit for their accomplishments, credit risk

    d. Fundamental flaws in an entity's marketing plan, market risk

3. A quarterly internal control newsletter published by the CEO's office would most likely be related to which element(s) of the COSO *Internal Control* framework?

    a. Risk assessment, monitoring

    (b.) Control environment, information, and communication

    c. Risk assessment, control environment

    d. Monitoring, information, and communication

4. Which of the following is most likely to benefit from a lockbox system as a form of internal control?

    a. Mortgage lender

    (b.) Convenience store

    c. The IRS

    d. Home Depot's corporate office

5. All of the following have a responsibility for promoting strong internal control in organizations except:

    a. Independent auditors.

    b. Internal auditors.

    c. Executive management.

    (d.) Stockholders.

15. *Statement evaluation.* Indicate whether each of the following statements is (i) always true, (ii) sometimes true, or (iii) never true. For those that are (ii) sometimes true, explain when the statement is true.

    a. Audits are less time consuming and less expensive in organizations with strong internal control systems.

    b. Document matching concepts can be applied to purchases of and payments for office supplies.

    c. In companies with strong internal control, only one person has the authority to sign checks.

    d. In the COSO *Internal Control* framework, control activities can be preventive, detective, or corrective.

    e. Information technology eliminates the need for internal control systems.

    f. Internal controls prevent fraud.

    g. Liquidity risk is more important than other types of risk.

    h. Preventive controls are more expensive than detective or corrective controls.

    i. Properly implemented lockbox systems eliminate the need for bank reconciliations.

    j. Reported weaknesses in internal control will lead to reductions in stock prices.

Chapter **Four**

Management Concepts

AIS in the Business World

Woburn Safari Park

Woburn Safari Park (www.woburn.co.uk/safari/) is an "up close and personal" experience with animals from a variety of habitats around the world. As part of a research project focused on business process management (BPM), Julien and Tjahjono (2009) offered the following comments about the park:

> WSP opened in 1970 as the second safari park in UK. From 1974, WSP was managed by a circus family; the facilities in the park were originally designed to last 25 years, and during that time no attempt was made to renew the facilities. When the current management took over in 1993, apart from very low staff morale, the park was losing money and the facilities needing replacement. Today, WSP is an award-winning attraction that makes a valuable contribution to conservation and research. The 121-hectare safari park offers customers a full day out providing fun, entertainment, and a relevant educational message. A day out combines the excitement of the Safari Drive with the fun of taking the Foot Safari around the Wild World Leisure Area. A day out allows meeting the animals, enjoy the many demonstrations, keeper talks, and feeding times.

The purpose of their research was to re-engineer WSP's business processes to focus more on "lean thinking."

Discussion Questions

1. Why is the study of management concepts, such as BPM, relevant to AIS?
2. What is BPM? What steps do managers commonly follow in a BPM project?
3. What risks are associated with WSP's operations? How can those risks be managed?

Source: D. M. Julien and B. Tjahjono, 2009. "Lean Thinking Implementation at a Safari Park," *Business Process Management Journal* 15, no. 3.

The accounting information system is a subset of an organization's overall management information system. And, it needs to be managed using similar tools and techniques. I'm therefore including this new chapter in this edition to introduce some important management ideas and their relationship to accounting information systems.

In this chapter, we'll look at three major topics: enterprise risk management (ERM), business process management (BPM), and behavioral issues in AIS. When you've finished studying the chapter, and completing the activities at its conclusion, you should be able to:

1. Summarize and explain the importance of COSO's *Enterprise Risk Management—Integrated Framework.*
2. Define business process management, including a generalized model of BPM.
3. List and discuss some basic principles of business process management.
4. Explain expectancy theory.
5. Apply all three topics within the context of accounting information systems.

ENTERPRISE RISK MANAGEMENT

In Chapter 3, you learned about COSO and its *Internal Control—Integrated Framework.* According to COSO:

> Enterprise risk management is a process, effected by an entity's board of directors, management and other personnel, applied in strategy setting and across the enterprise, designed to identify potential events that may affect the entity, and manage risk to be within its risk appetite, to provide reasonable assurance regarding the achievement of entity objectives.

Notice that the definition of ERM mentions entity objectives. COSO discusses five categories of objectives for most organizations: strategic, operations, reporting, compliance, and safeguarding of resources. The objectives and categories overlap, of course; also, not all categories are always under the direct control of management. Strategic and operations objectives, for example, can be profoundly influenced by political and economic events around the world.

Whereas the integrated framework for internal control had five components, the ERM framework has eight, as shown in Figure 4.1. Like the five elements of the internal control framework, the eight ERM elements are intimately linked to one another. Here's the way COSO describes them in the executive summary of the ERM documents:

> **Internal Environment**—The internal environment encompasses the tone of an organization, and sets the basis for how risk is viewed and addressed by an entity's people, including risk management philosophy and risk appetite, integrity and ethical values, and the environment in which they operate.
>
> **Objective Setting**—Objectives must exist before management can identify potential events affecting their achievement. Enterprise risk management ensures that management has in place a process to set objectives and that the chosen objectives support and align with the entity's mission and are consistent with its risk appetite.
>
> **Event Identification**—Internal and external events affecting achievement of an entity's objectives must be identified, distinguishing between risks and opportunities. Opportunities are channeled back to management's strategy or objective-setting processes.
>
> **Risk Assessment**—Risks are analyzed, considering likelihood and impact, as a basis for determining how they should be managed. Risks are assessed on an inherent and a residual basis.

FIGURE 4.1
Enterprise Risk Management Framework

Risk Response—Management selects risk responses—avoiding, accepting, reducing, or sharing risk—developing a set of actions to align risks with the entity's risk tolerances and risk appetite.

Control Activities—Policies and procedures are established and implemented to help ensure the risk responses are effectively carried out.

Information and Communication—Relevant information is identified, captured, and communicated in a form and time frame that enable people to carry out their responsibilities. Effective communication also occurs in a broader sense, flowing down, across, and up the entity.

Monitoring—The entirety of enterprise risk management is monitored and modifications made as necessary. Monitoring is accomplished through ongoing management activities, separate evaluations, or both.

The objectives (strategic, operations, reporting, compliance, and safeguarding assets) represent what the organization is trying to accomplish. The eight components of the enterprise risk management framework help managers formulate plans for accomplishment.

A few years ago, I was a consultant for Dreambox Creations Inc. (www.dreambox-creations.com/), a technology-based firm in Diamond Bar, California. My job was to work with Dreambox's management to develop an enterprise risk management plan. After some discussion, we decided to use COSO's framework as the basis for the plan. Check out the company's Web site, which will give you some context for the following excerpt from their ERM plan.

1. *Internal environment.* Dreambox's management had committed to developing an ERM plan. It was growing as an organization and wanted to present a more sophisticated image to clients and employees—both current and prospective.

2. *Objective setting.* Dreambox had set a strategic goal of acquiring at least three new clients every year.

3. *Event identification.* If Dreambox lacked the staff with the skills and desire to pursue new clients, it might not be able to achieve its strategic goal.

4. *Risk assessment.* The potential impact of that risk was great. At an inherent level, it was also high. (*Inherent risk* is the "raw" risk, while *residual risk* is the risk that remains after management takes some action. The higher the risk level, the greater the need to address it.)

5. *Risk response.* Dreambox chose two of the four generic risk responses discussed in the COSO framework: reducing and sharing.

6. *Control activities.* To reduce the risk of not achieving its strategic goal, Dreambox developed a plan to hire additional marketing professionals whose main job would be to

pursue new clients. It also chose to share the risk by offering incentives to current clients for referrals that resulted in additional business for Dreambox.

7. *Information and communication.* Dreambox planned several meetings with its staff to explain the importance of ERM, the development of the ERM plan, and its implications for the firm.

8. *Monitoring.* Dreambox assigned one of its three corporate officers the responsibility for annually reviewing the plan. If updates were needed, they would be discussed with the other corporate officers.

COSO's internal control framework was well received in the business community. The ERM framework was more sharply criticized because it was much more general. From my point of view, the ERM framework had to be more general: The kinds of risks organizations face and the ways they respond to them are much more diverse than matters related to internal control. While not every organization has identical internal controls, all internal control systems are attempting to respond to the same four purposes we discussed in Chapter 3.

In early 2011, COSO released some additional documents related to ERM:

- *Embracing Enterprise Risk Management: Practical Approaches for Getting Started* by Frigo and Anderson
- *Developing Key Risk Indicators to Strengthen Enterprise Risk Management* by Beasley, Branson, and Hancock.

You can access both documents on the COSO Web site (www.coso.org). The next two sections of this chapter look at ideas related to business process management.

NATURE OF BUSINESS PROCESS MANAGEMENT

Business process management has been defined in many different ways, including:

- A business improvement strategy based on documenting, analyzing, and redesigning processes for greater performance (SmartDraw.com, 2008).
- A method of efficiently aligning an organization with the wants and needs of clients (Wikipedia.com, 2008).
- A systematic approach to analyzing, redesigning, improving and managing a specific process (Harmon and Wolf, 2008, p. 12).

Notice the important ideas in each definition of BPM: improving performance, promoting efficiency, responding to the needs of clients, and analyzing processes systematically and strategically.

Reflection and Self-Assessment   4.1

Consult at least two other sources that provide definitions of business process management. Based on those sources and what you've just read, develop your own definition of BPM.

Although every BPM project is unique in some way, certain generic activities are common to most of them. Seppanen, Kumar, and Chandra (2005) suggested the following sequence as a **generalized model of BPM**.

1. Select the process and define its boundaries.
2. Observe, document, and map the process steps and flow.
3. Collect process-related data.
4. Analyze the collected data.
5. Identify and prioritize potential process improvements.
6. Optimize the process.
7. Implement and monitor process improvements.

How is BPM related to your study of accounting information systems? Good question! Consider the following points to help understand why AIS students should know something about business process management:

1. BPM can assist managers in providing accounting information that conforms to elements of the FASB Conceptual Framework. Refer back to Figure 1.1, which illustrates the conceptual framework. Managing business processes can ensure that relevant, reliable information is furnished in a cost-effective way.
2. BPM can help managers promote strong internal control. You probably recall that internal control has four main purposes, one of which is enhancing operating efficiency. Periodically examining business processes to see how they can be improved helps achieve that goal.
3. BPM frequently involves strategic uses of information technology, such as relational databases, enterprise resource planning systems, and general ledger software.
4. BPM is a natural outgrowth of accountants' intimate involvement with business processes. As a future accounting professional, your work will frequently focus on business processes: documenting them (flowcharts, data flow diagrams, REA models), designing inputs and outputs for them (sales invoices, purchase requisitions, production cost reports), and auditing them (financial, operational, compliance).

Next, let's turn our attention to some fundamental ideas associated with business process management.

BASIC PRINCIPLES

As part of my background research for this chapter, I interviewed my friend and former student, Robert J. Eppele II. Robert is the chief information officer (CIO) for ERP Solutions LLC; you can learn more about his company on its Web site: www.erpsolutions.net. He shared these important ideas about business process management:

1. *Understand how business processes interact with/support organizational strategy.* As you may have learned in a management class, "strategy" refers to the ways an organization gains a competitive advantage in its markets. In today's on-demand, knowledge-driven economy, organizations' business processes can be key to creating and sustaining a competitive advantage in the marketplace.
2. *Move away from the "we've always done it this way" mentality. Be open to alternatives.* Business processes often originate based on some organizational need. For example, many medical offices have historically relied on paper documents for things like patient

charts and prescriptions; in the last decade, however, IT professionals have developed cost effective, efficient ways to maintain those records electronically.

3. *Enlist top management support; ensure that top management can describe current business processes before trying to reengineer/maintain/modify the processes.* We've already talked about the COSO frameworks for internal control and enterprise risk management; in both frameworks, the "tone at the top" is an important factor. The same is true for BPM: Without top management support, most efforts will be doomed to failure. In addition, to support and lead BPM efforts effectively, top management needs to understand the way things currently work in the organization.

4. *Managing business processes is fundamentally about people, not technology or documents. It's important to hire people who can think beyond their little piece of the world and see how what they do fits into the "bigger picture."* BPM requires a holistic view of the organization—one that moves beyond thinking about what's best for your department to thinking about how the organization as a whole can create value for its stakeholders.

5. *Don't rely on external consultants to the exclusion of internal employees; value the experience of people in the organization who are close to the process.* This point might strike you as a bit odd, since both Robert and I have worked as external consultants in many organizations. But it is 100 percent true! Far too many managers, when confronted with a complex problem, advocate hiring an external consultant as a first step. While doing so has many advantages, external consultants rarely have the intimate familiarity of internal employees when it comes to BPM. I've often found that a team approach, combining both employees and consultants, produces very positive results.

6. *When using consultants, make sure the task is well defined, with specific deliverables defined by the company.* This idea reminds me of something Lewis Carroll wrote in *Alice's Adventures in Wonderland:* "If you don't know where you are going, any road will take you there." In other words, outcomes for a BPM project should be defined in advance; otherwise, the project may grow out of control, costing both time and money without achieving solid results.

7. *Communicate early; communicate often. Deal immediately with objections/issues as they arise.* BPM, like most important organizational initiatives, needs to be an open, transparent process. The best plans are developed by a team of people through a process of dialogue and feedback, not by one or two people sitting in an office for several hours.

We'll take a closer look at how the steps and principles of BPM are applied later in the text.

BEHAVIORAL ISSUES IN AIS

In Chapter 1, we took a brief look at the FASB conceptual framework; you'll probably recall "cost effectiveness" as one of the constraints on financial reporting. Costs associated with an accounting information system come in at least three forms: behavioral, psychological, and financial. In this section of the chapter, we're going to take a quick look at behavioral issues in AIS. People have been trying to understand and explain human behavior in organizations practically since organizations first existed. While this section alone won't make you an expert on the matter, it will provide a framework for understanding some of the behavioral issues you'll face in designing, implementing, and using accounting information systems.

So what are some of the behavioral issues associated with AIS? Consider the following list:

- Many people are uncomfortable with change. So, if you are moving an AIS from paper-based to technology based, making a business process more efficient, or introducing new internal controls, some folks will resist "on principle."
- Fraud is a serious problem in all types of organizations. In its 2010 Report to the Nations on Occupational Fraud and Abuse, the Association of Certified Fraud Examiners (www.acfe.com) "estimated that the typical organization loses 5% of its annual revenue to fraud. Applied to the estimated 2009 Gross World Product, this figure translates to a potential global fraud loss of more than $2.9 trillion" (ACFE, 2010).
- Business today is a global endeavor. So, people in organizations must learn new languages, cultures and customs.
- When elements of an AIS change, people need to be trained in new technologies, processes and procedures to be effective. Whether the training is done in a classroom or online format, it involves human behavior.

Dozens, perhaps hundreds, of theories exist to help us understand human behavior. One I've used a lot is Vroom's expectancy theory (1964). It has stood the test of time both in research and in practice—probably because it is easy to understand and practical. **Expectancy theory** says that motivation is the product of three factors:

- *Expectancy:* If I put in the effort toward achieving a goal, will I be successful?
- *Instrumentality:* If I achieve the goal, will I be rewarded?
- *Valence:* Do I value the reward?

Vroom put them together in a simple, yet elegant, formula to emphasize their relationship:

$$\text{Motivation} = \text{Expectancy} \times \text{Instrumentality} \times \text{Valence}$$

Notice that the three factors are *multiplied,* not added, to achieve motivation. So, if just one of the three factors is zero, motivation will be zero as well.

How would Vroom's expectancy theory be applied within the context of accounting information systems? Earlier in this chapter, you read about Dreambox Creations' enterprise risk management plan. The officers of Dreambox were highly motivated to develop and implement the plan; Table 4.1 shows how the three elements of expectancy theory might look in that context:

TABLE 4.1   **Application of Expectancy Theory**

Factor	General Question	Application to Dreambox
Expectancy	If I put in the effort toward achieving a goal, will I be successful?	If we work with a consultant, will we be able to develop an ERM plan?
Instrumentality	If I achieve the goal, will I be rewarded?	If we successfully develop the ERM plan, will we manage risk and achieve our goals?
Valence	Do I value the reward?	Will managing risk and achieving our goals give us something we want?

Think about a goal you have tried / are presently trying to achieve—perhaps earning your accounting degree. Use the elements of Vroom's expectancy theory to ana-lyze your motivation for achieving it. Be as honest as you can be.

Summary

This chapter has been all about the management issues you'll need to consider in AIS work. Here is a summary of its main points, organized based on the expected outcomes from the beginning of the chapter:

1. *Summarize and explain the importance of COSO's Enterprise Risk Management—Integrated Framework.* COSO's ERM framework comprises eight elements: internal environment, objective setting, event identification, risk assessment, risk response, control activities, information and communication, monitoring. The framework is important because it gives business professionals a structured, concrete way to manage risk throughout the organization. It also allows them to change and adapt their risk management procedures over time as internal and external environments change.

2. *Define business process management, including a generalized model of BPM.* BPM has been defined in many different ways. Fundamentally, it is a set of ideas associated with making virtually any business process more effective and efficient—helping ensure that it creates value for organizational stakeholders. The generalized model of BPM discussed in the chapter comprises seven steps:

   a. Select the process and define its boundaries.
   b. Observe, document, and map the process steps and flow.
   c. Collect process-related data.
   d. Analyze the collected data.
   e. Identify and prioritize potential process improvements.
   f. Optimize the process.
   g. Implement and monitor process improvements.

3. *List and discuss some basic principles of business process management.* The chapter also presented seven basic principles of BPM:

   a. Understand how business processes interact with/support organizational strategy.
   b. Move away from the "we've always done it this way" mentality.
   c. Enlist top management support.
   d. Managing business processes is fundamentally about people, not technology/documents.
   e. Don't rely on external consultants to the exclusion of internal employees.
   f. When using consultants, make sure the task is well defined, with specific deliverables defined by the company.
   g. Communicate early; communicate often.

4. *Explain expectancy theory.* Vroom's expectancy theory is a way to understand and explain human motivation in organizations. It comprises three elements: expectancy, instrumentality, and valence. Motivation is the product of the three; if any one of the factors is zero, motivation will also be zero.

5. *Apply all three topics within the context of accounting information systems.* All three areas can be applied in various ways when working with accounting information systems. The ERM framework can be used to assess and respond to the various types of risk discussed in Chapter 3 (financial, operational, strategic, hazard). Business processes are central to AIS, as you'll see later in the text. The principles of BPM outlined in this chapter can be used to make those processes more effective and efficient. Since every AIS involves people in some way, expectancy theory can be used to assess and increase motivation.

Key Terms

basic BPM principles, *66*

business process management, *65*

Enterprise Risk Management— Integrated Framework, *63*

expectancy theory, *68*

Generalized model of BPM, *66*

Chapter References

Association of Certified Fraud Examiners. 2010. *Report to the Nations on Occupational Fraud and Abuse.* Downloaded 31 January 2011 from www.acfe.com.

Committee of Sponsoring Organizations of the Treadway Commission. 2004. *Enterprise Risk Management—Integrated Framework.* New York: Committee of Sponsoring Organizations of the Treadway Commission.

Harmon, P., and C. Wolf. 2008. *The State of Business Process Management.* San Francisco: Business Process Trends.

Seppanen, M., S. Kumar, and C. Chandra. 2005. *Process Analysis and Improvement: Tools and Techniques.* 1st ed. New York: Irwin/McGraw-Hill.

SmartDraw.com. 2008. "Standards and Methodologies." www.smartdraw.com/tutorials/bpm/methodologies.htm (August 27).

Vroom, V. H. 1964. *Work and Motivation.* Jossey-Bass.

Wikipedia.com. 2008. "Business Process Management." http://en.wikipedia.org/wiki/Business_process_management (August 27).

End-of-Chapter Activities

1. *Reading review questions.*

   a. What are the elements of COSO's enterprise risk management framework?

   b. What is business process management? List and discuss the steps managers often use to change a business process.

   c. List and discuss seven principles of business process management.

   d. What are the elements of expectancy theory? Give examples of each one.

   e. In a format specified by your instructor, respond to the questions for this chapter's "AIS in the Business World."

2. *Reading review problem.*

   America Online (AOL) describes itself as "a leading global advertising-supported Web company, with the most comprehensive display advertising network in the U.S., a substantial worldwide audience, and a suite of popular Web brands and products. The company's strategy focuses on increasing the scale and sophistication of its advertising platform and growing the size and engagement of its global online audience through leading products and programming" (http://corp.aol.com/about-aol/company-overview). Given the size of its staff and operations, you can probably imagine the transaction volume AOL's accounting information system handles on a daily basis.

In 2004, AOL used the principles and processes of business process management to develop an electronic funds transfer system (EFTS) for processing employee expense reimbursements and vendor invoices. Prior to the EFTS, such requests were processed manually, consuming a lot of time and resources while offering very little flexibility for customers. As a result of the EFTS implementation, AOL experienced improvements in time, cost, customer satisfaction, and management control.

Source: America Online, Inc., Financial Services white paper, http://interfacing.com/uploads/File/aol.pdf (September 9, 2008).

a. Use COSO's enterprise risk management framework to create an ERM plan for AOL.

b. How might AOL's management apply the steps and principles of business process management to develop their EFTS?

c. Consider an AOL employee who was fully supportive of the EFTS. Use expectancy theory to explain the employee's support.

d. In expectancy theory, all three elements must be present to provide motivation. Based on AOL's EFTS project, suggest a scenario in which one or more of the elements is not present.

3. *Multiple choice review.*

1. All of the following are elements of COSO's enterprise risk management framework except:
   a. Fraud detection.
   b. Objective setting.
   c. Control activities.
   d. Monitoring.

2. Which of the following steps typically occurs first in business process management?
   a. Analyze collected data.
   b. Monitor process improvements.
   c. Define process boundaries.
   d. Optimize the process.

3. When considering a business process management project, managers should:
   a. Understand how business processes interact with organizational strategy.
   b. Be open to alternatives.
   c. Ensure that top management can describe current business processes before the project starts.
   d. All of the above.

4. All of the following are elements of expectancy theory except:
   a. Expectancy.
   b. Instrumentality.
   c. Valence.
   d. Conditioning.

5. Which of the following best exemplifies expectancy theory?
   a. Motivation = Expectancy $\times$ Instrumentality $-$ Valence
   b. Motivation = Expectancy $+$ Instrumentality $+$ Valence
   c. Motivation = Expectancy $\times$ Instrumentality $\times$ Valence
   d. Motivation = Expectancy $\times$ Instrumentality / Valence

4. *Making choices and exercising judgment.*

In Chapter 3, you learned about COSO's internal control framework. In this chapter, we took a look at COSO's enterprise risk management framework. COSO went to great lengths to explain why the ERM framework was needed and how it relates to the internal control framework. Read their explanation at www.coso.org. Are both frameworks needed? Do both frameworks add value to organizations? Justify your responses.

5. *Field exercises.*

   a. The chapter discussed expectancy theory as a way of explaining motivation. But, researchers and practitioners have suggested many other theories, such as Maslow's hierarchy of needs, Herzberg's two-factor theory, and McClelland's needs theory. Research one or more of those theories (or others suggested by your instructor). Compare and contrast them to expectancy theory.

   b. Search the Internet and/or your school's library to find an example of a successful BPM project. Summarize the project. To what extent does the case follow the seven basic steps suggested by Seppanen, Kumar, and Chandra? The BPM principles suggested by Eppele?

   c. If you're like students at my university, you may be frustrated by some of your school's processes—such as the process of registering for classes, purchasing textbooks, or paying fees. Use the steps and principles of business process management to suggest a way to improve a process that frustrates you.

6. *Enterprise risk management.* Which element of the COSO ERM framework is most closely associated with each of the following?

   a. ALG Corporation bonds key employees.

   b. Based on previous experience, TRG Corporation's management believes the risk of inventory shortages is moderate.

   c. BPC Corporation implements a profit-sharing plan as a way to motivate managers to control costs.

   d. BRN Corporation's board of directors hires a consultant to explain ERM.

   e. CNV Corporation's managers accept the risk of stock price decreases.

   f. DTI Corporation holds quarterly staff lunches where employees discuss how they manage risk.

   g. EIV Corporation's president organizes monthly meetings for managers to discuss books and articles related to ERM.

   h. FLM Corporation operates manufacturing plants on three continents.

   i. FPO Corporation follows a top-down model for strategic planning.

   j. HRP Corporation's internal audit department assesses and tracks the effectiveness of its ERM plan.

   k. Management at CNV Corporation determines the probability of a decrease in stock value is very high.

   l. MGG Corporation occasionally hires a consultant to provide feedback on its ERM plan.

   m. RCH Corporation's enterprise risk management department prepares and distributes a monthly ERM newsletter.

   n. SSO Corporation reviews and revises its strategic plan annually.

   o. TRG Corporation's managers want to avoid inventory shortages.

   p. WRL Corporation does not use data encryption in its wireless network.

7. *Expectancy theory elements.* Which element of expectancy theory is described in each of the following independent scenarios?

   a. Anh completed the steps for licensure as a Certified Public Accountant and received a pay raise.

   b. Claudia completed a BPM project early; her boss said she could either have extra time off or a small pay raise. Claudia chose the pay raise.

   c. Ethan put in many extra hours in January and was pleased to be named "employee of the month."

   d. Lupe believes her company's new general ledger software is too complex to master.

   e. Mark changed his major from finance to accounting because he heard jobs are more plentiful in accounting.

   f. Richard has stopped suggesting business process improvements because his ideas are never implemented.

8. *Expectancy theory and employee motivation.*

In the previous problem, you identified one relevant element of expectancy theory. Consider each scenario again; "fill in" the other two elements. Here's an example:

> Expectancy: Anh studied hard and took a review course that enabled her to pass the CPA exam on her first attempt. Instrumentality: Anh completed the steps for licensure as a Certified Public Accountant and received a pay raise. Valence: Anh celebrated her pay raise with her family and close friends.

9. *Business process management principles.*

Which of Eppele's seven principles is violated in each of the following independent cases? Justify your responses. (Each case may violate more than one principle.)

   a. Amanda objected to her company's new approach to training because they had never used it before.

   b. Esther started a BPM project by looking for appropriate information technology tools.

   c. Eugene, an entry-level employee, implemented a new system for taking inventory.

   d. Jeff decided to change his company's purchasing process because the current process seemed too cumbersome.

   e. Minh told the consultants for a BPM project to prepare and submit reports as they felt appropriate.

   f. Molly told employees that all their concerns would be addressed at the end of the BPM project.

   g. Raul argued strongly that a proposed BPM project be managed by a consulting firm.

10. *ERM plan.*

In Chapter 3, Exercise 8, you developed a risk/control matrix for two of the Fortune 100 companies. Develop a full enterprise risk management plan for one of them; use the COSO framework to structure your plan.

11. *Terminology.* Match each item on the left with the most appropriate item on the right.

1. Behavioral issues	a. First step in BPM
2. Control activities	b. Fraud & resistance to change
3. Define boundaries	c. Key idea when using consultants
4. Expectancy	d. Reduce, accept, avoid, share
5. Instrumentality	e. Second step in BPM
6. Internal environment	f. Specific actions taken to respond to risk
7. Map steps and flow	g. The belief that effort will lead to success
8. Risk responses	h. The idea that goal achievement leads to reward
9. Valence	i. The value placed on a reward
10. Well-defined tasks	j. Tone at the top

12. *Multiple choice questions.*

   1. In business process management, decision makers must collect and analyze data. Which of the following tools would best be used to collect useful data?

      a. Journal entries

      b. Interviews

      c. Financial statements

      d. Expectancy theory

2. Employees of BRN Corporation are trying to convince the CEO of the importance of enterprise risk management. The CEO comments: "I can't really support this idea. Too many organizations develop ERM plans, then put them on the shelf instead of implementing them." Which element of expectancy theory is reducing the CEO's motivation?

   a. Expectancy
   b. Valence
   c. Instrumentality
   d. Motivation

3. The first step in business process management is to select the process and define its boundaries. Which of the following is the best defined process within the context of BPM?

   a. Selling assets
   b. Posting journal entries to the ledger
   c. Purchasing inventory
   d. Financing operations

4. Which of the following is a key idea in both business process management and enterprise risk management?

   a. Defining the boundary
   b. Accepting things as they are
   c. Increasing efficiency
   d. Involving company executives

5. Which of the following statements best exemplifies one of the principles of BPM?

   a. First, we need to think about the software we're going to use.
   b. Let's develop a proposal, then inform the CFO.
   c. We'll need to select the BPM team carefully.
   d. This project should be quick and easy; we can wait and let everyone know about it when we're done.

13. *Statement evaluation.* Please indicate whether each of the following statements is (i) always true, (ii) sometimes true or (iii) never true. For those that are sometimes true, explain when/under what circumstances they are.

   a. Accountants are in the best position to determine reward valence.
   b. Both BPM and ERM require strong support from top management to be successful.
   c. Both the COSO internal control and ERM frameworks include monitoring.
   d. BPM projects result in lower costs because they use information technology strategically.
   e. Companies should avoid external consultants at all costs in BPM projects.
   f. Cost variance analysis can be used to analyze data in BPM.
   g. In developing an ERM plan, managers should always attempt to reduce risk.
   h. Production workers are in the best position to add value to a BPM project.
   i. The COSO ERM framework is the only viable way of managing risk.
   j. Vroom explained that human motivation depends on three factors.

Chapter **Five**

Information Systems Concepts

AIS in the Business World

Systems Development in an Insurance Company

Jones and Rastogi provided the following brief description of a systems development project they completed:

> A large insurance company engaged us to implement a Web single sign-on solution (WSS). The implementation required upfront analysis of six Web applications that the WSS would support, along with analysis of the network environment, security policies, procedures, and standards. Our analysis of the applications revealed totally distinct and different approaches to identity authentication. This posed a problem for the WSS; this problem was only the symptom. The root cause was the organization's "official" SDLC process. Yes, the company had an established SDLC process. But it was, effectively, shelfware; none of the developers, system architects, or project managers used it. Worse yet, some of their people used no formal SDLC at all. They simply "winged it." Other project teams used established software development processes. But they did not consistently document design and code artifacts.

You can probably tell, just from that brief description, why they chose to keep the company anonymous!

Discussion Questions

1. Why is the study of information systems concepts, such as the systems development life cycle, relevant to AIS?
2. What is the SDLC? How is it used in developing an accounting information system?
3. How would you describe the insurance company's overall process for systems development?

Source: R. L. Jones and A. Rastogi, "Secure Coding: Building Security into the Software Development Life Cycle," *Information Systems Security,* November/December 2004.

Early in your study of accounting information systems, you learned that most AIS have five parts: inputs, processes, outputs, storage, and internal controls. But did you ever wonder how those elements of the AIS come into existence in the first place? After all, they don't "spring full blown" like Minerva from the brow of Jupiter! (That's your multicultural, interdisciplinary lesson for this chapter. Hope you liked it.) And once the elements are in place, how can we judge, in a macro sense, the extent to which an organization's processes need improvement? Finally, what factors should professionals take into account when choosing which information technology to implement?

In this chapter, we're going to explore three topics that help answer those questions: the systems development life cycle (SDLC), the capability maturity model (CMM), and software selection.

When you've finished studying this chapter, you should be able to:

1. List and discuss, in order, the steps in the systems development life cycle.
2. Explain the advantages and disadvantages of using the SDLC.
3. Apply the SDLC in accounting contexts.
4. List and discuss the levels of the capability maturity model.
5. Classify organizations' processes according to the CMM.
6. Explain factors managers should consider when choosing IT for an AIS.

SYSTEMS DEVELOPMENT LIFE CYCLE

As the name implies, the **systems development life cycle** (SDLC) is a methodology for designing, implementing, and maintaining virtually any kind of information system. It's certainly not the only such methodology; it may not even be the best methodology. But many organizations use the SDLC in their systems projects, so you're highly likely to run across it in your career.

The SDLC comprises seven parts (see Figure 5.1):

1. Initiation/planning
2. Requirements analysis
3. Design
4. Build
5. Test
6. Implementation
7. Operations and maintenance

Although the seven steps appear very linear in nature, the SDLC is actually highly **iterative** in practice—similar to systems documentation. In other words, information systems professionals don't move from one step to another in a rigid way. Rather, they move back and forth between the steps as needed in a specific project. So, for example, an organization might be engaged in testing, only to find that it must change the way a system is built; or, a team might be partially done designing a system when it discovers that the requirements analysis needs additional work.

Let's look at each of the seven steps in more detail, along with how you might apply them in an accounting information system:

1. *Initiation/planning.* Most systems development projects start because someone in an organization recognizes an unfilled need. For example, a small organization might

FIGURE 5.1
Systems Development Life Cycle

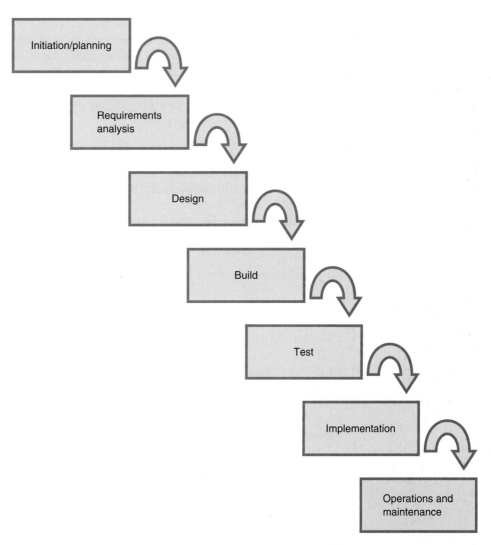

have been using a checkbook as its only accounting information system. But if the organization is growing, its needs for accounting information will quickly outpace the capabilities of a simple checkbook. This first phase of the SDLC often includes a feasibility study to determine if the project is possible from economic, operational, and technical perspectives. The feasibility study results may be used to try to get the project funded.

2. *Requirements analysis.* In requirements analysis, systems designers figure out what the new system needs to accomplish. They may use a variety of tools at this stage, including flowcharts and interviews with system users. The fundamental goal of requirements analysis is to develop a clear set of objectives for the new system—in much the same way that every chapter in this book starts with a set of objectives. The requirements analysis for our fictional small organization, which we'll call MCL Company, could include objectives like "produce general purpose financial statements" or "prepare end-of-year tax returns."

3. *Design.* With the requirements analysis in hand, systems designers can begin to think about how the system should look—how will screen layouts look, what kinds of documents are

Enterprise resource planning systems come in different versions based on generic organizational types. For example, PeopleSoft has one version designed for the needs of colleges and universities.

needed, what forms of internal control will be involved. Very often, the overall AIS is broken down into modules for design purposes; modules could be based on business processes (sales/collection, for example) and/or stakeholders (such as customers and employees). At this point, MCL may decide to build a system "from scratch" or to evaluate "off-the-shelf" software. Both approaches have costs and benefits. Building a system from scratch takes time and may be expensive; off-the-shelf software may not be completely customizable to a specific organization.

4. *Build.* If the system is being built "from scratch," this phase involves writing the actual computer code. If an organization is using off-the-shelf software, like Peachtree, building probably includes customizing it to the particular organization. If you've worked with general ledger software in your AIS course, you probably customized things like the chart of accounts, inventory records, and personnel information. As a small organization, MCL Company may be more likely to use off-the-shelf software, particularly if its needs are as generic as those mentioned in (2) above.

5. *Test.* You probably wouldn't want to buy a new car without test driving it first, right? The same holds true for information systems! During the testing phase, users can critique the system and make suggestions for its improvement. One of my former students works for the U.S. Navy; when the Navy was preparing to implement new software for procurement/purchasing, the software was installed on a few machines. Users had the opportunity to work with the new software and make suggestions about it. If MCL's management decided to build a system from scratch using relational database software, testing would involve setting up the database so users could "check it out" before starting to use it. It's much easier to make design changes at this stage than it would be after the system has been implemented. If the information system has been designed in modules, testing also helps ensure that the modules work well together.

This step may help you understand the iterative nature of systems development more clearly, as it may involve revisiting earlier phases of the SDLC.

6. *Implementation.* After any revisions based on testing, the system is at last ready for implementation—for actual use by the organization to achieve the purposes set out in requirements analysis. Managers have many choices when it comes to systems implementation. They may, for example, run the old system and the new system simultaneously for a time (parallel implementation). They may completely take down the old system and put the new system in its place (direct cutover or "big bang"). They may implement the system in modules, as well. MCL's management could continue using its simple checkbook system alongside its newly developed/purchased system for a time. Even with such a parallel approach, MCL could use modular implementation for the new system. Every implementation approach has costs and benefits; there's no "one right way" or even "one best way" to approach this important task.

7. *Operations and maintenance.* Information systems, particularly accounting information systems, are dynamic. As people, processes, products, and services of the organization change, the AIS should change along with them. For example, MCL's management might decide to incorporate at some point; at a minimum, incorporation would require a change in the chart of accounts. Other issues to consider over the life of a new system include internal control, accessibility for the disabled, and hardware and software requirements.

Some descriptions of the SDLC break it down into more than seven phases. The U.S. Department of Justice lists 10 steps in its SDLC (www.usdoj.gov/imd/irm/lifecycle/ch1 .htm#para1.2); regardless of the level of detail, the same basic tasks are involved.

The SDLC has both strengths and weaknesses. Some of its strengths include strong control and opportunity for user input; weaknesses include rigidity and difficulty estimating costs. What other strengths and weaknesses can you identify for the SDLC?

Now, we'll turn our attention to the capability maturity model.

CAPABILITY MATURITY MODEL

Humphrey first wrote about the CMM in Managing the Software Process.

The **capability maturity model** (CMM) was first suggested by **Watts Humphrey** in the late 1980s. Humphrey was a software engineer, and he developed the CMM as a framework to assess business processes in an objective way—with particular reference to government contractors and software projects. In the intervening years, the CMM has been applied in many other organizational contexts: project management, software maintenance, risk management, and business school accreditation. Whatever the context, the CMM has five levels: chaotic, repeatable, defined, managed, and optimized (see Figure 5.2). Let's look at each level's characteristics and apply them to accounting information systems.

- *Level one: chaotic.* These processes are unstable and noncohesive; think of this level as an "every person for him/herself" mentality, or like a bunch of Lone Rangers in an organization. Individuals may be highly motivated and put forth extraordinary effort in making a process "work," but the organization's processes as a whole are jumbled and confused. As a graduate student, I did some consulting with small businesses that often had chaotic

FIGURE 5.2
Capability Maturity Model

Level Five
Optimized

Level Four
Managed

Level Three
Defined

Level Two
Repeatable

Level One
Chaotic

79

accounting information systems. I recall one client, a marine supply business, in which the AIS consisted of a shoebox full of receipts, check stubs, and other documents. And, as a reviewed them, I discovered that the collection was incomplete. Hopefully, in your professional career, you won't run across an organization with such a chaotic AIS.

- *Level two: repeatable.* This level involves some planning; it may result in consistent results over time. One way to recognize this maturity level is the development of "major milestones" for projects and/or processes, with specific deliverables at each milestone. If the marine supply business wanted to move from its chaotic AIS to this level, managers might focus on producing monthly financial statements. They could establish a process for collecting source documents, making journal entries, and keeping accounting records up-to-date to achieve that goal.

- *Level three: defined.* In describing this level, Hurst (2007, p. 4) noted:

  > At maturity level 3, the standards and procedures for an individual project are derived from organizational standards to suit that particular project. This is a key distinction between levels 2 and 3. Both levels require project standards, procedures, and process descriptions. In level 2, they might be unique to a project. In level 3, they are tailored from broader organizational standards. It is expected in level 3 that processes will be described in more detail and with more rigor. Management is expected to understand relationships between processes and to collect detailed metrics of performance.

  So, in the marine supply business, the accounting information system moves from being a "necessary evil" to something that supports the organization in other ways. The business would likely develop a procedures manual to standardize the way the AIS is maintained; such a manual would be particularly useful during times of transition and expansion.

- *Level four: managed.* In level three, processes are defined but not measured. When an organization moves to level four, its management develops metrics to establish goals and control processes. When a process doesn't achieve those goals, management can look for ways to improve the process. The management of the marine supply business might, for example, set a goal of producing quarterly financial statements within one week of the end of each quarter. If the quarterly financials took longer than a week, management would look for ways to improve the process to achieve that goal.

The idea of continuous improvement is called *kaizen* in Japan. You may have encountered this idea in a cost accounting or operations management course.

- *Level five: optimized.* This level is characterized by a "continuous improvement" mentality in the organization. At this level, organizations look at the "big picture" of process improvement. Hurst (2007, p. 4) offered these comments: "A key distinction between level 4 and level 5 is the types of process variation that are addressed. At level 4, the concern is with individual projects experiencing delays and variations. Level 5 organizations develop processes to address the common causes of process delay and variation, and to change processes to improve performance." If our marine supply business moved to this level, managers would think beyond the accounting information system, considering ways to improve other business processes. Level five is really about an attitude of improvement—one that permeates the organization and affects nearly everything it does.

Reflection and Self-Assessment   5.2

You've started the process of entering the accounting profession by going to college. Based on the CMM levels, how would you describe that process? Why?

We'll look more closely at business processes in Part Four of the text.

Ideally, an organization will move all of its business processes sequentially through the levels. Since each level builds on those that precede it, skipping levels can be frustrating and counterproductive. At the same time, processes at different levels within the same organization can create problems; for example, a sales/collection process at level four would be problematic if the acquisition/payment process was at level two.

INFORMATION TECHNOLOGY SELECTION

The eight issues here are but a small subset of many considerations managers must weigh in IT decisions. Later, you'll have a chance to research and/or brainstorm additions.

Managers need to consider two kinds of issues when they think about selecting an appropriate form of information technology for their AIS: **macro-level issues** and **micro-level issues.** Figure 5.3 provides a list of all the factors we'll consider in this section.

Managers must first specify the *need* they are trying to meet with a new form of information technology. Often, company personnel want the "latest and greatest" form of information technology just because it looks cool or is fun to play with. But IT resources represent a major investment of time and money for most firms, so establishing a clear need is critical. Johnston (2003) offered the following insights in this area:

Notice how Johnston's comments tie into the phases of the SDLC.

> Assign the managers . . . to prepare a [needs analysis] for their sections. It should include all the things they do—from invoice preparation to inventory operations. Using the data, ask them to prepare flowcharts to diagram how they perform those tasks . . . or even how they get bottled up. During this analysis have the managers gather samples of every form . . . and every report the current software produces. From this analysis you will be able to develop a requirements definition—a detailed document that defines what your business needs.

Strategic fit is also important when investing in new information technology. As you may know, a strategy indicates how an organization competes in its markets. Most good strategic plans begin with a strong, yet concise, mission statement. For example, the mission of the McGraw-Hill Companies (www.mcgraw-hill.com) is to provide essential information and insight that help individuals, markets, and societies perform to their potential. A mission statement, as part of a strategic plan, explains why an organization exists; it outlines how the organization plans to differentiate itself from its competitors. Information technology investments should align with (support) the organization's strategic plan; that is, managers and employees should be able to state clearly how a given information technology fulfills the organizational mission.

Personnel involvement is another key factor in new IT investments. Johnston (2003) recommended two items in this area: a technology advisory committee and independent consultants. While he considers a technology advisory committee essential, he states that hiring an independent consultant may or may not be a good idea. A technology advisory committee should, according to Johnston, comprise five to seven members from various

FIGURE 5.3
Factors to Consider in IT Selection

Macro-Level Factors	Micro-Level Factors
Need	Cost
Strategic fit	Adaptability
Personnel involvement	Training
Financing	Vendor reliability

departments/functions/offices of the organization. Subcommittees also may be in order to manage more focused tasks and involve more personnel. Employees on the committee need not necessarily be technology experts, but they should be able to think globally for the good of the company, rather than representing the (perhaps) parochial interest of their own area.

Reflection and Self-Assessment   5.3

Under what circumstances would you want to hire an independent consultant for an IT investment project? Suggest three questions you would ask during a selection interview for an independent consultant; also, identify and discuss three adjectives that would describe the ideal consultant.

Finally, on the macro side of the equation, managers need to consider *financing*—how do they plan to pay for the IT? Key questions here include

- Will external funding be required for the investment?
- If so, how will the company raise it: debt or equity?
- Is leasing an option? If so, what are its advantages and disadvantages?
- Are any tax credits available based on the investment?

Well-developed, detailed operational and capital budgets will help address those issues.

Now, let's look at some of the *micro-level issues* involved in IT investments. Most managers will immediately consider *cost* when they think about micro-level issues. Cost, however, is much broader than just the money spent for the investment. Managers need to consider the total cost of information technology: its upfront cost, training, maintenance, and customization, to name a few.

Adaptability is another micro-level issue managers need to consider. In other words, can the proposed information technology be adapted effectively to the organization? Or will its adoption involve major business process redesign? Investments in new IT are challenging under most circumstances. But, if they disrupt or create change in the way a company does business, they become even more so.

Employees need to learn to use a new information technology, so *training* becomes another issue. How easy will it be to learn to use new hardware and/or software? Will the training be provided by the vendor as part of the contract, or will the company have to pay extra for it? Can the training be made available online, or does it require classroom attendance to be effective? While a hardware or software vendor will certainly have answers to most of those questions, many organizations seek answers from companies that have already implemented the same or similar systems.

Finally, what about *vendor reliability?* Is the supplier of the technology a well-established, reputable company? You don't want to make a significant investment with a company only to find them bankrupt or out of business within a few months or years. Naturally, no one can predict those kinds of events with perfect certainty, so managers have to rely on their judgment and independent data collection as assessment tools.

Sylla and Wen (2002) proposed a three-stage process for evaluating information technology investments; their ideas are depicted in Figure 5.4.

FIGURE 5.4
Sylla and Wen Framework

So how can you make sense of all those factors in an IT investment situation? I've often used a **weighted-rating technique** as a guide. Here's how it works:

1. Develop a list of factors that are important in your decision. I generally stick with around five factors, but you could use fewer or more depending on the circumstance.
2. Weight each factor on a scale from 1 to 10 based on its importance, with higher numbers assigned to factors that are more important.
3. Evaluate each piece of hardware and/or software on each factor. Assign each item a score (again from 1 to 10) based on how well it fulfills the factor.
4. Multiply the weightings by the ratings and add everything up to determine an overall "score" for an individual item.
5. Use the weighted ratings as one input to your investment decision.

Here's an example:

Factor	Factor Weighting
Adaptability	7
Cost	8
Strategic fit	9
Training	9

	Ratings				
Software package	**Adaptability**	**Cost**	**Strategic Fit**	**Training**	**Weighted Score**
1	6	10	8	5	239
2	10	10	9	7	294
3	8	7	10	9	283

So, in the preceding analysis, the numeric results argue in favor of software package 2. Notice, though, that its "score" is very close to that of package 3. In cases such as this, where the scores are so close, managers need to use judgment in making the final choice—rather than slavishly following the numeric results.

CRITICAL THINKING

We've looked at three important information systems concepts in this chapter: the systems development life cycle, the capability maturity model, and factors to consider in selecting software for the AIS. To develop your critical thinking skills about the topics, let's first look in more detail at how the SDLC would be applied in the design of an accounting information system.

While pursuing my Ph.D., I worked as a consultant for a small medical practice in Claremont, California. The doctor was an osteopathic physician who had just left teaching to reenter medical practice; she had no accounting system to speak of, and contacted me through a mutual friend to accomplish that goal. Here's how I used the SDLC to design and implement her AIS:

1. *Initiation/planning.* The doctor recognized her need for an accounting information system. She knew she didn't have the expertise herself to design it, so she contacted me for assistance. I explained the process I'd be using and got her promise to cooperate.

2. *Requirements analysis.* I interviewed both the doctor and her office staff over a period of several days. The basic questions were always the same: What information do you need to run the medical practice? What reports will you need to produce, including those for insurance companies, tax agencies, and other entities? The answers were fairly straightforward; the practice had to have sufficient data to generate income statements and balance sheets; they also needed to justify and track insurance billings from both private- and public-sector agencies.

3. *Design.* Because her accounting needs weren't out of the ordinary for that type of business, I recommended an off-the-shelf general ledger software that could be customized to her practice. You're probably using something like Peachtree Complete Accounting in your AIS course; the software we finally settled on was very similar.

4. *Build.* After installing the software on the office computers, I created a block-coded chart of accounts. The doctor had a few patients from the outset, so I also created an accounts receivable subsidiary ledger for them and an accounts payable subsidiary ledger for vendors. The practice was organized as a sole proprietorship, so two equity accounts were needed: Capital and Drawing.

5. *Test.* I worked with the office manager for several days, inputting a few transactions. I showed both the office manager and the doctor the reports, confirming that they had all the information she needed.

6. *Implementation.* The first five steps of the SDLC took about two months to complete; after that, the system "went live." Because it was a brand new system where none had existed before, we didn't have to worry about modular/direct cutover/parallel implementation.

7. *Operations and maintenance.* I worked with the doctor and her office manager for about a year after implementation, ensuring that everything was running smoothly and according to plan.

To choose the software in the design stage of the SDLC, I used the weighted-rating technique discussed in the chapter. In consultation with the doctor, I considered three fairly common factors: cost, ease of learning and use, and adaptability to her business. Ease of learning and use was weighted most heavily, followed by cost and adaptability.

How does all that information relate to the capability maturity model? We can look at it in at least two ways: (1) the maturity of the design process itself and (2) the maturity of the operations. The design process itself could best be characterized by the CMM as repeatable. The project had some standards with respect to time, cost, and efficiency, but the doctor viewed the project as a stand-alone endeavor. She didn't have generalized organizational standards for systems development, which was probably appropriate in her case. The project involved specific deliverables and a time line, which means it had progressed beyond chaotic. But, it hadn't yet risen to *defined* because the doctor left most of the details to me.

On the other hand, the system's operation could best be described as *managed*. The processes associated with entering data and extracting reports were described in a procedures manual and in the software's documentation; after the system had been operating a few months, the doctor and her office staff set goals for the length of time spent doing accounting tasks.

Notice that neither the design nor the operation of the accounting information system had become optimized within the first year. As you read in the chapter, the last level of the CMM involves a "culture of improvement," which often takes quite a while to establish.

Summary

Here's a look back at what we've covered in this chapter:

1. *List and discuss, in order, the steps in the systems development life cycle.* The SDLC is a methodology many organizations use to develop and implement information systems. It comprises seven steps, which are highly iterative in nature: initiation/planning, requirements analysis, design, build, test, implementation, and operations and maintenance.

2. *Explain the advantages and disadvantages of using the SDLC.* The SDLC is very structured and offers organizations a lot of control over information systems projects; in addition, it is widely recognized and used in business. On the other hand, the steps in the SDLC can take a lot of time to complete, thereby resulting in high costs relative to other systems development strategies.

3. *Apply the SDLC in accounting contexts.* Since accounting is fundamentally an information system, the SDLC steps can be applied to it. In the *initiation/planning* stage, an organization would recognize the need for changes in its AIS—for example, the need to generate a variance analysis or consolidate results from subsidiary companies. *Requirements analysis* focuses on what the system needs to accomplish; staying with the variance analysis example, the system would probably need to generate quantity and cost variances for product costs. *Designing* such a system gets still more specific: What would a user see on the screen? Which source documents, paper or electronic, would be required to collect the data? How would the data be input? Systems professionals would move next to *building* the system—actually putting together the screens, documents, and programming code for computing variances. Users would have the opportunity to *test* the system prior to it being *implemented* with a parallel approach, direct cutover approach, or some other approach. Finally, in *operations and maintenance,* the system would be changed as the organization and its information needs change.

4. *List and discuss the levels of the capability maturity model (CMM).* The capability maturity model consists of five levels, each more sophisticated than the previous level: chaotic, repeatable, defined, managed, and optimized.

5. *Classify organizations' processes according to the CMM.* When an organization's processes are *chaotic,* they lack cohesion; each individual in the organization does what seems best to him/her. *Repeatable* processes involve some standards and procedures, but they are probably applied to a single project. When processes are *defined,* they are connected to broader organizational standards; standards are developed and data are collected about the process. Processes move to the *managed* stage when the collected data are used to improve and control the process. When the idea of managing and improving business processes is ingrained in the organization, becoming part of its culture, it moves to the last level of the CMM: *optimized.*

6. *Explain factors managers should consider when choosing IT for an AIS.* The chapter considers both macro- and micro-level factors. Macro-level factors include need, strategic fit, personnel involvement, and financing. Micro-level factors are cost, adaptability, training, and vendor reliability. The weighted-rating technique can be used to balance the factors.

When accounting information systems courses started becoming a part of undergraduate accounting programs, they often focused on ideas common to all information systems like the SDLC. Although the content of AIS courses has become more specific over time, those ideas can still be an integral part of AIS study.

Key Terms

capability maturity model, *79*
iterative, *76*
macro-level issues, *81*

micro-level issues, *81*
systems development life
cycle, *76*

three-stage process, *82*
Watts Humphrey, *79*
weighted-rating technique, *83*

Chapter References

Hurst, J. 2007. *The Capability Maturity Model and Its Applications.* www.giac.org/resources/whitepaper/application/242.php (last visited September 15, 2008).

Johnston, R. 2003. "A Strategy for Finding the Right Accounting Software." *Journal of Accountancy,* September, pp. 39–46.

Sylla, C., and H. J. Wen. 2002. "A Conceptual Framework for Evaluation of Information Technology Investments." *International Journal of Technology Management,* pp. 236–61.

End-of-Chapter Activities

1. *Reading review questions.*

   a. What are the steps in the systems development life cycle? What activities does each step involve?

   b. What are the costs and benefits of using the SDLC?

   c. How can the SDLC be useful in accounting information systems?

   d. What are the levels in the capability maturity model? What characteristics distinguish each level?

   e. What factors should managers consider when choosing information technology resources?

   f. Respond to the questions for this chapter's "AIS in the Business World."

2. *Reading review problem.*

   As organizations grow and change, their information systems must change as well. Consider these examples:

   - Gazing more at the rowers on the [Schuylkill River] below than on the automobiles ahead, a [Center City Philadelphia] driver slams into the car in front of him, causing an accident that increases the ride home for many commuters—and sets in motion a series of legal and insurance steps. Such a traffic incident is only one of more than 70,000 automobile accidents reported each year in Philadelphia, and the city's police department prepares a report for each one. Accident reports are necessary for insurance companies to process claims and ultimately pay settlements to their customers. Until recently, processing an accident report was a costly, time-consuming process, taking up to six weeks for a paper copy to become available. Thanks to the efforts of a unique public/private partnership and the power of Internet technology, Philadelphia accident reports are now available to insurance companies in less than one week. [Coghlan and vonMechow, 2004]

• When Wacoal [Corporation] analyzed their information technology systems, what they found wasn't very encouraging. Their technology had been growing as the company grew—systems were added on an as-needed basis, which resulted in a patchwork quilt of 32 independent legacy systems. Many of these legacy systems were more than 10 years old. To improve the quality of business-decision information, Wacoal sought a solution that would connect its disparate systems together in a seamless data flow. These system changes would allow the company to achieve operational efficiency and concentrate on its core competence. The question was how to accomplish a seemingly complex task of system and platform integration in a very short time frame with a limited project budget. The answer came from Wacoal's technology partner—Hitachi—and the freely available eXtensible Business Reporting Language for General Ledger (XBRL-GL), the Journal Taxonomy. [Hasegawa et al., 2004]

Sources: T. Coghlan and T. vonMechow, "Driving Auto Accident Costs Down," *Strategic Finance,* January 2004; M. Hasegawa, T. Sakata, N. Sambuichi, and N. Hannon, "Breathing New Life into Old Systems with XBRL-GL: The Wacoal Story," *Strategic Finance,* March 2004.

Considering either the accident report case or the information technology case, respond to the following questions:

 a. How would workers in the case have used the SDLC to make the changes described?
 b. Compare the "before" and "after" processes in the case you chose. How would you classify each one using CMM?
 c. Which macro- and micro-level factors for IT selection are indicated/implied in the case?

3. *Multiple choice review questions. Please select the best answer for each question.*

 1. Which of the following SDLC steps occurs first?
    a. Build
    b. Design
    c. Test
    d. Operations/maintenance

 2. Which phase of the SDLC is most likely to include a feasibility study?
    a. Initiation/planning
    b. Requirements analysis
    c. Design
    d. Operations and maintenance

 3. At which level of the CMM are project standards first derived from broader organizational standards?
    a. Chaotic
    b. Repeatable
    c. Defined
    d. Managed

4. Which of the following phrases is most closely associated with the "optimized" level of the CMM?
   a. Lone Ranger
   b. Continuous improvement
   c. Necessary evil
   d. Information technology

5. All of the following are macro-level issues to consider in IT selection except:
   a. Financing.
   b. Need.
   c. Strategic fit.
   d. Training.

4. *Making choices and exercising judgment.*

   a. Business professionals have debated whether or not an organization should strive to ensure that all its processes are "optimized" according to the CMM. What do you think? Regardless of your response, what benefits might an organization realize at the earlier levels?

   b. Common forms of information technology in AIS include spreadsheets, databases, general ledger software, and ERP systems. List and discuss three AIS-related tasks you could accomplish with each type of software; for example, you could develop a budget with spreadsheet software.

   c. FTP (file transfer protocol) software is used to transfer files between a computer and the Internet. In considering an FTP package, managers might consider factors such as cost, popularity, documentation, and ease of use. Point your Web browser to www.download.com and identify three FTP software packages available there. Evaluate them using the weighted-rating technique described in the chapter.

5. *Field exercises.*

   a. The SDLC is only one methodology for designing and implementing information systems. Others include rapid application development, open source development, joint applications design, and prototyping. Investigate one or more of those alternatives. Describe it, then compare and contrast it to the systems development life cycle.

   b. Arrange an interview with an accounting or information systems professional in an environment where you'd like to work after earning your degree. Ask your interviewee to describe a business process in his/her organization. On your own, based on that description, classify the process according to the capability maturity model. Explain your classification.

   c. Read "Commercializing the Back Office at Lloyds of London: Outsourcing and Strategic Partnerships Revisited" in *European Management Journal* (April 2004, pp. 127–40). Summarize the article's contents in no more than one single-spaced page. Did Lloyds use IT strategically? Justify your response.

6. *Capability maturity model classification.* Several business processes are described below. Which CMM level best characterizes each one?

   a. Alastor owns a lawn care business. Each time he mows a client's lawn, he sets a goal for how long it should take.

   b. Big State University was engaged in three building projects simultaneously: an addition to the library, a new parking structure, and upgrades to the student center. Although each project was over budget for both time and money, the university president focused on analyzing the situation for the parking structure only.

   c. CHL Corporation's management team meets monthly to address issues of process improvement and product quality.

    d. Christina is a sales representative with clients all over eastern Michigan. At the beginning of each day, she decides which clients she will contact that day and whether she will contact them in person, over the phone, or via e-mail.

    e. Hong and Meihua build wooden doghouses based on requests from clients. They frequently disagree about the best way to build each one.

    f. Magdy is the vice president of finance at TCH Corporation. At the end of each year, he consults with the president and other vice presidents to determine the corporation's optimal capital structure. He then compares the optimal structure to the actual one, making recommendations for needed changes.

    g. Rodrigo, Miguel, and Ana own a mobile pet grooming service with eight employees. Every quarter, as part of their overall quality improvement plan, they send two employees to a continuing education seminar.

    h. Sebastian is a manager at PPK Corporation. The last time he hired a new employee, he asked his favorite current employee if any of her relatives were looking for a job; he then hired one based on that conversation.

    i. The payroll manager at BHN Corporation has proposed outsourcing part of the payroll function. In accordance with BHN policy, the manager prepared a flowchart of how the new process would work.

    j. When the production manager at STK Corporation suggested converting from a process-costing system to a job-costing system, the vice president of operations asked how the change would affect the amount of inventory available for sale.

7. *Systems development life cycle.* Which phase of the SDLC is described by each independent case below?

    a. Dolores used design specifications to create database tables for employee records.

    b. Eric works at a "help desk" answering questions about patching issues in World of Warcraft.

    c. Esther must decide how many "action buttons" to put on an Access form for entering purchase requisitions.

    d. Liliane completed several simulations of a new inventory control system, then made recommendations for changes in how the system was designed and built.

    e. Marcel prepared a leveled set of data flow diagrams for a new sales/collection process, then used the set as a basis for discussion with the sales staff.

    f. Tony wants to move from incremental budgeting to zero-based budgeting.

    g. When the accounting staff of CHF Corporation arrived at work on Monday morning, their old manual accounting system had been replaced.

8. *Requirements analysis.*

    a. Jeff is the warehouse manager for Alta Pasa Unified School District; he wants an online inventory tracking system for computers and other technology resources in the warehouse. List and discuss at least five questions you would ask Jeff and his staff as part of the requirements analysis for the project.

    b. Amanda is a hypnotherapist in Dallas, Texas. She currently maintains her appointment schedule in a paper-based calendar but wants to start using information technology for that purpose. List and discuss at least five questions you would ask Amanda as part of the requirements analysis for the project.

9. *Designing, building, and testing an information system.* Working on your own or with a group of students, consider one of the cases from the reading review problem above. Design and build at least one database table with an associated form for the case you select.

10. *AICPA Top Technology Initiatives.* Do a Google search for the AICPA Top Ten Technologies. Investigate the most recent list; describe the process used to develop the list.

Work with a group of students to investigate one or more of the technologies, summarizing your work in a form specified by your instructor.

11. *Terminology.* Match each item on the left with the most appropriate item on the right.

1. "Ad hoc" processes	a. Test (SDLC)
2. Business rules	b. Risk of SDLC
3. Consistent project standards	c. Repeatable (CMM)
4. Cost overrun	d. Optimized (CMM)
5. Discrete project standards	e. Managed (CMM)
6. Feasibility study	f. Initiation/planning (SDLC)
7. Improvement part of organizational culture	g. Design (SDLC)
8. Modular programming code	h. Defined (CMM)
9. Simulations	i. Chaotic (CMM)
10. Statistical project control	j. Build (SDLC)

12. *Multiple choice questions.*

1. As a future accounting professional, which phase of the SDLC are you least likely to be involved in?

   a. Build

   b. Requirements analysis

   c. Operations/maintenance

   d. Test

2. If a system does poorly during the testing phase of the SDLC, it may be due to issues in

   > I. Requirements analysis.
   > II. Design.
   > III. Build.

   a. I and II only

   b. II and III only

   c. I and III only

   d. I, II, and III

3. Which of the following is the best example of the "initiation/planning" stage of the SDLC?

   a. "We need to use XBRL to produce financial statements."

   b. "We should adopt Peachtree as our general ledger software."

   c. "Let's compare PeopleSoft with SAP."

   d. "Our inventory controls are weak."

4. Which of the following statements is most true?

   a. Failure of a new system is a bigger risk in direct cutover implementations than in parallel implementations.

   b. Failure of a new system is a bigger risk in parallel implementations than in direct cutover implementations.

   c. Smaller organizations should use parallel implementation more often than direct cutover.

   d. Larger organizations should use direct cutover implementation more often than parallel.

5. John plans to use the SDLC to develop a balanced scorecard for his department. Which stage of the capability maturity model is John's organization in?

   a. Chaotic

   b. Repeatable

   c. Managed

   d. Cannot be determined from the information given

13. *Statement evaluation.* Indicate whether each of the following statements is (i) always true, (ii) sometimes true, or (iii) never true. For those that are (ii) sometimes true, explain when the statement is true.

a. The systems development life cycle is the best way to develop new information systems.

b. The SDLC can never be used as a tool for managing business processes.

c. Interviews with system users can be an important element of requirements analysis.

d. Results in the build stage of the SDLC may require an organization to revisit its requirements analysis.

e. Cost growth and schedule delays are risks associated with using the SDLC.

f. If the business processes in Department X are optimized, the business processes in Department Y are also optimized.

g. An organization can move from repeatable processes to managed processes without having defined processes.

h. An organization should move through the stages of the CMM sequentially.

i. An organization using activity-based management is at the managed stage of the CMM.

j. Publicly traded corporations are required to optimize their business processes for SOX and the Foreign Corrupt Practices Act.

Documentation Techniques

Part One presented some fundamental ideas about accounting information systems. In Part Two, we'll look at ways to document the AIS. Systems documentation is an important part of auditing; in addition, you'll need to be able to prepare and interpret graphic representations of the AIS. This section discusses three techniques: flowcharting, data flow diagramming, and REA modeling. Depending on your work environment and the task at hand, you may be called upon to use any one (or more) of the three.

Chapter **Six**

Flowcharting

AIS in the Business World

Billing Process

The "AIS in the Business World" for Chapter 4 discussed the implementation of "lean thinking" at Woburn Safari Park. Tatikonda (2008) applied the concepts of lean thinking to the customer billing process most companies use. She provided the following illustration as part of her discussion:

In this chapter, we'll begin discussing methods for documenting accounting information systems. We'll start with the most commonly used method: flowcharting.

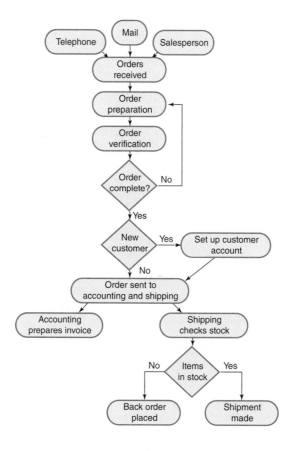

Discussion Questions
1. How are flowcharts used in accounting information systems?
2. What are the strengths and weaknesses of Tatikonda's flowchart?

Source: L. Tatikonda, "A Less Costly Billing Process," *Quality Progress,* January 2008.

I am indebted to my colleague, Dr. Kathy Hurtt of Baylor University, for focusing my thinking and providing valuable insights in the revision of this chapter. (And no, she's not related to me.)

In practice, you may often be called upon to evaluate a system's risk exposures; recommend ways to achieve stronger internal control; and/or suggest one or more ways to make a system more efficient and effective. In those situations, you'll want a way to encapsulate the essential features of an accounting information system: its documents, personnel involved, information flows, and related technologies.

When you complete your study of this chapter, you should be able to:

1. List and discuss the purpose and use of systems flowcharts, document flowcharts, program flowcharts, and hardware flowcharts.
2. Explain the basic parts of and design considerations common to all types of flowcharts.
3. Identify and describe common symbols and information technology tools used in flowcharting.
4. Discuss ways flowcharts impact the design, implementation, and evaluation of accounting information systems.
5. Create and interpret systems flowcharts.

A good flowchart is like a snapshot of an information system. It can tell you, at a glance, where information originates, who handles the information, and how it is summarized for decision making. Like most of the rest of AIS, flowcharting is at least as much art as science. The keys are to make your flowcharts as easy to read and as understandable as possible and to develop them in sufficient detail to provide an accurate picture of what's going on in an accounting information system.

FLOWCHART TYPES AND CONVENTIONS

Basically, a flowchart is a graphical representation of some part of an information system. The information system might be focused on accounting, production, human resources, or marketing; it might be related to a particular project such as launching the space shuttle or evaluating employee performance. Flowcharts have been used by information technology professionals for years to document computer programs; they also can be used to depict the hardware associated with a computer information system.

Flowcharts often are classified by their overall purpose and function:

- **Systems flowcharts** give the user a "big picture" look at an information system. Consider, for example, the process you use to register for classes each term. You use certain documents and types of information technology to select and register for classes; a systems flowchart would combine all of those resources with their related business processes.
- **Program flowcharts** show the logic associated with a computer program. As an accountant, you probably won't have much to do with program flowcharts.

- **Document flowcharts,** as you might expect, show the various documents involved in a system; they also portray the procedures performed on those documents. So, for example, a document flowchart might show your federal income tax return from the time you receive a blank form through its eventual disposition with the Internal Revenue Service.
- **Hardware flowcharts** will probably be a minor concern in your accounting career as well. They show the computers, printers, monitors, input devices, and other hardware elements associated with an information system.

Reflection and Self-Assessment   6.1

What type of flowchart would be most appropriate in each of the following situations?

1. Steps in a Visual Basic program for producing financial statements.
2. Steps associated with purchasing inventory.
3. Relationships between a central server and desktop computers.
4. Path of a sales invoice through an information system.
5. Origination, processing, and termination of a payroll check.
6. Local area network configuration.
7. Employee evaluation process.

Although two different people can look at the same business process and draw flowcharts that are significantly different, they should generally observe some very common conventions (habits) associated with good flowcharting:

1. Flowcharts should be read from top to bottom and left to right—the same way you read a page in a book. Flowcharting, though, is a highly iterative process, meaning that most folks don't "get it right" the very first time. So, the design may not proceed in such a neat and orderly fashion. But, when the final flowchart is produced, users should be able to follow it easily.
2. Flowcharts should have plenty of "white space." In other words, they shouldn't be too crowded on the page. If you're like most accounting students, you're thinking, "How do I know if it's too crowded? Is there a rule?" Well, no. Generally, if you think a flowchart looks too crowded, it probably is. In that case, it needs to be broken up into more than one page for easier reading.
3. Flowcharts should have a title. A bunch of symbols on a page can be confusing to read and evaluate if you don't know what they're trying to present. So, it's a good idea to title your flowchart based on what it represents; for example, "Systems flowchart of the employee evaluation process." The title should also include the name of the company, the date the flowchart was prepared, and the preparer's name. If the flowchart spans multiple pages, they should be numbered as "1 of x, 2 of x," and so on.
4. Flowcharts should be organized in columns that depict areas of responsibility. For example, purchasing inventory in most organizations involves departmental managers, purchasing agents, and vendors. So, a systems flowchart that shows the purchasing process would typically have three columns—one for each area of responsibility. Areas of responsibility will most commonly be the names of departments/functions/job titles within the organization; we don't typically use a person's name as a column heading.

5. Documents involved in a business process should have a clear origin and a clear termination. They shouldn't appear "by magic" in the middle of a flowchart, nor should they disappear from the system. A "clear origin" means the document first appears in the column where it enters the system. Documents typically originate in one of two ways: (a) they enter the system from some external entity or (b) they are created by some process within the system.

6. Rough drafts of flowcharts should be discussed by people involved in the process. Such discussions serve as a "reality check." They also help ensure that the flowchart is easily understood by someone other than the designer.

Adhering to those six conventions will make your flowcharts a lot easier to read and understand; they'll also be considerably more useful in the design, evaluation, and implementation of accounting information systems.

FLOWCHARTING TOOLS AND SYMBOLS

Flowcharts can be designed using a variety of tools, both high-tech and low-tech. On the low-tech end, you can draw a flowchart with paper and pencil. You also can use a flowcharting template, which includes many common flowcharting symbols. While manual methods are useful for "quick and dirty" starts at a flowchart, they can become tedious and messy over time.

You can find more information about Visio at http://support .microsoft.com/ph/2529. Check out SmartDraw on its Web page: www .smartdraw.com. It comes with a free trial that you might find useful for your AIS course.

Fortunately, numerous software programs facilitate the preparation of good flowcharts. Two programs I've found useful are **Microsoft Visio** and **SmartDraw.** Visio is part of the Microsoft Office Suite, so it interfaces fairly well with other programs such as Word, PowerPoint, and Excel. SmartDraw is an independent software program, but it also does a good job with designing all kinds of flowcharts; generally, they also can be read by Office software. Of course, you can use just about any software package that has some graphics capability to design a flowchart—even something as simple as PowerPoint! The advantage of using a program specifically designed for flowcharting, like SmartDraw or Visio, is its adherence to the flowcharting conventions discussed earlier. Additionally, flowcharting programs typically have a wider variety of flowcharting symbols in their libraries than other programs designed for different purposes.

Reflection and Self-Assessment   6.2

Point your Web browser to www.download.com. Search for flowcharting programs. Identify and describe two other programs you could use to create flowcharts.

Because flowcharts represent a kind of "universal language" in information systems design, implementation, and evaluation, they have some common symbols with specific meanings. According to the American National Standards Institute (ANSI), flowchart symbols can be divided into four groups: data, process, line, and special. Consider the **symbols** shown in Figure 6.1, which are just a small subset of the many symbols associated with flowcharting.

Now, let's take a look at how the symbols are put together to construct an actual flowchart.

FIGURE 6.1
Selected
Flowcharting
Symbols

On-page connector (special): shows where a document or process continues on the same page.

Multiple copies of a single document (data): shows that a single document, such as a purchase order, has several copies, which would be numbered and tracked separately in the flowchart. If a document doesn't have copies, the "top layer" only would be enough.

Disk storage (data): denotes storage on a hard drive, CD, or similar medium.

Manual process (process): used when data are processed manually, such as writing a check or preparing a sales invoice.

Terminator (special): starts or ends a business process; also can be used to show destinations such as "the bank."

Reflection and Self-Assessment   6.3

Which flowcharting symbol is used to depict each item below? Give an example as well as a description. (You'll need to do some outside research for this exercise. You could start by examining the "auto shapes" in Word or PowerPoint.)

- Annotation
- Decision
- File (merge)
- Generic process
- Off-page connector
- Predefined process

FLOWCHART DESIGN STEPS

As you might suspect, there's no "one right way" to design a flowchart. But, my AIS students often ask me the steps I use to prepare one, so I'm adding this section. When I prepare a flowchart, I normally follow this seven-step process:

1. *Establish the system boundary.* The system boundary is critical in designing a flowchart. Without a well-established system boundary, you end up "analyzing the world" every time you draw a flowchart. The system boundary puts a virtual "box" around the system; this process is sometimes called "delimiting."

    For example, if I'm flowcharting the process a company uses to purchase inventory, the system boundary is likely to be the company itself. The outside vendor (i.e., inventory supplier) is only important to the extent that it interacts with the company. So, while the flowchart is likely to include a column titled "vendor," the actions in that column do not include how the vendor processes the purchase order. The vendor column would include receiving the purchase order, shipping the goods, and billing the client.

2. *Determine column headings.* As mentioned above, column headings should focus on areas of responsibility—usually department names, functions, or position titles.

   For example, in a "purchase inventory" flowchart, column headings would include requesting departments, purchasing department, accounting department, receiving department, and vendor.

3. *List actions performed within each column.* In this step, list what each department does within the system. Notice that we haven't yet begun thinking about how to represent those actions with flowcharting symbols. It's important to have a good, clear idea of what goes on in the system before thinking about the symbols. Because flowcharting is a highly iterative process, you might find it necessary to revisit the column headings at this stage—always keeping in mind the system boundary so the flowchart doesn't grow out of control.

   For example, the purchasing department would: (a) receive purchase requisitions from requesting departments; (b) prepare a purchase order; (c) send the original purchase order to the vendor; and (d) send copies of the purchase order to the requesting department, the accounting department, and the receiving department.

4. *Select appropriate symbols.* Once I have the list of actions, I think about what flowcharting symbols will best represent them. As you'll see in the flowchart examples throughout the text, I tend to focus on a small group of commonly recognized symbols. Refer to Figure 6.1 and Reflection and Self-Assessment 6.3 for the actual symbols. Here are a few comments about each one:

   a. *Annotation.* This symbol is used to add descriptive comments or explanations to a flowchart.

   b. *Decision.* Decision symbols have a single point of entry, but multiple exits. For example, in a personnel selection process, the entry point might be "receive application documents." The decision symbol itself would be labeled "Meets qualifications?" and the two exits would be "yes" and "no."

   c. *Document.* Figure 6.1 shows multiple copies of a document. The same symbol would be used alone if a document had no copies.

   d. *File.* Sometimes referred to as "merge," this symbol should always indicate how the documents are filed. Examples include by name or by date.

   e. *Generic process.* This symbol can be used for any process in a flowchart. Because it symbolizes a process, it should always be labeled with a verb phrase, such as "receive applications" or "prepare purchase order."

   f. *Manual process.* If you know a process is manual (i.e., doesn't involve IT), you can use this symbol instead of the generic process.

   g. *On- and off-page connectors.* Readability is a critical feature of flowcharts. To avoid crossed lines on a page, use an on-page connector. To avoid overcrowding and move the action of a flowchart between pages, use an off-page connector. On- and off-page connectors always come in pairs with the same label. You can use letters for on-page connectors and numbers for off-page, or vice versa—just be consistent.

   h. *Predefined process.* Use this symbol to encapsulate a named process with multiple steps. The multiple steps should either be readily understood by the person reading the flowchart, OR they should be specified elsewhere (such as in a separate flowchart). "Complete the steps in the accounting cycle" is an example of a predefined process.

i. *Terminator*. I tend to use the terminator symbol only to mark the start and end of a flowchart. But, it can also be used to show entry from/exit to some point outside the system boundary.

5. *Prepare a first draft*. Once I've decided on symbols, I draw a first draft of the flowchart, keeping in mind the design conventions listed above.

6. *Discuss the flowchart with others*. Because flowcharting is somewhat subjective and highly iterative, the first draft is rarely the final product. It's important to get feedback on the draft from other people, because they can tell you what seems unclear from an outsider's point of view. Although there's no "magic number" of people you should consult, I usually try to ask two or three colleagues about the draft.

7. *Revise as needed*. Based on those suggestions, I revise the flowchart as necessary to make it clearer. For your first few flowcharts, you might need several rounds of revision. As you become more experienced, you might be able to cut them down to just one or two.

In the next section, we'll look at an example flowchart.

SAMPLE FLOWCHARTS

In this section, we'll look at an example flowchart for common parts of an accounting information system. Carefully read and study the example. As an AIS professional, you'll need to be comfortable in "both directions" with flowcharts; that is, looking at a flowchart and describing it in narrative form *and* reading a narrative description and preparing a flowchart.

As a student, you see a "finished product" when your professor comes into the classroom at the start of a new term. But, have you ever thought about what happens in preparation for that first class meeting? Even for a class a professor who has taught repeatedly, most of us spend considerable time "up front" designing a course. In this section, we'll use the first five flowchart design steps listed above to create a systems flowchart of the course design process. (I'm omitting the last two steps from the discussion because they are fairly self-explanatory.)

1. *Establish the system boundary*. This flowchart begins with an already established course; that is, a course that already has a title, a description, a course number, and other details. It's already been through whatever approval process the university has established. The task before us is to figure out how to apply the general ideas from the approved documents to design a particular offering of a class. The process will end when all the course materials are ready; it will not include the delivery of the course to students.

2. *Determine column headings*. Given that system boundary, what parties are involved in course design? We'll include two in our flowchart: the designer (i.e., the faculty member teaching the course) and the publishers (who will provide materials like textbooks).

3. *List actions performed within each column*. Here are the actions commonly performed by each party identified above:
   a. Designer
      i. Establish expected student outcomes. (generic process)
      ii. Develop preliminary list of possible textbooks/articles/cases. (generic process)
      iii. Order exam copies. (predefined process and document)
      iv. Review exam copies. (predefined process)
      v. Select course materials. (manual process)

     vi. Determine topic sequence. (generic process)

    vii. Develop grading plan. (predefined process)

   viii. Choose/create additional course materials. (decision, predefined process, document)

    ix. Write syllabus. (generic process and document)

     x. File course materials. (file)

  b. Publisher

     i. Receive and process orders for exam copies. (predefined process)

    ii. Send exam copies to the designer. (document)

4. *Select appropriate symbols.* The symbol we'll use for each action above is shown in parentheses after the action.

5. *Prepare a first draft.* See Figures 6.2 and 6.3 for the flowchart.

Does every professor follow those exact steps to design a course? Probably not. Would every flowchart of those exact steps look like Figures 6.2 and 6.3? Definitely not. But, you could use the flowchart as a basis for teaching someone how to design a course or for helping someone (like an AIS student) understand what happens before their professor sets foot in the classroom each term.

Here are some additional notes about the flowchart:

1. In this example, the on-page connectors are labeled with numbers. You could also use letters instead.

2. The off-page connector has two important pieces of information. In Figure 6.2, it shows the destination page (p. 2) and an identifier (A). In Figure 6.3, it shows the source page (p. 1) and the same identifier (A). If you use letters for on-page connectors, it's a good idea to use numbers for off-page connectors.

FIGURE 6.2   Systems Flowchart of Course Design Process Page 1 of 2

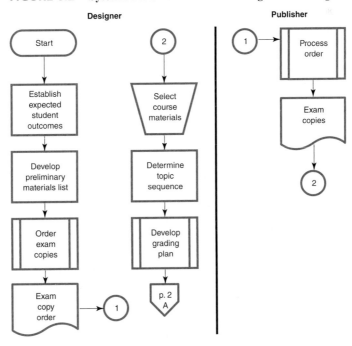

FIGURE 6.3   Systems Flowchart of Course Design Process Page 2 of 2

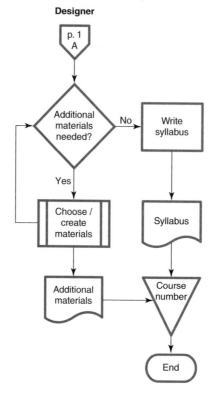

3. The document, "exam copy order," appears only in the first column. Some flowchart designers would also put it in the second column just to clarify what's entering the publisher's part of the system.

4. The file symbol indicates how the documents are filed. If they were stored in a computer database, you would use a cylindrical symbol labeled with the name of the database.

5. Figure 6.3 (the second page of the flowchart) includes only the designer column. Because no actions take place on that page for the publisher, you don't need a "publisher" column on the second page.

6. Although the designer makes several decisions along the way, only one is represented with a decision symbol. My general guideline is to use the decision symbol when an action has a fixed number of outcomes—usually two, but sometimes more than two.

FLOWCHARTING AND ACCOUNTING INFORMATION SYSTEMS

So how does all this material relate to your study of accounting information systems? AIS professionals use flowcharts in many different ways, including confirming how a system is currently operating, suggesting improvements to an accounting information system, evaluating internal control deficiencies, and designing procedures manuals.

In your very first accounting job after you graduate, you'll likely be coming into an unfamiliar environment. You may wonder "how things work" in the accounting information system, especially if you're in charge of a particular function such as accounts payable or accounts receivable. Additionally, if you're working for a CPA firm or as a consultant, you may need to confirm how a system is operating currently before you start an audit or make recommendations regarding operational efficiency. In all those cases, a flowchart can be a useful way to conceptualize the big picture of a system. You'd probably want to look over any existing procedures manuals and talk with employees familiar with the system already. Then, you can try designing a flowchart to model a business process. Once you've completed a first draft, discuss it further with others in the organization. Explain to them what it says and ask if that's the way things "really work" in the company, or if you're misunderstanding something. Remember: The overall goal of a flowchart in this situation is to understand the current state of things—the way they are, not necessarily the way they should be.

If you're looking at a previously constructed flowchart, whether you've created it or not, you can try to spot opportunities for improvement. Critically analyzing a flowchart is a tough job—there are no hard-and-fast rules for doing it. You'll need to draw on your training, experience, and ordinary business sense to identify and describe possible improvements in an accounting information system. Once again, interviewing and other kinds of research will help in this task. Ask employees, for example, what their biggest complaint is about the current process. If they've thought about ways to improve it, listen to those as well. You could ask employees in one-on-one or small group interviews; written surveys, e-mail exchanges, and employee suggestion boxes also can help in gathering ideas about process improvements. In many cases, the employees closest to a process can provide the best suggestions for making things better; in some cases, a system outsider can provide a new, fresh idea based on experience in other organizations. Opportunities for improvements might include redesigning forms, increasing or decreasing the number of copies of a particular form, obtaining authorizing signatures for transactions, filing in a different way (for example, based on date rather than customer name or vice versa), or changing a form from paper-based to electronic (or vice versa).

> Systems risk relates directly to information technology. As organizations become increasingly dependent on computers and related IT to deliver goods and services to customers, they risk the possibility that IT resources will fail at a critical moment.

Flowcharts also can be used to spot internal control deficiencies in an accounting information system. A flowchart can enhance a risk analysis by providing a concrete picture of an accounting information system. To use a flowchart to spot internal control deficiencies, start by making a list of the system's risk exposures. Then, look at the flowchart with those risk exposures in mind. Do any of the organization's processes or documents increase its exposure to specific risks? For example, if a company maintains only an electronic record of inventory purchases, you'll see that in a flowchart. In that case, the company is exposed to a systems risk. What controls has the company implemented to reduce its exposure to systems risk? Are the controls strong and adequate given the level of the risk? For example, does the company also maintain a paper file that is not shown on the flowchart? Or is a paper file missing from the flowchart because it doesn't exist?

Finally, flowcharts can be a starting point for the development of procedures manuals. A procedures manual is simply an "instruction book" that explains how everyday tasks in an organization are accomplished. Halbert (2003) recommends that "every staff member . . . document his or her duties and write a procedures manual—a time-consuming effort but worth doing." A well-constructed flowchart can easily be "translated" into regular, step-by-step text for use by future employees.

CRITICAL THINKING

As you read earlier in this chapter, developing flowcharts is as much "art" as "science." Therefore, learning to create good, descriptive flowcharts is often a challenge for accounting students—knowing the rules and conventions only takes you part of the way, in just the same way that you can't really learn to drive a car simply by reading a book. So, for this section, I'm going to show you how I usually go about creating a flowchart; please keep in mind that the way I do it is a result of my own experience and training. It's not the "one right way" to develop flowcharts.

If you've had some intermediate accounting already, you probably know the process the Financial Accounting Standards Board uses to develop new accounting pronouncements. In case you haven't studied that yet, here's a summary (Spiceland et al., 2009, p. 14):

1. *Identification of problem.* A measurement or reporting issue is identified by the Emerging Issues Task Force and placed on the FASB's agenda.
2. *The task force.* A task force of approximately 15 knowledgeable persons is appointed to advise the Board on various matters.
3. *Research and analysis.* The FASB's technical staff investigates the issue.
4. *Discussion memorandum (DM).* The DM, a detailed analysis of the problem along with alternative solutions, is prepared and disseminated to interested parties.
5. *Public response.* Public hearings are held to discuss the issue and letters of response are sent to the FASB, which then analyzes this feedback.
6. *Exposure draft (ED).* A preliminary draft of a proposed statement, called an exposure draft, is issued. The ED details the proposed treatment for the problem.
7. *Public response.* Written responses to the ED are accepted and analyzed. The ED is revised, if necessary, depending on the Board's analysis.
8. *Statement issued.* An SFAS [Statement of Financial Accounting Standards] is issued if four of the seven FASB members support the revised ED.

So how would you encapsulate those eight steps in a systems flowchart? First, I usually decide how many columns the flowchart will have, keeping in mind that you need one column for each area of responsibility. In the eight-step process, the groups involved are the Emerging Issues Task Force, the advisory task force, technical staff, the public, and the FASB. So, the flowchart will need five columns. Next, I normally consider what each group does and how to translate those actions into flowcharting symbols. The Emerging Issues Task Force identifies issues; a generic process symbol could be used to represent that. The Board does several things: appoints the advisory task force (generic process or predetermined process symbol), prepares documents (document symbol), analyzes feedback (generic process), and votes (decision symbol). The advisory task force advises the Board, while the technical staff conduct research. The process also involves several documents, each of which should be depicted with a document symbol.

Once I know how many columns and what kinds of symbols to use, it's time to start drawing the flowchart. I usually use graphics software like Visio or SmartDraw; you could also start with a paper-and-pencil sketch. Keep in mind that the flowchart should have a single "start" symbol and a single "end" symbol; it should also follow the rules and conventions discussed at the beginning of this chapter. Once the first draft is done, I discuss it with other people, make any needed changes, and then discuss it again; the flowchart is "done" when it fairly represents the process involved.

Reflection and Self-Assessment   6.4

Try drawing a flowchart of the standard-setting process based on the preceding description. Share your work with at least one other person—perhaps someone in your AIS course. Then, revise the flowchart as needed.

Summary

Here is a summary of the chapter:

1. *List and discuss the purpose and use of systems flowcharts, document flowcharts, program flowcharts, and hardware flowcharts.* A systems flowchart provides a top-level view of an information system; it shows the "big picture" of what is happening. A document flowchart, as the name implies, shows how documents (paper and electronic) flow through an information system, while a program flowchart details the steps in a specific computer program. A hardware flowchart lays out the computers, printers, monitors, and other hardware devices used in an information system.

2. *Explain the basic parts of and design considerations common to all types of flowcharts.* In general, a flowchart should be read from top to bottom and left to right. Since flowcharts are communication tools, they should be easy to read, incorporating plenty of white space. Every flowchart should have a title to make it easier to reference after its creation; flowcharts also should be organized into columns based on areas of responsibility in the information system. Documents should have clear beginning and ending points as well. Finally, flowcharts are usually the product of discussion among colleagues, rather than the product of a single individual.

3. *Identify and describe common symbols and information technology tools used in flowcharting.* Figure 6.1 shows various flowcharting symbols; your individual research (Reflection and Self-Assessment 6.3) revealed more. Two popular IT tools for flowchart creation are SmartDraw and Visio.

4. *Discuss ways flowcharts impact the design, implementation, and evaluation of accounting information systems.* A well-constructed flowchart can give a new accountant or consultant a quick overview of how a system works. Flowcharts also can be used as part of the auditing process and/or to suggest process improvements in the accounting information system, particularly when combined with a risk/control matrix. They also can inform recommendations regarding internal controls.

5. *Create and interpret systems flowcharts.* Three key ideas are important in creating flowcharts: (*a*) strive to achieve a clear representation of the system, not a deterministic response to a particular problem or case situation; (*b*) practice will increase your skill in flowcharting; and (*c*) seldom will your first creation be your final one—flowcharts can almost always be improved via dialogue and consultation with other professionals.

Flowcharting is one commonly used documentation techniques for accounting information systems. For accounting students, who typically like dealing with numbers better than words and symbols, they can be challenging. But, with time, practice, and patience, you can learn the art of developing clear, meaningful flowcharts and using them as analytical tools in the accounting information system.

Key Terms

document flowcharts, *96*	program flowcharts, *95*	symbols, *97*
hardware flowcharts, *96*	SmartDraw, *97*	systems flowcharts, *95*
Microsoft Visio, *97*		

Chapter References

Egerdahl, R. 1995. "A Risk Matrix Approach to Data Processing Facility Audits." *Internal Auditor,* June, pp. 34–40.
Halbert, J. 2003. "Mining Back-Office Operations May Bolster the Bottom Line." *Los Angeles Business Journal,* April 14, www.findarticles.com (last visited November 4, 2004).
Spiceland, J. D., J. Sepe, M. W. Nelson, and L. A. Tomassini. 2000. *Intermediate Accounting,* 5th ed. New York: Irwin/McGraw-Hill.

End-of-Chapter Activities

1. *Reading review questions.*

   a. What is a flowchart? Describe four different kinds of flowcharts and explain which are most often used in an accounting information system.
   b. Summarize the rules and conventions commonly observed in the preparation of flowcharts.
   c. List and explain the meaning and use of 10 common flowcharting symbols. What sources would you consult for learning about additional symbols not on your list?
   d. How are flowcharts used in working with accounting information systems?
   e. Respond to the questions for this chapter's "AIS in the Business World."

2. *Reading review problem.* The Sarbanes-Oxley Act of 2002 (SOX) was a reaction to the corporate accounting scandals of the late 20th century. In discussing some of the positive results of SOX, Harrington stated:

   > Companies can find additional uses for Sarbanes-Oxley documentation as a tool for audit committees, a way to enhance employee decisions based on cross-function process information and a means of increasing efficiencies by eliminating duplicate controls. Alltel Corporation (www.alltel.com) documented 100 company processes within the scope of [SOX]. Alltel's internal audit team reports to the company's audit committee. Its process documentation includes six flowcharts per process, supported by memos and narratives. The audit committee can use this information to support its decisions.

   She concluded her article with these summary comments:

   > CPAs can use the documentation to provide audit committees with more detailed information, to empower all employees to consider cross-functional processes and to lead the entire company in using section-404-type documentation. Since there is no way to avoid the cost, companies might just as well find ways to spread the expenditures over this greater array of benefits.

   So, flowcharts aren't just something you study in AIS class. In fact, in a survey conducted by Bradford, Richtermeyer, and Roberts, nearly half of the respondents reported using flowcharts to document accounting information systems.

   Sources: Cynthia Harrington, "The Value Proposition," *Journal of Accountancy* (September 2005), pp. 77–81; Marianne Bradford, Sandra B. Richtermeyer, and Douglas F. Roberts, "System Diagramming Techniques: An Analysis of Methods Used in Accounting Education and Practice," *Journal of Information Systems* (Spring 2007), pp. 173–212.

   a. Which type(s) of flowcharts discussed in the chapter would be relevant in this case? Explain your response.
   b. SOX imposes serious requirements regarding internal control on publicly-traded corporations. Those requirements include the CEO and CFO personally reviewing the company's internal control system, identifying weaknesses and known cases of fraud. Suppose you were creating a systems flowchart depicting a typical SOX process; identify three or four symbols you would expect to use in that flowchart, and explain how you would use them.

3. Multiple choice review questions. Please select the best answer for each question.

   1. Which of the following best describes a systems flowchart?
      a. Shows the flow of documents through an information system.
      b. Shows the logic used to create a program.
      c. Shows the "big picture" view.
      d. Shows how hardware elements are configured in a system.

   2. Which of the following statements about "white space" in a flowchart is most true?
      a. White space prohibits the use of color in flowcharts.
      b. At least 50 percent of the page should be devoted to white space.

c. White space is unimportant in document flowcharts.

d. Adequate white space is a matter of judgment.

3. In a systems flowchart, columns denote:

a. Areas of responsibility.

b. People's names and titles.

c. That the flowchart is unfinished.

d. A lack of adequate white space.

4. In a systems flowchart, a terminator symbol can be used to indicate: (i) the start or end of a business process or (ii) a destination outside the system boundary.

a. i only

b. ii only

c. Both i and ii

d. Neither i nor ii

5. In creating a systems flowchart, selecting appropriate symbols comes immediately after:

a. Determining column headings.

b. Establishing the system boundary.

c. Discussing the flowchart with others.

d. Listing actions performed within each column.

4. *Making choices and exercising judgment.* Compare and contrast SmartDraw and Microsoft Visio. Prepare a paper and/or PowerPoint presentation that includes a recommendation regarding your preferred flowcharting software; justify your recommendation.

5. *Field exercises.* Visit a local restaurant for lunch or dinner. Pay close attention to the steps involved in ordering, receiving, and paying for a meal. Create a flowchart that depicts the process. List and discuss one or two internal controls you observe in the process; also suggest one or two ways the system could be improved.

6. *Flowchart creation.* Create a flowchart based on each of the following independent situations (one flowchart per situation).

a. *Cori's Catering Services.* Cori is the owner and manager of a catering company. CCS provides complete meals (breakfast, lunch, and dinner), as well as an assortment of hot and cold appetizers and drinks, for groups of 12 to 500. CCS receives orders in three main ways: e-mail, telephone, and personal office consultation. In some cases, the customer has an idea of what he/she wants; in others, the customer relies on Cori's expertise to select appropriate items. For each catering job, Cori prepares an estimate for the client; she files one copy of the estimate and sends the other to the client for approval. The client may make changes to the estimate over the phone, via e-mail, or through a personal consultation. Once the estimate has been finalized, Cori prepares a catering contract for the client's signature. She requires a 50 percent deposit with the signed contract; the remaining catering fees can be paid within 30 days of the catering event. Cori accepts cash and checks; she does not accept credit cards. The client signs the contract and sends it back to Cori. Cori also signs it, files a copy for her own records, and sends a copy with both signatures back to the client. Cori and her staff deliver the catering order as scheduled, and she bills the client for any remaining fees. The client pays the invoice within 30 days and Cori deposits the funds in her bank account.

b. *University Bookstore.* Ordering textbooks in a university bookstore is a massive undertaking that requires good organizational, communication, and coordination skills. The process begins with faculty deciding which textbooks they want to use. Professors communicate relevant information about the textbook (title, author, ISBN, edition, publisher, copyright date) to a department chair or secretary, who consolidates all the orders. That communication may take place with a paper form or an e-mail. In either case, the departmental representative prepares a standard university book requisition form in triplicate: one copy for the requesting faculty member, one for the department, and one for the bookstore. The bookstore receives and consolidates requisition forms from all across the university and prepares purchase orders for textbook publishers. Each purchase order has three copies: one for the publisher, one for the purchasing department, and one for the accounting department. When the publisher sends the books, the bookstore's receiving department prepares two copies of a receiving report; one is filed to indicate that the goods were received, while the second is forwarded to the accounting department. The publisher sends a billing statement (invoice) directly to the accounting department. Once all three documents have been matched and verified, the accounting department writes a check or sends an electronic funds transfer to the publisher. The bookstore staff then sort the books based on class and stock the shelves, where the books await purchase by students.

c. Horacio is a college student at Feng Shui University. He rents an apartment from the university for $600 a month. On the 15th of every month, Horacio writes a check for the rent. He mails the check to the Housing Services office on campus; in turn, Housing Services sends an e-mail receipt back to Horacio. The mailroom staff in Housing Services makes a copy of the check for Horacio's file and sends the original, with all the other rent checks for the month, to the bank. Once a month, the treasurer of Housing Services reconciles the bank statement. Prepare a flowchart of the preceding scenario.

d. Visit the Web site of the International Accounting Standards Board. Summarize the process the Board uses to develop International Financial Reporting Standards (IFRS), then create a systems flowchart of the process.

7. (CMA adapted) *Narrative preparation from a flowchart.*

a. Consider the Richards Furniture Company flowchart presented below in Figure 6.4. Write a narrative description of the business process it depicts.

b. Consider the PriceRight Electronics Inc. flowchart presented below in Figure 6.5. Write a narrative description of the business process it depicts.

FIGURE 6.4   Flowchart for Richards Furniture Company

FIGURE 6.5   Flowchart for PriceRight Electronics Inc.

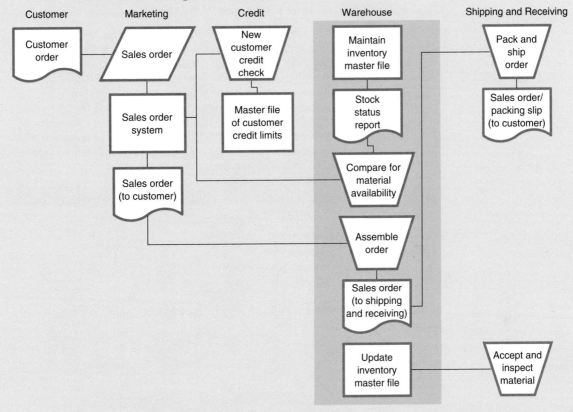

8. *Flowchart and system critiques.*

   a. Consider the Richards Furniture Company flowchart again. Describe at least two strengths and at least two weaknesses of the flowchart itself. Then, identify and describe at least two strengths and at least two weaknesses of the process it depicts. For each process weakness, suggest a way to correct it.

   b. Consider the PriceRight Electronics Inc. flowchart again. Describe at least two strengths and at least two weaknesses of the flowchart itself. Then, identify and describe at least two strengths and at least two weaknesses of the process it depicts. For each process weakness, suggest a way to correct it.

9. *Terminology.* Please match each item on the left with the best item on the right.

   1. Areas of responsibility
   2. Document flowchart
   3. Hardware flowchart
   4. Inverted triangle
   5. Origin and termination
   6. Overlapping shapes
   7. Program flowchart
   8. Spotting internal control deficiencies
   9. Systems flowchart
   10. Title

   a. A flowchart depicting the process of buying a car
   b. Based on lines of computer code
   c. Can trace remittance advices and invoices through a system
   d. Documents in a flowchart should have these
   e. Every flowchart should have one of these
   f. One application of flowcharting in AIS
   g. Represents a file in a flowchart
   h. Shows monitors, input devices, and computers
   i. Used to show multiple copies of a document
   j. What columns represent in a flowchart

10. *Multiple choice questions.*

Consider the following narrative as you respond to these questions:

> When staff at IGV Corporation need to travel on company business, they first submit a travel request to their immediate supervisor. The travel request includes the employee's identifying information; dates, location, and purpose of the trip; and a budget. The supervisor compares the travel budget to the department's total travel budget; if sufficient funds are available, the supervisor evaluates the need for the trip by comparing it to the department's strategic plan. If the trip is approved, the supervisor submits the budget to the cash expenditures department, where a staff member issues a travel advance to the employee. After the trip, the employee submits receipts and either pays back any excess advance funds or receives additional reimbursement for expenses incurred. If insufficient funds are available or if the trip does not support the strategic plan, the request is filed by employee name.

In each question, assume you are creating a systems flowchart of the narrative.

1. All of the following would be column headings except:
   a. Cash expenditures department.
   b. Department strategic plan.
   c. Staff member.
   d. Supervisor.

2. Which of the following actions would require the use of this symbol?

   a. Compare travel budget to total budget
   b. File request
   c. Issue travel advance
   d. Prepare budget

3. Which of the following actions would require the use of this symbol?

   a. Compare travel budget to total budget
   b. File request
   c. Issue travel advance
   d. Prepare budget

4. Which of the following is most likely to fall outside the system boundary?
   a. Supervisor
   b. Receipts
   c. Conference hotel
   d. Additional reimbursement

5. Which of the following actions is most likely to be depicted with this symbol?

   a. Evaluate the need for the trip
   b. File receipts
   c. Prepare strategic plan
   d. Issue travel advance

11. *Statement evaluation.* Indicate whether each statement below is (i) always true, (ii) sometimes true, or (iii) never true. For those that are (ii) sometimes true, explain when the statement is true.

   a. Columns in a systems flowchart denote areas of responsibility.
   b. Flowcharts are focused on business documents.
   c. Flowcharts should include off-page connectors for easier reading.
   d. Monthly bank reconciliations ensure that no one embezzles cash.
   e. Once designed, flowcharts do not need to be revised.
   f. On-page connectors help keep flowcharts uncluttered and easy to read.
   g. Process symbols should be sandwiched between an input and an output.
   h. The first step in drawing a flowchart is to decide which software package to use.
   i. Two designers would independently create identical flowcharts for the same business process.
   j. Visio is the best tool for drawing flowcharts.

Chapter Seven

Data Flow Diagramming

AIS in the Business World

Billing Process

Consider the billing process flowchart presented in Chapter 6's AIS in the Business World. While it does a fairly good job of outlining the steps in the billing process, it says almost nothing about the data involved and how they flow between steps in the process. An information systems professional might use a different technique to illustrate the same process: a data flow diagram (DFD). Here's an example of how that same billing process might be depicted using a DFD:

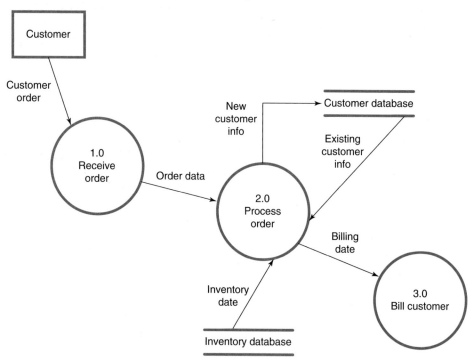

DFDs, while not as widely used in accounting information systems as flowcharts, can provide a valuable alternative way to document the AIS.

Discussion Questions

1. What are the basic principles and design considerations for a DFD?
2. What do the four symbols in the DFD mean?
3. How are DFDs similar to flowcharts? How are they different?

In the previous chapter, you learned about the first of three documentation techniques often used in accounting information systems: flowcharting. In this chapter, we consider the second of the three: data flow diagramming. The third technique, REA modeling, is discussed in the next chapter.

The concepts and ideas of data flow diagramming originated in the broader field of systems analysis and design. Since the accounting information system is a subset of an organization's complete management information system, we can borrow the ideas and techniques for our purposes here. Data flow diagrams (DFDs) incorporate fewer symbols and different "rules" than flowcharts, but they do share many similarities. When you finish studying this chapter, you should be able to:

1. Explain the symbols and design considerations associated with DFDs.
2. Compare and contrast flowcharts and DFDs with regard to purpose, content, structure, and use in accounting information systems.
3. Discuss ways DFDs are used in AIS work.
4. Construct a leveled set of DFDs.
5. Design normalized database tables from a DFD.

Some AIS professionals prefer one documentation method over another, but many use both flowcharts and data flow diagrams depending upon the situation and tasks at hand. In research conducted by Bradford, Richtermeyer, and Roberts (2007), just over 20 percent of respondents reported using data flow diagrams to document information systems. Managers use them to describe business processes, evaluate the current system, design or change a system, and assess the internal control environment.

DFD SYMBOLS AND DESIGN CONSIDERATIONS

Data flow diagrams can be prepared with the same software tools as flowcharts.

Unlike flowcharts, which incorporate a plethora of symbols, data flow diagrams incorporate only four (DeMarco, 1979), which are shown in Figure 7.1.

A **process** is any set of procedures an organization uses to gather data, change the data into information, or report the information to system users. Every process in a data flow diagram has two identifying characteristics: a number and a name. Numbers follow specific conventions, which we'll examine later in this chapter. Process names should always be verb phrases; that is, they should start with an "action word," like approve, record, calculate or check.

FIGURE 7.1
Data Flow Diagram Symbols

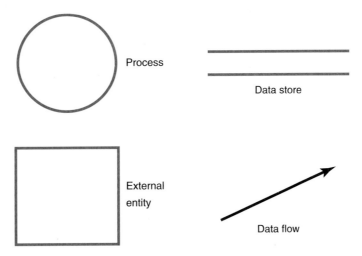

An **external entity** is any person or organization outside the boundary of an information system. Establishing a clear, appropriate system boundary is essential to the construction of a good data flow diagram. Without such a boundary, you'll end up analyzing "the world" every time you want to solve a problem in an accounting information system. Boundaries are a matter of management judgment, and external entities lie outside boundaries. So, for example, if you were constructing a data flow diagram for an organization's cash management system, external entities might include customers, suppliers, or the bank. But whether or not a person or an organization is an external entity depends upon your definition of the system, not your definition of the organization. So, for example, if you are processing travel expenses for a marketing staff member, the marketing staff member might be an external entity—even though she is employed in the same organization. You might want to refer back to Chapter 6 for additional comments on establishing the system boundary.

A **data store** is a place for collecting data; you might think of it as a "file," whether paper-based or electronic. Data stores are labeled with noun phrases such as customer data, vendor data, or inventory data. Data stores can be linked to processes or external entities in a data flow diagram; they cannot be linked to one another. Later in this chapter, we'll consider some of the issues involved in creating database files based on the data stores in a DFD.

Finally, a **data flow** is represented by a directional line in a data flow diagram. Data flows should have only one arrow on one end to conform to DFD design conventions. Data flows, like data stores, are labeled with noun phrases: desired information, accounts payable data, customer order data, and the like. When a data flow is labeled in that way, we're referring to the content, not the format. So, for example, a data flow labeled "approved order" could indicate a piece of paper, an e-mail, or an electronic purchase order. Students often try to label data flows with verb phrases—that's a bad idea. Remember, processes are verbs—they tell what happens to data in an information system. A data flow refers to the data itself, not what happens to it.

Hoffner, George, and Valacich (1996) suggested the following **rules/conventions** associated with good data flow diagrams:

1. All processes should have unique names. If two data flow lines (or data stores) have the same label, they should both refer to the exact same data flow (or data store).
2. The inputs to a process should differ from the outputs to a process.
3. Any single DFD should not have more than about seven processes.
4. No process can have only outputs. (This would imply that the process is making information from nothing.) If an object has only outputs, then it must be an external entity.
5. No process can have only inputs. If an object has only inputs, it must be a data store.
6. A process has a verb phrase label. Examples include *prepare check* or *register for classes.*
7. Data cannot be moved directly from one data store to another data store. Data must be moved by a process.
8. Data cannot move directly from an external entity to a data store. Data must be moved by a process that receives data from the entity and places the data into the data store.
9. Data cannot move directly to an external entity from a data store. Data must be moved by a process.
10. A data store has a noun phrase label.
11. Data of any concern to the system cannot move directly from one external entity to another external entity. They must be moved by a process. If data flow directly between external entities without processing, then they are outside the system boundary and omitted from the DFD.
12. An external entity has a noun phrase label.

FIGURE 7.2   **Registration Process Level Zero DFD**

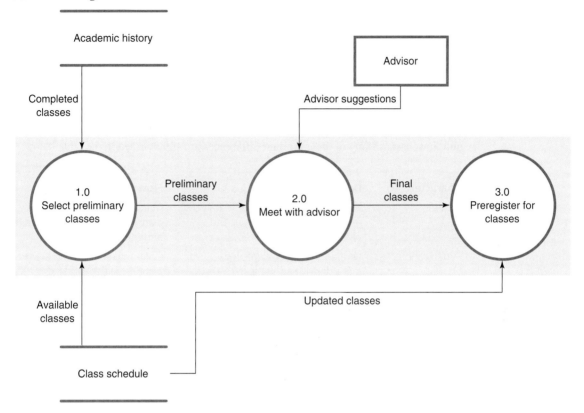

13. A data flow has only one direction between symbols.
14. A data flow cannot go directly back to the same process it leaves. There must be at least one other process that handles the data flow, produces some new data, and returns the original data to the original process.
15. A data flow can go directly into a data store. When it does, it signifies an update (delete, add, or change). Likewise, a data flow can come directly from a data store; in that context, it refers to a retrieval or use of the data in the store.
16. A data flow has a noun phrase label.

Consider the data flow diagram in Figure 7.2, which shows a basic process for registering for classes. The DFD contains three processes associated with registration: selecting preliminary classes, meeting with an advisor, and preregistering for the classes. It has two data stores: academic history (which is the record of all the classes a student has taken and the grades earned in them) and class schedule. Keep in mind that the data stores don't necessarily refer to physical documents—we're focused here on the *data,* not the *format.* The one external entity is the advisor; including the advisor as an external entity is a design judgment.

Data flow diagrams represent a very new way of thinking for most accounting students, so expect a bit of frustration as you become comfortable with this important method of documenting an accounting information system. When my own students experience that frustration, I often remind them of how they may have struggled initially to remember the rules of debit and credit in the AIS. By the time they take an AIS course, however, debiting and crediting accounts seem as routine as driving a car. In time and with practice, you'll develop that same level of comfort regarding designing and interpreting data flow diagrams.

Write a narrative description of the process depicted in Figure 7.2. Also, clearly describe and differentiate the four data flows associated with classes: available, preliminary, final, and preregistered. In other words, how do the four data flows differ from one another? How are they similar?

DATA FLOW DIAGRAMS AND FLOWCHARTS

So now that you know a bit about both, what are the differences between data flow diagrams and flowcharts? Many of the important differences are summarized in the table below:

Characteristic	Data Flow Diagram	Flowchart
Symbols	Four: circle (process), line (data flow), rectangle (external entity), and parallel lines (data store).	Many: rectangle (process), diamond (decision), triangle (file), and others.
Organization	Leveled sets, each depicting more detail than the last.	Columns representing areas of responsibility.
Numbers	Processes are numbered in the following formats: Level Zero, 1.0; Level One, 1.1; Level Two, 1.1.1; and so on.	Numbers can be used for on- and off-page connectors, not for processes.
Focus	DFDs focus on data and how they move between business processes, external entities, and data stores.	Flowcharts are concerned with data, but also with documents and processing tools.
Use of "lines"	Lines represent data; they are labeled with noun phrases (e.g., account balance, customer data).	Lines represent movement between processes, areas of responsibility, and the like; they are not labeled.

Both data flow diagrams and flowcharts are useful in the design and implementation of accounting information systems; but systems flowcharts typically provide more detail than a data flow diagram. In a data flow diagram, for example, a business process, such as "receive payment," would be represented with a single numbered circle, a single data flow, and a single external entity:

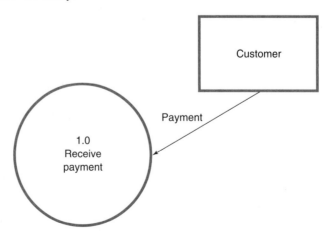

Someone looking at that portion of a Level Zero data flow diagram would not know

- How is the payment transmitted?
- What documents are used in the transaction?
- Who receives the payment?

A flowchart of that same process, on the other hand, might look like this:

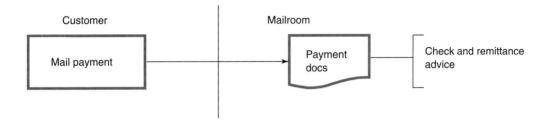

From that flowchart excerpt, we know

- Payments are made through the mail.
- They are received in the company's mailroom.
- Documents include both the customer's check and the remittance advice.

In the DFD, notice that the rectangle denotes the customer (an external entity); in the flowchart, the rectangle denotes a process (mail payment). In the data flow diagram, the process is depicted with a numbered circle. And, in the DFD, the data flow (arrow) has a name; in the flowchart, the data are represented with the document symbol, while the arrow shows the movement of the documents between areas of responsibility.

At this point, you might be wondering why it's necessary to learn more than one systems documentation technique; many students feel that knowing one should be enough. In practice, you might be called upon to create a flowchart as part of a financial statement audit to assess internal controls; you also might need to use a data flow diagram if you want to focus on the data you're auditing, regardless of their format (paper, electronic). Additionally, you will probably need to interpret both kinds of documents at some point in your career. For example, if you were hired by an entrepreneur to design an accounting information system "from scratch," you might first use a data flow diagram to focus on the data and how they are manipulated; the DFD might later be supplemented with a systems flowchart to iron out the details of who is responsible for different tasks, how documents will be named, how many copies of documents will be required, and other detailed issues.

LEVELED SETS OF DFDS

You probably recall from our discussion of flowcharting that flowcharts often span more than one page; the pages are connected with off-page connectors. The point of creating multipage flowcharts is to make them easy to read and interpret.

In the same way, data flow diagrams should be uncluttered and easy to read; but systems analysts use a slightly different method to achieve that goal: **leveled sets** of DFDs. A leveled set of DFDs refers to a collection that models related business processes. The various levels provide increasing detail about the processes in the system.

Table 7.1 shows an overview of the components of a leveled set of DFDs.

TABLE 7.1
Components of a
Leveled Set of DFDs

Level Name	Number of DFDs in a Leveled Set	Numbering Format
Context	One	0
Zero	One	1.0, 2.0
One	As many as necessary	Process 1.0 is subdivided into 1.1, 1.2, 1.3 Process 2.0 is subdivided into 2.1, 2.2, 2.3
Two	As many as necessary	Process 1.1 is subdivided into 1.1.1, 1.1.2 Process 2.3 is subdivided into 2.3.1, 2.3.2, 2.3.3
Three	As many as necessary	Process 1.1.2 is subdivided into 1.1.2.1, 1.1.2.2 Process 2.3.1 is subdivided into 2.3.1.1, 2.3.1.2

Just before I sat down to write this evening, I was doing some baking: fudge, pound cake, and ginger cookies. If I wanted to create a set of DFDs for that process (which wouldn't be nearly as much fun as doing the baking itself), the set might have labels and numbers that look like Table 7.2.

Table 7.2 is only talking about the processes—not the external entities, data stores, and data flows. Also notice how the system boundary is defined; it does not include driving to the grocery store or buying all the ingredients. As I mentioned earlier, defining the system boundary is a critically important judgment when preparing DFDs.

TABLE 7.2
DFD Description and
Numbering
Conventions

Level	Processes
Context	0: Bake tasty treats.
Zero	1.0: Make fudge. 2.0: Make pound cake. 3.0: Make ginger cookies.

One	Process 1.0 is broken down into
	    1.1: Combine chocolate chips, vanilla, butter, and nuts in a large bowl.
	    1.2: Cook marshmallows, sugar, and milk in a saucepan.
	    1.3: Pour mixture from saucepan over mixture in large bowl.
	    1.4: Stir vigorously until combined.
	    1.5: Lightly grease pan.
	    1.6: Pour combined mixture into greased pan.
	    1.7: Cool and cut.
	Process 2.0 is broken down into
	    2.1: Prepare oven and pan.
	    2.2: Whisk together dry ingredients.
	    2.3: Mix wet ingredients.
	    2.4: Combine wet and dry ingredients.
	    2.5: Pour batter into pan.
	    2.6: Bake.

Two	Process 2.1 is broken down into
	    2.1.1: Preheat oven to 375 degrees.
	    2.1.2: Lightly grease and flour cake pan.
	Process 2.3 is broken down into
	    2.3.1: Beat together butter, sugar, and vanilla.
	    2.3.2: Mix in eggs.

FIGURE 7.3
Registration Process
Context Diagram

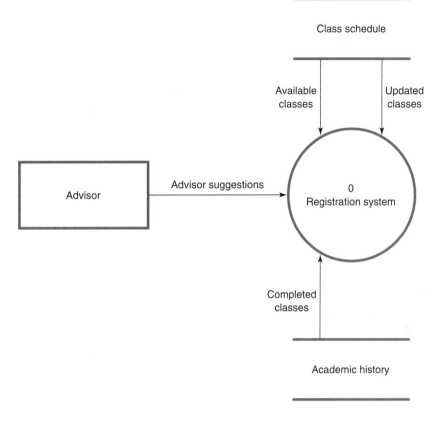

Figure 7.3 shows a **context diagram** for a registration system. (I showed you the **Level Zero diagram** first because it's more detailed; in practice, you'd prepare the context diagram first, then the Level Zero diagram.) Figure 7.2 showed a Level Zero diagram with three processes that are part of the registration system: select preliminary classes, meet with advisor, and preregister for classes.

Figure 7.4 shows a Level One diagram; it breaks down the "select preliminary classes" process from Level Zero into three parts: determine needed classes, determine time constraints, and prepare list for advisor meeting.

Reflection and Self-Assessment   7.2

Try your hand at creating a DFD that decomposes Process 3.0 (Preregister for classes) from Figure 7.2. The processes should have numbers like 3.1 and 3.2.

Here are some questions students often have when they first learn about DFDs:

1. *How many processes should a single DFD have?* There's really no "one right answer" for this question. But most analysts would try to limit the number of processes to seven in a single DFD.

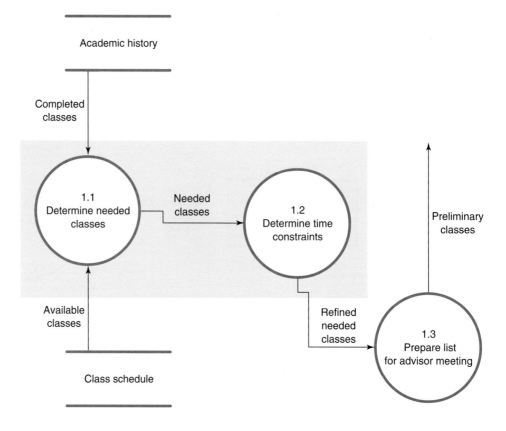

FIGURE 7.4
Registration Process
Level One DFD for
Process 1.0

2. *How many levels should be in a leveled set?* Again, it's a matter of judgment and the complexity of the process. For your work in class, you shouldn't need to go past Level Three—most of the time, Level Two will be plenty.

3. *When do you stop breaking down a process?* You stop breaking down a process when it's "self-explanatory." At that point, the process is said to be **primitive,** meaning it cannot be broken down any further. If you were preparing a leveled set of DFDs of the accounting cycle for a group of experienced accounting students, a process called "make journal entries" might be considered primitive; but, if the audience for that same set was a group of students in introductory accounting, you might decompose "make journal entries" into its component parts in a new DFD.

4. *Does each process have to be decomposed to the same level?* No. In the cooking example above, notice that Processes 2.1 and 2.3 are broken down further; Process 2.2 is not.

5. *What other documents support the leveled set of DFDs?* In most information systems, you'll find some specialized terminology that needs to be defined. In the cooking example, those terms might include *dry ingredients* from Process 2.2 and *wet ingredients* from Process 2.3. In Figure 7.2, *academic history* might need to be defined. You'd normally prepare a systems dictionary for that purpose; a systems dictionary is very similar to a regular dictionary—it includes terms and their definitions as a reference.

6. *What's the relationship between the levels?* The DFDs at various levels must be **balanced.** In other words, things cannot magically appear and disappear between the levels. For example, look at the context diagram in Figure 7.3; notice that it includes a data flow called "advisor suggestions." Now, look at the Level Zero diagram in

What other data flows are balanced between Figures 7.2, 7.3, and 7.4? Look back at the DFD you created in Reflection and Self-Assessment 7.2; is it balanced?

Figure 7.2; you see that same data flow. In Figure 7.2, two data flows go into Process 1.0: completed classes and available classes. Look now at Figure 7.4, which breaks down Process 1.0. Both data flows are inputs to Process 1.1.

DATABASE DESIGN

Constructing a data flow diagram is part of "requirements analysis" in the systems development life cycle (discussed in Chapter 5). Later steps in the systems development life cycle (such as design and build) call on designers and users to collaborate in deciding what kind(s) of data to capture and how to organize them in an information system; in most cases, that organization is accomplished with relational database software. The fundamental element of a database is a table. **Database tables** are organized in rows and columns, much like the rows and columns of a spreadsheet. Columns are referred to as "fields," while rows are referred to as "records." So, a database record typically comprises many different fields. For reasons that will become apparent in a few paragraphs, systems designers often say that "new rows are cheap, but new fields are expensive." In other words, it's fairly easy to add rows to a table once the structure has been established; on the other hand, it's fairly difficult and time-consuming to add new fields.

Arguably, the most commonly used relational database software for small and medium-sized businesses today is Microsoft Access. We'll just touch the surface of database applications in this text, but you'll know enough to interact successfully with other information systems professionals about their design, use, and maintenance.

Each field in a database captures a single type of information. Consider our ongoing example of a class registration process. One of the data stores in Figure 7.2 is called "Class schedule." In a typical class schedule, you'd find information like

Course prefix	Meeting days
Course number	Meeting times
Course title	Class location
Section number	Instructor last name
Number of units	Instructor first name

So, each of the 10 elements above constitutes a field in the class schedule database. Each record in the database would have a particular value associated with it. For example, at my university, all accounting courses have an "ACC" prefix. Our basic accounting information systems course is ACC 304; its title is "Introduction to Accounting Information Systems."

Each record in a database must have a unique identifier, referred to as a **primary key.** In a database of student information, for example, the primary key might be your student

Consider the data store labeled "Academic history" in Figure 7.2. What fields would you establish in a table to capture that information? What primary key would you use to identify each record in a unique way?

identification number. The Internal Revenue Service uses your Social Security number as a primary key; it identifies you and only you, uniquely and clearly. In a class schedule database, an individual course would probably have a unique reference number, although you could also use a *compound primary key* made up of the course prefix, course number, and section number as well.

In practice, a single database is likely to contain multiple tables. For example, a credit card company might have one table with customer information, a second table with information about current period charges, and a third table with information about customer payments. Each table captures different information, yet all three are related to one another. For that reason, database tables often include one or more **foreign keys.** A foreign key in one table is nothing more than another table's primary key. For example, the primary key in the customer information table might be the customer's credit card number. When a payment comes in, the credit card company needs to record not only the amount and date of the payment, but also who the payment is from. So, the customer's credit card number (the primary key in the customer information table) would become a foreign key in the payment table.

For the sake of convenience and clarity in talking about database tables, we'll use an underline to denote a primary key and [brackets] to denote a foreign key. Here's an example:

Check number	Payee number
Date written	Payee name
[Payee number]	Payee address
Amount	Payee city
Date paid by bank	Payee state
	Payee ZIP code
	Payee phone number
	Contact person

The column on the left might be called the "check table," while the column on the right could be labeled the "payee table." Organizing the data in a relational database would allow users to ask questions (referred to as **queries**) and create output reports that reflect information. For example, in our two-table database above, we could generate a query as the basis for a report that contains the check number and amount for each payee in the database. Relational databases also can do simple arithmetic operations, such as calculating the average check amount or the number of checks written but not yet paid by the bank as of a certain date. Database queries store instructions, not data. Each time the query is "run," it looks at the current data to get the answer to its question. Storing just the instructions, and not the results, helps keep the database compact and manageable (we'll come back to that idea at the end of this section).

Databases also can contain forms that facilitate data entry. If, for example, you've ever purchased anything on the Internet, you probably filled out a form with information such as your name, address, items ordered, and credit card number. That form would store the data in a table. Experienced users can also enter data directly into a table, whether a form exists or not.

Databases of accounting information can grow very large, very quickly. And database users want to be able to access the data quickly and easily. The process of making a database efficient and easy to use is referred to as *data normalization*. In short, data

You can get more information about data normalization at www .datamodel.org or by doing a Web search on "data normalization."

normalization allows database creators and users to minimize database size, optimize table design, and access data more quickly and efficiently. When a database follows the rules of data normalization, it is said to be in "normal form." Altogether, database specialists have conceptualized six normal forms, although the first three typically satisfy most business requirements. And normal forms are "additive"; that is, if a database is in second normal form, it is by definition in first normal form as well. Let's look at the rules for the first three normal forms in more detail.

First Normal Form (1NF): Eliminate Repeating Groups

A database table is in first normal form if it *eliminates repeating groups.* Suppose, for example, you wanted to show which customers had purchased which inventory items. If you attempted to create an "inventory items purchased" field in the customer table, at least two problems would result. First, the field would have to be updated every time a customer purchased a new type of inventory. Second, searching the database for that information would be time-consuming and cumbersome. Succinctly stated, the table would contain repeating groups—inventory item names would be repeated in several customer records.

Customer Name	Inventory Items
Brown	Paper, pens
McLaughlin	Pens, notebooks
Silva	Paper, pens, notebooks
Truong	Paper, notebooks
Zarineh	Notebooks

So how could you eliminate the repeating groups and put the database in first normal form? You could create two tables—one for inventory items and one for customers. The inventory table would have one field for the inventory item name and another field for the customer name. The inventory table would have a compound primary key; each record would be uniquely identified with the combination of the inventory item name AND the customer name.

Inventory Item	Customer
Notebooks	McLaughlin
Notebooks	Silva
Notebooks	Truong
Notebooks	Zarineh
Paper	Brown
Paper	Silva
Paper	Truong
Pens	Brown
Pens	McLaughlin
Pens	Silva

Second Normal Form (2NF): Eliminate Redundant Data

A table is in second normal form if it *eliminates redundant data.* In the table above, both customer names and inventory item names are repeated, although not in groups. (Eliminating repeating groups is the point of 1NF.) Because data items are repeated individually, the 1NF table contains redundant data. If the number of products and/or the number of customers expanded significantly, the database table would take up a lot of "space" on a computer network.

How could we fix that problem and put the database in 2NF? By splitting the 1NF table into separate tables again: one for inventory items, one for customer names, and a third that "marries" the two. The inventory item table would have three records (notebooks, paper, and pens); the customer table would have five records (Brown, McLaughlin, Silva, Truong, Zarineh). The third table, often referred to as a "junction table," would combine the data, thus making searches more efficient. A junction table is required in this case because each inventory item can be associated with many customers, and each customer can be associated with many inventory items. The three tables would look like this (notice the addition of "identification numbers" for each inventory item and each customer):

Inventory Table		Customer Table		Inventory/Customer Table	
Item	**ID**	**Name**	**ID**	**Inventory ID**	**Customer ID**
Notebooks	1	Brown	1	1	2
Paper	2	McLaughlin	2	1	3
Pens	3	Silva	3	1	4
		Truong	4	1	5
		Zarineh	5	2	1
				2	3
				2	4
				3	1
				3	2
				3	3

The tables above are in 2NF; they eliminate data redundancy in that they do not repeat inventory item names and customer names. The data redundancy is eliminated by introducing a third table that stores the ID numbers rather than the full names; the junction table would have a compound primary key, comprised of both fields displayed in the table above.

Third Normal Form (3NF): Eliminate Columns Not Dependent on the Primary Key

A table is in third normal form if it *eliminates columns not dependent on the primary key.* In other words, each field in a table should provide additional information about its primary key. So, if you wanted to include more information about each customer (address and phone number, for example), where would you put it? In the customer table, *not* in the junction table. Although the junction table contains one piece of data about a customer (the customer ID), additional data about the customer does not help us understand more about the relationship between customers and inventory; additional data about the customer help us understand more about the customer and therefore should be included in the customer table. Likewise, additional data about inventory transactions (such as the date and number of items purchased) help us understand more about the data in the junction table and therefore should be included there.

One other note about database design: Never store derivable data in a database table. Derivable data refer to anything that can be calculated, such as a customer's account balance, an employee's age, or the number of inventory items on hand. Use a query to get derivable data. Recall that a query stores instructions, not output. Storing the instructions takes up a lot less room than storing the data itself; also, using a query to derive data allows database users to get current results each time the query is run. So, for example, the junction table above would not contain a field for "total sales." It would contain a field for number of items sold and price per item; you would use a query to calculate the total of each sale.

As noted above, we've barely scratched the surface of using databases in accounting information systems. While data flow diagrams can be used in AIS work regardless of the technology that underlies the system, they are arguably used most often as the basis for designing a relational database. Depending upon the emphasis your instructor places on software in your AIS course, you may develop a basic to intermediate skill level with databases; either way, such knowledge will give you a competitive edge in your accounting career.

CRITICAL THINKING

The "AIS in the Business World" vignette in this chapter presents a DFD of the same business process discussed in Chapter 6. You might want to take time to compare the two once you've read through this section.

In the last chapter, we talked about drawing a flowchart of the FASB's new standards approval process; if you completed Reflection and Self-Assessment 6.4, you actually drew the flowchart. To help you understand the similarities and differences between flowcharts and DFDs, let's look at a Level Zero data flow diagram of the same process.

I usually start drawing a DFD by thinking about the system boundary. In this case, I'm going to define the system boundary as the FASB itself; that is, the actual Board members. As a result, the following will be external entities: Emerging Issues Task Force, advisory task force, technical staff, and the public. An alternative definition of the system boundary would be the entire FASB organization, which would include the Board, the EITF, and the technical staff. In that case, external entities would be the advisory task force and the public.

The processes involved in standard setting are described fairly clearly by the steps listed in Chapter 6. They would include (1) develop the agenda, (2) appoint advisory task force, (3) assign technical staff, (4) develop discussion memorandum, (5) get feedback on the DM, (6) develop the exposure draft, (7) get feedback on the ED, and (8) vote. Notice that the list involves seven processes, so we'd really be pushing the limit to include all of them in a single DFD. The good news is not all seven processes need to be shown in the Level Zero diagram. Some of them could potentially be combined, with the detail provided in subsequent levels.

Based on that, a Level Zero DFD might look like Figure 7.5. From the Level Zero DFD, you could decompose Process 3.0 into three processes: 3.1, prepare discussion memorandum; 3.2, obtain DM feedback; and 3.3, prepare exposure draft. Notice how, in the Level Zero diagram, the data flow leaving Process 3.0 is labeled "exposure draft." In the Level One decomposition of Process 3.0, that same data flow should leave Process 3.3 as one way of balancing the diagrams. You also could decompose Process 5.0 into two processes: 5.1, revise exposure draft; and 5.2, vote on revised draft.

At this point, you may be thinking: But what if the FASB votes and the potential new standard doesn't pass? The Board probably wouldn't conduct a vote until they were fairly certain the standard would pass; revision would continue until that point.

Developing data flow diagrams, just like constructing flowcharts, requires practice; in fact, I made three different drafts of Figure 7.5 before it was ready. And another systems professional might suggest additional changes, too. So, try not to be discouraged as you're learning—use constructive feedback to make your diagrams clearer and more readable, keeping in mind the "art versus science" comments from Chapter 6.

FIGURE 7.5   Level Zero DFD of FASB's Standard Development Process

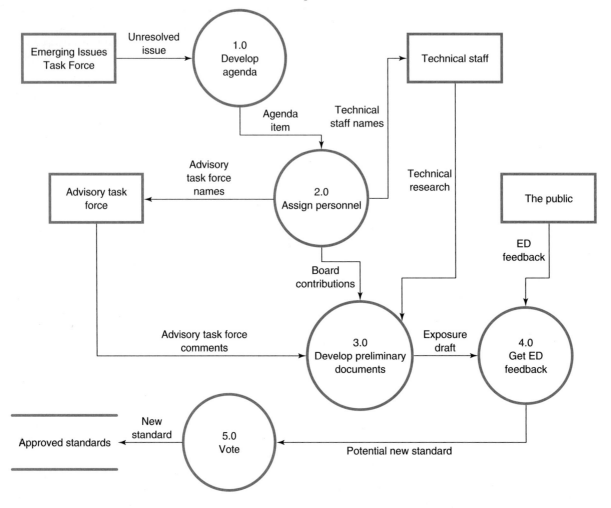

Summary

Data flow diagrams and relational databases are powerful tools in the design, implementation, use, and evaluation of accounting information systems. Here is the chapter summary:

1. *Explain the symbols and design considerations associated with DFDs.* Data flow diagrams incorporate four symbols. Processes are represented with circle, data flows are depicted by arrows, parallel horizontal lines denote data stores, and rectangles represent external entities. DFDs are prepared in leveled sets, with each set revealing more detail than the one before it.

2. *Compare and contrast flowcharts and DFDs with regard to purpose, content, structure, and use in accounting information systems.* Both flowcharts and DFDs are methods of conceptualizing an information system. Flowcharts incorporate more symbols than DFDs, but both are read from top to bottom and left to right (generally). DFDs can be used more easily to design relational databases.

3. *Discuss ways DFDs are used in AIS work.* DFDs can be used in at least four ways in accounting information systems design, development, and implementation. They can (*a*) ensure an adequate understanding of an accounting information system, (*b*) help accountants make process improvements to the system, (*c*) help others understand the

flows of data and information, and (*d*) assist in designing relational database tables that capture data and report information.

4. *Construct a leveled set of DFDs.* As with flowcharting, DFDs are designed iteratively and cooperatively. Two different systems professionals can create two different DFDs based on the same situation; as usual, there is no deterministic solution for most DFD problems.

5. *Design normalized database tables from a DFD.* Many elements of a DFD require database tables in an accounting information system. Tables should be normalized; each must include a primary key that uniquely identifies each record within the table. Foreign keys can link tables together in a database. Junction tables are used when items in two separate tables have a many-to-many relationship, such as the relationship between customers and inventory or purchasing agents and vendors.

As noted in the conclusion for the flowcharting chapter, you will likely be challenged as you develop familiarity and skill in using DFDs. Keep in mind that, like flowcharting, data flow diagramming and database design are at least as much "art" as "science." The point isn't to get to the "one right answer"; it probably doesn't exist anyway. The point here is to produce DFDs and database tables that are both effective and efficient from multiple points of view.

Key Terms

balanced, *120*
context diagram, *119*
data flow, *114*
data store, *114*
database tables, *121*

external entity, *114*
foreign keys, *122*
Level Zero diagram, *119*
leveled sets, *117*
primary key, *121*

primitive, *120*
process, *113*
queries, *122*
rules/conventions, *114*

Chapter References

Bradford, M., S. Richtermeyer, and D. Roberts. 2007. "System Diagramming Techniques: An Analysis of Methods Used in Accounting Education and Practice." *Journal of Information Systems,* Spring, pp. 173–212.

DeMarco, T. 1979. *Structured Analysis and Systems Specifications.* Englewood Cliffs, NJ: Prentice Hall.

Hoffner, J., J. George, and J. Valacich. 1996. *Modern Systems Analysis and Design.* Reading, MA: Benjamin/Cummings.

Ricciardi, S. 1994. "Database Design: Redundancy and Normalization." *PC Magazine,* January 25, pp. 285–89.

End-of-Chapter Activities

1. *Reading review questions.*

   a. What is a data flow diagram? How are data flow diagrams used in accounting information systems?

   b. List and discuss the four symbols used in the development of data flow diagrams. Give an example of each symbol in an AIS context.

   c. What rules/conventions should accountants follow when creating DFDs?

   d. Define the following terms as they relate to the material presented in this chapter: relational database, table, primary key, foreign key, field, record, and query.

   e. Respond to the questions for this chapter's "AIS in the Business World."

2. *Reading review problem.* Consider the following summary of a risk analysis conducted from May to July 2003 (den Braber et al., 2005):

   > NetCom is one of the main mobile phone network providers in Norway. Their "MinSide" application offers their customers access to their personal account informa-

tion via the Internet, enabling them to view and change the properties of their mobile phone subscription. "MinSide" deals with a lot of sensitive customer information that needs to be secure, while at the same time being easily available to the customer in order for the service to remain usable and competitive. The goal of the analysis was to identify risks in relation to the use of the "MinSide" application and, where possible, suggest treatments for these risks. This was achieved through two model-driven brain-storming sessions based on system documentation [including] data flow diagrams.

You can find NetCom's Web page (written in Norwegian) at http://www.netcom.no.

Source: F. den Braber, A. Mildal, J. Nes, K. Stolen, and F. Vraaslsen, "Experiences from Using the CORAS Methodology to Analyze a Web Application," *Journal of Cases on Information Technology* (July–September 2005), pp. 110–30.

a. Data flow diagrams incorporate four symbols. Identify those symbols and suggest how each might be applied in the NetCom case.

b. NetCom would need to maintain a database of customer records; that database would likely include (at a minimum) a customer table and a subscription table. Create specifications (field names) for both tables, indicating primary keys by underlining and foreign keys with brackets.

3. *Multiple choice review questions.* Please select the best answer for each question.

1. All of the following are rules for preparing DFDs except:
   a. No process can have only inputs.
   b. A DFD can never have more than seven processes.
   c. External entities and data stores have noun phrase labels.
   d. A data flow can go directly into a data store.

2. How many context diagrams are in a properly prepared leveled set of DFDs?
   a. One, with its process numbered 0
   b. One, with its processes numbered 1.0, 2.0 and so on
   c. No more than seven
   d. As many as the preparer thinks necessary.

3. What term is used to describe the relationship between levels in a set of DFDs?
   a. Primitive
   b. Decomposed
   c. Context
   d. Balanced

4. Every ___ in a database table must be uniquely identified with a ___.
   a. field, primary key
   b. primary key, field
   c. record, primary key
   d. primary key, record

5. The process of making a relational database efficient and easy to use is called:
   a. Normalizing.
   b. Balancing.
   c. Leveling.
   d. Combining.

4. *Making choices and exercising judgment.* Bumble Beasley is a recently enrolled accounting major at your university. In a conversation about accounting information systems, he said: "I don't know why we have to learn about flowcharts *and* data flow diagrams. One documentation technique should be enough; besides, both techniques give basically the same information if you know how to read them." Do you agree or disagree with Bumble? Why?

5. *Field exercises.*

  a. Contact an information systems professional such as a professor or systems analyst. Ask him or her about how flowcharts and data flow diagrams could be used in the design and evaluation of an accounting information system.

  b. Point your Web browser to www.download.com and search for flowcharting and/or data flow diagramming software there. Identify and describe two pieces of software that are capable of creating *both* flowcharts and data flow diagrams.

  c. Look up the Bradford article listed in the chapter references. Summarize its main points.

6. *Data flow diagram creation.*

  a. The Geek Squad (www.geeksquad.com) offers a variety of telephone, in-office, and in-home computer services. When a call for assistance comes into their 800 number, the Geek Squad determines its geographical origin and routes the call to an agent in the area. The agent confers with the customer by phone, determining the nature of the problem and the type of service desired. The agent also will find out if the customer has previously done business with Geek Squad. The agent will respond to the customer's request and report the problem's resolution to the corporate office. The corporate office bills the customer and collects payment; a fixed fee is remitted to the local agent based on the type and nature of the service call. Point your Web browser to the Geek Squad Web site to get more information about their operations. Then, prepare a context diagram, Level Zero diagram, and one Level One diagram for Geek Squad.

  b. Every year, the Institute of Management Accountants sponsors a student case competition to help students build their technical, analytical, and communication skills. In the student case competition, the IMA solicits cases from accounting faculty; an IMA committee chooses the best case and publishes it in an issue of *Strategic Finance.* Teams of students prepare video-taped responses to the case and submit them to the IMA. The videotaped presentations are evaluated and the team with the best presentation in each geographic region presents their case "in person" to a panel of judges at the IMA annual meeting. The team with the best presentation receives an award; all teams presenting at the annual meeting receive an engraved plaque with the members' names on it. The IMA maintains a database of case topics and authors; it also keeps a record of the name and university affiliation of all teams submitting videotapes as well as the status of those submissions. (For more information about the IMA student case competition, point your Web browser to www.imanet.org.) Consider the preceding narrative, and prepare a leveled set of data flow diagrams (context, Level Zero, and Level One).

  c. Consider the narratives presented in Problem 6 of Chapter 6 for Cori's Catering Services and University Bookstore. Use those narratives to prepare a leveled set of data flow diagrams.

7. *Critiquing database tables.* Bumble Beasley attempted to design a database to capture data about inventory purchases. He thought it would be easier to create one table with all the data rather than separate tables for different data items. The table he created contained the following fields:

Vendor phone	Inventory description
Purchasing agent ID	Cost per item
Vendor ID	Vendor code
Purchasing agent home address	Invoice total (number of items × cost per item)
Vendor state	Payment terms (e.g., 2/10, n/30)
Vendor address	Inventory ID
Vendor city	Purchasing agent first name
Purchasing agent last name	Transaction number
Transaction date	Quantity purchased
Vendor ZIP	

a. Is Bumble's database table in normal form? Discuss.

b. How many normalized database tables would be required for the data?

c. Group the data into the required number of normalized database tables. Specify a primary key for each table.

8. *Creating database tables.*

a. Create at least two database tables for each Level One data flow diagram you created in Problem 6 (data flow diagram creation).

b. In most states, the Department of Motor Vehicles keeps records of individual driver's licenses and vehicle license plates. Create two database tables that capture relevant information for the DMV; information in the driver's license table would include, but not be limited to, an individual's name, license number, and birth date. Information in the vehicle license plate table would include, but not be limited to, the license plate number and information about the vehicle itself. What foreign key(s) would you use to link the two tables together?

c. Robert Half International (www.roberthalf.net) pairs up potential employees with companies seeking accountants and other financial information professionals. Their Web site states: "With 325 offices and 55 years of experience, Robert Half is the world's first and largest specialized financial recruiting firm, placing quality candidates at all levels." Point your Web browser to the company's Web site and click the link for Robert Half United States. What information does Robert Half collect on new job seekers? Organize that information into a database table.

9. *Terminology.* Please match each item on the left with the most appropriate item on the right.

1. Data flow	a. A compilation of fields in a database
2. Data store	b. A primary key posted to another table
3. External entity	c. Accounts receivable file
4. Field	d. Customer last name
5. Foreign key	e. First detailed look at an information system
6. Level Zero	f. First National Bank
7. Primary key	g. Paid invoices
8. Process	h. Prepare financial statements
9. Query	i. Uniquely identifies records in a database
10. Record	j. Which customers have balances over $500?

10. *Multiple choice questions.* Consider the following narrative in responding to the questions that follow:

The Rancho Cucamonga Humane Society (RCHS) is open from 7 a.m. to 7 p.m., seven days a week. It maintains a computerized inventory of animals available for adoption, which includes animal type (dog, cat, bird), breed (basset hound, parakeet), gender, approximate age, date placed at the shelter, notes, and date adopted. People interested in adopting animals can visit the Society at any time; they complete an application, which is reviewed by the Society staff. A staff member discusses the potential adopters' wants and needs for a pet, then takes them to see appropriate animals. The potential adopter can see and interact with up to five animals in a single visit. If the customer chooses an animal, the staff member fills out appropriate paperwork before the customer takes the pet home. A staff member makes a follow-up call two weeks later to ensure that everything is satisfactory with both the pet and the adopter.

You have been asked to prepare a leveled set of DFDs for RCHS.

1. Which of the following is most likely to be an external entity?

   a. People interested in adopting animals
   b. Humane Society staff
   c. Animals
   d. Rancho Cucamonga Humane Society

2. Which of the following is most likely to be Process 1.0?

   a. Open from 7 a.m. to 7 p.m.
   b. Maintain computerized inventory of animals.
   c. Complete application.
   d. Review application.

3. The Level Zero DFD is likely to have how many processes?

   a. Two
   b. Three
   c. Four
   d. Five

4. How many data stores would be depicted in the Level Zero DFD?

   a. One
   b. Two   Animal + Customer
   c. Three   Database
   d. Four

5. Which of the following is most likely to be the primary key for the "animal" table?

   a. Type
   b. Breed
   c. Name
   d. Intake number

11. *Statement evaluation.* Specify whether each statement below is (i) always true, (ii) sometimes true, or (iii) never true. For those that are (ii) sometimes true, explain when the statement is true.

    a. A context diagram does not include data stores.
    b. A database table in 2NF is in 3NF as well.
    c. A salesperson is an external entity in a data flow diagram.
    d. Data flow diagrams are better than flowcharts for documenting accounting information systems.
    e. Database forms can be used to look up information in a table.
    f. Database queries store instructions, not data.
    g. Database tables are needed for processes, external entities, and data stores in a DFD.
    h. Database tables in 3NF are, by definition, also in 1NF and 2NF.
    i. Decomposing a process numbered 2.0 would lead to numbers like 2.1, 2.2, and so on.
    j. Lines in a data flow diagram should be labeled with verb phrases to show the movement of data.

Chapter Eight

REA Modeling

AIS in the Business World

Billing Process

In the last two chapters, we've looked at two ways of documenting the accounting information system: flowcharts and data flow diagrams. Each method has its strengths and weaknesses, along with times when it's most appropriately used. In this chapter, we look at one of the newest additions to the world of AIS documentation: REA modeling. A REA model of the billing process we've been working with would look like this:

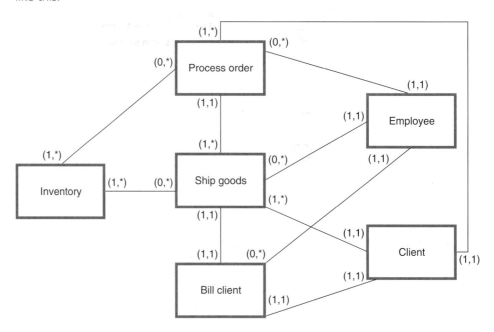

Although it looks a lot more cluttered and "busy" than either a flowchart or a DFD, the REA model provides a lot of useful information—particularly when it comes to designing a relational database.

Discussion Questions

1. What are the basic principles and design considerations for a REA model?
2. What are cardinalities? How are they interpreted?
3. How are REA models similar to flowcharts and DFDs? How are they different?
4. How does the REA model facilitate the design of a relational database?

So far, we've looked at two documentation techniques for accounting information systems: flowcharting and data flow diagramming. In this chapter, we'll examine a third technique: REA modeling (we discuss the meaning of the "REA" term later in the chapter). A relative newcomer to accounting information systems, REA modeling is an important part of designing event-driven accounting information systems.

McCarthy (1982) is considered by many to be a pioneer in the development of event-driven accounting systems. Event-driven systems capture a broader range of data than view-driven systems; relational database technology underlies most event-driven systems. Enterprise resource planning (ERP) systems are a sophisticated version of event-driven AIS. In this chapter, we'll take a closer look at event-driven accounting information systems and REA modeling, the documentation technique often used in their development.

When you finish studying this material, you should be able to:

1. Compare and contrast view-driven and event-driven accounting information systems.
2. Use REA modeling to represent an event-driven AIS.
3. Use a REA model to design a relational database for an event-driven AIS.

In some accounting curricula, professors devote entire courses to the topic of event-driven AIS. Although REA modeling is used less frequently in accounting practice than systems flowcharts, it represents an important way of thinking about the AIS. As with flowcharting and data flow diagramming, two people may come up with slightly different REA models for the same event-driven AIS. And, as with the other two systems documentation techniques, skill in REA modeling is developed with practice over time.

TYPES OF ACCOUNTING INFORMATION SYSTEMS

At a very basic level, accounting information systems can be divided into two broad groups: view-driven and event-driven. Think of view-driven systems as traditional accounting systems—they may incorporate some forms of information technology, but their defining characteristic is their focus on the general purpose financial statements. If a manager or other decision maker is interested in producing an income statement, a balance sheet, a statement of changes in equity, or a statement of cash flows, the task can be accomplished with a few simple, well-defined steps (i.e., completing the accounting cycle).

Stove piping refers to separating organizational functions and their information systems; for example, treating accounting as though it is unrelated to marketing, operations, or human resource management.

However, managers and other organizational stakeholders frequently need different and/or additional information for effective decision making. As business processes have become more integrated, the need for information has grown exponentially. Business professionals no longer have the luxury of "stove piping" the disciplines. And, unfortunately, view-driven accounting systems foster the idea that departments can remain separate and unrelated.

Walker and Denna (1997) summarized five key problems with view-driven accounting information systems:

1. They focus on a very small, well-defined group of important business events—those that are recordable in the accounting information system with debits and credits.
2. They often process data in batches, frequently at the end of the month. Thus, the data in a view-driven accounting system are often outdated.
3. Even for those transactions described in (1), the system captures a very limited set of data—dates, accounts, and amounts. Other transaction details, such as product characteristics, are omitted.

4. Data in a view-driven system are highly aggregated and stored in multiple places. Important data from source documents such as purchase orders and customer invoices are summarized and rearranged to conform to generally accepted accounting principles. Those changes may facilitate the production of financial statements, but they limit the information available for making decisions.

5. In view-driven systems, the internal control process is often protective and expensive. Controls such as separation of duties are focused on preventing collusion in an effort to safeguard assets.

Consider, for example, a simple, common transaction in most businesses: the sale of inventory on account. If the cost of inventory was $100 and the selling price was $150, a view-driven accounting information system would record the sale as follows:

Accounts receivable	$150	
Cost of goods sold	100	
Sales		$150
Inventory		100

And, while that information is vital for the production of financial statements, consider the following questions related to the transaction: Was the merchandise delivered on time? Was its quality acceptable to the customer? Has this customer ordered similar merchandise before? How close is the customer to reaching/exceeding its established credit limit? Those questions are virtually impossible to answer with a view-driven accounting information system.

In contrast to view-driven systems that capture, organize, and summarize data by business function, event-driven accounting systems focus on business processes. Processes may cut across disciplinary lines, so the data captured about business processes must be more comprehensive than in a view-driven system.

Walker and Denna (1997, p. 24) offer the following comments about event-driven accounting information systems:

> The event-driven approach assumes that the purpose of accounting (and other) information systems is to provide information about economic events that is useful in a variety of decision contexts. Events proponents say, "Let's collect raw business data that can be used by a variety of information customers, each with its own set of values and weights to assign to the data." It is the events view that provides an avenue to the next generation of business information systems.

So, in contrast to view-driven systems, event-driven systems

1. Capture more data about individual transactions.
2. Organize the data so that they can be accessed and understood by people from a variety of organizational functions.
3. Are equipped to answer questions like those posed above regarding the inventory transaction.

By their nature, event-driven systems are more complex than view-driven systems. They must be designed to meet the information needs of many groups of users—not just accountants interested in preparing general purpose financial statements. Because of that complexity and the importance of following good design principles, systems professionals needed a new modeling tool. In the next section, we'll look at REA modeling—a documentation technique that facilitates the design and implementation of event-driven accounting information systems.

REA MODELING

REA is an acronym referring to the *r*esources, *e*vents, and *a*gents in an event-driven accounting information system. Most AIS designers and auditors find it best to start a REA model by identifying its relevant events. In general, "events" come in three broad categories:

- *Operating events* focus on activities involved with providing goods and services to customers. Examples include purchasing and selling inventory, paying employees, and converting raw material into finished goods.
- *Information events* deal with recording and maintaining data, as well as reporting information. Think of information events as preparing financial statements or updating accounting records.
- *Decision/management events* are concerned with human decision making. They can range from simple things, such as which software and hardware to buy, to more complex decisions such as changing compensation packages.

REA models capture data on strategically significant operating events; they do not incorporate information events or decision/management events. Once strategically significant operating events have been identified, the rest of the details (resources, agents, and, when necessary, locations) can be filled in around them.

Agents are the people involved in the information system. Internal agents include employees in all departments; external agents refer to customers, vendors, and other stakeholders "outside" the business. Resources are the things agents need to complete the events: cash, inventory, equipment, supplies, and other assets. Some texts, including previous editions of this one, refer to REAL models rather than REA models. In those cases, the "L" stands for "location." But, most systems designers now focus on just the first three elements, so I'm omitting the discussion of locations here.

REA models are organized in columns, with the **events** appearing in the middle, **resources** to the left, and **agents** to the right. The REA model presented in Figure 8.1 has one event: rent car for cash. It includes one resource—automobile—and it incorporates two agents: client (an external agent) and a rental agent (an internal agent). That REA model describes the process of renting a car to a client.

So how do you develop a REA model? Hollander, Denna, and Cherrington (2000) recommend a **six-step process:**

1. *Understand the organization's environment and objectives.* To become trusted business advisors, accounting professionals need to have a thorough grasp of what the

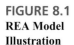
FIGURE 8.1
REA Model
Illustration

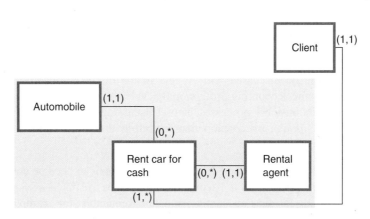

organization does. In 1995, I was privileged to work in Swaziland, a small country next to South Africa. Part of my job there was to consult with local organizations about the development and implementation of activity-based costing systems. One such organization was Mhlume Sugar Company. But, before I could help the organization as a consultant, I had to understand how sugar is manufactured—everything that happens from the time the sugar cane is planted until the sugar is in its final form. The same logic applies to REA modeling. You'll have to observe the operations, read manuals and articles from the literature, and talk with managers and workers before developing a REA model.

2. *Review the business process and identify the strategically significant operating events.* REA modeling focuses on business processes—the everyday activities employees undertake to create value for their customers and other stakeholders. Every business process is made up of events; the focus in REA modeling is on the strategically significant operating event. I'm fortunate to be able to travel a bit, both personally and professionally. So, I spend more time than many people in airports. The strategically significant operating events associated with the flight process would include checking baggage, checking in passengers, and boarding the airplane. Identifying the strategically significant operating events for a REA model is both subjective and iterative. The process is subjective because two different designers might come up with two slightly different sets of events and/or give them different names. The process is iterative because you'll normally need several "tries" to capture all the events.

3. *Analyze each strategically significant operating event to identify the event resources and agents.* For example, checking in passengers would include two agents (a passenger and an airline employee) and two resources (a computer and a boarding pass).

4. *Identify the relevant behaviors, characteristics, and attributes of the REA model elements.* This step helps you create database tables. For example, what data would you want/need to capture about an airline employee in your database? Fields in the "employee" table might include last name, first name, Social Security number, phone number, address, job position, and emergency contact. The relevant data for a boarding pass would include the passenger's name, seat assignment, departure and destination cities, gate assignment, and boarding and departure times.

5. *Identify and document the direct relationships among elements of the REA model.* Look again at Figure 8.1; notice the lines between the various REA model elements and the symbols on the end of each line. The lines show which elements are related to one another; the symbols are called *cardinalities*. We'll look at how to establish cardinalities in more detail in the next section. Cardinalities help systems designers, auditors, and fraud examiners (among others) understand how a relational database should be constructed.

6. *Validate the REA model with businesspeople.* Once the REA model is constructed, it should be discussed with people in the organization. Discussing the REA model helps the accounting professional develop a deeper understanding of the organization and its business processes. Those discussions will probably result in changes to the REA model, once again demonstrating that REA modeling is a highly iterative process.

You won't be able to complete this step in homework problems, but it is vital in practice.

You'll need to practice developing REA models to become comfortable and proficient at the process. Try not to become discouraged or frustrated—REA modeling is a new way of thinking for most accounting students. Remember, for example, when you first started making journal entries in introductory accounting? You may have thought you'd never remember that debits are on the left and credits are on the right; now, though, you probably don't give that whole process a lot of conscious thought—it's second nature to you. REA modeling will likely be the same: some initial confusion and discomfort leading to success in the long term.

Reflection and Self-Assessment   8.1

If you're like most accounting students, you love pizza. Think about the process of ordering and making a pizza. Identify the strategically significant operating events associated with those two processes; then identify the relevant resources and agents. What information would you want to capture in a relational database about each item you identify?

Now, let's take a closer look at establishing relationships between the elements of a REA model by creating cardinalities.

CARDINALITIES

As you read earlier, **cardinalities** tell an accounting professional about the relationships between elements of a REA model. A well-constructed set of cardinalities is a huge help in using a REA model to create a relational database. Ask yourself four questions when establishing cardinalities for a REA model:

1. *For each* x*, what is the minimum number of* y *involved?* Consider, for example, the relationship between "rent car for cash" and "rental agent" in Figure 8.1. If "rent car for cash" is *x* and "rental agent" is *y,* you're asking: for each "rent car for cash" transaction, what is the minimum number of rental agents involved? In this case, the answer is one. Could the minimum number of rental agents ever be zero? Sure—if the process was entirely automated; for example, a client might access a Web site to make a reservation for a car. Situations such as that illustrate why it's important to understand an organization's environment when you develop a REA model.

2. *For each* x*, what is the maximum number of* y *involved?* Extending that illustration, this question becomes: for each "rent car for cash" transaction, what is the maximum number of rental agents involved? Assuming that each transaction is handled by only one agent, the answer here is also one. Setting the maximum number of agents to "one" promotes strong internal control; if two or more agents were involved in a transaction, collusion between them could lead to errors and/or fraud.

Once you've answered the first two questions, record the cardinalities on the *y* side of the relationship. So, the (1,1) notation next to the "rental agent" box in Figure 8.1 explains how many rental agents are involved in each "rent car for cash" transaction.

3. *For each* y*, what is the minimum number of* x *involved?* In our example, this question is asking about the minimum number of rental transactions each rental agent could complete. To answer this question, envision a rental agent who just stands around behind the counter or sits behind the desk, reading magazines and surfing the Internet instead of helping customers. If you had an employee like that, who never completed a rental

transaction, you'd want to know it! So, the minimum number of rental transactions for a given rental agent is zero.

4. *For each* y, *what is the maximum number of* x *involved?* On the other hand, envision an employee who works tirelessly—who handles each rental transaction effectively and efficiently. Would you limit the number of transactions that agent could complete? Probably not. When there's no upper limit on a relationship between two elements of a REA model, we refer to the maximum as *many,* and symbolize it with an asterisk (*).

After answering questions 3 and 4, note the cardinalities on the *x* side of the relationship. So, the (0,*) notation next to "rent car for cash" tells us that each rental agent can complete from zero to many car rental transactions.

If you're like most students who read this material for the first time, you're saying to yourself, "Hmmm, maybe I don't want to be an accounting major after all." But don't give up! Remember: cardinalities are a very new way of thinking for most accounting students. You've probably never encountered anything like this notation in your other accounting classes. You'll need to practice and think very deliberately about establishing cardinalities for a while—after that, it'll become as second nature to you as creating a balance sheet.

Reflection and Self-Assessment   8.2

Examine the remaining relationships in Figure 8.1. Write out, in plain English, what each relationship means. Use the four questions as a guide.

The final element of our discussion of REA modeling involves how to translate the REA model into a **relational database.** We'll take up that topic in the next section.

DATABASE CREATION FROM A REA MODEL

In general, you're going to need at least one table for each "box" in the REA model. So, in our ongoing rental car example, you'd need the tables listed on the next page. Possible fields in each table are indicated, with the primary key signified by an underline. The rules for data normalization, explored earlier in the text, also apply to creating databases for event-driven accounting information systems based on REA models. When finished, database tables should be in third normal form; they should contain neither repeating groups (1NF) nor redundant data (2NF). In addition, every field in the table should provide additional information about its primary key (3NF). As you may recall from your study of data flow diagramming, the rules of **normalization** are

1. Focus each database table on a single "thing," such as customer data or inventory data. Each table must have a primary key that uniquely identifies each record.
2. Eliminate redundant data in each table. If a table has a compound primary key, each data element in the table must depend on both parts of the primary key. If a data element depends on only one part of the key, it should go in a separate table.

3. Ensure that all fields in a database table contain data that describe the table's primary key. If a field is not dependent on the primary key, it should be removed to a separate table.

- Automobile table

  <u>Identification number</u> Model

  Make Year

- Client table

  <u>Client last name</u> City

  <u>Client first name</u> State

  Client date of birth ZIP

  Street address Phone

- Rental agent table

  <u>Employee ID</u> First name

  Address Job classification

  Date of birth Last name

  Emergency contact information Phone

- Rental transaction table

  <u>Transaction number</u> [Client last name]

  [Automobile identification number] [Employee ID]

  [Client first name] Transaction date

In the rental transaction table, notice the presence of primary keys from the other three tables. Referring to the REA model in Figure 8.1, notice the cardinalities between the automobile table and rental transaction table (as well as the others). The maximum cardinalities between the automobile and rental transaction are one and many, bringing us to the first "rule" of creating database tables from a REA model:

When the maximum cardinalities between two elements of a REA model are one and many, include the primary key from the "one side" in the table on the "many side."

In our example, that rule tells us to put the primary key from the automobile table (the "one side") into the rental transaction table (the "many side").

In some REA models, relationship cardinalities include maximums of many on both sides. Consider, for example, a database that tracks the academic progress of students in your AIS class. Each student can take many classes; each class includes many students. The REA model relationship between student and class would look like this:

The cardinalities there indicate that every class can have from 10 to many students; every student can take between one and many classes. Situations like that one bring us to the second important rule of creating database tables from a REA model:

When the maximum cardinalities between two elements of a REA model are many and many, create a separate junction table to reflect the combined relationship.

So, in creating a database to reflect the relationship above, you would need three tables: a student table, a classes table, and a student/classes table. The student/classes table is referred to as a **junction table.** Junction tables don't normally contain more than a few fields; many of them will simply comprise the primary keys from the other two tables. So, if the primary key of the student table is the student identification number and the primary key from the classes table is the class identification number, the student/classes table would look like this:

- Student/classes table

    [Student identification number]

    [Class identification number]

In creating a relational database table, you would enforce referential integrity between the tables (i.e., between the student and student/classes table and between the classes and student/classes table). Enforcing referential integrity tells the database to update the junction table whenever the separate tables are updated. Junction tables are necessary to make databases more efficient. Consider the alternative: creating separate fields in the student table for each class a student takes. The problem is not knowing the maximum number of fields to create. If you created 10, for example, where would you record information about an 11th class? On the other hand, creating too many fields (i.e., enough so that you never "run out") makes the database too large to store and search.

Reflection and Self-Assessment   8.3

Suppose one of the strategically significant operating events for a pizza restaurant is "sell pizza." Assume the agents involved are "customer" and "employee," and the one resource is "pizza." Create a REA model, including cardinalities, for those four items. Then, create specifications for the "sell pizza" database table.

Remember: it takes patience and practice to get comfortable with creating REA models and databases for event-driven accounting systems. The idea is to create a workable model that reflects an organization's **strategically significant operating activities**—not to search for the "one right answer" in any particular situation.

CRITICAL THINKING

So now, let's take a look at a different example of REA model and database creation. Netflix (www.netflix.com) is an online service that supplies DVDs to its clients. We'll use the six-step process outlined above to create a REA model for Netflix.

1. *Understand the organization's environment and objectives.* In the company's sales/ collection process, clients subscribe to Netflix and create a "rental queue" of DVDs they want. The client pays a fixed monthly fee, and Netflix ships the DVDs one at a time. When a client returns one DVD to Netflix, Netflix ships the next DVD on the list.

2. *Review the business process and identify the strategically significant operating events.* From Netflix's point of view, the strategically significant operating events in the sales/ collection process are

a. Subscribe new clients.

b. Ship DVDs.

c. Collect payment.

d. Receive returned DVDs.

So, at this point, the REA model would look like the diagram shown in Figure 8.2.

3. *Analyze each strategically significant operating event to identify the event resources, agents, and locations.*

a. Subscribe new clients.
   i. Agent: client
   ii. Resource: DVDs

b. Ship DVDs.
   i. Agents: client, Netflix employee
   ii. Resource: DVDs

c. Collect payment.
   i. Agents: client, Netflix employee
   ii. Resource: cash

d. Receive returned DVDs.
   i. Agents: client, Netflix employee
   ii. Resource: DVDs

I've put all Netflix employees into a single table; as a result, the table must include information about the employee's position. Another option would be to create separate tables for different kinds of employees (mailroom, cash receipts, receiving, and so on). So, we can add the resources and agents to the REA model, as shown in Figure 8.3.

4. *Identify the relevant behaviors, characteristics, and attributes of the REA model elements.* (In anticipation of creating the database, primary keys are underlined; foreign keys are in brackets.)

a. Resources
   i. DVDs: <u>DVD ID,</u> Title, year, genre, director, synopsis
   ii. Cash: <u>Account number,</u> bank, beginning balance date, beginning balance

b. Events
   i. Subscribe new clients: <u>Subscription date,</u> [client ID], number of DVDs per month
   ii. Ship DVDs: <u>Shipping transaction number,</u> shipment date, [client ID], [Netflix employee ID], [DVD ID]
   iii. Receive returned DVDs: <u>Receipt transaction number,</u> receipt date, [client ID], [Netflix employee ID], [DVD ID]

c. Agents
   i. Client: <u>Client ID,</u> last name, first name, address, city, state, ZIP, area code, phone, e-mail address, credit card number, credit card expiration date
   ii. Netflix employee: <u>Employee ID,</u> last name, first name, address, city, state, ZIP, area code, phone, emergency contact, department, date employed, pay rate, date terminated, reason for termination

5. *Identify and document the direct relationships among elements of the REA model.* In this step, we'll create cardinalities using the four questions noted above. Note that "client" has a relationship with "DVDs" outside of any event because the client

FIGURE 8.2
Strategically Significant Operating Events—Netflix

Subscribe new clients

Ship DVDs

Collect payment

Receive returned DVDs

FIGURE 8.3
REA Model without Cardinalities— Netflix

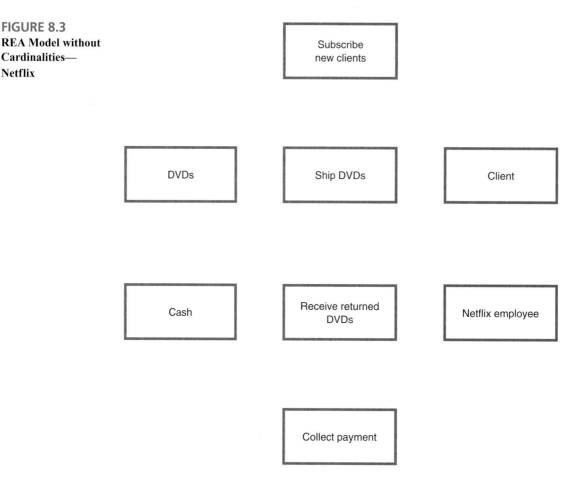

establishes a rental queue as part of the subscription event. The REA model with cardinalities is shown in Figure 8.4.

6. *Validate the REA model with businesspeople.* In practice, you would review the REA model with Netflix employees and others to ensure that it portrays the business rules clearly and accurately.

After creating the REA model, you'd be ready to construct a relational database. Notice how step four above helps you create the database—if you've completed it diligently, you have the field names for most of the database tables. In this case, let's assume that DVD ID refers to a specific title—not a specific copy. Netflix could create as many copies as it needs to distribute to clients; tracking each copy separately would involve extensive record-keeping. If you didn't want to create a separate DVD ID, you could use a compound primary key of title *and* year for the DVD table—the title alone wouldn't be enough because of the common practice of "remaking" films in different years.

The REA model in Figure 8.4 would require one junction table to document the relationship between client and DVDs. Again, recall that those two have a relationship independent of any event because the client establishes a rental queue during the subscription process. The client/DVD junction table would have just a few fields: client ID, DVD ID, position in queue, date added. It would have a compound primary key (client ID and

FIGURE 8.4   **REA Model with Cardinalities—Netflix**

DVD ID); in the Access table, you'd have to specify "duplicates OK" for both the client and DVD ID fields, as each client can have many DVDs in the queue *and* each DVD can be associated with multiple clients.

Summary

In this chapter, then, we've examined event-driven accounting information systems and REA modeling. Here's a summary of the chapter's important points, seen through the lens of its learning objectives:

1. *Compare and contrast view-driven and event-driven accounting information systems.* Both types of systems are designed to collect data and process it into information; both typically involve various forms of information technology. View-driven systems are designed to present that information in one principal way: the general purpose financial statements. Event-driven systems are built on relational database technology; they capture more data and offer greater flexibility in terms of reporting via queries and reports.

2. *Use REA modeling to represent an event-driven AIS.* REA modeling begins by understanding an organization's environment and business processes. Then, for each process, it identifies the resources, events and agents needed to capture the essential nature of transactions. System designers use cardinalities to explain the relationships between the elements of a REA model.

3. *Use a REA model to design a relational database for an event-driven AIS.* Once the REA model has been established and validated, it can be translated into a series of relational database tables. In most cases, each element of a REA model requires at least one table in a relational database. Where the maximum cardinalities between elements of the model are many to many, system designers create a junction table to denote the relationship.

The relational database technology that forms the basis for REA modeling is also the basis for enterprise resource planning systems. So, a solid understanding of this area of AIS will give you an appreciation for that important technology, as well as help you "speak the same language" as the IT professionals with whom you'll be working.

Key Terms

agents, *135*
cardinalities, *137*
events, *135*
junction table, *140*

McCarthy, *133*
normalization, *138*
relational database, *138*
resources, *135*

six-step process, *135*
strategically significant
operating activities, *140*

Chapter References

Hollander, A. S., E. L. Denna, and J. O. Cherrington. 2000. *Accounting, Information Technology, and Business Solutions.* 2nd ed. New York: Irwin/McGraw-Hill.

McCarthy, W. E. 1982. "The REA Accounting Model: A Generalized Framework for Accounting Systems in a Shared Data Environment." *Accounting Review,* July, pp. 554–77.

Walker, K. B., and E. Denna. 1997. "Arriveder ci, Pacioli? A New Accounting System Is Emerging." *Management Accounting,* July, pp. 22–30.

End-of-Chapter Activities

1. *Reading review questions.*

   a. What are the similarities and differences between view-driven and event-driven accounting information systems?

   b. What does the acronym REA stand for? Give examples of each element.

   c. List the six steps for creating a REA model.

   d. Explain how to establish a set of cardinalities between two elements of a REA model.

   e. How would you use a REA model to design a relational database?

   f. Prepare a response to the questions for this chapter's "AIS in the Business World."

2. *Reading review problem.* Beta Alpha Psi (www.bap.org) is the international honor society for students and professionals in accounting, finance, and information systems. According to its Web site:

   > The primary objective of Beta Alpha Psi is to encourage and give recognition to scholastic and professional excellence in the business information field. This includes promoting the study and practice of accounting, finance and information systems; providing opportunities for self-development, service and association among members and practicing professionals, and encouraging a sense of ethical, social, and public responsibility.

   Each BAY chapter is required to complete certain activities each year; they also may earn extra recognition and rewards by going beyond the minimums specified by the national office. Events include things like meet the firms, professional speaker meetings, community service projects, and national and regional meetings. Each BAY chapter tracks its members' participation in the various events, reporting periodically to the national office via BAY's reporting intranet.

As you can tell, the information needs of a typical BAY chapter go far beyond general purpose financial statements. To facilitate information gathering and decision making, a BAY chapter might choose to develop a REA model as the basis for an event-driven accounting information system.

1. What is a REA model? How are REA models used in accounting information systems?
2. What are cardinalities? How are they incorporated in a REA model?
3. Every BAY chapter has multiple members; each member must participate in multiple activities. Explain how you would show that relationship in both a REA model and in a relational database.

3. *Multiple choice review questions.* Please select the best answer for each question.

1. All of the following are criticisms of view-driven accounting information systems except:
   a. The information technology tools to implement them are not widely available.
   b. They often process data in batches.
   c. They focus on a very small, well-defined group of important business events.
   d. The internal control process is often protective and expensive.

2. In contrast to view-driven AIS, event-driven systems:
   a. Capture more data about individual transactions.
   b. Organize the data so they can be accessed and understood by people throughout the organization.
   c. Are equipped to answer a broader range of questions relevant to running a business.
   d. All of the above.

3. Events can be classified into three broad groups. Which of the following is not one of them?
   a. Decision/management events
   b. Financial events
   c. Information events
   d. Operating events

4. Cardinalities:
   a. Are not necessary in a well-designed REA model.
   b. Are required by GAAP.
   c. Explain relationships between elements of a REA model.
   d. Can be developed without human judgment.

5. Which of the following statements is (are) true in using cardinalities to construct a relational database?
   a. When the maximum cardinalities between two elements of a REA model are one and many, include the primary key from the "many side" in the table on the "one side."
   b. When the maximum cardinalities between two elements of a REA model are many and many, create a separate junction table to reflect the combined relationship.
   c. Both a and b.
   d. Neither a nor b.

4. *Making choices and exercising judgment.* Coral's See-the-Reef, located on the Gulf of Mexico, is famous for its fast service. Coral's business is renting scuba and snorkeling gear. Coral needs someone to analyze her business and help her use that analysis to plan and design a new information system. Coral employs four fitting clerks, three rental clerks, and four cashiers. The fitting clerks enter equipment items, sizes, and experience codes into the computer. The computer searches the rental inventory, by experience code, for the requested equipment. For example, a beginner is code one, which tells the computer to locate the oldest equipment available in the requested size. Once the requested equipment is located, a duplicate rental invoice is printed. The

rental clerk uses the second copy to retrieve the equipment. While this clerk gets the equipment, the customer pays the rental fee to a cashier. A deposit is added to the rental fee, and a code indicating the condition of the equipment is noted.

Source: A. S. Hollander, E. L. Denna, and J. O. Cherrington, *Accounting, Information Technology, and Business Solutions*, 2nd ed. (New York: Irwin/McGraw-Hill, 2000).

a. Create a REA model for Coral's See-the-Reef. Create database tables for one resource, one event, and one agent.

b. Suggest two queries Coral should incorporate in her database; justify your suggestions. Which tables and fields would she need to create the queries you suggest?

c. Design a form a fitting clerk could use for entering equipment items, sizes, and experience codes.

5. *Field work.*

a. Enterprise resource planning (ERP) systems are an advanced form of the event-driven concepts discussed in this chapter. Examples of ERP systems include PeopleSoft, SAP, and Oracle. Use your school's library resources to find case examples of ERP systems in action. Prepare a brief PowerPoint presentation of your findings.

b. Relational database software can be used very effectively in detecting fraud in the accounting information system. Use your school's library resources to find and read R. Marden and R. Edwards, "Internal Controls for the Small Business: Skimming and the Fraud Triangle," *Internal Auditing* (January/February 2005). If Pinewoods of the Blue Ridge Mountains (the company discussed in the article) captured transactions in a relational database based on a REA model, what queries and reports would you construct in an attempt to discover the fraud?

6. *Constructing REA models.* (Case situations (*a*) through (*d*) come from Hollander, Denna, and Cherrington, 2000.) In each independent case situation below, construct a REA model and a database structure.

a. *Tom's Trailers.* Tom owns a small recreational trailer business in a suburban community located close to the mountains. The community is relatively small but growing at a fast rate. Tom's business is growing, not because of his effective sales style and personality, but by growth of the community. Currently, Tom's competition has been nearly nonexistent but, as the area grows, he expects to encounter increasing competition.

Tom sells mostly trailers for vacationing and camping. When customers arrive on Tom's lot, they are greeted by a salesperson. The salesperson may show the customers the trailers on the lot, but the salesperson need not be present during the entire showing. Depending on customer preference, either the salesperson will take the customer on a tour or the customer may roam the lot freely, inspecting trailers at his or her leisure.

Since recreational trailers are fairly large-ticket items, customers often will leave the lot without making a purchase, only to return another day after making the decision to purchase a trailer. When a customer decides to make a purchase, the salesperson initiates a series of procedures to properly document the order and sale transaction. First, the salesperson determines the model of the selected trailer and offers the customer a list of options that correspond to the particular model. The customer may (1) purchase a trailer off the lot with no added features, (2) purchase a trailer off the lot with additional features, or (3) special order a trailer not currently on the lot.

In most cases, customers do not pay cash for their trailers. If, however, the customer pays cash, a simple sales contract is prepared and the customer drives off with his or her trailer. The majority of customers use an installment method of purchase. Before an installment purchase is authorized, the customer's credit must be verified to determine creditworthiness.

With an installment purchase, an installment agreement is prepared in addition to the sales contract. Tom has arranged financing through a local bank for all installment sales. When an installment sale is made, the bank sends Tom a lump-sum payment equal to the price of the trailer. Instead of making a payment to Tom, customers pay the bank plus interest. In either case, Tom receives a lump-sum payment for each trailer sold, whether that lump sum comes from the customer or the bank.

Once the customer's credit is approved, the customer can take delivery of the trailer. This involves a delivery person who checks the trailer before delivering it to the customer. The customer may pick up the trailer or have it delivered by Tom.

b. *Maple Bluff Pharmacy.* Maple Bluff Pharmacy sells prescription drugs and over-the-counter medications and supplies. All prescriptions and over-the-counter items are sold using a cash register. Each cash register retains on the cash register's journal tape a record of the transactions and who performed them. This information is subsequently entered into a computer.

Prescriptions received over the phone are taken by the pharmacist and recorded on a prescription slip. Also, prescriptions received over the phone are entered into a computer that matches the prescription with guideline dosage levels and instruction information and prints the necessary information for the prescription. After entering the prescription information into the computer, the prescription is filled and a hard copy of the prescription slip is filed numerically for future reference.

All sales items are paid for with cash, check, or credit card. On occasion, credit is extended to a customer, but he or she must be approved through the chief pharmacist. If credit is extended, a separate billing account is established. If a customer does not pay the bill within 120 days of the initial billing date, the account is turned over to a collection agency.

At the end of the day, cash in the register till is counted and compared with the total amount of credit card receipts and accounts receivable slips. This check is performed by two employees in the safe room and is always monitored on camera. In addition, total cash receipts recorded in the computer are compared with the deposit totals each day before Deposits Express picks up the money for deposit.

c. *Western Steel Company.* Western Steel Company produces steel for a variety of customers. When customers order steel, an order clerk enters information into a computer that prepares a purchase order to track the order from production to collection of payment. If the customer's credit has been approved, production of the order begins immediately. If the customer is new, a credit check is performed.

After the order is filled, a tally count is made of the produced steel and the steel is shipped to the customer. If the steel is to be shipped by railroad, rail cars are checked for weight before shipping the order. The weight of the load is then compared to the order to ensure an accurate delivery. Accompanying the shipment is a computer-generated bill of lading and a copy of the purchase order.

Shortly after shipping an order, Western invoices the customer using prices on an approved price list. The invoice total is obtained by multiplying the quantity ordered and shipped by the standard price. Steel prices are set by the Sales Department, which determines competitive prices based on market conditions and cost information.

Customers send payments directly to a lockbox account in selected cities across the United States. The bank where a particular customer sends payment is located in the city closest to the customer's location. Western receives no payment, but Western receives a record of customer deposits from the bank maintaining the lockbox account. Accounting personnel maintain the billing and collection accounts, while the Credit Department issues credit to customers and follows up on past due accounts.

d. *Payroll process for a CPA firm.* The payroll and personnel function represents a large expense for many companies—especially the audit divisions of accounting firms. Clients are frequently billed based on staff, manager, and partner involvement in the audit. Firms bill clients based on a predetermined rate for each person involved. For example, a company bills a partner's hours at a substantially higher rate than it bills the staff's hours. Partners also trade employees to work on different projects for different clients. Careful tracking and planning go into each audit to maintain both audit quality and the lowest possible cost to the client.

For each client engagement, an audit plan is developed to identify the type and quantity of hours necessary to complete each audit step. For example, the audit plan might specify 30 hours to count warehouse inventory. Each week, auditors record their time on a time-and-expense report and submit it to the audit supervisor. The supervisor compares the actual time to the budgeted time in the audit plan. The time-and-expense reports are then submitted to the Payroll Department, which prepares paychecks for the auditors. Each week, the Payroll Department calculates pay based on a yearly salary and overtime for each employee. In addition, the Payroll Department must track deductions for taxes, insurance, and benefits. Once the deductions are withheld, the net pay is deposited into the employee's checking account, or a check is issued in the name of the employee.

e. *Textbook ordering and purchasing process.* Six weeks before the start of each academic term, accounting instructors at AIS University of America inform the department secretary of the books they're planning to use for each class. Instructors may use one or more books for an individual class; different instructors may use different textbooks for various sections of the same course. The department secretary compiles the instructor-provided data and transmits them via e-mail to the bookstore's purchasing agent. The purchasing agent prepares a purchase order and sends it to the textbook publisher; a single purchase order may combine textbooks for several different courses, so long as all the textbooks come from the same publisher. When the publisher ships the books, the bookstore's receiving department records the shipment; stock clerks put the books on the shelves. The textbook publisher invoices the bookstore, which then writes a check in payment; unused textbooks are returned to the publisher roughly one month after the term begins.

7. *Interpreting a REA model.* Consider the REA model presented below. Write a narrative description of the business process it depicts.

8. *Terminology.* Match each item on the left with the most appropriate item on the right.

1. Cardinality	a. Unique record identifier in a database table
2. Decision/management event	b. Supports the preparation of financial statements
3. Enterprise resource planning	c. Purchasing supplies
4. Information event	d. Preparing journal entries
5. Junction table	e. Opening an office in a new city
6. Primary key	f. Internal agent
7. Purchasing agent	g. External agent
8. Strategically significant operating event	h. Combines the primary keys of two tables
9. Vendor	i. A sophisticated form of event-driven AIS
10. View-driven AIS	j. (1,*)—(1,1)

9. *Multiple choice questions.* Consider the following REA model in responding to the questions below; it represents the system by which members of the accounting club at Big State University are reimbursed when they incur expenses on the club's behalf.

1. Which of the following is an external agent?

   a. Member
   b. Officer
   c. Advisor
   d. Financial services

2. How many junction tables are indicated in the REA model?

   a. Zero   └→ only when max ; max
   b. One
   c. Two
   d. More than two

3. Which of the following statements is most true?

   a. A disbursement request can be split into one or more checks.
   b. A check can cover multiple disbursement requests.
   c. Neither a nor b.
   d. Both a and b.

4. All of the following statements are true except:

   a. An advisor must sign every disbursement request.
   b. At least one officer must sign every disbursement request.
   c. All disbursement requests must be signed by two officers.
   d. Receipts may be presented by either an officer or a member.

5. Which of the following would be a foreign key in the "prepare disbursement request" table?

   a. The primary key from the "present receipt" table

   b. The primary key from the "receipt" table

   c. Both a and b

   d. Neither a nor b

10. *Statement evaluation.* Please indicate whether each of the following statements is (i) always true, (ii) sometimes true, or (iii) never true. For those that are (ii) sometimes true, explain when the statement is true.

   a. "Choose AIS software" would be included as an event in a REA model.

   b. Events can be related to one another in a REA model.

   c. Events in a REA model are shown in the second column.

   d. If an accountant can construct a REA model, data flow diagrams and flowcharts are unnecessary.

   e. Most REA models will include both internal and external agents.

   f. REA models include decision/management events.

   g. Resources and agents are unrelated in a REA model.

   h. Strong internal controls are evident in a REA model.

   i. Understanding an organization's environment is important in designing a REA model.

   j. View-driven accounting systems do not provide information for decisions.

Part Three

Information Technology in the AIS

As you learned in Part One, information technology is a processing tool in the AIS—the technology is not the system itself. Now that you've learned some fundamental ideas about AIS in Parts One and Two, we'll turn our attention to the role IT can play in the accounting information system.

This part comprises three chapters:

9. XBRL

10. E-business and Enterprise Resource Planning

11. Computer Crime and Information Technology Security

XBRL is an acronym for the eXtensible Business Reporting Language. It is an information technology tool that allows accounting and IT professionals to tag (mark up) financial data. Once marked up, the data and tags can be read and interpreted across diverse hardware and software platforms. All companies that file documents with the SEC are required to use XBRL.

Next, we'll turn our attention to e-business, the essence of which is conducting business via computer networks. Enterprise resource planning systems are often associated with e-business; they are relational databases that capture comprehensive data about an organization and allow managers and others to access that data for improved decisions.

Finally in this section, we'll reconsider issues of internal control within an IT-enabled environment. As you can likely imagine, using information technology creates new risks for organizations; thus, they need to create internal controls to address those risks. This chapter also introduces the CoBIT framework, a widely used, well-respected framework that shares some similarities with the COSO internal control framework you learned about in Chapter 3.

Chapter **Nine**

XBRL

AIS in the Business World

SEC and FFIEC

Consider the following comments from Gray and Miller regarding XBRL:

> The use of financial reporting data identification technology known as eXtensible Business Reporting Language (XBRL) continues to grow since its public introduction in April 2000. For example, since April 2005, the U.S. Securities and Exchange Commission (SEC) has been encouraging corporations and mutual funds filing financial reports through its Electronic Data Gathering, Analysis, and Retrieval (EDGAR) system to voluntarily furnish XBRL-related documents as attachments to traditional EDGAR filings. The SEC has begun phasing in a program requiring that all corporations and mutual funds include XBRL instance documents as part of their EDGAR filings where all public companies will be required to furnish XBRL documents by 2011. The U.S. Federal Financial Institution Examination Council (FFIEC) completed a $39 million project in October 2005 that required over 8000 banks to submit their quarterly call reports to the FFIEC using XBRL.

Although accounting was an information system long before the advent of any form of information technology, most AIS today incorporate technology at some level. XBRL is a powerful IT tool that you'll hear about more and more as you continue your education and start your professional career.

Discussion Questions
1. What is XBRL?
2. What is the relationship between XBRL and accounting information systems?
3. Why should organizations adopt XBRL?

Source: G. L. Gray and D. W. Miller, "XBRL: Solving Real World Problems," *International Journal of Disclosure and Governance*, August 2009.

One of the really interesting things about accounting information systems is its dynamic nature. Because AIS involves information technology, there are always new ideas, new tools, and new topics to explore. We'll look at one of those topics in this chapter: XBRL. XBRL is an acronym for the eXtensible Business Reporting Language; the basic purpose of XBRL is to facilitate information exchange, particularly financial information, between all different kinds of organizations, regardless of the hardware and software platforms they use individually.

XBRL is a "standard" in the broadest sense of the term. It is not, however, a new accounting standard in the FASB sense. XBRL is simply a way to code information for easier interpretation.

You may have heard of HyperText Markup Language (HTML), the language used to develop Web pages on the Internet. **XBRL** is to financial information what HTML is to Web page development. XBRL is a subset of a much broader language, XML (eXtensible Markup Language). As an accountant, you will likely be called upon to convert standardized financial statements into XBRL format; you also may have to interact with information technology professionals in organizations about this important standard.

When you've finished studying this chapter, you should be able to:

1. Define the following terms as they relate to XBRL: *extensible, specification, taxonomy, namespace,* and *instance document.*
2. Explain the history and structure of XBRL.
3. Discuss ways XBRL can benefit organizations.
4. Identify software tools for creating XBRL-tagged documents.
5. Discuss internal control issues for XBRL.

According to the Web site of XBRL International (www.xbrl.org):

> XBRL is a language for the electronic communication of business and financial data which is set to revolutionize business reporting around the world. It provides major benefits in the preparation, analysis and communication of business information. It offers cost savings, greater efficiency and improved accuracy and reliability to all those involved in supplying or using financial data. XBRL is being developed by an international non-profit consortium of approximately 250 major companies, organizations and government agencies. It is an open standard, free of license fees. It is already being put to practical use in a number of countries and implementations of XBRL are growing rapidly around the world.

Except where specifically stated otherwise, the material in this chapter is based on material found on that Web site as well as materials provided at the first American Accounting Association workshop on XBRL Teaching.

TERMINOLOGY

I often tell my students that accountants (and other professionals) invent new words for things people already understand, and new meanings for words they already know.

As you may have learned in your very first accounting course, accounting is often referred to as the "language of business." And, like most languages, accounting has some specialized terminology/idiomatic expressions that should be mastered. Consider, for example, the term *depreciation.* If you ask a friend who is a nonaccounting major what depreciation is, he or she likely will talk about a loss in value—as in "when you drive a new car off a lot, it depreciates 50 percent." But, in accounting, *depreciation* takes on a completely different meaning: the periodic allocation of an asset's cost to the periods that benefit from its use. In accounting, we say that depreciation is a process of allocation, not valuation.

In the same way that accounting (and most "regular" languages) involves specialized terminology, so does XBRL. You should understand at least five terms before you begin reading about XBRL in the rest of this chapter.

- *Extensible.* The "X" in XBRL stands for *extensible.* In other words, the XBRL language is "able" to be "extended." The same is true for English. Think about words and expressions we use in the 21st century that hadn't even been invented a decade ago: WiFi, iPod, and the like. In the same way that English grows and changes, users can add new ideas and phrases to the basic XBRL without changing its fundamental purpose, structure, or existing terminology. This idea is critically important in any discussion of XBRL. The original creators of the language could not possibly have anticipated every term needed by every organization over the course of even a few years—let alone a longer time period.

- *Specification.* Think of a specification as a particular (specific) example of a larger group. For example, "California" is a specification of "United States." Or "goodwill" is a specification of "assets." XBRL is part of a larger group of languages referred to as XML (eXtensible Markup Language). One common feature of all XML specifications is their "extensible" nature; another is their use as "markup" languages. So, XML consists of a series of descriptors added to various kinds of information that help users make sense of the information. As a specification of XML, XBRL is focused on descriptors of business reporting information—most often, accounting information.

- *Taxonomy.* Broadly speaking, a taxonomy is a way to organize knowledge. The table of contents of a book is a taxonomy. If someone asked you about the information contained in a balance sheet, you would likely describe it as "assets, liabilities, and equity." Those three elements of financial statements are a taxonomy—they are a way of grouping items together for ease of presentation and discussion. XBRL is made up of several taxonomies, which, for the most part, are focused on specific industry groups. For example, the terminology that describes financial information in a manufacturing firm (such as material, labor, overhead, work in process) has some significant differences from financial terminology in a government entity (fund, encumbrance).

- *Namespace.* If you were reading and ran across a word you didn't know, where would you look to find its meaning? Probably a dictionary—online or in book form. A namespace is like an XBRL dictionary. Remember what the "X" stands for: *extensible.* So, if someone invents a new XBRL term (i.e., extends XBRL), he or she has to let others know what it means. The meaning (definition) of the new term would reside in a namespace. Namespaces have Internet addresses (URLs) just like Web pages.

- *Instance document.* An instance document is a specific example of properly tagged XBRL information. For example, a publicly traded company like Microsoft might mark up its balance sheet with XBRL tags. The balance sheet, then, would be an instance document.

Those five terms will come up again as you read the chapter. You might find it helpful to mark these pages in some way in case you need to refer back to them later.

HISTORY AND STRUCTURE

Take a look at this number:

59.77.85.91

What do you suppose it means? If you're like most students, you're thinking "it could mean anything!" The problem is you don't have any *context* for interpreting the number. On the other hand, if I provide you the following facts, the number might make more sense:

I'm grateful to Dr. Roger Debreceny (University of Hawaii, Manoa) for providing a similar illustration at the AAA XBRL Teaching workshop (Debreceny and White, 2005).

- I was born in 1959.
- I graduated from high school in 1977.
- I earned my master's degree in 1985.
- I defended my doctoral dissertation in 1991.

Now, extrapolate the difficulty of interpreting a relatively simple number in a relatively easy-to-understand language to the complexity of an accounting information system.

- Organizations can have significantly different structures and titles in their chart of accounts.
- Every account in the system has its own balance.
- The balances can be measured in hundreds of world currencies.
- Some of the numbers in the system reflect results for a period of time (e.g., revenues), while others reflect position at a point in time (e.g., assets).
- The numbers in an accounting system can be produced with or without information technology. When information technology is used, the specific hardware and software variations are practically limitless.

Reflection and Self-Assessment   9.1

Consider the list of complexities inherent in accounting information presented above. Suggest one or two more items that make it difficult to interpret accounting information without some context.

Suppose, for example, ASR Corporation has two divisions: RBE Division in the United States and CLG Division in Mexico. RBE collects and processes accounting information using an enterprise resource planning system; CLG is a much smaller division and keeps its accounting records in Peachtree. At the end of a recent accounting period, RBE sent the following accounting information to corporate headquarters:

Account Number	Account Title	Balance
101	Cash	$80,000
105	Accounts receivable	15,000
108	Inventory	7,000

At the same time, CLG sent this information:

Account Number	Account Title	Balance (pesos)
102	Seguro	10,000
107	Seguridades comerciales	9,000
109	Fuentes	5,000

How could ASR's corporate controller combine the information from RBE and CLG to produce corporate financial statements? One solution might be to reenter all the information into Excel or some other piece of software—but that would be time-consuming and inefficient. In addition, reentering the information creates the risk of making an error that could impact the corporate financial statements.

Enter XBRL—the eXtensible Business Reporting Language. XBRL is one application of XML, the eXtensible Markup Language. According to the XBRL Web site (www.xbrl.org), XML "is a standard for the electronic exchange of data between businesses and on the Internet. Under XML, identifying tags are applied to items of data so that they can be processed efficiently by computer software." Let's dissect the pieces of the name *XBRL* to understand it more clearly.

1. XBRL is *extensible.* In other words, users can "extend" the language beyond its original parameters based on their own needs. Certain terms are commonly used in accounting: assets,

liabilities, revenue, gross profit, and the like. But suppose a company has its own unique labels for its financial information: revenue from the southern division, gross profit on products, gross profit on services, and similar terms. If XBRL wasn't extensible, users would be "stuck with" whatever labels its creators built into the language. As it stands, users can create their own unique tags for financial data as the need arises.

2. XBRL is for *business reporting.* It is specifically designed to tag and transmit financial information—the kind produced by an accounting information system. Other languages in the XML family include the Resource Description Framework (RDF), Rich Site Summary (RSS), Mathematical Markup Language (MathML), and Scalable Vector Graphics (SVG).

3. XBRL is a *language.* Just like English, French, or Visual Basic, XBRL has its own rules regarding things like syntax and punctuation. The XBRL Web site provides this example of how the language looks:

```
<ifrs-gp:AssetsHeldSale contextRef="Current_AsOf" unitRef="U-Euros"
  decimals="0">100000</ifrs-gp:AssetsHeldSale>
<ifrs-gp:ConstructionProgressCurrent contextRef="Current_AsOf"
  unitRef="U-Euros" decimals="0">100000</ifrs-
  gp:ConstructionProgressCurrent>
<ifrs-gp:Inventories contextRef="Current_AsOf" unitRef="U-Euros"
  decimals="0">100000</ifrs-gp:Inventories>
<ifrs-gp:OtherFinancialAssetsCurrent contextRef="Current_AsOf"
  unitRef="U-Euros" decimals="0">100000</ifrs-
  gp:OtherFinancialAssetsCurrent>
<ifrs-gp:HedgingInstrumentsCurrentAsset contextRef="Current_AsOf"
  unitRef="U-Euros" decimals="0">100000</ifrs-
  gp:HedgingInstrumentsCurrentAsset>
<ifrs-gp:CurrentTaxReceivables contextRef="Current_AsOf" unitRef="U-
  Euros" decimals="0">100000</ifrs-gp:CurrentTaxReceivables>
<ifrs-gp:TradeOtherReceivablesNetCurrent contextRef="Current_AsOf"
  unitRef="U-Euros" decimals="0">100000</ifrs-
  gp:TradeOtherReceivablesNetCurrent>
<ifrs-gp:PrepaymentsCurrent contextRef="Current_AsOf" unitRef="U-Euros"
  decimals="0">100000</ifrs-gp:PrepaymentsCurrent>
<ifrs-gp:CashCashEquivalents contextRef="Current_AsOf" unitRef="U-
  Euros" decimals="0">100000</ifrs-gp:CashCashEquivalents>
<ifrs-gp:OtherAssetsCurrent contextRef="Current_AsOf" unitRef="U-Euros"
  decimals="0">100000</ifrs-gp:OtherAssetsCurrent>
<ifrs-gp:AssetsCurrentTotal contextRef="Current_AsOf" unitRef="U-Euros"
  decimals="0">1000000</ifrs-gp:AssetsCurrentTotal>
```

Keep in mind that the preceding example of XBRL is designed to be read by computers, not people. In fact, the XBRL Web site says: "Ordinary users of XBRL may be largely or totally unaware of the technical infrastructure which underpins the language. However, software companies, such as accountancy software providers, need to take account of XBRL and its features when producing their products." We won't get further into the technical details of XBRL as a language in this text; we'll focus the rest of our discussion on XBRL at a conceptual level.

XBRL, then, is a **specification** of XML. XBRL itself is comprised of several **taxonomies;** taxonomies are developed by professional organizations and industry groups based on their unique accounting standards and needs. The XBRL Web site defines taxonomies as

> The dictionaries used by XBRL. They define the specific tags for individual items of data (such as "net profit"). Different taxonomies will be required for different financial reporting purposes. National jurisdictions may need their own financial reporting taxonomies to reflect their local accounting regulations. Many different organizations, including regulators, specific industries or even companies, may require taxonomies to cover their own business reporting needs.

As of February 2011, XBRL International had approved 13 XBRL taxonomies in the United States, including:

Most current software, such as Microsoft Excel and Great Plains Dynamics, can interpret XBRL tags. Namespaces must be "declared" at the beginning of an XBRL document so the software knows where to look on the Internet for its interpretive rules.

- U.S. Accountants' Report Taxonomy 2009
- U.S. Country Taxonomy 2009
- U.S. Currency Taxonomy 2009
- U.S. GAAP Taxonomy 2009

Figure 9.1 shows the relationship between XML, XBRL, and the XBRL taxonomies. The rules and terminology associated with a specific taxonomy reside in a **namespace** on the Internet; that way, XBRL-enabled software can reference the taxonomy simply by locating its namespace.

FIGURE 9.1
Basic XBRL Concepts

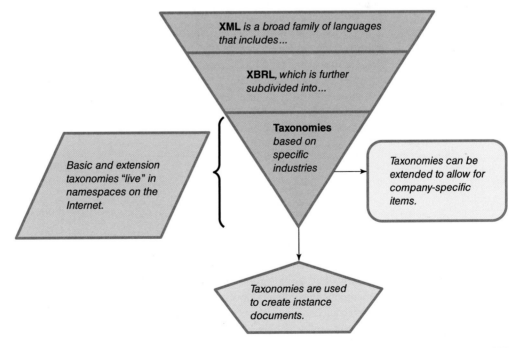

Here's one more piece of terminology associated with XBRL: **instance document.** One of the Big Four CPA firms, KPMG International, provides the following definition of an instance document (www.kpmg.com/xbrl/jargon.asp):

> A business report in XBRL form that provides information in context, complying with the definitions set down in a taxonomy and one or more extension taxonomies. For example, a company's financial statements might be published as an instance document in compliance with the U.S. GAAP commercial and industrial taxonomy. Quarterly, half yearly, weekly or hourly business reports also take the form of an instance document.

So, for example, the illustration provided in item 3 on page 156 ("XBRL is a language") is part of an XBRL instance document.

GLOBAL TAXONOMIES AND TAGGING TOOLS

Many XBRL taxonomies are country-based; that is, approved taxonomies in the United States are different from approved taxonomies in, for example, China or Ireland. But two taxonomies cut across national borders: the International Financial Reporting Standards (IFRS) taxonomy and the Global Ledger (GL) taxonomy.

As of February 2011, the IFRS taxonomy was *acknowledged* by XBRL. An acknowledged taxonomy has to conform to a specific version of XBRL. Acknowledged taxonomies are differentiated from *approved* taxonomies; the latter must conform to a specific version of XBRL and XBRL guidelines for the specific taxonomy type (e.g., financial reporting). The official name of the IFRS taxonomy is "International Financial Reporting Standards Taxonomy 2008," but people commonly refer to it as IFRS-GP. The purpose of IFRS-GP is to allow for-profit organizations to prepare XBRL-tagged financial statements based on International Financial Reporting Standards.

The Global Ledger taxonomy, commonly known as XBRL-GL, helps organizations manage internal information. According to the XBRL Web site discussion of XBRL-GL, "the XBRL Global Ledger taxonomy allows the representation of anything that is found in a chart of accounts, journal entries or historical transactions, financial and non-financial. It does not require a standardised chart of accounts to gather information, but it can be used to tie legacy charts of accounts and accounting detail to a standardised chart of accounts to improve communications within a business." Like other XBRL taxonomies, XBRL-GL cuts across organization types, hardware/software combinations, and languages.

U.S.-based taxonomies, along with IFRS-GP and XBRL-GL, are going to become more and more important as time goes on. The Securities and Exchange Commission (SEC) published its final rules for XBRL in December 2008. The SEC has phased in mandatory XBRL reporting according to the following schedule:

Type of Filer	XBRL Reporting Deadline
Large, accelerated filers using U.S. GAAP	2009
All other accelerated filers using U.S. GAAP	2010
All remaining filers using U.S. GAAP	2011

If you access the SEC's EDGAR database, XBRL-based filings will be marked "Interactive Data."

As you can tell, XBRL is massive. And if organizations had to tag every piece of data manually, they would probably need an entire staff devoted to that one task! Thankfully, there are many automated tools available for that purpose.

You can check out www.xbrl.org/Tools/ for more examples of tagging software. The use of tagging software doesn't eliminate the need to understand the purpose, nature, and structure of XBRL, any more than the use of general ledger software eliminates the need to understand principles of debit and credit, the accounting cycle, and the purpose and structure of financial statements. Rather, tagging software is a tool that helps organizations tag their documents more efficiently than they could with manual coding.

ORGANIZATIONAL BENEFITS

Fundamentally, XBRL helps organizations in two major ways. First, it allows for more efficient data collection and reporting. Consider, for example, a corporate controller in an international organization. The controller would be receiving reports from all over the world that are prepared using a multitude of software packages. If all the information came into the controller's office with appropriate XBRL tags, it could be collected and summarized quickly and easily, then reported to both internal and external stakeholders in a relatively short time.

Second, XBRL facilitates data consumption and analysis. Using XBRL, our corporate controller can collect data and report information much more quickly and easily—leaving more time for analysis and interpretation. Additionally, XBRL-tagged documents can be searched for specific kinds of information, such as sales revenue by geographic region.

The XBRL Web site lists 10 specific **benefits** organizations can derive from implementing this important new technology:

- Save costs by preparing data in one form and automatically generating many outputs. Companies will avoid re-keying of data and other manual tasks.
- Consolidate results across divisions and subsidiaries with much greater speed and reliability.
- Improve accuracy and reliability of financial data.
- Focus effort on analysis, forecasting, and decision making, rather than on laborious tasks in gathering, compiling, and preparing data.
- Achieve quicker and more efficient decisions.
- Make more effective use of the internet in communicating with investors. Companies will benefit from the growing importance of web sites as a means of communication.
- Improve investor relations through provision of more transparent and user-friendly information.
- Simplify the process and reduce the costs involved in regulatory reporting to tax and other authorities.
- Obtain quicker responses from counterparties, including banks and regulators.
- Free themselves from proprietary systems and software which are difficult and costly to replace.

As accountants, we can benefit from XBRL as well. Again, XBRL International cites the following advantages for accountants using XBRL:

- Obtain more rapid and reliable data on company financial performance.
- Greatly reduce effort and costs in gathering and analyzing data.
- Simplify and automate tasks.
- Focus effort on analysis and value-added work.
- Make better use of software to improve efficiency and speed.

The XBRL Web site also identifies specific advantages for other kinds of organizations and groups of financial information professionals.

Reflection and Self-Assessment   9.3

Point your Web browser to www.xbrl.org. Click the "XBRL and Business" link on the left side of the page. Choose one of the groups listed there (e.g., regulators and government, stock exchanges, and investment analysts) and prepare a summary of XBRL's specific advantages.

INTERNAL CONTROL

First, a bit of review. In general, internal control has four main purposes: safeguard assets, ensure reliable financial statements, encourage adherence to management directives, and promote operating efficiency. And, with respect to information technology, recall the C-I-A triad; we want to ensure that data are *c*onfidential, have *i*ntegrity, and are *a*vailable when needed.

What risks, then, do organizations face when they use XBRL? Consider the list below:

- XBRL moves data between and within information systems electronically. Therefore, the data are subject to theft, loss, and manipulation in the same ways all electronic data are.
- XBRL tagging, while not complex, is detail oriented. So, the coding process is subject to the risk that humans will make errors in coding.
- Since XBRL is so technology dependent, we also must consider the risks of hardware and software failure in an XBRL environment.

Trites (2002), working under the auspices of the Canadian Institute of Chartered Accountants (www.cica.ca), suggested two additional risks associated with XBRL: inappropriate/missing authorizations for document changes and selection of an inappropriate taxonomy. Given those five risks, then, what internal controls should organizations consider when adopting XBRL? Here are some suggestions:

Risk	Suggested Control(s)
Compromised data	Daily data backups
	Firewalls
	Mandatory password changes
	"Strong" password requirements
	Password-protected access
	Virus protection software
Tagging errors	Electronic tagging (as opposed to manual)
	Independent review after tagging (e.g., by internal auditors)
	Periodic user training
Hardware and software failure	Disaster recovery plan
	Physical security (e.g., locked doors, alarms)
	Uninterruptible/backup power supplies
Inappropriate/missing authorizations	Internal audit review of selected transactions
	Periodic user training
	Up-to-date procedures manuals
Selection of an inappropriate taxonomy	Periodic review and approval of taxonomies used
	Centralized approval process for taxonomy additions

Does XBRL create new risks for organizations that adopt it? Yes. But, with strong internal controls (such as those listed above), the benefits of adopting XBRL far outweigh its associated costs and risks.

CRITICAL THINKING

Consider the following data about current assets, drawn from the XBRL International Web site (www.xbrl.org).

Assets Held for Sale	100,000
Construction in Progress, Current	100,000
Inventories	100,000
Other Financial Assets, Current	100,000
Hedging Instruments, Current [Asset]	100,000
Current Tax Receivables	100,000
Trade and Other Receivables, Net, Current	100,000
Prepayments, Current	100,000
Cash and Cash Equivalents	100,000
Other Assets, Current	100,000
Current Assets, Total	1,000,000

Here's the XBRL coding that would produce it:

```
<ifrs-gp:AssetsHeldSale contextRef="Current_AsOf" unitRef="U-Euros"
  decimals="0">100000</ifrs-gp:AssetsHeldSale>
<ifrs-gp:ConstructionProgressCurrent contextRef="Current_AsOf"
  unitRef="U-Euros" decimals="0">100000</ifrs-
  gp:ConstructionProgressCurrent>
<ifrs-gp:Inventories contextRef="Current_AsOf" unitRef="U-Euros"
  decimals="0">100000</ifrs-gp:Inventories>
<ifrs-gp:OtherFinancialAssetsCurrent contextRef="Current_AsOf"
  unitRef="U-Euros" decimals="0">100000</ifrs-
  gp:OtherFinancialAssetsCurrent>
<ifrs-gp:HedgingInstrumentsCurrentAsset contextRef="Current_AsOf"
  unitRef="U-Euros" decimals="0">100000</ifrs-
  gp:HedgingInstrumentsCurrentAsset>
<ifrs-gp:CurrentTaxReceivables contextRef="Current_AsOf" unitRef="U-
  Euros" decimals="0">100000</ifrs-gp:CurrentTaxReceivables>
<ifrs-gp:TradeOtherReceivablesNetCurrent contextRef="Current_AsOf"
  unitRef="U-Euros" decimals="0">100000</ifrs-
  gp:TradeOtherReceivablesNetCurrent>
<ifrs-gp:PrepaymentsCurrent contextRef="Current_AsOf" unitRef="U-Euros"
  decimals="0">100000</ifrs-gp:PrepaymentsCurrent>
<ifrs-gp:CashCashEquivalents contextRef="Current_AsOf" unitRef="U-
  Euros" decimals="0">100000</ifrs-gp:CashCashEquivalents>
<ifrs-gp:OtherAssetsCurrent contextRef="Current_AsOf" unitRef="U-Euros"
  decimals="0">100000</ifrs-gp:OtherAssetsCurrent>
<ifrs-gp:AssetsCurrentTotal contextRef="Current_AsOf" unitRef="U-Euros"
  decimals="0">1000000</ifrs-gp:AssetsCurrentTotal>
```

Notice a few things about the XBRL coding:

1. XBRL tags are enclosed in brackets.
2. Every tag has both a beginning, such as <ifrs-gp:AssetsHeldSale contextref="Current_ AsOf" unitRef="U-Euros"decimals="0">, and an ending, such as </ifrs-gp:Assets HeldSale>.
3. Elements of an XBRL tag include capital letters within a label, such as "AssetsHeld-Sale." We refer to that style as *camelCase.*
4. Each tag includes the following information:
   a. The taxonomy used. In this example, "ifrs-gp" stands for General Purpose International Financial Reporting Standards.
   b. The element name from the taxonomy. In this example, those element names include AssetsHeldSale and ConstructionProgressCurrent.
   c. Time data. Since we're looking at a schedule of current assets, we're dealing with data at a point in time—not data for a period of time.
   d. Currency data. Each item in the schedule is measured in euros.
   e. Number of decimals to display. In this example, we're displaying zero decimals.

Keep in mind that you're looking at a *partial* instance document. The full document would "declare" a namespace—that means telling a computer where to look on the Internet to find the "translation" of the IFRS-GP taxonomy. The taxonomy is quite extensive—over 700,000 bytes of data. And the PDF file that lists the taxonomy elements is 189 pages long! Nevertheless, if an organization needed to extend the IFRS-GP taxonomy, it could definitely do so. The organization would then have to create a namespace for the extension and identify ("declare") it within the XBRL instance document.

Summary

Here is a summary of the chapter's main points for your review:

1. *Define the following terms as they relate to XBRL:* extensible, specification, taxonomy, namespace, *and* instance document.
   a. *Extensible:* The characteristic of XBRL that allows users to create new tags as the need arises.
   b. *Specification:* Describes the relationship between XBRL and its parent language (XML). XBRL is a specification (example) of the eXtensible Markup Language.
   c. *Taxonomy:* The organizational unit of XBRL. Taxonomies typically are linked to industry groups, such as commercial and industrial or investment management.
   d. *Namespace:* An XBRL dictionary. This is an Internet location that defines some of the tags used in a taxonomy.
   e. *Instance document:* A specific example of properly tagged XBRL information.

2. *Explain the history and structure of XBRL.* The eXtensible Business Reporting Language grew out of a need for increased efficiency in collecting, analyzing, and reporting financial information. XBRL is one specification of XML, the eXtensible Markup Language. XBRL comprises several approved taxonomies that are used to create individual instance documents.

3. *Discuss ways XBRL can benefit organizations.* XBRL allows organizations to collect data from disparate accounting systems, combining it quickly and easily. It smoothes the data collection process and automates many tasks previously completed by hand. Just as general ledger software allowed accountants to automate many repetitive tasks, XBRL helps managers accomplish the same goal. Automating tedious tasks such as consolidating financial statements provides more time for analysis and decision making.

4. *Identify software tools for creating XBRL-tagged documents.* Accountants can avail themselves of a plethora of software tools for creating XBRL-tagged documents. Tagging software does not replace human judgment on preparing instance documents. Rather, it is a tool that makes such preparation more efficient and less tedious.

5. *Discuss internal control issues for XBRL.* XBRL exposes an organization to many risks commonly associated with any information technology. Internal controls to combat those risks include proper authorizations and approvals, periodic user training, virus protection software, password procedures, and up-to-date procedures manuals.

XBRL is here to stay. It provides a language for understanding financial information that transcends national borders, differences in GAAP, languages, currencies, and software packages.

Key Terms

benefits, *159*
instance document, *158*
namespace, *157*
specification, *156*
taxonomies, *156*
XBRL, *153*

Chapter References

Debreceny, R., and S. White. 2005, June. *XBRL Working Paper.*
Trites, G. D. 2002. *Audit and Control Implications of XBRL.* Toronto, Ontario: Canadian Institute of Chartered Accountants.
XBRL International, www.xbrl.org.

End-of-Chapter Activities

1. *Reading review questions.*
   a. What is XBRL? How is it related to XML?
   b. Define the following terms related to XBRL: *specification, taxonomy, instance document.*
   c. How can XBRL benefit organizations?
   d. Will most accountants need to learn to write "code" in XBRL? If not, how can they create XBRL-tagged documents?
   e. Respond to the questions for this chapter's "AIS in the Business World."

2. *Reading review problem.* According to its Web site (www.fdic.gov), "The Federal Deposit Insurance Corporation (FDIC) is an independent agency created by the Congress that maintains the stability and public confidence in the nation's financial system by insuring deposits, examining and supervising financial institutions, and managing receiverships."

   On a quarterly basis, banks submit a Report of Condition and Income, otherwise known as a "Call Report," to the FDIC. The Web site provides the following information about the Call Report:

   > FDIC collects, corrects, updates and stores Reports of Condition and Income data submitted to us by all insured national and state nonmember commercial banks and state-chartered savings banks on a quarterly basis. Reports of Condition and Income data are a widely used source of timely and accurate financial data regarding a bank's condition and the results of its operations. The Reports of Condition and Income data are the only publicly available source of information regarding the status of U.S. banking system; therefore, the FDIC's actions in this regard are of paramount importance, and every precautionary measure is taken to preserve data integrity and accuracy.

   In 2004, the FDIC began requiring member banks to use the eXtensible Business Reporting Language in filing Call Reports. XBRL has been particularly useful in Call Report formulas, which check for logical consistency in the reports.

1. Suppose you were talking to a finance major at your school who had never heard of XBRL, but had recently gone to work for the FDIC. Briefly explain what XBRL is and how it is useful to the FDIC and other organizations.

2. Explain the following terms as they relate to XBRL: taxonomy, namespace, instance document. Which taxonomy would banks likely use for their call reports?

3. What internal controls should banks institute to address the risks associated with XBRL? What internal controls should the FDIC institute for that same purpose?

3. *Multiple choice review questions.* Please select the best answer for each question.

1. XBRL is:
   a. A new GAAP standard that must be used for SEC filings.
   b. A tool for labeling financial information and providing context for it.
   c. Owned by the SEC.
   d. All of the above.

2. As the term is used in XBRL, a namespace is:
   a. A URL created by a company that wants to extend XBRL.
   b. A dictionary for finding definitions of new XBRL terms.
   c. Both a and b.
   d. Neither a nor b.

3. Tagging software:
   a. Is a requirement for using XBRL.
   b. Removes the need for human judgment from XBRL coding.
   c. Often functions as an add-on to other software.
   d. All of the above.

4. Implementing XBRL entails some risks for organizations; internal controls are needed to address those risks. Which of the following correctly pairs a risk with an internal control that addresses it?
   a. Hardware failure, disaster recovery plan
   b. Compromised data, electronic tagging
   c. Tagging errors, mandatory password changes
   d. Software failure, internal audit review

5. In the SEC's EDGAR database, documents that have been tagged with XBRL are labeled as:
   a. Tagged data.
   b. Contextualized data.
   c. Taxonomies.
   d. Interactive data.

4. *Making choices and exercising judgment.* The chapter discussed several benefits of implementing XBRL. What are the costs associated with an adoption? Think in terms of financial, organizational, and behavioral costs.

5. *Field work.*

a. Interview a practicing accountant, in either a CPA firm or a corporate environment. Find out what your interviewee knows about XBRL and its advantages for accounting firms and their clients.

b. Refer to the list of XBRL tagging software at www.xbrl.org/Tools. Choose two or three of the software packages on the list; apply the software evaluation methodology discussed earlier in the text. As your evaluation criteria, use cost (weight = 5), ease of use (weight = 3), and support services (weight = 2).

c. Complete the XBRL tutorial developed by KPMG, which you'll find at www.us.kpmg .com/microsite/xbrl/train/86/86.htm. Prepare a summary of what you learned to discuss in class.

6. *Contextual categories of XBRL.* The purpose of XBRL is to provide a context for understanding financial information. Several contextual categories associated with financial information are listed below; for each category listed, give at least two examples of how it might vary across organizations and financial reporting systems. The first item is done as an example.

   a. Type of balance: debit, credit
   b. Time period
   c. Currency
   d. Account type
   e. Accounting rules (i.e., GAAP)
   f. Reporting language
   g. Preparation tools

7. *XBRL tags.* Consider the sample of XBRL tags shown in the chapter. Use your critical-thinking skills and accounting background to suggest what each of the following pieces of information might denote. The first item is done as an example.

   a. IFRS: International Financial Reporting Standards
   b. ContextRef
   c. UnitRef
   d. Decimals

8. *XBRL tagging.* Read "Six Steps to XBRL" by Phillips, Bahmanziari, and Colvard in the February 2008 issue of *Journal of Accountancy.*

   a. Is XBRL relevant to companies that don't file with the SEC? Justify your response.
   b. List the six steps the authors recommend for creating XBRL-tagged documents.
   c. How many XBRL-tagged filings did the SEC receive as part of its voluntary program?
   d. With respect to Dragon Tag software:
      i. What are the elements of an entity profile?
      ii. What is a "hopper"?
      iii. What is "validation"? Why is it important?

9. *Benefits of XBRL.* Fill in the blanks below with terminology that describes the benefits of XBRL for organizations and accountants.

   a. Consolidate results across ___ with much greater speed and reliability.
   b. Focus effort on ___, rather than on laborious tasks in ___ data.
   c. Free themselves from ___ and software that are difficult and costly to replace.
   d. Greatly reduce ___ in ___.
   e. Improve ___ through provision of more ___ information.
   f. Make better use of ___ to improve ___.
   g. Make more effective use of the ___ in ___.
   h. Obtain ___ data on company financial performance.
   i. Save costs by ___ and automatically generating many ___.
   j. Simplify the process and reduce the costs involved in ___ to tax and other authorities.

10. *Internal control issues for XBRL.* Point your browser to the Web site of the Canadian Institute of Chartered Accountants (www.cica.ca). Find and download Trites' paper on

audit and internal control issues. In consultation with your instructor, and working with a group of students, write a paper or prepare a presentation that summarizes at least one of the following sections of the Trites report: control issues, assurance issues, emerging issues.

11. *Terminology.* Please match each item on the left with the most appropriate item on the right.

1. Acknowedged and approved	a. "Levels" of XBRL taxonomies
2. Business exchange technology	b. AICPA Top Ten Technology that describes XBRL
3. Context	c. Dragon Tag item that specifies "as of" or "duration"
4. Dragon Tag	d. An Excel add-on that facilitates tagging
5. Focus effort on analysis	e. An XBRL taonomy
6. NAICS 1.0	f. Marking up data with XBRL codes
7. Namespace	g. Relationship between XBRL and XML
8. Open source	h. What XBRL provides for information
9. Specification	i. Why no one "owns" XBRL
10. Tagging	j. XBRL "dictionary"

12. *Multiple choice questions.* This series of questions deals with XBRL's Global Ledger taxonomy. Before attempting to answer them, point your Web browser to www.xbrl. org. Locate the slide presentation on "Key Features of XBRL-GL." Reference it as you respond to these questions.

1. XBRL-GL follows information:
   a. From an initial transaction directly to financial reporting.
   b. From operational systems to transaction recording.
   c. From initial transaction through operational systems to reporting.
   d. From a taxonomy to a namespace.

2. How does XBRL-GL relate to tax filings?
   a. It provides supporting data to substantiate the filing.
   b. It eliminates the need for tax software like Turbo Tax.
   c. It ensures error-free tax reporting.
   d. All of the above.

3. Operational systems that tie into an organization's general ledger include all of the following except:
   a. Project accounting.
   b. View-driven AIS.
   c. Accounts payable.
   d. Fixed assets.

4. The URL gl.iphix.net presents:
   a. The global ledger taxonomy specifications.
   b. Instructions for extending the global ledger taxonomy.
   c. A summary of how operational systems feed into the general ledger.
   d. Material to help people learn more about XBRL-GL.

5. Which of the following statements is most true?
   a. XBRL cannot be adapted for use in filing tax returns.
   b. XBRL without XBRL-GL does not go deep enough to support tax audit processes.
   c. XBRL-GL is unrelated to SOX and IFRS recordkeeping.
   d. All of the above statements are true.

13. *Statement evaluation.* Indicate whether each of the following statements is (i) always true, (ii) sometimes true, or (iii) never true. For those that are (ii) sometimes true; explain when the statement is true.

    a. All necessary XBRL tags were developed by the XBRL Consortium.
    b. Companies should use Dragon Tag to create XBRL documents.
    c. Companies that do business in a single country do not need XBRL.
    d. Diversified organizations should use XBRL.
    e. General ledger software can create XBRL tags.
    f. Organizations that adopt XBRL must create their own namespace.
    g. Publicly traded companies can use XBRL for SEC reporting.
    h. XBRL adopters must create specific internal controls for XBRL.
    i. XBRL is a nonproprietary system.
    j. XBRL is an example of business exchange technology.

14. *Prior material application.* You'll see a problem of this type in every chapter from here through the end of the text; this problem type is brand new to this edition. In these problems, you'll be considering the relationship between the current chapter's material (XBRL in this case) and material discussed in earlier chapters (such as transaction process, internal controls, and systems documentation). My goal in including problems like these is to encourage you not to do a "memory dump" as you finish each chapter. These problems should also help you develop your critical thinking skills.

    a. Earlier in the text, you learned that most AIS have five generic parts. The chapter talked about internal controls related to XBRL; give an example of each additional part related to XBRL. (For example, a 10-K report to the SEC would be an example of an AIS output.)
    b. When an organization incurs a cost, it can be recorded in one of two basic ways in the AIS: it can be debited to an asset (capitalized), as when a company buys a piece of equipment, or it could be debited to an expense (expensed), as with salaries. Suppose a company hired a consultant to help with XBRL implementation. If the company expects to use XBRL for at least five years, should the cost of the consultant be capitalized or expensed? Use the FASB conceptual framework to justify your response.
    c. In our discussion of management concepts, you read about Vroom's expectancy theory, which helps us understand and analyze motivation in organizations. With respect to an XBRL project, someone with low expectancy might say: "Why should I invest the time and energy to learn about XBRL? I'm lousy with computer stuff, and I probably can't learn it anyway." Create a similar statement for the other two elements of expectancy theory (instrumentality and valence). Then, explain how you would improve someone's motivation by addressing each objection.
    d. The systems development life cycle comprises seven steps; the development and implementation of XBRL is a systems development project. Work with a group of students to develop a paper/presentation that explains how the SDLC would apply to an XBRL project. For example, the initiation/planning phase might begin when the CFO attends an XBRL workshop/presentation.
    e. Consider the article referenced in Problem 8 ("Six Steps to XBRL"). Create a systems flowchart/Level Zero DFD/REA model documenting the process described in the article. Clearly specify any assumptions you make.

Chapter **Ten**

E-business and Enterprise Resource Planning Systems

AIS in the Business World

KEO

KEO (www.keogroup.com) produces and distributes a variety of alcoholic and nonalcoholic beverages; its headquarters are on the beautiful island of Cyprus, located on the eastern end of the Mediterranean Sea. As the company expanded, its need for better, more integrated information about sales, inventory levels, and other important items grew more profound. KEO's management decided to implement an enterprise resource planning system to help address that need.

Tsamantanis and Kogetsidis examined the ERP implementation process at both KEO and a sister company. They pointed out the following goals achieved through the project: planning production volumes more accurately to respond to market demand; controlling raw materials inventory more tightly; setting prices more effectively; controlling both revenue and costs more efficiently.

In spite of the overall success of the ERP implementation, the authors offer the following cautionary conclusion:

> In order to function properly an ERP system has increased demand for information input. Since it integrates different functions of the company and uses data from several departments, delays in updating the system by one department have a direct impact on the operations of the others. Because of this, discipline should be imposed with regard to the various operations of the company.

In this chapter, we'll take a closer look at enterprise resource planning systems and e-business.

Discussion Questions

1. What is an enterprise resource planning system?
2. Is ERP required if a company wants to engage in e-business?
3. What basic principles and terminology are commonly used when discussing e-business and ERP systems?

Source: V. Tsamantanis and H. Kogetsidis, "Implementation of Enterprise Resource Planning Systems in the Cypriot Brewing Industry," *British Food Journal*, 2006.

E-business systems have become a fact of life in most sectors of the economy; we truly live in a networked world. Think of all the ways information technology impacts your life today, from the hundreds of television and radio stations available via satellite, to the process of registering for classes and ordering textbooks at your university, to the ways you've done research and completed assignments for your AIS class.

When you've finished studying this chapter, you should be able to:

1. Explain the nature of e-business, comparing and contrasting it with traditional "brick-and-mortar" organizations.
2. Discuss major forms of e-business, including business-to-business, consumer-to-consumer, business-to-consumer, government-to-business, and government-to-consumer.
3. Describe the basic nature, purpose, and structure of enterprise resource planning systems.
4. Give examples and analyze the causes of ERP system failures.
5. List and discuss steps associated with successful ERP implementations.
6. Discuss the role of application service providers in e-business.

While this chapter won't make you an expert on these topics, it will give you sufficient background to ask the right questions and engage in intelligent professional conversation about them.

E-BUSINESS

We'll use the terms *e-business* and *e-commerce* interchangeably throughout this chapter.

Encarta (www.encarta.msn.com) offers the following definition of e-business:

E-commerce is the exchange of goods and services by means of the Internet or other computer networks. E-commerce follows the same basic principles as traditional commerce—that is, buyers and sellers come together to exchange goods for money. But rather than conducting business in the traditional way—in stores and other "brick and mortar" buildings or through mail order catalogs and telephone operators—in e-commerce buyers and sellers transact business over networked computers.

The central feature of e-business is business is transacted over computer networks. Completing business transactions over **computer networks** offers many costs and benefits, including those summarized in the following table.

Benefits of E-business	Costs of E-business
• Marketing: geographic market expansion, hard-to-reach markets, more targeted marketing	• Financial costs associated with setting up networks
• Reduced operating costs: marketing, telecommunications, transaction processing	• Need to develop different, better internal control systems
• Streamlined operations	• Potential for customer distrust
• Quicker, easier product and service delivery	• Severe consequences for technology breakdowns

From a *marketing* point of view, e-business allows companies to reach customers they might never be able to contact in a traditional brick-and-mortar operation. Late in 2005, I visited Budapest, Hungary, for a week of consulting and teaching with MBA students at the Budapest University of Technology and Economics (www.bme.hu/en/). Part of my travels included a flight on Malev, the Hungarian national airline (www.malev.hu/bp/eng/index.asp). Without the benefit of e-business, I might never have known about or considered flying with Malev; their routes are restricted to a few geographic areas.

E-business also can help organizations *reduce their operating costs.* Consider, for example, Moviefone.com, which allows moviegoers to purchase their tickets before arriving at the theater. Moving a significant portion of ticket sales to the Internet would help theaters reduce personnel costs in the box office; such systems also would reduce the costs of transaction processing, since online ticket sales could be fed directly into the company's accounting information system or enterprise resource planning system, lessening the need for employees to make manual journal entries and updates to the accounting records. You may also have seen ticket kiosks at large chain movie theatres—that's another form of e-business.

Companies also can *streamline their operations* using e-business. For example, tourists in southern California can purchase tickets to Disneyland and other attractions online. They can print them out on their own computers, thus eliminating the need to stop at a ticket booth once they arrive at the park. The same is true for airlines; most carriers now offer the option of printing boarding passes before arriving at the airport.

Finally, e-business can promote *quicker, easier product and service delivery.* I'm reminded of this advantage every year during the holiday season. Most of my family and friends live in the Midwest, not in southern California. Prior to the advent of e-business, holiday shopping was extremely stressful: Pick out gifts, fight traffic to shop for them, package them securely, and ship them well in advance to ensure they would arrive on time. With e-business, the process is much simpler; I can complete virtually all of my holiday shopping in just an hour or two at home.

Of course, almost everything in business that has a benefit also involves a cost. Organizations that are just starting their venture into e-business may experience *significant financial costs* associated with developing, purchasing, and configuring software and hardware to support the e-business operation. In addition, e-business systems necessarily require different kinds of *internal controls* than brick-and-mortar operations. Such controls would probably include customer identity authentication via usernames and passwords. Many e-business operations also require customers to input the "control number" from the back of a credit card. A control number is typically a three-digit number printed next to the card number itself, above the signature panel on the back of the card. Billing addresses must match the credit card company's records as a preventive internal control as well. Most companies engaged in e-business operations also process their transactions using a secure server dedicated to that purpose. You may have seen the VeriSign logo on Web pages, indicating an added layer of security for online transactions.

The AICPA's WebTrust and SysTrust projects also provide extra security. The AICPA Web site (http://infotech.aicpa.org) offers the following comments about trust services, WebTrust, and SysTrust:

You can get more information about both services at www.cpawebtrust.org.

Trust Services (including WebTrust® and SysTrust®) are defined as a set of professional assurance and advisory services based on a common framework (that is, a core set of principles and criteria) to address the risks and opportunities of IT. Trust Services principles and criteria are issued by the Assurance Services Executive Committee of the AICPA.

WebTrust is the accounting profession's answer to concerns relating to electronic commerce. WebTrust is based on Trust Services Principles and Criteria, which constitute professional guidance and serve as best practices for electronic commerce. Using these Principles and Criteria either separately or in combination, CPAs can offer a range of advisory and assurance services to help either clients or employers address security, online privacy, availability, and confidentiality needs.

SysTrust is the accounting profession's answer to concerns relating to system reliability. SysTrust is based on the Trust Services Principles and Criteria, which constitute professional guidance as well as serving as best practices for system reliability. Using these Principles and Criteria either separately or in combination, CPAs can offer a range of advisory and assurance services to help either clients or employers address their security, availability, processing integrity, and confidentiality needs.

Data encryption is another common internal control found in e-business systems. With data encryption, the party that receives data over the Internet must have a decryption key to make it understandable; without encryption, computer criminals can use high-tech techniques to intercept data as they are transmitted electronically. Finally, e-business systems also can incorporate their own form of segregation of duties. You may recall reading about segregation of duties earlier in the text; for any asset, three important responsibilities should be vested in three different people: physical custody, authorization for use, and recordkeeping. In e-business operations, designers can restrict access to various parts of the system based on organizational level and/or job function. For example, faculty members can access certain student information that is unavailable to others at a university.

Beyond the development and internal control costs of e-business, doing business online can create significant amounts of *customer distrust*—particularly for customers who are accustomed to doing business in a traditional brick-and-mortar context. Perhaps you know someone who simply refuses to buy things on the Internet because of concerns over data security and related issues. Finally, the effects of *technology breakdowns* can be severe in an e-business environment: Loss of customer confidence, lost sales, overloaded customer service phone lines, and generalized damage to a company's reputation are just a few.

Reflection and Self-Assessment   10.1

Which of the above benefits and costs have you experienced in doing business on the Internet? What other items could you add to the list based on your experience and/or previous study?

Business professionals and researchers have developed many taxonomies, or **e-business categories,** to describe e-business. I've generally found it helpful to classify e-businesses by the parties they connect, leading to a five-part classification system:

Type	Abbreviation	Example
Business-to-consumer	B2C	Travelocity
Business-to-business	B2B	Dell Computers
Government-to-consumer	G2C	Internal Revenue Service
Government-to-business	G2B	EDGAR (SEC)
Consumer-to-consumer	C2C	eBay

You may have experienced examples of one or more categories of e-business as a consumer. For example, if you've ever purchased anything online, you've been a part of a B2C transaction. C2C transactions are associated with organizations like eBay (www.ebay .com), where people deal with each other directly in selling goods and services. B2B transactions take place when two organizations do business over a computer network; for example, your university bookstore may use e-business techniques to order textbooks from publishers each semester.

Government at all levels is moving head on into the networked economy as well. For example, the Internal Revenue Service (www.irs.gov) provides a lot of information to taxpayers on its Web site; taxpayers also can file their taxes electronically there. And the U.S. Securities and Exchange Commission's EDGAR database (www.sec.gov/edgar.shtml)

Suggest one other specific example for each of the five categories presented in the table above.

allows publicly traded companies to file their required SEC reports. Investors, researchers, and potential investors also can access companies' documents via EDGAR.

How would e-business impact the accounting information system? Let's go back to the basic model of AIS discussed earlier in the text: inputs, processing tools, storage media, outputs, and internal controls.

We've already discussed a few of the internal controls associated with an e-business environment (data encryption, segregation of duties, access restrictions). From an input perspective, e-business can cut down on the number of paper documents in an accounting information system; it also can shift data entry responsibilities from accounting clerks to customers, since transaction data can be captured directly from a Web site. Consider the process of buying a book from a retail bookstore such as Barnes and Noble. In a brick-and-mortar environment, the steps might include

1. Customer locates book and brings it to a cash register.
2. Register clerk rings up the sale and provides the customer with a paper receipt.
3. At the end of the day, the register clerk retrieves data on the day's sales from the cash register and transmits them to a corporate office or an accounting department.
4. Clerks in the accounting department make journal entries to record the day's transactions.

Contrast those steps with purchasing a book online:

1. Customer identifies books and adds them to an electronic "shopping cart."
2. Customer provides billing and shipping information electronically.
3. E-business system creates and posts journal entries and related inventory information in the accounting information system.

The flowchart in Figure 10.1 depicts the brick-and-mortar process. Figure 10.2 shows what the process would look like in an e-business environment.

Purchasing airplane tickets is another business process that has been profoundly streamlined via e-business. In a brick-and-mortar environment, most people who wanted to purchase airline tickets would consult a travel agent. The travel agent would communicate with the airline, then present options to the client. The client would make a choice; the agent would buy the tickets from the airline, sometimes charging an additional fee for the service. The process could often take several days, and paper tickets were required in the overwhelming majority of transactions.

Consider the process you probably follow now if you want to fly. You log on to an airline or travel-related Web site (for example, www.jetblue.com or www.travelocity.com). You put in the parameters of your travel; the computer searches for tickets and can even compare nearby airports. You submit your payment information on a secure server, and an e-mail arrives in your mailbox confirming the transaction. When you get to the airport, you don't need a paper ticket in most cases.

While e-business probably cannot remove the need for human intervention in an accounting information system, it can significantly reduce that need—and all the attendant problems that accompany it (e.g., data entry mistakes, billing problems, incorrect journal entries).

FIGURE 10.1
Brick-and-Mortar Sales Process

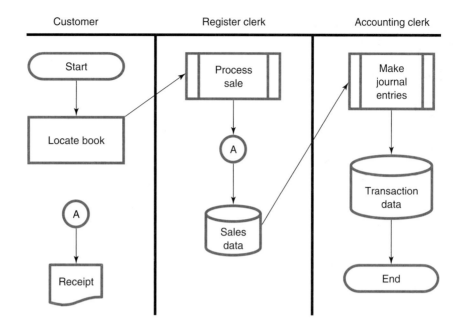

From an output perspective, e-business systems facilitate the preparation of general purpose financial statements and other reports. In an early job in my accounting career, I worked for a heavy-equipment manufacturer with consistently large amounts of outstanding accounts receivable. At the end of each business day, I manually prepared an accounts receivable aging, showing each customer's name, balance owed, and length of time the balance had been outstanding. In an e-business system, generating an accounts receivable aging is normally a matter of "pushing a button." The computer does the analysis and prints out the results with little or no human effort.

FIGURE 10.2
E-business Sales Process

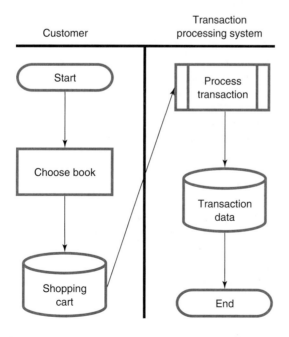

So, with that very brief overview of e-commerce as background, let's turn our attention to one of the most important, yet most controversial, technologies associated with the networked economy: enterprise resource planning systems.

ERP SYSTEMS

An **enterprise resource planning system** is a modular, relational database designed to provide internal organizational stakeholders with more timely, comprehensive information for decisions. Arguably, the two best-known ERP systems today are PeopleSoft (www .peoplesoft.com) and SAP (www.sap.com). Because most ERP systems are modular, they can be implemented one piece at a time according to an organization's needs and budget. Because they are relational in nature, they organize information in database tables, much like those you learned about earlier in this text.

Typical modules in an ERP system include

Customer relationship management

Financial management

Human resource management

Supply chain management

The modules depicted above are not unique to any particular ERP vendor; rather, they provide a broad organizational structure for most ERP systems.

Think back to your study of database development earlier in the text. Since ERP systems are built on relational databases, the principles we discussed there apply here as well. Customer relationship management, as the name implies, helps organizations manage customer data. Beyond basic data such as customer name, address, and phone number, organizations also can capture data on credit limits, transaction histories, contacts, and appointments and referrals. For example, when I log on to Amazon.com to buy books, the system has recommendations for me based on my past purchases; the same is true for Netflix.

Human resource management concerns itself with employee data. Again, an organization can track "mundane" data such as name and address. However, an HRM module also might include details on work goals, disciplinary problems, and training and development plans. For example, the university where I work maintains a database of faculty experts for the media and other purposes. So, if a newspaper reporter wants a quote on the impact of recycling on the environment, public affairs personnel can consult the database and give them some recommendations.

Supply chain management focuses on vendors—the usual data, plus transaction histories, comments about product quality, and personnel interactions, among other items. Financial management would incorporate the accounting information system, but also would go far beyond the basic general purpose financial statements. For example, organizations can input their budget data into a financial management module, then generate variance reports quickly and easily at any point in time. In universities, a financial management module also might track scholarship records. Financial forecasting is another important function of most financial management ERP modules.

Notice that the four parts of most ERP systems provide information associated with four key stakeholder groups: customers (customer relationship management), employees (human resource management), vendors (supply chain management), and stockholders (financial management). Most ERP systems help managers stay aware of the importance of those relationships; they also allow an individual manager to concentrate on the relationship(s) that are most important to him or her, while simultaneously providing access to comprehensive information throughout the organization.

Reflection and Self-Assessment   10.3

Suggest three pieces of information an ERP system should capture in each module shown above.

Many organizations experience significant difficulty in implementing ERP systems; consider the example below:

> [A major soft drink bottler], which implemented a major ERP system, completed the implementation, but not without losing significant personnel and system functionality. After committing millions of dollars to purchase ERP software, the soft drink maker tried cutting corners during implementation. Relying too heavily on its own people instead of consultants, the bottler expected too much from its already-taxed employees. Trying to minimize setup costs and reduce expenses, the company overlooked many of the planning team's recommendations regarding the project. This ERP implementation created high turnover and communication problems, which led to the termination of key people and animosity among employees. All of these factors, in turn, led to a system that was grossly underused, and in the beginning, a hindrance to the overall business. (Barker and Frolick, 2003)

Umble and Umble (2002) identified 10 major **causes of ERP implementation failures:**

1. *Poor leadership from top management.* Selecting and installing an ERP system is an enormous undertaking in terms of time, money, and energy. Clear, strong leadership and support from top management are essential for a successful implementation—without them, employees are likely to view the ERP system as just another "initiative du jour."

2. *Automating existing redundant or non-value-added processes in the new system.* An ERP implementation project is a terrific time to reconsider the company's business processes. In other words, do policies, procedures, document flows, and internal controls make sense from a business point of view? Do the processes add value to organizational stakeholders? In most organizations, at least a few policies and processes will need to be changed to make the most of the ERP system. Otherwise, managers will be doing the same, ineffective things—only faster.

3. *Unrealistic expectations.* An ERP system is designed to collect, process, and report data and information for making management decisions more effectively. Systems are not a panacea for problems with organizational culture, poorly designed business processes, or inadequate internal controls. Expecting an ERP system to fix those kinds of problems is a forlorn hope and will seriously jeopardize the project's success.

4. *Poor project management.* ERP system selection, testing, and implementation are time-intensive, long-term projects. To be successful, managers have to apply solid project management techniques for selecting the right people, completing tasks in the right order, and staying on schedule.

5. *Inadequate education and training.* This failure cause is linked to many of the others in this list. Without good training and education, employees may have unrealistic expectations of what the ERP system can do; they also may see the ERP implementation as solely an information technology project, rather than as an opportunity to analyze business processes and make them better.

6. *Trying to maintain the status quo.* Since an ERP system is such a major undertaking, implementation will almost always create fear and uncertainty throughout an organization. When people are fearful about their job security and future in the firm, they will likely act in very dysfunctional ways, either intentionally or unintentionally. To avoid this problem, be upfront and honest from the start about the purpose and possible results of implementing the ERP system.

7. *A bad match between ERP software and organizational processes.* Every organization has its own ways of doing business. And, while ERP systems can be customized to a degree based on specific organizational contexts, such modifications are time-consuming and expensive. Managers would be well advised to consult with colleagues in the field about which ERP software has worked well, and which has worked poorly, in a specific industry.

8. *Inaccurate data in the system.* As the old saying goes: "garbage in, garbage out." The reports and information generated by an ERP system are only as valid and useful as the data that undergird them. Faulty or inaccurate data in the ERP system can be even worse than the same condition in less-integrated systems, since they will be used throughout the organization for decision making. Once inaccurate data have been discovered in a system, every other prior and future output are called into question until the situation has been resolved.

9. *ERP implementation viewed as an IT project.* As discussed above, implementing an ERP system goes far beyond the information technology requirements. Fundamentally, an ERP project needs to be viewed as holistic, touching not only information technology, but also business processes and organizational behavior issues.

10. *Significant technical difficulties.* Of course, even though an ERP project is not solely concerned with IT issues, some technical problems may arise. Bugs in the software, problems interfacing with existing information systems, and hardware difficulties are just three identified by Umble and Umble.

Similarly, Umble and Umble (2002) discussed six necessary **conditions for a successful ERP implementation:**

1. *Obtain organizational commitment.* This condition speaks most clearly to poor leadership from management and trying to maintain the status quo. The ERP project team needs to get a clear, strong commitment to the project throughout the organization, but especially from top management. Without a psychological and financial commitment to see the project through to its completion, the project may "lose steam" when encountering difficult problems.

2. *Communicate strategic goals clearly.* This idea also relates to two of the common causes of ERP implementation failure: unrealistic expectations and inadequate education and training. Employees in all functions at all levels of the organization need to understand the goals of the ERP project—typically, providing better information more quickly for decision making.

3. *View ERP as an enterprisewide venture.* An ERP system will eventually touch every aspect of operations; therefore, it must be viewed as a companywide project. If the project is viewed as "just another information technology initiative," managers will lose the opportunity to examine business processes thoughtfully and critically—possibly leading to automating redundant or non-value-added processes.

4. *Select a compatible ERP system.* Here, we're talking about items 7 and 10 from the list of common causes of failure: a bad match between ERP software and organizational processes and significant technical difficulties. The bottom line: Don't believe everything the software vendor or implementation consultants tell you! Do your own research; ask for other companies that have had successful (and unsuccessful) implementations.

5. *Resolve multisite issues.* ERP implementations are inherently complicated. But they become more complicated when an organization is geographically dispersed. The project management plan (see item 4 in the preceding list) must deal specifically with multisite issues.

6. *Ensure data accuracy.* The final key to success in ERP implementation is directly related to item 8 on the previous page. The project team needs to do significant employee education about the importance of accurate data entry; test runs with fictitious data before the system "goes live" also can help achieve this goal.

Many of those conditions were found at Marathon Oil, leading to a successful implementation of SAP ERP software (Stapleton and Rezak, 2004). Marathon used a change-management approach in implementing its ERP system, recognizing that the goal was "the transfer of ownership from the project team that designed and configured the new system and processes to the end users, the internal clients who would employ these tools and processes in their day-to-day operations." Other keys to Marathon's successful experience included constant communication via newsletters, workshops, and hands-on interaction to increase employees' comfort level with the software.

APPLICATION SERVICE PROVIDERS

Organizations that want to move into an e-business environment have two basic choices for doing so: create applications "from scratch" or hire an **application service provider** (ASP). ASPNews.com (2002) offers the following comments about application service providers:

An ASP is a third party entity that deploys, hosts and manages access to a packaged application and delivers software-based services and solutions to customers across a wide area network from a central data center. Applications are delivered over networks on a subscription or rental basis. In essence, ASPs are a way for companies to outsource some or almost all aspects of their information technology needs.

ASPnews.com breaks the industry into five subcategories:

- Enterprise ASPs—deliver high-end business applications.
- Local/Regional ASPs—supply wide variety of application services for smaller businesses in a local area.
- Specialist ASPs—provide applications for a specific need, such as Web site services or human resources.
- Vertical Market ASPs—provide support to a specific industry such as healthcare.
- Volume Business ASPs—supply general small/medium-sized businesses with prepackaged application services in volume.

COSO's *Enterprise Risk Management—Integrated Framework* discusses ASPs as a form of risk sharing, one way of responding to risks in an organization's environment. (Refer back to Chapter 4 for a complete discussion of the COSO ERM framework.)

Organizations and individuals have used ASPs to

- Process insurance claims (www.processclaims.com).
- Complete the steps in the accounting cycle (www.epeachtree.com).
- Manage stock market transactions electronically (www.tradingtechnologies.com).
- Provide personal financial planning (www.naviplan.com).
- Prepare income tax returns (www.taxslayer.com).

Just as with e-business in general, ASPs offer both benefits and risks to organizations. The table below summarizes a few:

ASP Benefits	ASP Risks
Less costly than purchasing software outright	Psychological and behavioral factors
Increased flexibility	Service interruptions
Potentially improved customer service	Compromised data
Role in disaster recovery plans	Inability to pay monthly fees

Internal controls like those listed below can help address some of those risks:

- Establishing a budget for the ASP project.
- Backing up data on a daily basis.
- Providing ongoing training for employees using the ASP.
- Creating firewalls and encryption protocols.

Application service providers are one type of service organization addressed by Statement of Auditing Standards 70, developed by the AICPA in 1992. Here's part of what www.SAS70.com has to say about the standard:

> Statement on Auditing Standards (SAS) No. 70, *Service Organizations,* is a widely recognized auditing standard developed by the American Institute of Certified Public Accountants (AICPA). A service auditor's examination performed in accordance with SAS No. 70 ("SAS 70 Audit") is widely recognized, because it represents that a service organization has been through an in-depth audit of their control objectives and control activities, which often include controls over information technology and related processes. In today's global economy, service organizations or service providers must demonstrate that they have adequate controls and safeguards when they host or process data belonging to their customers. In addition, the requirements of Section 404 of the Sarbanes-Oxley Act of 2002 make SAS 70 audit reports even more important to the process of reporting on the effectiveness of internal control over financial reporting.

So, if an ASP has had a service audit, its clients can have more confidence that their data are safe, secure, and accessible when they need them.

CRITICAL THINKING

In the next few paragraphs, I'm going to show you how to apply two of the concepts we've discussed in other chapters in an e-business environment: systems documentation and database design.

FIGURE 10.3
You Bars Ordering
Process

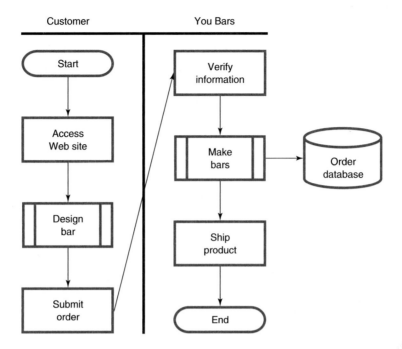

Check out www.youbars.com, the Web site for You Bars and You Shakes; the company makes custom-designed nutrition bars and shakes. Here are the steps that might go into receiving an order of You Bars:

1. Customer accesses Web site.
2. Customer completes 10-step process for designing a nutrition bar.
3. Customer submits billing, shipping, and other information.
4. You Bars verifies information submitted.
5. You Bars prepares product.
6. You Bars ships the product.

The "other information" in step three includes options for overnight shipping, gift wrapping, and personalized greeting cards. A systems flowchart of those steps could look like Figure 10.3.

I've used a predefined process symbol for "design bar" and "make bar" to indicate that there are predefined steps associated with each process; additional systems flowcharts would spell out those details. The details could be included in Figure 10.3, but the flowchart would rapidly become crowded and difficult to read.

If you wanted to do a leveled set of data flow diagrams, it would definitely include one context diagram and one Level Zero diagram. At Level One, you could decompose "design bar" and "make bars" into their separate steps. The table below suggests elements for a REA model of the same process:

REA Model Element	Examples
Events	Design bar, place order, make bar, ship order
Resources	Bar ingredients
Agents	Customer, production employee, shipping employee

You Bars' accounting information system would need several database tables: customer, order history, product, employee. It also might include a raw materials table for the various ingredients in the finished product. Customer and employee tables are fairly common; their design doesn't change much from one company to another.

The product table, though, would be unique. As you can see on the Web site, the last step in creating a bar is to give it a name. But the name alone won't uniquely identify each bar; two customers might independently come up with the same bar name. So, the product table would need a compound primary key composed of the customer ID and the bar name. Customer ID would be a foreign key in the product table; it would be the primary key in the customer table. The product table would need fields for the various ingredients: Base 1, Base 2, Protein 1, Protein 2, Protein 3, and such.

The order history table would include data like order number (as the primary key), order date, and customer ID. Since each order can comprise many products, and since each product can be ordered many times, the database would need an order/product junction table as well.

I hope this example has reinforced some of the ideas we've examined in previous chapters. As always, I encourage you to e-mail me with suggestions for improvement.

Summary

After reading the chapter, I'm confident you can see that e-business and ERP systems, like most other aspects of AIS, are full of judgments—they are almost certainly a blend of "art" and "science," at the very least. Here's a summary of the chapter's main points in terms of its learning objectives:

1. *Explain the nature of e-business, comparing and contrasting it with traditional "brick-and-mortar" organizations.* The essential feature of e-business is the computer network. It is otherwise very similar to traditional businesses in terms of its stakeholder groups, information needs, and organizational structures.

2. *Discuss major forms of e-business, including business-to-business, consumer-to-consumer, business-to-consumer, government-to-business, and government-to-consumer.* E-businesses often are classified by the types of entities connected via computer networks. B2B arrangements partner organizations, such as when a company purchases inventory from a supplier. B2C transactions are characterized by operations such as Travelocity or Amazon. G2B partners government agencies with businesses, as with EDGAR. G2C operations allow consumers to obtain information from the government; consider the Web site of the Internal Revenue Service (www.irs.gov) in this category. C2C sites, like eBay, facilitate business between individuals.

3. *Describe the basic nature, purpose, and structure of enterprise resource planning systems.* An ERP system is a relational database designed to capture data and provide for reports and analyses via queries. Common modules include financial, human resources, vendors, and customer relationships.

4. *Give examples and analyze the causes of ERP system failures.* ERP implementations fail for one or more of a few common reasons, including poor leadership from top management, failure to analyze business processes thoroughly, unrealistic expectations, poor project management, inadequate education and training, bad match between software and organization, technical problems, and inaccurate data.

5. *List and discuss steps associated with successful ERP implementations.* Successful ERP implementations commonly follow a six-step implementation process: (1) Obtain organizational commitment. (2) Communicate strategic goals clearly. (3) View ERP as an enterprisewide venture. (4) Select a compatible ERP system. (5) Resolve multisite issues. (6) Ensure data accuracy.

6. *Discuss the role of application service providers in e-business.* Application service providers can facilitate an organization's entry into the networked economy. ASPs deliver a wide range of applications on a subscription or rental basis: managing elements of the human resource function, preparing tax returns, and completing the steps in the accounting cycle. Organizations using ASPs must modify their internal control systems to address the risks they present. SAS 70 audits help promote the integrity of an ASP's accounting information system.

Now, please proceed to the end-of-chapter activities assigned by your instructor to get some practical applications of the concepts discussed in this chapter.

Key Terms

application service provider 177
causes of ERP implementation failure, *175*

computer networks, *169*
conditions for a successful ERP implementation, *176*
e-business categories, *171*

e-commerce, *169*
enterprise resource planning system, *174*

Chapter References

ASPNews.com. 2002. "ASPNews Glossary." www.aspnews.com/strategies/asp_basics/article .php/759691 (January 11).

Barker, T., and M. Frolick. 2003. "ERP Implementation Failure: A Case Study." *Information Systems Management,* Fall, pp. 43–49.

Stapleton, G., and C. Rezak. 2004. "Change Management Underpins a Successful ERP Implementation at Marathon Oil." *Journal of Organizational Excellence,* Autumn, pp. 15–22.

Umble, E., and M. Umble. 2002. "Avoiding ERP Implementation Failure." *Industrial Management,* January/February, pp. 25–34. Reprinted with the permission of the Institute of Industrial Engineers. 3577 Parkway Lane, Suite 200, Norcross, GA 30092, 770-449-0461. Copyright © 2002.

End-of-Chapter Activities

1. *Reading review questions.*
   a. What is the distinguishing characteristic of e-business that makes it different from traditional brick-and-mortar businesses?
   b. The chapter discusses five basic types of e-business arrangements. Identify and describe each one; give an example of each type other than the example in the chapter.
   c. What is an enterprise resource planning system?
   d. What common problems cause ERP implementations to fail? What can managers do to promote successful ERP implementations?
   e. Prepare a response to the questions for this chapter's "AIS in the Business World."

2. *Reading review problem.* Information technology and computer networks have changed nearly every aspect of business in the last decade. Consider the following comments about human resource (HR) management:

   Large U.S. employers continue to take a selective approach to outsourcing their benefits administration, recruiting, payroll and other HR functions rather than relying exclusively on a single provider, according to research by consultancy Watson Wyatt. Selective outsourcing is popular because it can be tailored to meet an organization's exact needs. The key to successful outsourcing is finding the solutions that fit the organization's needs and culture, Hubbard notes. Watson Wyatt's Changing Strategies in HR Technology and Outsourcing survey of 182 U.S. companies found that many expect to do more outsourcing in areas such as health and welfare programs. However, few companies, 21%, direct their HR function to outsource programs automatically. The majority, 63%, look to use their internal or enterprise resource planning systems whenever possible to deliver HR services.

Source: Stephen Miller, "Companies Continue to Selectively Outsource HR Programs," *HRMagazine: SHRM's 2009 HR Trend Book*, January 2009, pp. 76–78, from ABI/ INFORM Global database (Document ID: 1607406711; accessed January 4, 2009).

a. How might an HR outsourcing company use e-business to attract new clients? To accomplish its goals for existing clients?

b. How would an HR outsourcing firm use the four ERP modules discussed in the chapter?

c. Would an HR outsourcing firm be considered an application service provider? Why, or why not?

3. *Multiple choice review.* Please select the best answer for each question.

1. All of the following are costs associated with e-business except:
   a. Potential for customer distrust.
   b. Financial costs associated with setting up networks.
   c. Need to develop different internal control systems.
   d. REA modeling requirements.

2. WebTrust and SysTrust are:
   a. Required for e-business.
   b. Always part of a SAS 70 audit.
   c. Tools for providing security in an e-business environment.
   d. Federal government programs.

3. Which ERP module is most concerned with vendor relationships?
   a. Customer relationship management
   b. Supply chain management
   c. Financial management
   d. Human resource management

4. All of the following are conditions for a successful ERP implementation except:
   a. Thinking of the implementation as an IT project.
   b. Obtaining organizational commitment.
   c. Ensuring data accuracy.
   d. Communicating strategic goals clearly.

5. An application service provider provides HR services for the health care industry. It can be considered:
   a. A specialist, vertical market ASP.
   b. An enterprise, specialist ASP.
   c. A local, specialist ASP.
   d. An enterprise, vertical market ASP.

4. *Making choices and exercising judgment.*

a. Point your Web browser to www.baselinemag.com. Locate and read "Hershey's Sweet Victory" by David F. Carr. In the blinding light of hindsight, which of the common causes of ERP failure did Hershey experience? What could management have done to avoid those problems?

b. The e-business model can be applied very effectively in some industries, but not as effectively in others. You may remember early attempts to establish online grocery shopping with companies such as Web Grocer and Net Grocer. Think of another industry where the value of e-business might be considered questionable. Explain your reasoning.

c. Chapter 5 discussed a weighted rating model for software evaluation. If you were using such a model to evaluate ERP systems, what factors would you want to consider? What relative weights would you assign each of them? Explain your choices.

5. *Field work.*

a. Conduct research into WebTrust and/or SysTrust. Prepare an oral or written report summarizing at least the following items: historical development, nature and purpose of the system, financial and nonfinancial benefits, and costs and examples of companies using the technology. You can start your research at www.webtrust.org.

b. Visit a company in your geographic area that uses an ERP system. Ask for a demonstration of the system (or at least one part of it) and prepare a brief oral or written presentation to the class on your findings.

6. *Internal controls in e-business.* The chapter mentioned three potential internal controls for an e-business environment: encryption, segregation of duties, and access restrictions. Consider your study of internal controls throughout this text; suggest five additional internal controls for e-business environments. Explain specifically how you would apply them.

7. *Types of computer networks.* As you read in the chapter, the presence of a computer network is the defining characteristic of e-business. Research the topic and define each of the following terms related to networks and networking.

a. Local area network
b. Network architecture
c. Network protocol
d. Network topology
e. Node
f. Server
g. Wide area network

8. *Forms of e-business.* Which category of e-business (B2B, B2C, G2B, or G2C) best describes each of the following items?

a. Buying materials for professional practice from www.aicpa.org
b. Electronic reporting of state unemployment taxes
c. Filing personal income taxes with TaxSlayer.com
d. Getting medical advice from www.webmd.com
e. Making appointments with the Department of Motor Vehicles
f. Online banking
g. Paying traffic citations online
h. Purchases from Amazon.com
i. Receiving the online newsletter from the Institute of Management Accountants
j. Registration for seminars sponsored by the Association of Certified Fraud Examiners

9. *Promoting ERP success.* Choose one of the Fortune 100 companies; investigate it on the Internet and through your university's library. Work with a group of students to prepare a PowerPoint presentation to fulfill the first three of Umble and Umble's six conditions for promoting ERP success (obtain organizational commitment, communicate strategic goals, and view ERP as an enterprisewide venture).

10. *Application service providers.*

a. Companies considering utilizing an ASP might start the process by identifying a need to lower costs and increase flexibility. What other steps would a manager likely take in selecting an ASP? Who should be involved in such a decision?

b. Refer to www.sas70.com to determine which of the following statements are true about service audits conducted under that standard.

i. The audit provides positive proof that an ASP is not vulnerable to fraud.
ii. An SAS 70 audit is sometimes called a "service auditor's examination."

      iii. An SAS 70 audit can be an important component of an internal control examination and assessment.

      iv. The audit consists of going through a checklist of required controls and activities.

      v. As defined in the standard, a "service organization" can be an ASP.

      vi. Service auditors can issue a Type I report or a Type II report.

      vii. A Type I report means that the service organization has good internal control; a Type II report indicates internal control problems.

      viii. Without an SAS 70 examination, an ASP may need to be audited by its clients' independent auditors.

      ix. SAS 70 audits are generally performed by professionals with a background in accounting, auditing, and information security.

      x. Section 404 of the Sarbanes-Oxley Act of 2002 has increased the importance and relevance of SAS 70 examinations.

c. All professional accounting certifications and licenses (such as the CPA and CFE) require continuing professional education (CPE) on an annual basis. Suppose you and a group of friends started an ASP designed to track CPE requirements for accounting professionals. Design a database that would capture the required information about your clients. What internal controls would you implement to promote the integrity of those data?

d. Point your Web browser to www.sas70.com. Work with a group of students to summarize, in a format specified by your instructor, the information in at least five of the site's Frequently Asked Questions about SAS 70 audits.

11. *Terminology.* Please match each item on the left with the best item on the right.

1.	Brick and mortar	a.	A well-known ERP system
2.	Computer network	b.	Another name for "old economy" organizations
3.	Financial management	c.	Associated with G2C and G2B e-commerce
4.	Hershey	d.	B2C e-commerce example
5.	Human resource management	e.	ERP module associated with employees
6.	Internal Revenue Service	f.	Had a "not so sweet" experience with ERP
7.	Multisite issues	g.	Module in an ERP system associated with stockholders
8.	Online banking	h.	Need to be resolved for a successful ERP project
9.	PeopleSoft	i.	Technology underlying ERP
10.	Relational database	j.	The salient feature of e-business

12. *Multiple choice questions.*

1. The Web site www.sco.ca.gov/upd.html is an example of which form of e-business?

    a. B2C

    b. G2C

    c. G2B

    d. C2C

2. WebTrust and SysTrust are forms of:

    a. Internal control.

    b. E-business.

    c. Systems documentation.

    d. Transaction processing software.

3. In February 2011, Pfizer Inc. authorized a $5 billion program to repurchase shares of its own common stock from investors. Which ERP system module is most likely to be involved in the transactions?

   a. Customer relationship management
   b. Financial management
   c. Supply chain management
   d. Human resource management

4. Which of the following can cause problems in ERP system implementation, internal control design, and enterprise risk management?

   a. Lack of strong positive signals from top management
   b. Assuming staff understand project goals and purposes
   c. Both a and b
   d. Neither a nor b

5. Which of the following is included in a SAS 70 Type II report, but is optional in a SAS 70 Type I report?

   a. Independent service auditor's report
   b. Service organization's description of controls
   c. Information provided by the independent service auditor
   d. Other information provided by the service organization

13. *Statement evaluation.* Indicate whether each of the following statements is (i) always true, (ii) sometimes true, or (iii) never true. For those that are (ii) sometimes true, explain when the statement is true.

   a. Companies involved in e-business report higher profit margins than traditional companies.
   b. Computer networks are the defining feature of e-business.
   c. E-business expands an organization's geographic markets.
   d. E-business removes the need for human intervention in accounting information systems.
   e. Every aspect of Porter's value chain can be impacted by e-business.
   f. Implementing an ERP system ensures that data will be accurate and accessible.
   g. Many enterprise resource planning systems are modular in nature.
   h. Organizations enter into relationships with stakeholders to get the resources they need to operate.
   i. Successful ERP implementations often require business process redesign.
   j. WebTrust and SysTrust can strengthen internal controls in e-business.

14. *Prior material application.*

   a. When an organization implements an ERP system or enters into the e-business arena, it is exposed to a variety of risks. Use the COSO ERM framework discussed in Chapter 4 to design a generic risk management plan for one of those two situations.
   b. A small bookstore wants to expand its operations to include e-business. Use the generalized model of business process management discussed in Chapter 4 to develop a plan for doing so.
   c. A business plan is essential for starting an e-business venture. Do some research on how to develop a business plan; you might start by consulting www.sba.gov or by asking a strategy/entrepreneurship professor at your university. Document the steps for developing a business plan using one of the formats discussed in Part Two of the book.

Chapter Eleven

Computer Crime and Information Technology Security

AIS in the Business World

Law firms

Have you ever heard of a movie called *War Games?* In it, a high school student (played by Matthew Broderick) accidentally hacks into a government computer and nearly starts a war. Although it came out in 1983, a lot of people still believe today's computer crimes follow a similar model. In reality, though, nothing could be further from the truth. One of the most important economic assets for any organization today is information. And, that information is frequently stored and transmitted electronically, making it very vulnerable to computer crime. Nowhere is that more true than in law firms.

Consider this excerpt from the Finkel article referenced below:

> Law firms are a very attractive target for cyberattacks by anyone seeking sensitive information, says Bradford A. Bleier, unit chief to the Cyber National Security Section in the FBI's Cyber Division. "Law firms have tremendous concentrations of really critical private information," says Bleier, and breaking into a firm's computer system "is a really optimal way to obtain economic and personal security information."

In this chapter, we'll take a closer look at the timely and important topics of computer crime and information technology security.

Discussion Questions

1. What is computer crime?
2. What broad principles should accountants apply to prevent, detect, and correct computer crime?
3. What is the CoBIT framework? How does it relate to the topics discussed in this chapter?

Source: E. Finkel, "Cyberspace Under Siege," *ABA Journal* (November 2010).

With individuals becoming more than simply computer literate and the emergence of the Internet as a tool for global information exchange, accounting information systems and the information they store and process will increasingly fall victim to computer crime and fraud. Computers also have become facilitators for criminals, providing them with new methods of perpetrating classic forms of crimes and creating many new "business opportunities" for these criminals. This chapter examines many facets of computer crime and fraud: associated risks and threats, the use of accounting information systems, and investigation of computer crime.

When you've finished studying this chapter, you should be able to:

1. Explain Carter's taxonomy of computer crime.
2. Identify and describe business risks and threats to information systems.
3. Name and describe common types of computer criminals.
4. Discuss ways to prevent and detect computer crime.
5. Explain CoBIT's information criteria and accountability framework.
6. Explain how CoBIT can be used to strengthen internal controls against computer crime.

Understanding the various types of computer crime will allow you to understand more clearly how the AIS can be affected by common malicious acts. Carter (1995) suggested a four-part **taxonomy for computer crime:**

- *Target.* This category is comprised of computer crimes where the criminal targets the system or its data. The objective of these crimes is to impact the confidentiality, availability, and/or integrity of data stored on the computer.
- *Instrumentality.* Computer as the instrumentality of the crime uses the computer to further a criminal end. In crimes *targeting* the computer, the data are the object of the crime; in this case, the computer is used to commit a crime.
- *Incidental.* This type of computer crime encompasses crimes where the computer is not required for the crime but is related to the criminal act. The use of the computer simplifies the criminal actions and may make the crime more difficult to trace.
- *Associated.* The simple presence of computers, and notably the growth of the Internet, has generated new versions of fairly traditional crimes. In these cases, technological growth essentially creates new crime targets and new ways of reaching victims.

The lines between each type of crime can be blurry at times and some criminal transactions may overlap the different types of crimes.

BUSINESS RISKS AND THREATS TO INFORMATION SYSTEMS

Organizations, both large and small, have come to rely heavily on information systems to provide timely information used in making critical business decisions. As such reliance on information systems grows, so do the risks the organization faces. So, anyone involved in decision making should understand those risks and how they can impact the organization.

We'll discuss the following business **risks and threats:**

- Fraud
- Error
- Service interruption and delays

- Disclosure of confidential information
- Intrusions
- Information theft
- Information manipulation
- Malicious software
- Denial-of-service attacks
- Web site defacements
- Extortion

Fraud

In 1989, the U.S. Department of Justice defined computer fraud as being any illegal act for which knowledge of computer technology is used to commit the offense. Fundamentally, computer fraud is people fraud; no computer system can perpetrate fraud without at least some human intervention.

Computer skills required will vary greatly depending on the type of fraud being perpetrated. Frauds such as data diddling—the intentional modification of information—require only basic skills; on the other hand, theft of information in a secure database will require more advanced computer skills from the fraudster.

Following a series of scandals and lapses in corporate governance, the Sarbanes-Oxley Act was introduced to restore customer confidence in the stock markets. It was introduced with the firm resolve to increase corporate responsibility and requires that companies establish extensive governance policies to prevent and respond to fraudulent activities. The act and the accompanying SEC regulations require that organizations produce a report of the internal controls it has in place to ensure compliance with the act itself.

Error

Losses associated with errors can vary widely depending on where the error originated and the time it may take to identify and correct it. A single error when entering a product code will lead to the wrong item being shipped; a programming error in a financial institution's transaction system could lead to many millions lost and some very angry customers. Implementing preventive controls that will detect and correct errors before they occur can prevent financial losses and negative impacts to the organization's image.

Service Interruption and Delays

A delay in processing information or a service interruption can bring an organization to a standstill; such delays can lead to missed deadlines for payables and receivables. Service interruptions can be due to many factors, but they all fall into three main categories: accidental, willful neglect, and malicious behavior. Accidental service interruption can be caused by someone shutting down the wrong machine. Willful neglect could be due to outdated antivirus software; a malicious service interruption could be caused by a hacker launching a denial of service attack against an organization's Web site.

Disclosure of Confidential Information

The disclosure of sensitive information can have major impacts on an organization's financial health. No organization wishes to imagine its customer or employee data being made available to all on the Internet, but such disclosure has become an important risk for most organizations. Privacy laws have made managers and other stakeholders aware of the critical need to protect information assets.

Intrusions

The main objective of an intrusion is to gain access to a network or a system by bypassing security controls or exploiting a lack of adequate controls. An intruder's motivations will vary widely: Some hack for profit while others hack for fun. Hackers for profit will often target specific organizations or specific information before beginning their attack; hackers looking for entertainment will often choose "low-hanging fruit": data and/or systems that are relatively unprotected and easy to access.

Information Theft

This form of computer crime targets the organization's most precious asset: information. Trade secrets, marketing plans, advertising campaigns, research and development data for new products, and customer lists are just a few examples of data in this category. These assets, which are represented in a numeric format, often have a higher value than other traditionally targeted assets, resulting in potentially higher losses for the organizations.

Information Manipulation

Information manipulation can occur at virtually any stage of information processing, from input to output. Input manipulation in computer systems is probably the most common form of fraud since it is easy to perform, requiring only basic computer skills. Furthermore, it is hard to detect, since the fraudulent input may look valid until an in-depth examination is performed. Such a situation could occur when an employee creates fake refunds in the payables system to benefit a family member.

Program manipulation is a complex task and is extremely difficult to detect as both the modification and detection require advanced computer programming knowledge. Manipulating computer programs involves the modification or insertion of specific functions in the computer information system.

Other forms of manipulation involve taking advantage of the automatic repetitions of a computer program. Such manipulation is characteristic of the "salami technique," where unnoticeable slices of a financial transaction are removed and transferred to another account. Under such a scenario, a computer programmer employed in a bank could redirect interest smaller then a penny to his own account. Over time, those fractional amounts can add up to a large sum.

Malicious Software

Malicious software, or malware, can take many different forms: a virus infecting a system and modifying its data, a worm replicating over the network causing a bottleneck, or a Trojan horse allowing an unauthorized backdoor into a system that directly impacts the confidentiality of the files residing on the system.

Logic bombs are another example of malicious software. In a payroll system, for example, software validates whether a specific employee's number is present or not when paychecks are issued. If the employee was ever dismissed, his employee number would no longer be present and, upon execution of the payroll application, the logic bomb would detect the missing employee number and trigger the deletion of all employee records.

Denial-of-Service Attacks

Denial-of-service (DOS) attacks prevent computer systems and networks from functioning in accordance with their intended purpose. These attacks cause loss of service to the users by consuming scarce resources such as bandwidth, memory, or processor cycles; they also can disrupt configuration information or physical components.

In a distributed denial-of-service attack, many compromised systems under the control of one or many attackers are used to multiply the impact by launching concurrent attacks against a determined target. These attacks can be devastating to an organization as they will bring computer operations to a complete standstill; in many cases, distributed DOS attacks are virtually impossible to block as they come from so many sources.

Web Site Defacements

Web site defacements are a form of digital graffiti where intruders modify pages on the site in order to leave their mark, send a message, or mock the organization. Politically motivated defacement, often called hacktivism, attempts to send a message to the organization or some part of the online community.

Extortion

Online extortion is often the result of the computer being the object of a crime; the extortionist contacts an organization after successfully stealing information or launching a DOS attack. The criminal then threatens either to reveal the information to the public or to launch a prolonged denial of service if demands are not met.

PERPETRATORS OF COMPUTER CRIME

A wide variety of individuals have been known to commit computer crimes: students, amateurs, terrorists, and members of organized crime groups. What distinguishes them is the intent of their crime: a youth attempting to break into a system without any further intent is much different than an employee embezzling funds. Any person of any age with computer skills, motivated by the technical challenge; by the potential for gain, notoriety, or revenge; or by the promotion of ideological beliefs is a potential computer criminal.

The following paragraphs discuss seven common types of computer criminals, or **perpetrators**:

- Script kiddies
- Hackers
- Cyber-criminals
- Organized crime
- Corporate spies
- Terrorists
- Insiders

A *script kiddie* describes a young, inexperienced hacker who uses tools and scripts written by others for the purpose of attacking systems. Most of them do not possess enough programming and system knowledge to write or understand such scripts and tools. The growth of the script kiddie has been exponential since the rise of the Internet, as it made available detailed information on breaking into systems and networks. Script kiddies will most often scan thousands of computers looking for those presenting vulnerabilities that they know how to exploit. They often act out of boredom, curiosity, or a desire to "play war" on the Internet.

Today, a *hacker* refers to someone who invades an information system for malicious purposes; for example, a hacker might steal clients' Social Security numbers or change student information. Originally, a hacker simply referred to a person who wanted to further his or her knowledge of computers and attempted to push the system to the limit.

Cyber-criminals are hackers driven by financial gain. These individuals possess advanced skills and have turned to hacking—not for the challenge, but for the money. Many of these cyber-criminals are members of or contractors for criminal organizations who have turned to the Internet to continue their rackets.

With computer crime being so profitable, it is no surprise that *organized crime* has expanded part of its operations into this new area. These criminal organizations have been getting into spamming, phishing, extortion, and all other profitable branches of computer crime. To assist them in their foray into computer crime, criminal organizations have begun recruiting talented hackers to handle the technical aspects of the crime, turning them into cyber-criminals.

As organizations have moved into the digital age, so have *corporate spies.* Information is now stored on network systems with physical access no longer required to access it. Corporate spies have begun taking advantage of this by turning to computer intrusion techniques to gather the information they desire.

As critical infrastructures become reliant on computers and networks for their operations, *terrorists* could seriously disrupt power grids, telecommunications, transportation, and others if they were to exploit vulnerabilities to disrupt or shut down critical functions. This new form of terrorism, known as cyber-terrorism, targets the underlying computers and networks of a nation's critical infrastructure with the intent of provoking public disturbances and threatening life and health.

According to many studies, *insiders* represent the largest threat to a company's information systems and underlying computer infrastructure, but, as the network perimeter gradually disappears, the threat from external sources is likely to increase. The insider threat is generally due to employees finding themselves in positions of extraordinary privilege in relation to the key functions and assets of their organization.

Less stringent supervisory controls over information systems personnel are often due to the highly technical and specialized nature of the work, which is difficult to understand and control. In addition, IS personnel often enjoy a degree of freedom quite different from that considered normal in a more traditional employment area.

Whether the threat is from malicious or subversive activities or from honest errors on the part of staff members, the human aspect is perhaps the most vulnerable aspect of information systems. In light of this, adequate controls should be implemented to ensure that employee wrongdoing is deterred and can be detected.

Reflection and Self-Assessment   11.1

Consult your university's library resources to find examples of one or more of the preceding types of computer criminals.

So, now that you know something about computer crime and computer criminals, let's examine ways to reduce the risk of computer crime in organizations.

INFORMATION SECURITY

The three principles are often referred to as the C-I-A triad.

Information security is defined as the protection of data in a system against unauthorized disclosure, modification, or destruction, and protection of the computer system itself against unauthorized use, modification, or denial of service. It is based on three fundamental principles: confidentiality, availability, and integrity. While the level of security varies from one organization to the next, controls are implemented to achieve one or more of these three **basic principles** (see Figure 11.1):

- *Confidentiality:* Condition that exists when data are held in confidence and are protected from unauthorized disclosure.
- *Data integrity:* State that exists when data stored in an information system are the same as those in the source documents or have been correctly processed from source data and have not been exposed to accidental or malicious alteration or destruction.
- *Availability:* Achieved when the required data can be obtained within the required time frame.

These three principles must be maintained throughout the information life cycle from creation to destruction.

Failure to protect the organization's information adequately could lead to financial losses, legal action, and loss of trust. Controls are thus implemented to protect the information. Much like the preventive/detective/corrective taxonomy we explored for internal controls, IT controls can be classified as physical, technical, or administrative (see Figure 11.2).

Physical security controls are required to protect computers, related equipment, and their contents from espionage, theft, and destruction or damage by accident, fire, or natural disasters (e.g., floods, earthquakes, and hurricanes). They involve the use of locks, security guards, badges, alarms, and similar measures to control access to computers, network equipment, and the processing facility. Other forms of controls such as smoke and fire detectors and generators are implemented to protect against threats such as fire and power outages.

Sometimes referred to as logical controls, **technical security controls** involve the use of safeguards incorporated in computer and telecommunication hardware and software. Firewalls, encryption, access control software, antivirus software, and intrusion detection systems fall into the category of technical security controls.

Firewalls are the first line of defense in protecting the corporate network from network-based threats. An access control policy determines which packets can flow between the network segments protected by firewalls; common techniques include examining packet information (such as source and destination address) and/or determining a message's transmission protocol. A firewall will only be as secure as the policy that it implements, the most effective being designed to restrict all traffic except that which is expressly permitted. You may be familiar with Windows Firewall or McAfee Security Suite, which incorporates firewall technology.

FIGURE 11.1
C-I-A Triad

FIGURE 11.2
Control Taxonomy

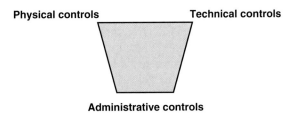

Physical controls   Technical controls

Administrative controls

Intrusion detection systems and intrusion prevention systems detect potentially malicious data and access patterns. Both system types operate at both network and individual computer levels. Network-based systems examine network traffic; they look for specific patterns of anomalous behavior or deviations from the standard behavior of the network. Individual systems detect malicious activity by examining system calls, event logs, critical system files, and other valuable system information.

Access controls protect the confidentiality, integrity, and availability of information resources. Access control can usually be seen as a three-step process: identification (the user provides information in order for the system to recognize him or her), authentication (once identified, the user must prove his or her identity), and authorization (the user is granted the privileges associated with his or her profile). Fundamentally, access controls ensure that only the "right" people have access to specific types of information. For example, as a faculty advisor at my university, I can access the records of any student, but an individual student has access only to his or her own academic records.

Cryptography transforms data to (*a*) hide them, (*b*) prevent them from being modified, and/or (*c*) prevent unauthorized access to them. Most cryptography uses mathematical functions (algorithms) to turn ordinary data into an incomprehensible format.

Management constraints, as well as operational and accountability procedures, are known as **administrative security controls.** Examples include security policies and procedures, security awareness and training, adequate supervision of employees, and security reviews and audits.

A security policy is a clear and concise set of guiding statements supported by management; it provides a framework that ensures that information assets are secured. It is the key component to an organization's information security management system; without it, internal stakeholders have no specific guidance with respect to information system security issues.

Security awareness training is an often-overlooked part of a security management program. Communicating the roles and responsibilities of employees as they are defined in the security policy is the first line of defense in protecting critical computing infrastructures.

Organizations should conduct security reviews in which they monitor the program to ensure compliance, fine-tune the security policy and controls in accordance with the organization's goals, and ensure that any deficiencies are corrected. Security audits will examine whether the information systems operate in accordance with the security policy and ensure that the controls are effective in protecting these systems. The information system auditing process collects and examines evidence to determine whether the information system possesses controls that adequately protect the organization's informational assets in an effective way.

Administrative security controls are established for three main reasons: (1) to provide supplemental controls, (2) to protect information processing resources, and (3) to ensure that all employees have proper authorization to access computing resources.

Physical, technical, and administrative controls can further be classified as preventive, detective, or corrective controls. Preventive controls are implemented to keep unwanted events from occurring, detective controls attempt to identify anomalous and unwanted events once they have occurred, whereas corrective controls remedy problems discovered by detective controls.

Reflection and Self-Assessment 11.2

Under what circumstances could each of the preceding information systems controls be classified as preventive, detective, and/or corrective?

Let's conclude our discussion of computer crime with a look at an important set of internal control ideas: ISACA's Control Objectives for Information and Related Technology (CoBIT).

CoBIT

You'll find ISACA's Web site at www.isaca.org.

ISACA is an acronym for the Information Systems Audit and Control Association, a professional group that bridges the gap between accounting and information technology. They offer the Certified Information Systems Auditor (CISA) credential along with other professional designations. ISACA's well-respected Control Objectives for Information and Related Technology framework gives accountants and other information systems professionals clear guidance in establishing strong internal controls, thereby deterring fraud. Earlier, we talked about COSO's (www.coso.org) contributions: *Internal Control—Integrated Framework* and *Enterprise Risk Management—Integrated Framework.* Singleton (2006, p. 12) explained the relationship between CoBIT and COSO as follows: "COSO does not directly provide guidance on assessing controls, especially IT controls, but CoBIT is well-suited to assess IT controls. Thus, a map from CoBIT to COSO is useful to IT auditors and managers alike in complying with Sarbanes-Oxley adequately and efficiently."

Now in Version 5.0, the **CoBIT framework** looks at the issue of internal control from three points of view: business objectives, information technology resources, and information technology processes. Further, CoBIT is organized in four "domains" of knowledge: plan and organize, acquire and implement, deliver and support, and monitor and evaluate. Poole (2006, p. 24) provides a context for the CoBIT framework by discussing CoBIT's seven **information criteria**:

- *Effectiveness.* The information is relevant and pertinent to the business process and is delivered in a timely, correct, consistent and usable manner.
- *Efficiency.* The information is provided through the optimal (most productive and economical) use of resources.
- *Confidentiality.* Sensitive information is protected from unauthorized [*sic*] disclosure.
- *Integrity.* The information is accurate and complete and is in accordance with business values and expectations.
- *Availability.* The information is available when required by the business process, now and in the future. It also concerns the safeguarding of necessary resources and associated capabilities.

- *Compliance.* The information complies with those laws, regulations and contractual arrangements to which the business process is subject, i.e., externally imposed business criteria.
- *Reliability of information.* Appropriate information is provided for management to operate the entity and exercise its financial and compliance reporting responsibilities.

Notice the way many of the information criteria relate to preventing and detecting computer crime. Computer crime often involves the disclosure of sensitive information—customer lists, employee records, and the like. By putting controls into place with sufficient confidentiality, managers can reduce the risk of computer crime. Such controls might include authorizing employees to access certain parts of the information system based on their position; for example, human resource employees would be able to access employee records, while purchasing department employees would not. The availability criterion talks about the importance of keeping resources safe; those resources would include hardware, software, and the information they contain. Internal controls in this area might include surveillance systems, locked and alarmed doors, and password protection with mandatory password rotation. As an accountant, you may be called upon to design or audit an information system for compliance with Sarbanes-Oxley. A strong internal audit function can be very helpful in achieving CoBIT's compliance criterion. Finally, information that has been compromised by computer crime, such as through Web site defacement, malicious software, or some form of information theft or manipulation, would violate the reliability of information criterion. Applicable internal controls here would include clear policy statements on installing software and various kinds of internal checks on data and information, such as validation rules in a relational database.

Poole also discussed the issue of accountability as it relates to information governance. Business professionals and other stakeholders need to understand the role and responsibilities of at least six parties in keeping information safe and combating computer crime. Those six parties are shown in the **CoBIT accountability framework** in Figure 11.3 (Poole, 2006, p. 24).

Notice how accountability flows downward from stakeholders, through the board of directors, to IT and information security management. In this context, *stakeholders* refers to anyone with an interest in the business; it therefore could refer to customers, employees, investors, and a host of other parties. How does the issue of accountability relate to the topic of computer crime? Stakeholders put their trust in the board of directors, who in turn rely on the expertise of IT and information security management, to guard the organization against the kinds of computer crime discussed in this chapter. When either or both parties fail to meet their responsibilities, stakeholders (including the public) can lose confidence in an organization; some of the officers might even be held legally accountable.

The three parties on the right (audit committee, internal audit, and external audit) work with one another and with IT and information security management to assess and attest to the scope and adequacy of internal controls over information technology. Your accounting degree probably includes at least one required course in auditing, so we won't go into a lot of depth with it in this text. But Figure 11.3 might be the first time you've run across the term *audit committee.* Whittington and Pany (2004, p. 74) offer the following comments about audit committees:

> The New York Stock Exchange, the American Stock Exchange and NASDAQ have established requirements for independent audit committees by all listed companies. According to these requirements, audit committees must consist of at least three independent and financially literate individuals, and the chairman must have accounting or financial management expertise. In addition, the Sarbanes-Oxley Act of 2002 makes the audit committee directly responsible for the appointing, compensating and overseeing [of] the public accounting firm. The SEC regulations require public companies to file a copy of the audit committee's charter every three years and disclose whether its members are independent of management.

FIGURE 11.3   CoBIT Accountability Framework

Source: Poole, 2006, p. 24.

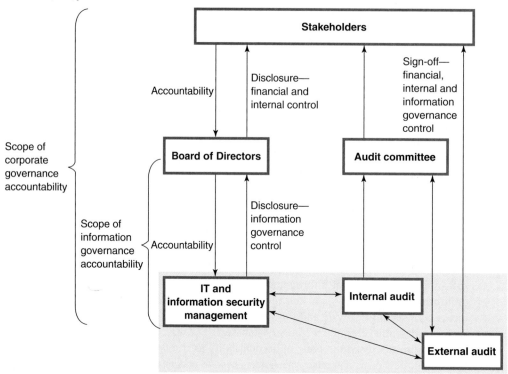

As you can see in Figure 11.3, the audit committee takes some responsibility for internal controls—including those that will prevent, detect, and correct computer crime. With most large accounting information systems employing some form of information technology, a clear understanding of computer crime and CoBIT will be helpful to you as an AIS professional.

CRITICAL THINKING

We've looked at several topics related to computer crime and IT security in this chapter: Carter's taxonomy, risks and threats, perpetrators of computer crime, internal controls, and CoBIT. In this section, I want to tie all of those together with an example.

Consider the following true account of a situation at Blue Security, an anti-spam firm that is now out of business (Lemos, 2006):

> Blue Security had created a small program called Blue Frog to turn a spam flood back on the advertiser, thus raising the cost of sending spam. The program would send a single opt-out request to the advertisers' Web sites for every registered user who received a spam message. Blue Security had about 500,000 subscribers to its service, so if a spam flood hit 20 percent of those users, then 100,000 opt-out requests would hit the advertisers who requested that the spam be sent. In revenge, one of the spammers—reportedly the one called PharmaMaster— attacked Blue Security and all Internet services associated with it for more than two weeks. The attack was so crippling that Blue Security was forced to close its doors.

How would the attack on Blue Security be classified using Carter's taxonomy of computer crime? As with many cases, it would fit in more than one category. We could think of it in

Carter's *target* classification; the attack targeted Blue Security's information system and its data to stop it from using Blue Frog. Since a computer was used to launch the attack, it also could be considered in the *instrumentality* classification. The incident wouldn't be appropriately classified as either incidental or associated; the computer was an integral part of the attack, but the attack was not simply a new version of an old crime.

The chapter discussed 11 business risks and threats associated with computer crime. The attack on Blue Security could be considered an example of any of the following:

- *Fraud.* According to the U.S. Department of Justice definition, the Blue Security case constitutes fraud. Knowledge of computer technology was critical in launching the attack.
- *Service interruption and delays.* During the attack, Blue Security's services were interrupted. If your campus has ever experienced a denial-of-service attack, as mine has, you know the kind of frustration those interruptions and delays can create.
- *Malicious software.* Attackers also sent incredible amounts of spam to Blue Security's customers. They were able to access customers' e-mail addresses by comparing e-mail lists based on responses to spam.
- *Denial-of-service attack.* The attack is a classic example of a distributed denial-of-service (DDOS) attack. SearchSecurity.com describes DDOS like this: "On the Internet, a distributed denial-of-service (DDOS) attack is one in which a multitude of compromised systems attack a single target, thereby causing denial of service for users of the targeted system. The flood of incoming messages to the target system essentially forces it to shut down, thereby denying service to the system to legitimate users."

In terms of perpetrators of computer crime, we could think of Blue Security's attackers as hackers; some sources also have suggested ties to organized crime in the Blue Security case.

Most experts agree that there is no 100 percent foolproof way to prevent situations like the one at Blue Security. But managers can still implement some internal controls to reduce their likelihood and lessen their effects on an information system. Here are some ideas:

- Develop a business continuity plan that lays out how the organization will respond to cyber-attacks.
- Ensure that the information system isn't stretched to its capacity limits. If a system has excess capacity, denial-of-service attacks may not be as severe.
- Purchase insurance to cover the costs associated with system attacks.
- Store data and Web pages on multiple servers so that attackers don't have a single focal point.
- Track activity on the system so that you can detect denial-of-service attacks and other forms of intrusion. By knowing what a system's traffic usually looks like, it's easier to determine when an attack has occurred.

While I was researching material for this section, I came across a good, comprehensive paper talking about DDOS attacks: "Managing the Threat of Denial of Service Attacks" by Householder et al., October 2001. You can find the paper on the Internet; I encourage you to read it if you'd like to know more about this important topic. You can also check out http://staff.washington.edu/dittrich/misc/ddos/ for a comprehensive set of references about DDOS attacks.

How does the Blue Security case relate to the CoBIT framework? The case really touches all four domains of knowledge from CoBIT. Organizations need to plan for such attacks and organize themselves to respond. They need to acquire and implement tools and policies, like those just suggested, to ensure that their response is efficient and effective. With regard to the third CoBIT domain (deliver and support), information systems professionals need to make sure that the tools are available to users. And someone in the organization (whether the IT staff, internal auditors, or some other group) must take responsibility for monitoring the protection plan and evaluating it periodically.

Developing a strong information security response plan helps fulfill CoBIT's information criteria as well. It also promotes the kind of accountability relationships illustrated in Figure 11.3. Finally, organizations can move through the stages of the CoBIT maturity model as their security plans become more sophisticated.

Summary

Here is a summary of the chapter's important points based on its learning objectives:

1. *Explain Carter's taxonomy of computer crime.* Carter identified four basic types of computer crime: target (where the object is to attack the computer itself, often with the intent of compromising its data), instrumentality (where the computer is used to commit the crime), incidental (where the computer is not necessarily required for the crime but is used to make it easier to complete and/or harder to detect), and associated (where the computer is used to commit old crimes in a new way).

2. *Identify and describe business risks and threats to information systems.* Computers expose businesses to at least four specific risks, some of which are also present in non-computerized information systems. First is the risk of fraud; while not unique to a computerized environment, the risk of fraud is increased because of the unique ways computers can be used to commit crime (refer to Carter's taxonomy for specific examples). Error is also an information systems risk; people can make data entry errors or create inaccurate processing instructions, just as they can in noncomputerized systems. Service interruptions and delays are unique to information technology environments; for example, without adequate internal controls, power failures can cause service interruptions. Finally, companies must consider the risk of disclosing confidential information; while not unique to a computerized environment, that risk is enhanced when data are stored electronically.

   The chapter discussed seven specific threats associated with computerized information systems. Intrusions allow a computer criminal to bypass information security and internal controls. Information theft is self-evident; it involves stealing sensitive or proprietary information from the system. Information manipulation doesn't necessarily mean that the information is stolen outright; however, it changes information, often resulting in inaccurate reports or less-than-optimal decision making. Malicious software, for example, a logic bomb, can exist in an information system benignly until a date, event, or condition activates it. At that point, it may change or delete data or cut off access to the information system. In a denial-of-service attack, a computer criminal bombards the information system with requests for information, thus preventing it from fulfilling its legitimate purpose. Think of Web site defacement as digital "tagging" or graffiti. Finally, extortion involves threats from a computer criminal (such as disclosing confidential information) unless the organization meets the criminal's conditions (such as paying cash).

3. *Name and describe common types of computer criminals.* A script kiddie is a relatively inexperienced computer criminal who uses techniques and code written by others. Hacker is a more generalized term referring to anyone who accesses an information system for any criminal/illicit purpose. Cyber-criminals are a subset of hackers; typically, cyber-criminals are motivated by financial gain. Organized crime groups have

taken advantage of information systems as well, often getting involved in phishing, extortion, and other profit-oriented types of computer crime. Corporate spies use computers and technology to gain access to confidential information, trade secrets, and the like. Terrorists may threaten life and public health by their actions, while insiders are employees of an organization who compromise the information system.

4. *Discuss ways to prevent and detect computer crime.* Internal control is at least as important in a computerized information system as it is in manual systems. Physical controls are perhaps the simplest type: locking doors, installing alarms, and requiring identification badges are some examples. Technical controls are part of the computer hardware and software themselves; think of firewalls, virus detection software, and access controls in this group. Finally, administrative controls refer to management policies and procedures designed to promote information security. For example, organizations may develop a clear information security policy and/or require periodic security training for employees.

5. *Explain CoBIT's information criteria and accountability framework.* The Information Systems Audit and Control Association (ISACA) developed and published a well-respected internal control framework specifically focused on IT security: Control Objectives for Information and Related Technology (CoBIT). The framework considers internal control from three perspectives: business objectives, information technology resources, and information technology processes. It identifies seven information characteristics essential to strong IT control: effectiveness, efficiency, confidentiality, integrity, availability, compliance, and reliability. CoBIT's accountability framework discusses the roles and responsibilities of six groups with respect to IT security: stakeholders, the board of directors, the audit committee, IT and information security management, internal audits, and external auditors.

6. *Explain how CoBIT can be used to strengthen internal controls against computer crime.* CoBIT's information criteria, accountability framework, and other components can help information systems professionals identify and assess risk. They also can help assign responsibility and designate authority for various tasks related to information systems security.

Key Terms

administrative security controls, *193*
basic principles of information security, *192*
CoBIT accountability framework, *195*
CoBIT framework, *194*
CoBIT information criteria, *194*
perpetrators, *190*
physical security controls, *192*
risks and threats, *187*
taxonomy for computer crime, *187*
technical security controls, *192*

Chapter References

Carter, D. 1995. "Computer Crime Categories." *FBI Law Enforcement Bulletin*, pp. 21–28.
Lemos, R. (2006, August). "Gangland Web Attacks; How Not to Get Whacked by the Botnet Mafia." *PC Magazine* 25(13), 116. ABI/INFORM Trade & Industry database (Document ID: 11070446111; February 1, 2009).
Poole, V. 2006. "Why Information Security Governance Is Critical to Wider Corporate Governance Demands—A European Perspective." *Information Systems Control Journal* 1, pp. 23–25.
Singleton, T. 2006. "CoBIT—A Key to Success as an IT Auditor." *Information Systems Control Journal* 1, pp. 11–13.
Whittington, R., and K. Pany. 2004. *Principles of Auditing and Other Assurance Services.* 14th ed. New York: McGraw-Hill/Irwin.

End-of-Chapter Activities

1. *Reading review questions.*

   a. What four common classifications are often associated with computer crime?

   b. What computer crime–related risks and threats are associated with information systems?

   c. What categories are commonly associated with computer criminals? Describe each category.

   d. How can organizations safeguard against computer crime? How can they detect it and recover from it if it happens? What role does CoBIT play in those tasks?

   e. What is CoBIT? What are the seven information criteria discussed in the CoBIT framework?

   f. Respond to the questions for this chapter's "AIS in the Business World."

2. *Reading review problem.* The growth of information technology has been a positive force in business; but, as with all innovations, it has a downside risk as well. Consider the following case of identity theft:

   > Federal prosecutors charged 11 men in five countries with orchestrating a high-tech operation that stole more than 40 million credit card numbers from U.S. retailers. The case is the biggest identity-fraud heist ever prosecuted in the U.S. The government said the defendants engaged in a sophisticated scheme involving wireless interception of retailers' data transmissions, "sniffer" programs that stole card numbers as they were being swiped at cash registers, bulk fencing of stolen cards at less than $1 apiece on the Internet, and encrypted computer servers that stored the thieves' digital plunder in Latvia and Ukraine. [One retailer] says it has set aside $202 million to cover costs including settlements with consumers and card-issuing banks. In a statement, the company said that the number of retailers attacked "demonstrates the much broader challenges in protecting sensitive consumer data from this increasing threat."

   As a future accounting professional, you may be called upon to help prevent, detect, or correct situations like that one in your career.

   Source: J. Pereira, J. Levitz, and J. Singer-Vine, "U.S. Indicts 11 in Global Credit-Card Scheme," *The Wall Street Journal* (Eastern Edition), August 6, 2008, p. A1.

   a. Use Carter's taxonomy for computer crime to classify the case.

   b. What business risk(s)/threat(s) are exemplified by it?

   c. Which element(s) of the C-I-A triad was/were compromised in the case?

   d. What internal controls would you recommend to address the problem?

   e. Discuss elements of the CoBIT framework that are relevant to this case.

3. *Multiple choice review.*

   1. Carter suggested a four-part taxonomy of computer crime, comprising:

      a. Technical, physical, administrative, and software crime.

      b. Target, instrumentality, incidental, and associated.

      c. Preventive, detective, corrective, and coercive.

      d. Motivation, expectancy, valence, and instrumentality.

   2. According to the U.S. Department of Justice, which of the following is defined as any illegal act for which knowledge of computer technology is used to commit the offense?

      a. Fraud

      b. Intrusion

      c. Information theft

      d. Malicious software

3. The largest threat to a company's information systems comes from:
    a. Hackers.
    b. Terrorists.
    c. Organized crime.
    d. Insiders.

4. The three fundamental principles that guide the development and implementation of IT controls are:
    a. Physical, technical, and administrative.
    b. Effectiveness, efficiency, and compliance.
    c. Confidentiality, availability, and data integrity.
    d. Preventive, detective, and corrective.

5. In the CoBIT accountability framework, disclosures about information governance control flow from ___ to ___.
    a. IT and information security management; board of directors
    b. Board of directors; stakeholders
    c. External audit; audit committee
    d. Audit committee, stakeholders

4. *Making choices and exercising judgment.*
    a. What would motivate someone to engage in computer crime?
    b. Do a Google search for the most recent list of AICPA Top Ten Technologies. Choose one and explain how it might be used to engage in computer crime.
    c. Suggest at least three specific internal controls you'd employ to prevent, detect, or correct the computer crime you identified above.
    d. Brad Willman contributed to the arrest of several pedophiles in Canada and the United States. But he collected evidence for his investigation by hacking into others' computers. Read about this case in Cori Howard, "Internet Vigilante," *Maclean's* (June 6, 2005). What model of ethics, discussed in Chapter 3, best describes Willman's actions? Were Willman's actions ethical? What legal action, if any, should be taken against Willman?

5. *Field work.*
    a. Use your university library or www.findarticles.com to locate and read T. McCollum, "Computer Crime Surveys Yield Mixed Results," *Internal Auditor* (August 2004). Prepare a brief oral or written report on the article, relating it to the material presented in this chapter.
    b. Point your Web browser to www.cybercrime.gov, the Web site for the U.S. Justice Department's Computer Crime and Intellectual Property section. Based on criteria provided by your instructor, summarize one or more of the press releases on the site.
    c. Use a literature search to investigate one or more of the following computer criminals. Describe each one's crime; also compare and contrast them in terms of personal characteristics and motivations.
        i.   Jeanson James Ancheta
        ii. Kevin Poulson
        iii. Robert Tappan Morris

6. *Applying Carter's taxonomy.* Which element(s) of Carter's taxonomy apply to each of the following situations? If more than one category applies, explain why.
    a. A bookkeeper steals cash as it comes into the company. The bookkeeper later falsifies accounting entries using general ledger software to cover the trail.
    b. A bored teenager initiates a denial-of-service attack on his Internet service provider's information system.

c. A disgruntled employee uses a previously installed "back door" into an information system to lock out other users by changing their passwords.

d. A gang of criminals breaks into a local retail store. They steal all the store's computers and then later hack into them for the purpose of identity theft.

e. A pair of computer criminals uses e-mail to contact victims for an illegal pyramid scheme. They use money from new investors, rather than profits, to pay off old investors, keeping most of the money themselves.

f. A recently fired employee laid the groundwork for corporate espionage by installing spyware on the company's network.

g. A student discovers the password to his university's information system. He then hacks the system to change grades for himself and his friends.

h. A woman impersonates her wealthy employer, stealing personal information about the employer from her bank's information system.

7. *Identifying business risks and threats.* Which type(s) of business risks/threats described in the chapter best applies to each situation below? If more than one applies, explain why.

a. Blackmail based on stolen information.

b. Concurrent attacks against a determined target.

c. Digital graffiti.

d. Discovery of customer Social Security numbers by external parties.

e. Hacking.

f. Intentional modification of information.

g. Mistakes in data entry.

h. Power failure.

i. Salami technique.

j. Stealing research and development data for new products.

k. Trojan horse.

8. *Classification of controls.* Classify each of the following controls as physical, technical, or administrative. Then, describe each control in your own words.

a. Access control software

b. Adequate supervision of employees

c. Badges

d. Encryption

e. Firewalls

f. Internal audits

g. Intrusion detection systems

h. Locks

i. Ongoing training regarding security issues

j. Security guards

k. Security policy

l. Smoke detectors

m. Universal power supplies

9. *CoBIT information criteria.* Indicate which of the CoBIT information criteria are violated in each of the following independent scenarios. Justify your choices.

a. Financial statements for the year ended December 31, 2011, are completed and published in June 2012.

   b. A company with $1 million in annual revenues maintains an accounting information system with paper journals and ledgers.

   c. Employee names, identification numbers, job classifications, and addresses are posted on a company Web site.

   d. A careless employee spilled a soft drink on a file server. The server was damaged and could not be used for three days.

   e. The CEO and CFO fail to provide the documents required by the Sarbanes-Oxley Act.

10. *Internal controls.* For each situation presented in the preceding problem, suggest one or more internal controls. Classify the controls as preventive, detective, or corrective.

11. *CoBIT.* Point your Web browser to www.isaca.org. Create a free account that will give you access to the CoBIT documents; then, work with a group of students to address one or more of the following questions:

   a. What are the five IT Governance Focus Areas identified in the framework? Describe at least one of them.

   b. How is CoBIT related to the COSO frameworks on internal control and enterprise risk management?

   c. What are the components of CoBIT? How do they relate to one another?

   d. How would managers apply the systems development life cycle to develop strong controls using CoBIT?

   e. Compare and contrast the CoBIT maturity model with the capability maturity model discussed earlier in the text.

12. *Terminology.* Please match each item on the right to the most appropriate item on the left.

1. Confidentiality	a. Computers used to carry out a crime
2. Creating fake refunds to benefit a friend	b. Crime classification that does not necessarily require a computer
3. Data diddling	c. Data are protected from unauthorized disclosure
4. Human element	d. Designed to help restore consumer confidence
5. Incidental	e. Information manipulation
6. Instrumentality	f. Intentionally changing information in a system
7. Logic bomb	g. Interest of less than one cent diverted to computer criminal's account
8. Salami technique	h. Most vulnerable part of an information system
9. Sarbanes-Oxley Act	i. One type of service interruption/delay
10. Willful neglect	j. Shuts down a payroll system if a specific employee number is deleted

13. *Multiple choice questions.* Consider the following short case in responding to these questions:

Tim was upset with his accounting instructor because of the grade he earned in her class. As an act of revenge, Tim used a computer program he downloaded from the Internet to discover the instructor's password for the university's information system. He used the password to infiltrate the system and introduced a program that would shut it down; he contacted his accounting instructor and threatened to activate the program if she did not change his grade.

  1. Which elements of Carter's taxonomy apply?

    a. Target and instrumentality

    b. Target and incidental

    c. Instrumentality and incidental

    d. Target, instrumentality, and incidental

2. The chapter discussed seven common types of computer criminals. Which types best describe Tim?

   a. Insider, script kiddie

   b. Script kiddie, hacker

   c. Insider, hacker

   d. Insider, hacker, script kiddie

3. Which of the following are administrative controls the university should implement to prevent such situations in the future?

   a. Backup files, strong passwords

   b. Backup files, mandatory password rotation

   c. Strong passwords, mandatory password rotation

   d. Backup files, strong passwords, mandatory password rotation

4. Because Tim is threatening his instructor, his actions are best described as:

   a. Extortion.

   b. Malicious software.

   c. Information theft.

   d. Service interruption.

5. If Tim activates the program, all of the following CoBIT information criteria will be compromised except:

   a. Compliance.

   b. Effectiveness.

   c. Availability.

   d. Reliability of information.

14. *Statement evaluation.* Indicate whether each of the following statements is (i) always true, (ii) sometimes true, or (iii) never true. For those that are (ii) sometimes true, explain when the statement is true.

   a. A specific instance of computer crime can involve multiple categories from Carter's taxonomy.

   b. Computer crime involves using a computer to commit a crime.

   c. Computer crime is perpetrated by organized crime groups.

   d. Confidentiality, availability, and data integrity comprise the C-I-A triad.

   e. Each element of the C-I-A triad is also mentioned in CoBIT's information criteria.

   f. Hackers may be motivated by profit or by entertainment.

   g. Information technology controls can be physical, technical, or administrative.

   h. Organizations that implement CoBIT are immune to computer crime.

   i. Perpetrators of computer crime come from outside the organization.

   j. The "salami technique" is an example of information manipulation.

15. *Prior material application.*

   a. Consider the five generic elements of most accounting information systems. For each element, suggest one way it could be compromised via computer crime.

   b. Read "Protect Small Business" by Joseph T. Wells in the March 2003 issue of *Journal of Accountancy;* consider the case presented in the opening paragraphs of the article (Denise, a bookkeeper for a small trucking firm). Work with a group of students and/or interview a forensic accountant/certified fraud examiner to suggest a series of steps you could use to investigate the fraud. Document your steps using one of the techniques described in Part Two of the text.

   c. Explain how the use of XBRL helps organizations respond to CoBIT's seven information criteria.

d. This chapter provided a three-part taxonomy for IT controls; earlier in the text, you learned that internal controls have four broad purposes. Fill in the table below with appropriate examples; be prepared to explain your reasoning.

Internal Control Purpose	Physical Controls	Technical Controls	Administrative Controls
Safeguard assets			
Ensure financial statement reliability			
Promote operating efficiency			
Encourage compliance with management directives			

Part **Four**

Business Processes

Many AIS courses focus on business processes. In this section, we'll explore a fundamental, comprehensive set of business processes. In addition, we'll apply many of the topics from previous chapters (e.g., AIS structure, transaction processing and internal controls) within the context of those processes. The first two chapters in this section are devoted to processes that generalize easily across organizations; the third chapter discusses processes that often vary in detail (i.e., conversion, financing, human resources).

Chapter **Twelve**

Sales/Collection Process

AIS in the Business World

World of Warcraft

If you don't have a World of Warcraft (WoW) account, the odds are good that you know someone who does. WoW is one of the most popular massively multi-user online roleplaying games today. (That's a mouthful, isn't it? It's MMORPG for short.) Developed by Blizzard Entertainment (www.blizzard.com), signing up to play WoW is a fairly straightforward process that goes something like this:

1. Purchase or download the software from a retail store or directly from Blizzard.
2. Create an account that includes personal data, including billing information.
3. Create a character based on game parameters and personal preference.
4. Begin leveling the character by completing various activities (called "quests") alone or with others.

From Blizzard's point of view, we would refer to those steps as the "sales/ collection" process. And, in this chapter, we'll apply many of the concepts we've discussed up until now within the context of the sales/collection process. The next two chapters in this section look at other business processes.

Discussion Questions

1. Why do we organize AIS courses in terms of business processes?
2. What are the steps involved in the sales/collection process?
3. How are the five generic parts of the AIS discussed in Chapter 1 applied/exemplified within the context of the sales/collection process?

In AIS study, we combine sales and collection activities because of their logical relationship to one another. But, as you're probably aware, a "collection" does not necessarily constitute a "sale" according to GAAP. The rules of accrual-basis accounting still apply—we just organize the knowledge a little differently in AIS.

This chapter, and the two that follow it, put together much of what you've already learned within the context of specific business processes. So what is a "business process"? At its most basic, a **business process** is a set of procedures and policies designed to create value for some organizational stakeholder. Those stakeholders might include customers, stockholders, employees or vendors.

Porter (1998) developed the **value chain** as a way to think about the processes organizations use to create value for their stakeholders. The value chain (shown in Figure 12.1) is organized into two parts: primary activities are directly involved in value creation, while support activities provide essential services to the organization.

Consider, for example, the value created by your university. If you were extraordinarily hardworking and diligent, you might be able to get the knowledge afforded by your degree on your own—but very few students have that kind of determination. So, instead, it's much more effective and efficient for you to gain that knowledge through an organization (your university) and its business processes.

While the details of processes can vary significantly from one organization to another, most of them share some common features. Those common features will be our focus in the next three chapters, starting here with the sales/collection process.

When you finish studying this chapter, you should be able to complete the following tasks within the context of the sales/collection process:

You might need to review some of the fundamental concepts from earlier chapters as you read and study this one.

1. Explain its role and purpose.
2. List and discuss, in order, the steps in the process.
3. Explain how the generic structure of most AIS applies to the process.

FIGURE 12.1
Porter's Value Chain

Primary activities

Inbound logistics: move raw materials

Operations: transform materials into finished products

Outbound logistics: move finished product

Marketing & sales: sell the product

Service: provide support as needed

Support activities

Procurement: purchasing function

Information technology: R & D, other forms of IT

Human resource management: personnel-related functions

Infrastructure: other aspects of the organization

4. Process common transactions.
5. Design and critique internal controls based on common risk exposures.
6. Develop and interpret process-related systems documentation.

PROCESS DESCRIPTION

The fundamental purpose of the sales/collection process is to provide goods and services to clients and to collect payment from them. Without an effective sales/collection process, an organization will soon cease to exist. Ineffective processes may arise from lack of demand for a company's product or service, inadequate exposure in the marketplace, and/or poor credit policies (with the attendant difficulty in cash collections).

So, what exactly are the **steps** involved in an effective sales/collection process? Consider the list below (Hollander, Denna, and Cherrington, 2000):

1. *Take a customer's order.* Sales staff can take a customer's order in a variety of ways: face-to-face, via the Internet, through the mail, over the phone, and others.
2. *Approve the customer's credit.* Once the customer's order is in hand, the organization often must approve his/her credit. When you shop in a store, credit approval comes from scanning your credit card. Organizations doing business with one another, though, often extend credit directly—without the use of a credit card.
3. *Fill the order based on approved credit.* If the customer's credit is approved, the warehouse staff can fill the order and prepare it for shipment.
4. *Ship the product (if necessary).* In the best-case scenario, a separate shipping department actually sends the product to the customer (we'll talk more about this idea when we consider internal controls later in the chapter). If a customer is paying cash, she might take the product on a cash-and-carry basis, rather than having it shipped. In some cases, a customer may be forced to pay cash for goods and services if his credit is insufficient or he has a poor payment history.
5. *Bill the customer.* When goods and services are sold on credit, the billing department will typically send an invoice or statement on a monthly basis. Your credit card company, for example, follows that process. They are a third-party intermediary between you and the company that sold the goods and services, but the process is basically the same.
6. *Collect payment.* In a perfect world, the client timely remits payment. The client may take advantage of cash discounts for early payment. Customers that fail to pay timely may undergo more extensive collection processes and/or be denied further credit. Systems for recording cash collections fall into two broad groups: open invoice and balance forward. In an open invoice system, a customer's remittance is tied to a specific invoice or set of invoices. While more complex to maintain, open invoice systems do provide more detail for decision making. In a balance forward system, remittances are not applied to a particular invoice; rather, they are simply applied to a customer's total outstanding balance.
7. *Process uncollectible receivables as necessary.* In a worst-case scenario, when all attempts to collect cash have failed, the organization may be forced to write off its bad debts using a method approved under GAAP.

Figure 12.2 presents a data flow diagram that captures the seven steps at a high level (we'll look at a more detailed flowchart later in the chapter).

FIGURE 12.2   Sales/Collection DFD

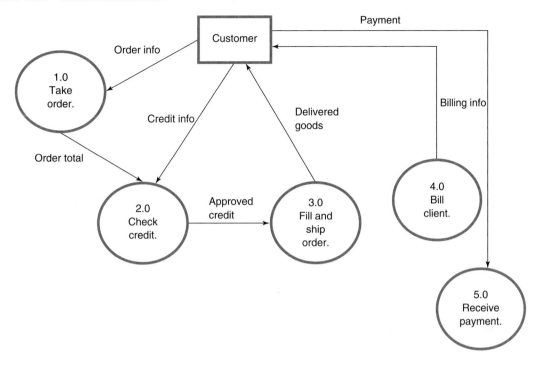

Keep in mind that the seven steps are very generic in nature. In your accounting career, you may be called upon to design an effective sales/collection process and/or to evaluate one as part of an audit. In either case, use the seven steps as a guide, but make allowances for individual company practices.

Next, let's consider some of the documents that are commonly involved in the sales/collection process.

Reflection and Self-Assessment   12.1

Consider the way your campus bookstore or other source sold you your textbooks this term. How did the transaction, from the bookstore's point of view, exemplify the steps in the sales/collection process?

AIS STRUCTURE

In Chapter 1, you learned that most accounting information systems comprise five parts: inputs, processes, outputs, storage, and internal controls. Let's take a look at how those five parts are applied to the sales/collection process.

From an AIS perspective, inputs and outputs most often refer to documents. Documents in the sales/collection process can be paper-based, electronic, or some combination of the two. Table 12.1 summarizes the most commonly used documents in the sales/collection

TABLE 12.1   **Documents Associated with the Sales/Collection Process**

Document Name	Basic Purpose	Originator	Recipient
Customer order	To summarize items ordered and prices	Sales department	Warehouse
Picking list	To guide selection of items from warehouse	Warehouse	Shipping department
Packing list	To specify contents of shipment	Shipping department	Customer
Bill of lading	To specify freight terms	Shipping department	Common carrier
Customer invoice	To bill client	Billing department	Customer
Customer check	To remit payment	Customer	Cash receipts department
Remittance advice	To provide a source document for AIS	Customer	Accounting department
Deposit slip	To transmit cash receipts to bank	Cash receipts department	Bank

process; we'll take a look at each of them in more detail in the following paragraphs. Note that an output from one step in the sales/collection process often serves as an input to subsequent steps; likewise, an output from one organization can serve as an input to another.

As we discuss **documents** associated with the sales/collection process, keep in mind that we're examining them from the point of view of the *selling* organization. The customer will have its own names and formats for the same documents; we'll explore those in the next chapter. Table 12.1 gives you a broad overview of the documents we'll be discussing in the next few pages.

In the first step of the sales/collection process (take customer order), a sales clerk (or someone with a similar title) notes the type and quantity of merchandise the customer is requesting. The customer's order, then, might be filled out by the sales staff or the customer him- or herself. In many cases, the customer may simply bring the needed merchandise to a cash register; in that situation, a formal "order" does not exist. See Figure 12.3 for an illustration of a customer order form.

The picking list comes into play when an order is filled based on approved credit. A picking list typically tells warehouse or stockroom staff what products to take (pick) off the shelves to fill the customer's order. If you've ever ordered any merchandise from the Internet or a catalog, you've probably seen a packing list. It serves as a final check of what is actually loaded into the box before the goods are shipped to the customer.

A bill of lading is used when the goods are shipped to the customer. A bill of lading is a contract between the seller (such as Amazon.com) and a common carrier (such as Federal Express or United Parcel Service). The bill of lading tells the common carrier where to deliver the goods. It also explains the freight terms associated with the shipment. **Freight terms** identify two important items: who is responsible for the goods while they're in transit and who ends up paying the freight bill.

Customer invoices vary as much as the companies that issue them. Typically, though, they will contain some key information: the customer's name and address, the mailing address for the company, the total amount due, and the due date. To foster good internal control (discussed later in the chapter), invoices should be prepared by a billing department once the goods have been received by the customer.

FIGURE 12.3 **Customer Order**

Your Name: _____

Shipping Address: _____
(No PO box, please)

City: _____ State: _____ ZIP code: _____

Phone (days): _____

Phone (eves): _____

Credit Card #: _____ Exp. Date: _____
(MasterCard, Visa, or Discover only, please)

Signature: _____
Your Distributor's ID #:   **Name:**
(Check on the e-rep's page for this name & number.)

_____

Please send a free Fuller Brush Master Catalog. ____Yes   ____ No

Item Number	Qty:	Description:	Price each	Total

Handling Charge Chart:

$0 to	$24.99	$3.95
$25 to	$49.99	$4.95
$50.00	and up	$5.95

Sales Tax Policy:
Since we have a business presence in all states, we are required by law to collect sales tax for every state. Need help finding your area's sales tax? Just call us at: 1-800-522-0499.

Merchandise total	
Handling from chart	
Merchandise subtotal	
Sales tax on subtotal	
Total amount due	

Make checks payable to: The Fuller Brush Company
PO Box 420130
Great Bend, KS 67530-1247

To motivate customers to pay as quickly as possible, a company may offer a cash discount. Cash discounts commonly look like this: 2/10, n/30. Read that notation as "two-ten, net thirty." In plain English, it says that the customer may take a 2 percent discount off the merchandise cost if the bill is paid within 10 days. Otherwise, the full (net) amount of the invoice is payable within 30 days. The discount will not apply to any freight charges included on the invoice.

Suppose, for example, CLM Corporation sends an invoice dated February 2, 2011, to a customer that includes $6,200 for merchandise and $100 for freight. If the cash discount is 2/10, n/30, the customer may pay the bill on or before February 12. The total remitted will be $6,200 \times 98\% + \$100$ for freight = $6,176. Otherwise, the full invoice amount ($6,300) is due within 30 days of February 2.

Collecting payment from a customer on open account involves two documents: the customer check and the remittance advice. While I'm sure you know what a check is, you may not be familiar with the term *remittance advice.* Basically, the purpose of a remittance advice is to *advise* the company that you are *remitting* payment on an invoice. Consider, for example, your monthly credit card bill. When you receive it, you tear off a portion to send back with your check. The portion you tear off is the remittance advice. It becomes the source document for journal entries related to cash receipts. The check itself goes to the bank; the remittance advice goes to the accounting department for recordkeeping. You can see a generic remittance advice in Figure 12.4.

Ideally, all cash received by a company is deposited daily in the bank. A deposit slip typically lists each item to be deposited with some identifying information (such as an ABA or routing number for checks), the account holder's name and account number, and the date. The bank issues a receipt as evidence that the deposit has been accepted.

How do organizations process the input documents to create outputs for the sales/collection process? They use th seven steps discussed earlier in this chapter. In addition, transactions must be appropriately recorded in the AIS.

Reflection and Self-Assessment   12.2

What journal entries would you make for each of the following transactions? Which input/output documents would trigger each one?

- Sale of inventory on account
- Sale of inventory for cash

- Cash collections for sales on account
- Inventory returns
- Payment of freight charges
- Bad debt write-offs

FIGURE 12.4
Remittance advice

REMITTANCE ADVICE FOR CPD INC.
CHECK # 3225 - CHECK DATE 04/14/11

INVOICE #	INV DATE	ORIG AMT	PAYMENT	REFERENCE
145216	03/12/11	$ 40.00	$ 40.00	WARRANTY REPLACEMENT
144540	03/04/11	158.00	158.00	SSI STOCK
146035	03/25/11	1,890.00	1,700.00	CIVIC PLAZA
TOTALS		$ 2,088.00	$ 1,898.00	

As you read in Chapter 1, "storage" in the AIS often happens in a computer database or other electronic medium. Even in the small number of cases where storage happens with paper files, though, the AIS still must capture certain basic information in master files and transaction files. Table 12.2 shows a list of the **common files**, along with the data they would contain.

In the next section, we'll turn our attention to the last generic AIS element: internal controls.

INTERNAL CONTROLS

Organizations commonly encounter various kinds of risks in the sales/collection process. Accountants, therefore, must design internal controls to ameliorate those risks as efficiently and effectively as possible.

The numbered items below are common risks faced in the sales/collection process. The associated lettered items represent **internal controls** that might lessen those risks. Keep in mind that the list is illustrative, not definitive; that is, each organization's risks and controls must be assessed and developed individually, based on time, money, and human constraints.

1. Granting credit to customers who are not creditworthy.

    a. *Relying on third-party vendors to grant credit.* A company may choose not to extend credit itself. Rather, it may rely on third parties such as Visa, Discover, or American Express to approve customers' credit.

TABLE 12.2   File Structures in the Sales/Collection Process

File name	File type	Primary key	Other data
Employee	Master	Employee ID	Last name, first name Street address, city, state, ZIP code Phone number Emergency contact Department Hire date
Customer	Master	Customer ID	Customer company name Street address, city, state, ZIP code Phone number Contact person name Credit limit Date of first sale
Inventory	Master	Product ID	Product name Beginning balance date Beginning balance quantity Beginning balance cost per unit Preferred supplier
Sales	Transaction	Transaction ID	Transaction date Customer ID Employee ID
Sales/inventory	Junction	Transaction ID	Product ID Quantity sold Selling price per unit

    b. Establishing a formal credit-approval process, independent of the sales function. In the best possible situations, salespeople will not have the authority to grant credit directly. If you've ever purchased a new car, for example, you may have observed that the salesperson does not handle the financing part of the transaction. Granting credit independently from sales is an example of separation of duties.

    c. Conducting a cash-only business. Smaller organizations may opt not to grant credit or accept third-party credit cards at all. While they may lose some sales as a result, they do not run the risk of inappropriately granting credit.

2. "Selling" products that are not available.

    a. Checking stock-on-hand before completing a customer's order. While salespeople should not grant credit, they should be able to check inventory levels directly or via an information system. Without that ability, customers may be frustrated and the organization may lose business.

    b. Maintaining adequate inventory. An organization must constantly balance the need to have sufficient inventory on hand with the costs of maintaining that inventory. Costs include tying up cash in inventory, insurance, maintenance (such as keeping perishable products cool), and supervision/security costs. Although beyond the scope of this text, you may be familiar with terms like just-in-time, economic order quantity, and reorder point as methods for maintaining adequate inventory.

3. Filling the customer's order incorrectly.

    a. Incorporating independent order checking. Warehouse personnel may misread the picking slip, select the wrong inventory from the shelves, or put incorrect quantities in the customer's order. Ideally, the organization should find and correct those errors before turning the merchandise over to the customer. An independent check by another member of the warehouse staff, or a member of the shipping staff, can reduce the chances that the wrong goods are shipped to the customer.

    b. Using information technology to fill orders. Computerized order-filling is becoming more and more common in some sectors of the economy. Many hospital pharmacies, for example, use computers to fill prescriptions. While the orders should still be checked by a pharmacist for accuracy, using IT first can be much more efficient.

4. Damaging goods in the delivery process.

    a. Packing merchandise adequately prior to shipment. Whether handled by a common carrier or the organization's own shipping department, goods should be properly packaged prior to shipment. Omaha Steaks (www.omahasteaks.com), for example, ships its products in Styrofoam containers with dry ice. The food therefore arrives at the customer's location fresh.

    b. Insuring goods in transit. If you have ever shipped anything valuable, you may have purchased insurance for it. While insurance cannot prevent damage to the goods, it can mitigate financial risk by providing the customer reimbursement for the insured value if the goods are damaged in transit.

5. Billing the customer incorrectly.

    a. Matching documents prior to billing. The customer should only be billed for what has been ordered and shipped. So, the billing department should receive a copy of both the customer's order and the bill of lading. Once those documents are received, billing clerks can generate customer invoices from the accounting information system.

    b. Using information technology to ensure numerical accuracy. In most accounting information systems, computers generate invoices. Mathematical errors are thus avoided.

6. Mishandling cash receipts.

The three basic duties to be separated include custody of an asset, its recordkeeping, and authorization for its use.

   a. *Separating duties.* As you learned in Chapter 3, separation of duties is a basic internal control in most accounting information systems. When it comes to the sales/collection process, cash should be deposited daily in the bank (custody). Accountants should use remittance advices as the source documents for journal entries (recordkeeping). And signatories on the checking account should not be allowed to handle cash received from customers (authorization).

   b. *Restrictively endorsing checks when they are received.* When you deposit checks in your bank account, you have to sign the back first—that's an endorsement. A restrictive endorsement includes the phrase "for deposit only" before the signature. Many banks encourage or require customers also to include their account number as part of the endorsement. Although managers should take great care not to lose or misplace checks once they have been endorsed, a restrictive endorsement can ensure that misplaced or lost checks are not cashed.

   c. *Reconciling the bank statement at least monthly.* At the very least, an independent accountant or someone who does not handle cash receipts or payments should reconcile the bank statement when it is received. The Association of Certified Fraud Examiners (www.cfenet.com) recommends that checking accounts be reconciled at least weekly—a process that is now entirely achievable with online banking records. As you may know, reconciling the bank statement involves accounting for timing differences in what the bank knows versus what the depositor knows; it also helps correct errors made by either the depositor or the bank.

Those six risks, and the suggested internal controls that accompany them, are by no means exhaustive. In designing and evaluating internal controls for the sales/collection process, you must develop an intimate knowledge of an organization's processes and personnel. Use your own creativity and critical-thinking abilities, coupled with your sense of cost–benefit issues, when confronted with the important task of internal control assessment in practice.

Reflection and Self-Assessment   12.3

Relate the six risks described above to Brown's taxonomy of risk. Explain whether each suggested control is primarily preventive/detective/corrective. Suggest one additional internal control for each risk.

SYSTEMS DOCUMENTATION

In Part Two of the text, we looked at three major ways to document the accounting information system: flowcharts, data flow diagrams, and REA models. Figure 12.5 shows a partial flowchart of the seven steps in the sales/collection process. (The partial flowchart ends in the warehouse, although the process continues through the shipping, billing, and cash receipts departments. You'll be asked to finish the flowchart in the end-of-chapter activities.) Figure 12.2 (presented earlier in the chapter) illustrates a Level Zero data flow diagram of the sales/collection process. We'll take a look at a REA model of the sales/collection process in the critical thinking application for this chapter.

FIGURE 12.5
Partial Flowchart of the Sales/Collection Process

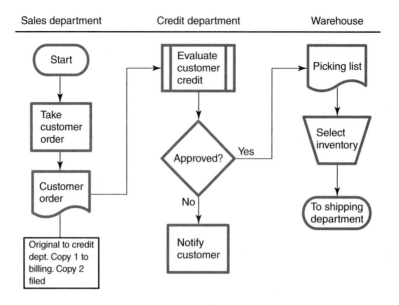

CRITICAL THINKING

Consider the following description of a sales/collection process:

Smoothies-R-Us prepares fresh, healthy fruit smoothies; at present, their menu includes six choices, each of which can be ordered in two sizes (small and large). Management expects to update and expand the menu as time goes on. When a customer enters the store, a staff member takes his/her order and inputs the details, including the customer's first name, into the cash register. The cash register is connected to a visual display in the smoothie-making area. The customer pays (cash, credit card, or gift card) and receives his/her order a few minutes afterward. All Smoothies-R-Us employees are cross-trained, so any one of them can perform any of the preceding tasks.

Let's look at how some of the concepts from this chapter would be applied to Smoothies-R-Us' sales/collection process. First, we can document the process with a REA model as shown in Figure 12.6.
Here are some examples of database tables for the process:

1. Take order table
   a. <u>Order number</u>
   b. Date
   c. [Customer name]

2. Smoothies table
   a. <u>Smoothie name</u>
   b. Small smoothie price
   c. Large smoothie price

3. Take order / smoothies table
   a. <u>[Order number]</u>
   b. <u>[Smoothie name]</u>
   c. Smoothie size
   d. Number ordered

FIGURE 12.6
REA model of Smoothies-R-Us sales / collection process

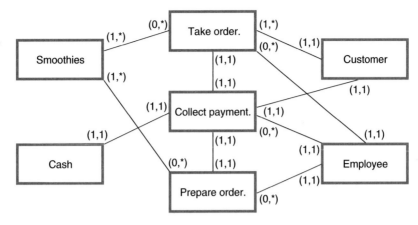

Smoothies-R-Us would use queries to calculate the total cost of each order; periodically, the store could run a report to determine the popularity of each smoothie.

The table below identifies some risks associated with the sales/collection process; it also shows internal controls to address each risk:

Risk	Control
Order taken incorrectly	• Repeating order back to customer • Visual display of order
Incorrect prices charged	• Prices programmed in cash register • Prices displayed on menu
Poor quality smoothies	• Employee training • Standardized recipes

How would you describe the Smoothies-R-Us sales/collection process using the capability maturity model? In the absence of other information, it would likely be considered "defined." Organizational standards for making the smoothies would be in place to ensure consistency and quality regardless of who is making a smoothie; other organizational processes (such as asking for a customer's name to identify his or her order) would also make the process defined.

Reflection and Self-Assessment   12.4

Add a few sentences to the Smoothies-R-Us description above that would suggest the process is managed.

Summary

This chapter began our discussion of business processes by looking at the sales/collection process. In addition to introducing new information about the process, we also saw how to apply other topics. Here's a summary of the chapter's main points, structured according to its learning objectives:

1. *Explain its role and purpose.* The sales/collection process helps accounting professionals track inventory sales and related cash collections. Because sales are the lifeblood of

most business organizations, fair, accurate, and complete accounting is critical. In addition, assets associated with the sales/collection process, such as inventory and cash, are more subject to fraud than other types of assets.

2. *List and discuss, in order, the steps in the process.* The sales/collection process comprises seven steps: (a) Take a customer's order. (b) Approve the customer's credit. (c) Fill the order based on approved credit. (d) Ship the product. (e) Bill the customer. (f) Collect payment. (g) Process uncollectible receivables as necessary.

3. *Explain how the generic structure of most AIS applies to the process.* As described in Chapter 1, a generic accounting information system has five elements: inputs, processes, outputs, storage, and internal controls. Inputs and outputs most often come in the form of paper-based or electronic documents, such as the customer order, picking list, packing list, bill of lading, customer invoice, customer check, remittance advice, and deposit slip. For each document, accountants should understand its content and purpose, where it originates and where it terminates. The sales/collection process includes three major types of storage files: master (e.g., customers and inventory), transaction (e.g., sales), and junction (e.g., sales/inventory). Common transactions can be processed with paper-based journals and ledgers, or with the benefit of information technology (such as ERP systems and general ledger software). XBRL also includes a multitude of tags for information related to the process. Internal controls for the sales/collection process help fulfill the four purposes of internal control: safeguarding assets, ensuring financial statement reliability, promoting operating efficiency, and encouraging compliance with management directives.

4. *Process common transactions.* Common transactions associated with the sales/collection process include sales of goods and services for cash and on account, cash collections for sales on account, inventory returns, freight payments, and bad debt write-offs.

5. *Design and critique internal controls based on common risk exposures.* Most sales/collection processes have at least six major risk exposures. Table 12.3 summarizes the information discussed in the chapter.

6. *Develop and interpret process-related systems documentation.* Figures 12.4, 12.5, and 12.6 in the chapter present, respectively, a flowchart, data flow diagram, and REA model of the sales/collection process.

TABLE 12.3
Risks and Internal Controls in the Sales/Collection Process

Risk	Recommended Controls
Granting credit inappropriately	Third-party vendors Formal credit approval process Cash-only business
Selling unavailable products	Inventory verification Maintaining adequate inventory
Filling the order incorrectly	Independent order checking Information technology
Delivering damaged goods	Adequate packing Insurance
Billing incorrectly	Document matching Information technology
Mishandling cash receipts	Separation of duties Restrictive check endorsements Bank reconciliations

Key Terms

business process, *209*
common files, *215*
documents, *212*

freight terms, *212*
internal controls, *215*
steps, *210*

value chain, *209*

Chapter References

Hollander, A. S., E. L. Denna, and J. O. Cherrington. 2000. *Accounting, Information Technology and Business Solutions.* 2nd ed. New York: Irwin/McGraw-Hill.

Porter, M. 1998. *Competitive Advantage: Creating and Sustaining Superior Performance.* New York: Free Press.

End-of-Chapter Activities

1. *Reading review questions.*

   a. What activities are accounted for in the sales/collection process?

   b. What are the steps in the sales/collection process?

   c. How are the five generic elements of the AIS exemplified in the sales/collection process?

   d. What recordable transactions are commonly associated with the sales/collection process? How are they recorded in the AIS?

   e. What internal controls do organizations use in the sales/collection process? What risks do they address?

   f. Respond to the questions for this chapter's "AIS in the Business World."

2. *Reading review problem.* Dean is the owner and manager of the AIM Mail Center in Rancho Cucamonga, California; the store is a franchise of AIM Mail Centers. The corporate Web site (www.aimmailcenters.com/index.html) provides a list of the company's services, which include an authorized UPS shipping outlet, packing needs, money orders, mail service, office gifts, money transfer, business cards, and office supplies.

   Often, a customer brings in material to be mailed without proper packaging. In that situation, Dean selects appropriate packaging from the store's inventory. He prepares the package for shipment and tells the customer how much shipping will cost based on the carrier and expected delivery date. The customer makes a choice; Dean prepares the shipping documents and collects payment. The store accepts cash and major credit cards, but not checks. Dean then puts the package with others to be shipped via the same carrier; major common carriers make daily visits to the store to pick up the packages.

   Consider the business process described above as you answer these questions.

   a. How does it align with the generic sales/collection process described in the chapter?

   b. Which documents discussed in the chapter are exemplified?

   c. What are AIM Mail Center's risk exposures? What are Dean's risk exposures?

   d. What internal controls would you recommend to address the risks?

   e. In a format specified by your instructor, document the business process.

3. *Multiple choice review*

   1. In a well-designed sales/collection process, the customer's credit should be evaluated:

      a. As the first step.

      b. Immediately after taking the customer's order.

      c. Immediately before billing the customer.

      d. By the salesperson taking the order.

   2. A remittance advice:

      a. Is the source document used to record cash receipts from a customer.

      b. Is the same as a sales invoice.

      c. Is not needed if payments are accepted only with checks.

      d. Is deposited in the bank.

3. Companies often rely on third-party vendors to avoid the risk of:

   a. Filling orders incorrectly.

   b. Selling products that are not available.

   c. Granting credit to customers who are not creditworthy.

   d. Billing the customer incorrectly.

4. A journal entry debits Cash and credits Accounts Receivable. Which of the following transactions is it recording?

   a. A cash sale

   b. Cash collected from a client

   c. Cash collected as deferred revenue

   d. Operating cash flow

5. All of the following are master files associated with the sales/collection process except:

   a. Employee.

   b. Customer.

   c. Inventory.

   d. Sales.

4. *Making choices and exercising judgment.* Rob, Teri, Kirk, and Peggy are students in the accounting program at Big State University. They have worked together on several projects throughout their classes and are considering starting a business together when they graduate. Their preliminary idea is a firm called Reliable Reminder Services (RRS). RRS would assist its clients in remembering important dates, purchasing and sending greeting cards, and providing specialized shopping services for important dates (birthdays, anniversaries, and the like). Using the seven generic sales/collection steps presented in the chapter, list and discuss the activities the students would likely incorporate in RRS's sales/collection process. Using one or more techniques specified by your instructor, create a document depicting the steps you develop.

5. *Field exercises.*

   a. Find examples of the documents discussed in the chapter. You may want to visit a local office supply store such as Office Depot or Staples or do an Internet search using the document names for your research.

   b. Contact a practicing accountant involved in auditing (either external or internal). Discuss the risks involved in the sales/collection process and internal controls he or she has observed in various organizations that address those risks.

6. *Modeling sales/collection processes.* In each of the following independent cases, use a systems documentation technique specified by your instructor to model the process.

   a. Dave's Pool Service is based in Upland, California; the firm offers a variety of pool- and spa-related services, including acid washing, routine maintenance, solar panel installation, and repair services. For regular customers, Dave prepares and mails paper invoices on a monthly basis; for one-time services, Dave leaves the invoice at the client's home. Dave accepts payment via check only; if a client fails to pay amounts billed within 30 days, Dave turns the case over to a collections firm. Dave deposits cash receipts in his personal checking account on a weekly basis; he does not maintain a separate business checking account.

   b. Steve and Mike Nauertz own an insurance agency with offices in Upland, Arcadia, and Pasadena, California; they offer several types of insurance, including automobile, motorcycle, homeowners, and whole life. When a client comes into one of the offices, one of the owners does a "needs assessment," which they record both on a paper form and in a relational database file. The client is then assigned to an office employee who presents the available options based on the needs assessment. Options include type of insurance, insurance providers, costs, and policy features. The client makes a choice; the employee writes the policy and collects the initial payment in cash or check. Thereafter, the insurance company bills the client directly; Nauertz Insurance collects a commission from the insurance company. Steve or Mike deposits client receipts in a business bank account daily; commissions are transmitted to the same account electronically.

c. Choose any organization where you do business regularly, such as a gas station, bookstore, or restaurant. Write a description of the sales/collection process, then document the process you described.

7. *Transaction processing.* BRN Corporation sells on credit with terms of 2/10, n/30. Freight charges are always paid by the customer when the goods are delivered by a common carrier. During the month of April 2011, BRN completed the following transactions:

Date	Transaction
2	Sold inventory with a cost of $300 on account to TRB Corporation, $1,000.
5	Sold inventory with a cost of $200 for cash to FOF Corporation, $900.
10	Received cash from TRB Corporation for the sale on 2 April.
15	Wrote off uncollectible receivables, $500.
19	Sold inventory with a cost of $500 on account to TRB Corporation, $2,000.
21	Sold inventory with a cost of $300 for cash to FOF Corporation, $1,100.
30	Received cash from TRB Corporation for the sale on 19 April.
30	Estimated bad debts as 1% of total credit sales.

a. Record the transactions in general journal form.
b. Compute BRN's gross profit for April.
c. Specify the source documents BRN would use for each transaction.
d. Beyond the journal entries, what information would you want to capture in a relational database?

8. *Internal controls.* Several potential problems in the sales/collection process are listed below. Indicate at least two internal controls that would address the problem. For each control you suggest, explain whether it is preventive/detective/corrective in nature. Also identify which of the four purposes of internal control it addresses.

a. A burglar takes cash while the office is closed.
b. A customer is unwilling to pay his bill.
c. A fire destroys inventory in the warehouse.
d. A sales clerk records incorrect items on a customer order.
e. An accounting clerk records cash received on account by debiting cash and accounts receivable.
f. Items ordered are missing from a shipment, although they appear on the packing list.
g. Merchandise is damaged during shipment.
h. Sales and warehouse clerks arrange to ship merchandise to their friends.
i. The cash receipts clerk steals money from incoming mail.
j. The customer invoice is sent before goods are shipped.

9. *Internal controls and risks.* Several risks are paired with potential internal controls in the list below. Place an "X" in the appropriate column to indicate if the internal control addresses the risk with which it is paired. Be prepared to explain your responses.

Risk	Control	Does the control address the risk? Yes	No
1. Sales are lower than expected	Echo checks		
2. Salesperson extends credit limit	Separation of duties		
3. Customer exceeds credit limit	Employee background checks		
4. Order is filled incorrectly	Adequate supervision		
5. Merchandise is damaged during shipment	Sequentially numbered bill of lading		
6. Merchandise is shipped to the wrong address	Shipping via common carrier		
7. Customer is billed prematurely	Document matching		
8. Customer bill contains mathematical errors	Bank reconciliation		
9. Mailroom clerk steals cash from bank deposit	Employee bonding		
10. Uncollectable accounts exceed estimates	Video surveillance		

10. *Internal controls.* (CMA adapted, December 1993) Abid and Company manufactures a variety of pumps and valves that it distributes through several thousand plumbing supply houses as well as 100 manufacturer's representatives. As a result of the less-than-favorable business conditions that have existed over the last several years, Abid's cash flow situation has deteriorated. Accounts receivable have continually grown due to creeping extensions of time that Abid's customers have been taking in remitting payments for supplies. In addition, as Abid has been easing credit to its customers, bad debts have grown to 3 percent of sales.

Abid's president has hired Joe Jackler, an experienced cash manager, to improve Abid's liquidity position. Jackler met with Dora Mooney, Abid's controller, and ascertained that Abid's (1) product sales prices have a 20 percent margin over the sum of direct operating costs and all delivery and selling costs; (2) production is currently slightly less than full capacity; (3) current credit terms are 2/12, n/45, which is in line with industry practices; and (4) dunning notices are sent monthly on all past due accounts with telephone follow-ups for delinquent accounts in excess of $8,000. On average, customers currently pay 35 days after the sale. Delinquent accounts are sent to collection agencies when they reach a past due status of 12 months.

From a review of credit records, Jackler was able to group Abid's customers into risk classes according to the probability of loss associated with sales to a customer, as follows:

Risk Class	Probable Loss (%)
1	None
2	0% to 0.5%
3	0.6% to 1%
4	2% to 3%
5	4% to 6%
6	7% to 12%
7	13% to 20%
8	Over 20%

After considering the available alternatives, Jackler has implemented the following changes to Abid's credit policies in order to improve cash flow:

- The credit terms extended to customers will change to 2/10, n/30. Jackler believes the current customers will accept this change as a sound business decision and, consequently, there will be minimal effect on sales. The overall effects of this change will be to improve accounts receivable turnover, reduce the opportunity costs of carrying receivables, and identify potentially troubled accounts sooner to minimize write-offs.

- Customers in risk groups 1 through 5 will continue to have the customary credit extended to them; selling to groups 6 and 7 will be under more stringent credit terms, such as cash on delivery; and sales to group 8 will require advance payments. Jackler believes this change will cause a reduction in sales; however, this reduction will come from the high-risk customer profile.

- Collection efforts will be increased to ensure better compliance with the new credit terms. Dunning notices will continue to be sent monthly; however, telephone follow-ups will be initiated for all delinquent accounts in excess of $2,000. Accounts outstanding nine months or more will be turned over to a collection agency. Jackler believes this action, coupled with the other changes in policy, will reduce bad debts to a level of 1 to 1.5 percent of sales.

Mooney is responsible for extending credit to customers who deal directly with the company and for establishing the guidelines under which manufacturer's representatives operate. Mooney has tailored credit to various customers to meet their needs and over time has developed a close relationship with a number of the larger customers. In view of the indicated impact the new policies will have on company sales and production, as well as on some of the larger customers, Mooney performed her own risk study. She concluded that some of Jackler's "risk classifications" were inappropriate and believes that some of the larger customers are better business risks than indicated in Jackler's analysis.

Mooney did not share her findings with Abid's president or with Jackler. She decided that to follow the policies in their entirety would reduce sales more than Jackler estimates and result in idle manufacturing capacity. Consequently, Mooney does not intend to totally comply with the new policies, particularly as they affect her larger customers.

What internal control strengths and weaknesses are indicated by the narrative? What additional internal controls would you recommend in this situation? Evaluate Mooney's actions using the IMA code of ethics.

11. *Flowchart interpretation and internal controls analysis.* (CMA adapted, June 1994) The flowchart below depicts the sales/collection process for Richards Furniture Company, a mid-sized retailer of living room and bedroom furniture. Use the flowchart to generate a narrative description of Richards' sales/collection process. Comment on

the company's strengths and weaknesses with regard to internal controls; suggest ways to address the weaknesses you identify.

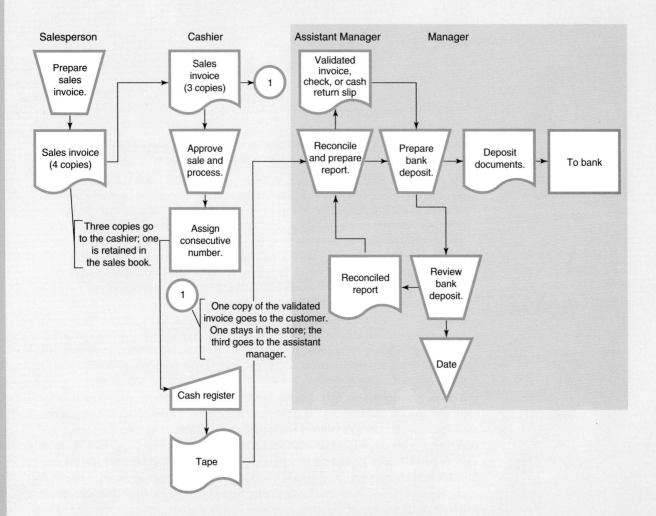

12. *Comprehensive problem.* Bonnie makes and sells her own jewelry over the Internet. A customer browses Bonnie's catalog online and fills out a sales order. The sales order is transmitted electronically to Bonnie, who checks her inventory for each item ordered. If the item is on hand, Bonnie packs it securely and ships it to the customer via a common carrier. If the item is not on hand, Bonnie e-mails the client with an expected shipment date; at that point, the customer must agree to wait until the expected shipment date or cancel the order. Bonnie encloses an invoice with all shipped merchandise; the client sends a check directly to Bonnie's bank for deposit. The bank reports all deposits to Bonnie on a weekly basis; Bonnie reconciles her bank account every day.

   a. In a format specified by your instructor, document Bonnie's sales/collection process.

   b. What are Bonnie's risk exposures? What internal controls does she have in place to address them? Which additional internal controls would you recommend?

   c. Create database specifications for Bonnie's inventory and customer tables. Also create database specifications for any required junction tables.

   d. Design a sales order form and a customer invoice for Bonnie.

13. *Terminology*. Match each item on the left with the most appropriate item on the right.

1. Bill of lading   b
2. Face-to-face, Internet, mail, phone   e
3. For deposit only   c
4. Independent order checking   g
5. Information technology   a
6. Outbound logistics   d
7. Picking list   H
8. Sales/inventory   f
9. Sales department, credit department, warehouse   i
10. Value chain   j

a. Support activity
b. Specifies freight terms
c. Restrictive endorsement
d. Primary activity
e. Order taking methods
f. Junction file
g. Internal control
h. Guides product selection from warehouse
i. Flowchart column headings
j. Comprises primary and support activities

14. *Multiple choice*. Please refer to the case in Problem 12 as you respond to these questions.

1. In a systems flowchart, which of the following is most likely to be depicted with a predefined process symbol?
   a. Browse catalog
   b. Make bank deposit
   c. E-mail client
   d. None of the above.

2. A Level Zero DFD showing Bonnie's interaction with her bank is likely to have how many circles?
   a. One
   b. Two or three
   c. Four or five
   d. More than five

3. At what point will Bonnie make a journal entry that debits accounts receivable and credits sales?
   a. When the order is transmitted
   b. When the goods are shipped
   c. When the cash is deposited
   d. None of the above.

4. Which of the following internal controls should Bonnie implement in the first step of the sales/collection process?
   a. Data encryption
   b. Separation of duties
   c. Lockbox system
   d. Bank reconciliation

5. All of the following are likely to be tables in Bonnie's relational database except:
   a. Customer.
   b. Inventory.
   c. Employee. → Least essential
   d. Order/inventory.

15. *Statement evaluation*. Indicate whether each of the following statements is (i) always true, (ii) sometimes true, or (iii) never true. For those that are (ii) sometimes true, explain when the statement is true.

a. A junction table would be required in a relational database for the sales/collection process.
b. Cash receipts clerks should reconcile a company's bank statement at least monthly.

c. Companies complete all activities in the value chain to serve their stakeholders.

d. Customers should borrow money to take advantage of cash discounts in paying their bills.

e. Documents in the sales/collection process can be paper or electronic.

f. In the sales/collection process, separation of duties can be applied to credit decisions.

g. Restrictive check endorsements eliminate the need for other internal controls over cash.

h. Separation of duties helps safeguard inventory in the sales/collection process.

i. Transactions in the sales/collection process require a bill of lading.

j. Web sites assist companies in the sales/collection process.

16. *Application of prior material.* Consider the following short case as you respond to the requirements for this problem:

The Institute for Computer Enthusiasts (ICE) sponsors four computer seminars each year: Access, Excel, PowerPoint, and QuickBooks. Participants can sign up for any or all of the seminars; pricing varies with the number of seminars and with the participant's membership and professional status as shown in the chart below:

Classification	Single-Seminar Price	Four-Seminar Price
Professional member	$40	$120
Student member	$30	$100
Non-member	$50	$150

ICE has a four-member executive board: president, vice president, secretary, and treasurer. The vice president processes all registrations for each seminar; the treasurer collects payment at the beginning of each seminar.

a. Use COSO's enterprise risk management framework to develop an ERM plan for ICE's computer seminars.

b. How could ICE use the principles of business process management to improve its sales/collection process with respect to the seminars?

c. ICE's board of directors is interested in expanding their seminar offerings to other IT-related topics. Consider the other topics we've discussed in previous chapters. Work with a group of students to develop materials for a seminar based on one of them.

Chapter **Thirteen**

Acquisition/Payment Process

AIS in the Business World

Home Depot

My brother used to work for a Home Depot Distribution Center (www.homedepot.com). The basic job of a distribution center (DC) is to coordinate inventory between suppliers and retail Home Depot stores. The corporate office orders merchandise from various suppliers and arranges for its shipment to a DC based on location and merchandise type. When it arrives at the DC, the merchandise is unloaded and processed by the receiving department; bar codes tell where the merchandise should be shelved within the DC, which is the size of several football fields.

Orders come in from the retail stores to the DC on a daily basis. DC inventory workers use handheld devices to locate the required merchandise; the DC's information system lists the merchandise for each order in a specific sequence to minimize travel time throughout the DC. Once all the related goods for an order have been "picked" from the shelves, the same inventory worker stages them. Shipping clerks then load the staged merchandise on trucks, which deliver it to the retail stores. Neither the trucks that bring the merchandise to the DC nor the trucks that carry the merchandise away from it are owned by Home Depot. Rather, they contract with independent carriers for that purpose.

From Home Depot's point of view, those steps are associated with our topic for this chapter: the acquisition/payment process. Note that the acquisition/payment process is the flip side of the sales/collection process we discussed in the last chapter.

Discussion Questions

1. Which activities in Porter's value chain are associated with the acquisition/payment process?
2. What are the steps involved in the acquisition/payment process?
3. How are the five generic parts of the AIS discussed in Chapter 1 applied/exemplified within the context of the acquisition/payment process?

The acquisition/payment process is the flip side of the sales/collection process. Like the sales/collection process, it follows a fairly common set of steps and uses some consistent documents and internal controls across a wide range of companies and industries.

The chapter follows the same structure as Chapter 12. When you finish studying this chapter, you should be able to complete the following tasks within the context of the acquisition/payment process:

1. Explain its role and purpose.
2. List and discuss, in order, the steps in the process.
3. Explain how the generic structure of most AIS applies to the process.
4. Process common transactions.
5. Design and critique internal controls based on common risk exposures.
6. Develop and interpret process-related systems documentation.

Although it can be applied to virtually anything an organization needs to acquire, our discussion of the acquisition/payment process will focus on inventory. We'll leave the discussion of payroll to the next chapter; although it can be considered part of the acquisition/payment process, its details are more complex than "ordinary" acquisition/payment activities and can vary significantly across companies and industries. In addition, the acquisition/payment process also incorporates noninventory purchases such as fixed assets (equipment, furniture, and similar items) and other current assets (such as supplies).

PROCESS DESCRIPTION

The primary purpose of the acquisition/payment process is to obtain the resources the organization needs and to pay for them. Fundamentally, organizations exist to create value for their stakeholders; the acquisition/payment process is one element of that basic purpose. In the last chapter, we looked at Porter's value chain as a way to think about business processes; the acquisition/payment process is principally related to procurement and inbound logistics. Procurement is a synonym for purchasing; inbound logistics refers to the process of getting resources from "where they are" to "where they are needed." For example, McGraw-Hill might use air and ground transportation to ship books to university bookstores.

Reflection and Self-Assessment   13.1

Other than inventory, what resources would an organization commonly need to create value for its stakeholders?

Although an acquisition/payment process can have slight differences across organizations and industries, its basic **steps** include (Hollander, Denna, and Cherrington, 2000)

1. *Request goods and services based on monitored need.* Organizations use all sorts of tools and techniques to establish the need for a good or service. Inventory levels, for example, might be monitored with a reorder point; orders could be based on an economic order quantity formula. Other resources may be time-sensitive; for example, your car insurance bill may be paid monthly or semiannually. A special project, such as the design and implementation of an accounting information system, may lead to a request for goods or services on a more episodic basis. In many organizations, requests for

inventory, supplies, and services are coordinated through a central purchasing department, thus creating economies of scale and discounted purchase prices.

2. *Authorize a purchase.* This step promotes good internal control (discussed in greater depth later in the chapter). For example, your AIS instructor may be authorized to select her own textbook for the course. Or the decision may be a collaborative one, with a department chair or course coordinator having the final authorization for placing a textbook order with your university bookstore. Even in the bookstore, not every employee is authorized to deal with publishers and other suppliers; rather, that right is probably vested in one employee or a small group of employees.

3. *Purchase goods/services.* Once a purchase has been authorized, the appropriate documentation must be submitted to the vendor/supplier. We'll look at purchase documentation requirements in more detail later in the chapter.

4. *Receive goods and services.* Major purchases of goods, particularly inventory, are received through a dedicated receiving department for stronger internal control. Individual employees, however, may be authorized to make small purchases using company credit or debit cards.

5. *Disburse cash.* Once the goods have been properly purchased and received, accounting personnel generate payment to the vendor. Keeping a solid audit trail is very important here, as it is in the other steps and in the sales/collection process.

6. *When necessary, process purchase returns.* If received goods are defective, do not meet quality standards, or are otherwise unacceptable to the buyer, they may need to be returned to the vendor.

As with our discussion of the sales/collection process, keep in mind that those six steps are very generic. Each organization will have its own modifications to the basic steps; the fundamental idea is purchasing the goods and services you need, when you need them, and paying for them timely. Figure 13.1 shows a Level Zero data flow diagram depicting the basic steps in the acquisition/payment process.

At Cal Poly Pomona, employees in the Facilities Planning and Management Department can use a departmental credit card to purchase small supplies such as light bulbs if none are available in the warehouse.

An audit trail consists of source documents, journal entries, and ledger postings; it also may involve electronic data in a computer-based accounting information system.

FIGURE 13.1
**Generic Acquisition/
Payment Process**

The steps in the sales/collection process are related to those in the acquisition/payment process as shown in the table below:

Sales/Collection	Acquisition/Payment
Take customer order	Purchase goods and services
Ship the product	Receive goods and services
Collect payment	Disburse cash

As we did in Chapter 12, let's take a look at how the five generic parts of an AIS are applied to the acquisition/payment process.

AIS STRUCTURE

Documents in the acquisition/payment process, as in the sales/collection process, can be paper-based, electronic, or some combination of the two. Table 13.1 summarizes the most commonly used documents in the acquisition/payment process; we'll take a look at each of them in more detail in the following paragraphs. Note that an output from one step in the acquisition/payment process often serves as an input to subsequent steps; likewise, an output from one organization can serve as an input to another.

Once an operating department establishes the need for a good or service, its personnel generate a purchase requisition. The purchase requisition, like all forms, should have a clear title and plenty of white space for easy reading. Information should be complete and logically laid out. In most cases, the operating department keeps a copy of the purchase requisition for its own files and sends a copy to the purchasing department. Figure 13.2 shows an example of a purchase requisition.

The purchasing department, then, will consolidate various purchase requisitions into a single purchase order. Consolidating purchase requisitions may allow the company to take advantage of quantity discounts. Creating a separate purchasing department also facilitates strong internal control through separation of duties. Purchasing agents may be in charge of dealing with a specific set of vendors, a certain group of parts or supplies, or the purchase requisitions from one or more operating departments. While the purchase requisition generated by the operating department is an informal, internal document, the signed purchase order functions as a "contract" between the company and the vendor. The purchase requisition will normally include the goods and quantities requested; the purchase order will

TABLE 13.1
Documents Used in the Acquisition/ Payment Process

Document Name	Basic Purpose	Originator	Recipient
Purchase requisition	To request that the purchasing department order goods or services from a vendor	Operating department	Purchasing department
Purchase order	To specify the items to be ordered, freight terms, shipping address, and other information for the vendor	Purchasing department	Vendor
Receiving report	To ensure that goods have been ordered and received in good condition	Receiving department	Various departments
Vendor invoice	To request payment from a customer	Vendor	Accounting department
Check	To pay the vendor	Accounting department	Vendor

FIGURE 13.2 **Purchase Requisition**

George Mason University

PURCHASE REQUISITION

Sample   Sample

835457

SUGGESTED VENDOR	DELIVERY INSTRUCTIONS	DEPARTMENTAL APPROVAL
	DELIVER TO:	DATE NEEDED:
	DEPARTMENT:	FUND CODE:
	TELEPHONE:	APPROVAL SIGNATURE:
	BUILDING:	
	ROOM NUMBER:	TITLE:
		DATE APPROVED:

ITEM NUMBER	DESCRIPTION OF ITEM/SERVICE DESIRED		QUANTITY	UNIT	UNIT PRICE	EXTENSION
			TOTAL AMOUNT OF REQUISITION:			

+++ FOR BUYER'S USE ONLY +++

VENDOR ADDRESS:	CONTRACT NO:
	FOB:
	DELIVERY:
CONTACT:	BUYER:
PHONE:	REMARKS
EIN/SSN:	

specify the vendor, the expected price, the freight terms, and other important data for the transaction. In most cases, the purchasing department keeps a copy on file; it also sends copies to the receiving department and the accounting department. Figure 13.3 shows an example of a purchase order.

Point your Web browser to www.ita.doc.gov/ ofm/forms/receiving _insp_text.htm for a summary of information commonly included in a receiving report.

When the goods arrive from the vendor, the receiving department prepares a receiving report. The goods should be matched and verified against an existing purchase order so that the company does not receive goods that were not properly ordered. The receiving personnel also may verify the quality and condition of the goods before accepting delivery. Commonly, the receiving department copies the accounting department and purchasing department as well.

Notice that the accounting department receives both a copy of the purchase order and a copy of the receiving report. When the vendor mails an invoice for payment, then, accounting personnel use those documents to ensure that the invoice reflects goods that were

FIGURE 13.3
Purchase Order

Purchase Order

Purchase Order No.:_____

Requisition No.:_____

Vendor Code:_____

Vendor Name:_____

Vendor Address:_____

Vendor Contact: Vendor Phone: (____) _____-_____

Order Description					
Product Item No.	Product Description	Quantity	Estimated Cost	Tax	Total

properly ordered and received before generating payment. The department then issues a check in payment of the invoice, taking advantage of any discounts offered.

How do organizations process the input documents to create outputs for the acquisition/ payment process? They use the seven steps discussed earlier in this chapter. In addition, transactions must be appropriately recorded in the AIS.

Reflection and Self-Assessment 13.2

What journal entries would you make for each of the following transactions? Which input/output documents would trigger each one?

- Purchase of inventory on account
- Purchase of inventory for cash
- Cash payments for payments on account
- Inventory returns

As you read in Chapter 1, "storage" in the AIS often happens in a computer database or other electronic medium. Even in the small number of cases where storage happens with paper files, though, the AIS still must capture certain basic information in master files and transaction files. Table 13.2 shows a list of the **common files,** along with the data they would contain.

TABLE 13.2 **File Structures in the Acquisition / Payment Process**

File Name	File Type	Primary Key	Other Data
Employee	Master	Employee ID	Last name, first name Street address, city, state, ZIP code Phone number Emergency contact Department Hire date
Vendor	Master	Vendor ID	Vendor company name Street address, city, state, ZIP code Phone number Contact person name Credit limit Date of first purchase
Inventory	Master	Product ID	Product name Beginning balance date Beginning balance quantity Beginning balance cost per unit Preferred supplier
Purchases	Transaction	Transaction ID	Transaction date Vendor ID Employee ID
Purchases / inventory	Junction	Transaction ID	Product ID Quantity purchased Purchase price per unit

Notice that both the sales/collection and acquisition/payment processes need data from the employee table. Although conceptually possible to create a separate employee table for each process/department, most organizations find it simpler to use a single employee table—that's why you need a field titled "department." The purchases/inventory table is needed because each inventory item can be involved in multiple purchase transactions, and each purchase transaction can include multiple inventory items.

In the next section, we'll turn our attention to the last generic AIS element: internal controls.

INTERNAL CONTROLS

As with the sales/collection process, our discussion is centered on the various risks managers confront in the acquisition/payment process. Many of the controls discussed in the last chapter also apply here, so don't consider the list that follows comprehensive or exhaustive. Remember: The idea is to implement internal controls that provide *reasonable* assurance—not *absolute* assurance. Even if the latter were possible, it almost certainly would not be cost-effective in most organizations.

As in the previous chapter, the numbered items below suggest risks to be addressed; the lettered items beneath them discuss possible **internal controls.**

1. Ordering unneeded goods.

   a. *Institute a system for monitoring inventory levels.* In addition to traditional systems like EOQ, many organizations use information technology to monitor inventory levels. Jonietz (2001) reported on the use of wireless systems in a Tulsa-based retail warehouse for inventory control.

   b. *Require justification for unusual orders or orders over a specified dollar amount.* If an employee is ordering goods unnecessarily, or is attempting to defraud the organization by ordering goods for personal benefit, an additional authorizing signature or approval process can be effective in detecting the problem.

   c. *Specify the business purpose for ordered goods.* This control is connected to the previous one. Consider, for example, a company with unusually high travel expenses; employees should be required to justify the business purpose of a trip before taking it.

2. Purchasing goods from inappropriate vendors.

   a. *Develop and enforce a conflict-of-interest policy.* Such policies make clear the actions that constitute a conflict of interest, as well as the consequences for engaging in those actions. The World Wide Web Consortium (www.w3.org) established a detailed policy in 2003; you may view it at their Web site: www.w3.org/2000/09/06-conflictpolicy.html.

   b. *Establish criteria for supplier reliability and quality of goods.* Managers may establish standards for delivery time, product quality, and availability for their suppliers. Home Depot (www.homedepot.com), for example, requires its vendors to maintain adequate inventory levels in their own operations so that they can fill Home Depot's inventory needs. Many organizations use a "preferred vendor list" for that purpose.

   c. *Create strategic alliances with preferred vendors.* Porter (1985, p. 33) conceptualized the value chain as a way of "examining all the activities a firm performs and how they interact. . . . The value chain disaggregates a firm into its strategically relevant activities in order to understand the behavior of costs and the existing and potential sources of differentiation." When an organization is particularly expert at one or more value chain activities, it may form a strategic alliance with organizations that are more adept at other value chain components. For example, an outstanding

The value chain consists of four support activities (infrastructure, human resource management, technology development, and procurement) and five primary activities (inbound logistics, operations, outbound logistics, marketing and sales, and service).

manufacturer may establish a strategic alliance with a particular common carrier, thus creating value for both organizations.

3. Receiving unordered or defective goods.

   a. *Match receiving reports with approved purchase orders.* Document matching is a fundamental internal control found in many organizations. In the acquisition/payment process, the receiving clerk should verify that goods have been ordered by an authorized company representative before accepting them. Goods received without a purchase order are suspicious; such receipts should either be refused outright or investigated more carefully to ensure that no fraud is involved.

   b. *Inspect goods before accepting a shipment.* This control is especially applicable when dealing with very specialized goods. Receiving clerks should have a clear grasp of acceptable quality standards and verify that (at least) a sampling of products meets those standards.

   c. *Insure products en route.* Purchasing transit insurance cannot necessarily prevent damage, but it can help organizations recover financially if goods are damaged in transit.

4. Experiencing theft of inventory and/or cash.

   a. *Establish an internal audit function.* The Sarbanes-Oxley Act of 2002 has done a lot to establish the importance of internal audits in organizations. Your university may have a separate class on internal auditing; you also can get more information about the field from the Institute of Internal Auditors (www.theiia.org/).

   b. *Reconcile bank statements promptly.* Consider the case of Wholelife Counseling Center (Hurt, 1994). In that organization, failure to reconcile bank statements promptly led to a major loss of cash due to embezzlement.

   c. *Separate authorization, custody, and usage functions for both inventory and cash.* Separation of duties is another common, and essential, internal control procedure. Three important duties should always be separated to foster good internal control: physical custody of an asset, authorization for its use, and recordkeeping associated with it.

   d. *Install employee monitoring systems.* Systems like these are controversial and may involve ethical and legal issues. Consider, for example, one company that put detection sensors in its employees' identification badges. The sensors allowed management to track employee movements inside the corporate headquarters.

   e. *Bond employees who handle high-value goods.* Fidelity bonding is a form of insurance focused on employee behavior. According to Kishel and Kishel (1993), three types of fidelity bonds are common. "Individual bonds cover theft by a specific named individual. Schedule bonds list every name or position to be covered. Blanket bonds, the most encompassing of the three, cover all employees without reference to individual names or positions."

5. Making errors in paying invoices.

   a. *Require document matching (purchase order, receiving report, invoice) before issuing a check.* This control technique is especially effective when incorporated with good separation of duties. When the accountant/cash payments clerk has all three documents in hand, he or she will know that goods were properly ordered and received. The invoice will show the amount due, and the accountant/cash payments clerk will cut a check for the vendor.

   b. *Employ information technology to take advantage of available discounts.* Most general ledger software packages, such as QuickBooks or Great Plains Dynamics, can prompt users to pay invoices before cash discounts expire.

   c. *Stamp documents "paid" to avoid duplicate payments.* This control seems simple (and it is!), but it is very effective in avoiding duplicate payments. Whether documents are stamped electronically or physically, they should be somehow marked so they are not paid more than once.

Those risks, and the suggested internal controls that accompany them, are by no means exhaustive. In designing and evaluating internal controls for the acquisition/payment process, you must develop an intimate knowledge of an organization's processes and personnel. Use your own creativity and critical thinking abilities, coupled with your sense of cost–benefit issues, when confronted with the important task of internal control assessment in practice.

Reflection and Self-Assessment   13.3

Relate the six risks described above to Brown's taxonomy of risk. Explain whether each suggested control is primarily preventive/detective/corrective. Suggest one additional internal control for each risk.

SYSTEMS DOCUMENTATION

Figure 13.4 shows a partial flowchart of the steps in the acquisition/payment process. (As in Chapter 12, you'll be asked to finish the flowchart in the end-of-chapter activities.) Figure 13.1 (from earlier in the chapter) illustrates a Level Zero data flow diagram of the acquisition/payment process.

FIGURE 13.4
Partial Flowchart of the Acquisition / payment process

Reflection and Self-Assessment   13.4

Use the steps in the acquisition/payment process listed above, along with the common files and their specifications from Table 13.2, to create a generic REA model of the acquisition/payment process.

CRITICAL THINKING

As you read at the start of this chapter, the acquisition/payment process can involve virtu-ally anything an organization needs to buy. Since our previous examples have involved inventory, I thought you might like to see something a bit different for this chapter's critical thinking exercise. This example focuses on an internal service; specifically, building and grounds maintenance.

The Facilities Management Department of ETR Corporation is in charge of all building and grounds maintenance; some tasks are completed routinely (e.g., weekly or monthly), while others are done based on service call requests from other ETR departments. Con-sider the systems flowchart of the process shown in Figure 13.5.

A narrative description of the process would look like this: When an ETR department needs a service call, the manager prepares a service request; the request becomes part of a master "service request database" in the Facilities Management Department. Each day, facilities employees consult a video display to determine which tasks will be addressed; those tasks include both routine maintenance and service requests. The facilities employee completes the required tasks. For each service request, the facilities employee prepares a "completed job report," which is sent back to the requesting manager; for both service requests and routine maintenance, the service request database is updated. The department manager who requested the service call files a copy of the original service request and a copy of the completed job report.

FIGURE 13.5
ETR Maintenance

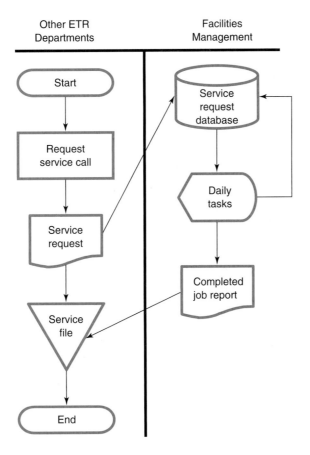

Here are some risks and associated internal controls for the process:

Risk	Control
Too many service call requests	Expand staffing. Hire temporary employees. Create a transfer pricing system.
Poor quality work	Periodic employee training Customer satisfaction reports Post-audits of completed jobs
Damage to database/files	Backup copies (electronic and hard copy)

Here are some sample specifications for the service request database:

<u>Request number</u>

Date requested

[Requesting manager]

Description

Date completed

[Facilities employee]

The primary key (request number) could be an auto-numbered field, thus promoting stronger internal control through sequential numbering. Since one manager can initiate many service requests, but each service request comes from only one manager, the primary key from the "requesting manager" table becomes a foreign key in the service request database; the same logic holds true for the "facilities employee."

BUSINESS PROCESS RELATIONSHIPS

So now we've looked at both the sales/collection process and the acquisition/payment process. Keeping in mind that the two complement one another in two different organizations, here's a comprehensive view of both processes:

1. An operating department in the buying organization requests goods and services. For example, the production department might need additional raw materials. Or the accounting department might need new computers. A purchase requisition is the relevant document in this step. The purchase requisition serves as an important internal control by allowing the organization to respond to legitimate needs, take advantage of quantity discounts, and establish relationships with suppliers based on objective criteria. A purchase requisition would indicate the items needed and their quantities; one copy would typically remain with the requisitioning department, while another copy would go to purchasing.

2. The purchasing department in the buying organization authorizes the purchase. Having a central location that handles all purchasing for an organization is an important element of internal control. It promotes adequate supervision, helping ensure that the organization is only buying things that are legitimately needed; in addition, it promotes operating efficiency through coordination. A purchasing agent would complete a serially numbered purchase order based on one or more requisitions; the purchase order would be transmitted to the supplier electronically and/or in paper form. One copy of

the purchase order, without the quantities of items ordered, would be sent to the receiving department; a second copy would go to the accounting department.

3. The sales department in the selling organization takes the customer's order. Taking a customer order can refer to receiving a purchase order; on the other hand, the selling organization can receive orders over the phone, electronically (such as through a Web site), or via electronic data interchange. The sales staff member would fill out an order form based on the data in the purchase order.

4. The credit department in the selling organization approves the customer's credit. Having a credit department promotes good separation of duties. If the sales staff is allowed to grant credit, internal control is weakened; customers might be allowed to purchase items on credit when they are not creditworthy, which can lead to collection problems later.

5. The warehouse in the selling organization fills the order based on approved credit. Again, we see good separation of duties here—physical custody of inventory is separated from its recordkeeping (handled in the accounting department) and from authorization for its use (which comes from the sales and credit departments). The warehouse employee would complete a picking slip to show what merchandise he or she took off the shelves.

6. The selling organization's shipping department ships the product. The shipping department would verify the customer's name and address; shipping also would fill out a packing slip to enclose with the goods, showing what was shipped. If the seller uses a common carrier such as UPS to ship the goods, a bill of lading also would be required. Insurance could be an important internal control here as well. The shipping department would send a copy of the shipping documents to the accounting department, as the shipment would trigger a journal entry recording the sale.

7. The buying organization's receiving department receives the goods. The receiving department would have a "blind copy" of the related purchase order(s). A blind copy contains all the usual information but not the quantities ordered. Thus, the receiving department can verify that the goods really were ordered (an important element of internal control) but would have to count the merchandise received physically, rather than simply verifying quantities against the purchase order. Receiving would send a copy of the receiving report to accounting and the merchandise itself to the warehouse or the location where it is needed.

8. The billing department in the selling organization bills the client. Document matching is an important internal control in this step and the ones that follow. Before issuing a bill, the selling organization needs to ensure that the client has indeed ordered the goods *and* that the goods have actually been shipped. Separation of duties also comes into play here, as the authorization to bill is separated from the physical custody of the inventory. The invoice (bill) could be mailed, faxed, and/or transmitted electronically; it would normally include the payment terms (e.g., 2/10, n/30) and the seller's address.

9. The cash disbursements department in the buying organization disburses cash. The cash disbursements department needs to ensure that the goods really were ordered (purchase order), that they were received (receiving report), and that the company is being billed for the correct amount (invoice). If all three documents match, the company could issue a check and/or an electronic funds transfer in payment of the invoice. The cash disbursements clerk would typically not be a signatory on the company's checking account; rather, the clerk would prepare the check and send it to an authorized signer—once again promoting good internal control through separation of duties. Checks would be sequentially numbered; they should ideally be kept in a locked filing cabinet until needed.

10. The cash receipts department in the selling organization collects payment. If the payment is mailed, it would be received in the selling organization's mailroom. Adequate supervision in the mailroom is an important internal control, as it is throughout most business processes. Most companies will not accept currency and coin through the mail, as it weakens internal control. The mail clerk would separate the check from the remittance advice; the check would be endorsed restrictively and prepared for deposit. The remittance advice would go to the accounting department to serve as a source document for the related journal entry.

So, that's a comprehensive picture of both the acquisition/payment and sales/collection business processes. I've described an "ideal" situation here; as an accounting professional, you might be called upon to audit or recommend improvements to similar systems in practice.

Summary

This chapter continued our discussion of business processes by looking at the acquisition/payment process. In addition to introducing new information about the process, we also saw how to apply other topics. Here's a summary of the chapter's main points, structured according to its learning objectives:

1. *Explain its role and purpose.* The acquisition/payment process is all about an organization acquiring the resources it needs to create value for its stakeholders. It's most often applied to inventory, but can be applied to virtually any resource.

2. *List and discuss, in order, the steps in the process.* The acquisition/payment process comprises six steps: (a) request goods and services based on monitored need; (b) authorize a purchase; (c) purchase goods/services; (d) receive goods and services; (e) disburse cash; and (f) when necessary, process purchase returns.

3. *Explain how the generic structure of most AIS applies to the process.* Inputs and outputs most often come in the form of paper-based or electronic documents, such as the purchase requisition, purchase order, receiving report, vendor invoice, and check. For each document, accountants should understand its content and purpose, where it originates, and where it terminates. The acquisition/payment process includes three major types of storage files: master (e.g., vendors and inventory), transaction (e.g., purchases), and junction (e.g., purchases/inventory). Common transactions can be processed with paper-based journals and ledgers or with the benefit of information technology (such as ERP systems and general ledger software). XBRL also includes a multitude of tags for information related to the process. Internal controls for the acquisition/payment process help fulfill the four purposes of internal control: safeguarding assets, ensuring financial statement reliability, promoting operating efficiency, and encouraging compliance with management directives.

4. *Process common transactions.* Common transactions associated with the acquisition/payment process include purchases of goods and services for cash and on account, cash payments for purchases on account, and inventory returns.

5. *Design and critique internal controls based on common risk exposures.* Most acquisition/payment processes have at least five major risk exposures. Table 13.3 summarizes the information discussed in the chapter.

6. *Develop and interpret process-related systems documentation.* Figures 13.1 and 13.3 present, respectively, a Level Zero data flow diagram and a partial flowchart of the acquisition/payment process.

TABLE 13.3   Risks and Internal Controls in the Acquisition / Payment Process

Risk	Recommended Controls
Ordering unneeded goods	Inventory monitoring system Order justification Business purpose specification
Using inappropriate vendors	Conflict of interest policy Supplier criteria Strategic alliances
Receiving unordered / defective goods	Document matching Inspection Insurance
Theft of inventory / cash	Internal audit Bank reconciliations Separation of duties Employee monitoring systems Employee bonding
Payment errors	Document matching Information technology "Paid" stamp

Key Terms

common files, *235*   internal controls, *236*   steps, *230*
documents, *232*

Chapter References

Hollander, A. S., E. L. Denna, and J. O. Cherrington. 2000. *Accounting, Information Technology, and Business Solutions.* 2nd ed. New York: Irwin/McGraw-Hill.

Hurt, R. 1994. "Wholelife Counseling Center." *Journal of Accounting Case Research,* pp. 97–98.

Jonietz, E. 2001. "Wireless Stockroom." *Technology Review,* July/August, p. 32.

Kishel, G., and P. Kishel. 1993. "Safeguarding Your Business." *Black Enterprise,* July, pp. 98–104.

Porter, M. 1985. *Competitive Advantage: Creating and Sustaining Superior Performance.* New York: Free Press.

End-of-Chapter Activities

1. *Reading review questions.*
   a. What is the basic purpose of the acquisition/payment process?
   b. What steps do companies commonly complete as part of the acquisition/payment process?
   c. How are the generic elements of the AIS exemplified in the acquisition/payment process?
   d. What risks do managers face as part of the acquisition/payment process? What internal controls help reduce exposure to those risks?
   e. Prepare a response to the questions for this chapter's "AIS in the Business World."

2. *Reading review problem.* Walmart is the largest retail organization in the world; in fiscal year 2008, its net sales were $374.5 billion, resulting in operating income of $22.0 billion. Earnings per share increased for the fifth consecutive year, and free cash flow increased by 25 percent from fiscal year 2007 to fiscal year 2008 (www.walmartstores.com). While there are many important factors leading to Walmart's impressive results, one of the firm's critical success factors is its ability to manage its inventory, which totaled more than $35 billion at the end of fiscal 2008. According to

Powanga and Powanga (2008), Walmart uses RFID technology to help manage its inventory. During its pilot test phase, stores using RFID had 16 percent fewer stock-outs than stores not using RFID.

Source: M. Powanga and L. Powanga, "Deploying RFID in Logistics: Criteria and Best Practices and Issues," *The Business Review*, Cambridge, Summer 2008.

a. What is RFID technology? How is it used in the acquisition/payment process?

b. RFID is a form of internal control. Which of the four purposes of internal control does it help Walmart achieve?

c. What documents would Walmart likely use in its acquisition/payment process? Which journal entries, if any, are triggered by each document?

3. *Multiple choice review.*

1. The acquisition/payment process can involve an organization buying:
   a. Inventory.
   b. Plant assets.
   c. Supplies.
   d. All of the above.

2. All of the following are methods for monitoring inventory levels except:
   a. Reorder point.
   b. FIFO and LIFO.
   c. Time.
   d. RFID.

3. Which of the following documents specifies items to be ordered, freight terms, shipping address, and other information for a vendor?
   a. Purchase requisition
   b. Purchase order
   c. Receiving report
   d. Bill of lading

4. Internal controls that address the risk of purchasing goods from inappropriate vendors include:
   a. Strategic alliances.
   b. RFID technology.
   c. Sequentially numbered purchase orders.
   d. Order justification.

5. The primary key for the inventory master file is most likely to be:
   a. Product name.
   b. Product description.
   c. Product ID.
   d. Quantity on hand.

4. *Making choices and exercising judgment.* Use your school's library to locate the Kishel and Kishel article in this chapter's references. Read the article and discuss the costs and benefits associated with each type of insurance coverage discussed. Considering the risks of the acquisition/payment process in the chapter, which risk management approaches would you consider most appropriate for each one? Why?

5. *Field exercises.*

a. Contact a practicing accountant involved in auditing (either external or internal). Discuss the risks involved in the acquisition/payment process and internal controls he or she has observed in various organizations that address those risks.

   b. Contact a practicing accountant in a corporate environment. Ask about forms of information technology the company employs in its acquisition/payment process. Also find out how various functional managers use the AIS data from the process for making decisions.

6. *Modeling acquisition/payment processes.*

   a. The library at Big State University routes all purchase requests through its requisitions department. Faculty, staff, and students can suggest titles for books, periodicals, electronic media, and other items via e-mail or by using a paper form sent to the requisitions librarian. The requisitions librarian tracks the various requests in a database; once at least 10 requests for the same item have come in, the requisitions librarian orders it from an appropriate vendor using a standard purchase order. The requisitions librarian e-mails the requestors to tell them the item has been ordered and files a copy of the purchase order by title. When the item is received, the receiving clerk matches it against the purchase order supplied by the requisitions librarian; if it matches, the item moves out of the receiving department into the library, where it is filed. A copy of the receiving report goes to the requisitions librarian and to the financial services department; financial services clerks match the invoice against the receiving report and purchase order. They also reconcile any differences between them with the vendor. Invoices are paid on a monthly basis according to the company name of the vendor; for example, vendors starting with A through C are paid the first five days of the month. The financial services clerk creates a payment packet of all relevant documents, stamps "Paid" on the top, and files it alphabetically by vendor name, and by date within vendor name. Create a flowchart or data flow diagram that depicts the preceding process.

   b. Goodkind Corporation replaces one-third of its desktop computers every year, so that every employee has a new computer every three years. In January of each year, Goodkind's information technology division accesses the corporate database to determine which computers are eligible for replacement. The information technology division manager consults with the chief financial officer to determine the budget for computer replacement, then asks each employee whose computer is eligible to be replaced for a list of three "must have" features and three "wish list" features for his or her new computer. A committee comprised of the information technology manager, the chief financial officer, and three employees prepares a request for proposal (RFP) to send to various computer vendors; vendors typically have about 30 days to respond to the RFP. At the end of the RFP period, the committee ranks the proposals based a on standard set of criteria. After discussion, they select the best proposal and contact the vendor. Goodkind's purchasing department issues a purchase order; the original goes to the vendor, while Goodkind's accounting department receives a copy. The receiving department gets a "blind copy" of the purchase order. When the computers arrive, the receiving department inspects them for quality; any computers that do not meet quality specifications are returned to the vendor. The receiving department prepares a receiving report for all good computers received. The computers are transferred to the information technology department; IT staff install them for the employees, typically in April of each year.

   c. Visit my AIS blog at http://bobhurtais.blogspot.com/. Access the entry titled "Acquisition/ Payment Process: Buying a Home," posted on 16 April 2011. Watch the video, then write a short description of the home buying process. In a format specified by your instructor, document the written description you prepared.

   d. Brooks Corporation strives to keep a minimum cash balance of $10,000 for its operating needs. When its actual cash exceeds that threshold by at least $5,000, Brooks' management frequently invests the excess cash by purchasing marketable securities. The board of directors' finance committee consults preestablished criteria for such investments, then conducts a search to identify potential investments. From the list of potential investments, the finance committee chooses the top three to present to the full board of directors. After discussion, the board approves up to two of the investments; Brooks' chief financial officer purchases the securities through the corporation's broker. Brooks maintains an electronic database of its short-term investments, liquidating them as necessary to meet the corporation's cash needs.

7. *Acquisition/payment transactions.* As of 30 April 2011, PLR Corporation's accounts payable subsidiary ledger included the following information:

Vendor	Invoice Number	Invoice Date	Invoice Amount	Terms
HRP Corp.	1398	15 April 2011	$12,890	n/30
VLD Corp.	432	10 April 2011	$ 5,780	2/10, n/30
RGN Corp.	848	21 April 2011	$ 4,500	1/15, n/45

PLR completed the following transactions in May 2011:

Date	Transaction
1	Paid half the amount due to HRP Corp.
3	Purchased inventory on account form VLD Corp., $1,220.
6	Paid the amount due to RGN Corp.
12	Purchased inventory on account form HRP Corp., $3,555
14	Paid the total amount due to HRP Corp.
18	Purchased supplies on account from QOC Corp., $600. Terms: 2/10, n/30.
21	Issued a check to VLD Corp. in payment of Invoice 432, including the applicable discount.
24	Purchased inventory on account form RGN Corp., $1,500.
25	Paid the total amount due to RGN Corp.
27	Purchased factory equipment, $20,000. Paid 20% down and financed the rest with a 6-month, 12% note payable.

   a. Record the May transactions in general journal format.

   b. Prepare a schedule of accounts payable as of 31 May 2011.

   c. Beyond the information in the journal entries, what information about the transactions would you include in a relational database?

8. *Document information.* The documents discussed in this chapter are listed below on the right. Various information items that might appear in them are listed on the left. For each information item listed on the left, indicate the document(s) in which it would most likely appear with the appropriate letter(s).

__ 1. Vendor name	a. Purchase requisition
__ 2. Items needed	b. Purchase order
__ 3. Vendor address	c. Receiving report
__ 4. Purchasing agent's name	d. Vendor invoice
__ 5. Operating manager's name	e. Check
__ 6. Transaction date	
__ 7. Cost per unit	
__ 8. Total cost of all items	
__ 9. P.O. number	
__10. ABA routing number	

9. *Internal controls.* (CMA adapted, June 1991) Brock Company is a manufacturer of children's toys and games. The company has been experiencing declining profit margins and is looking for ways to increase operating income. Because of the competitive nature of the industry, Brock is unable to raise its selling prices and must either cut costs or increase productivity.

   As the company purchases a variety of raw materials, the volume of paperwork in the Accounts Payable Department is very large, and there are several accounting clerks involved in processing and paying the invoices. The repetitive nature of this work leads to errors because of inattention to details such as part numbers and unit prices. These errors have led to double payments, payments for goods not yet received, and delays in the receipt of raw materials because suppliers that should have been paid have not been paid. These situations often require a great deal of supervisory time to resolve.

The department manager has recommended that increased emphasis be placed on quality control. This would be achieved by increased monitoring of daily output, curtailing talking among staff members, and strict adherence to work hours. All errors would be discussed with the employee, and the staff would be informed that performance evaluations will be negative if errors are not reduced.

Comment on the costs and benefits of Brock's proposed new internal control system in Accounts Payable. Suggest an alternative system that would achieve the same results.

10. *Internal control analysis.* (CMA adapted, December 1992) LCK Corporation manufactures small tools such as hammers and screwdrivers. Many of LCK's employees pocket some of the firm's manufactured tools for their personal use. Since the quantities taken by any one employee were typically immaterial, the individual employees did not consider their actions detrimental to LCK. As the company grew larger, management instituted an internal audit department. The internal auditor charted gross profit percentages for particular tools and discovered higher gross profit rates for tools related to industrial use than for personal use. Subsequent investigation uncovered the fraudulent acts.

As an internal auditor, what steps would you take to uncover the fraud? What additional internal controls should LCK Corporation institute to prevent this problem from occurring in the future?

11. *Terminology.* Please match each item on the left with the most appropriate item on the right.

1. Authorize a purchase	a. A way to monitor inventory needs
2. Bank reconciliation	b. Audit trail components
3. Purchase order	c. Internal control to manage the risk of embezzlement
4. Purchase requisition	d. One reason for consolidating purchase requisitions
5. Quantity discounts	e. Possible internal control for purchasing from inappropriate vendors
6. Receiving report	f. Prepared by purchasing department
7. Reorder point	g. Promotes separation of duties
8. Source documents, journal entries, ledger postings	h. Requests customer payment
9. Strategic alliance	i. Several can be combined on one purchase order
10. Vendor invoice	j. Step in the acquisition/payment process

12. *Multiple choice questions.*

1. PLP Corporation maintains an electronic database file for all its vendors and purchases. Which of the following amounts would you be least likely to find in the "vendor" table?

    a. Total amount owed

    b. Vendor name

    c. Part numbers commonly purchased

    d. All of the above would be included in the vendor table.

2. An accounting clerk debited inventory and credited accounts payable for $500. Which of the following is the most likely source document for that transaction?

    a. Purchase order

    b. Receiving report

    c. Vendor invoice

    d. Purchase requisition

3. In the context of an acquisition/payment process, the three-way match concept applies to which of the following sets of documents?

   a. Purchase requisition, vendor invoice, and remittance advice

   b. Vendor invoice, receiving report, and purchase requisition

   c. Receiving report, purchase order, and vendor invoice

   d. Remittance advice, purchase order, and receiving report

4. The difference between a purchase requisition and a purchase order is

   a. Purchase orders are paper, while requisitions are electronic.

   b. Purchase requisitions are electronic, while purchase orders are paper.

   c. Purchase requisitions are purely internal documents; purchase orders leave the company.

   d. Purchase requisitions often have different prices than purchase orders.

5. Which of the following is the best example of a conflict of interest?

   a. RKH Corporation established a list of preferred vendors.

   b. RKH's conflict-of-interest policy was developed by their auditors.

   c. RKH purchases 80 percent of its inventory from a firm where its purchasing agent is a stockholder.

   d. All of the above constitute conflicts of interest.

13. *Statement evaluation.* Indicate whether each statement below is (i) always true, (ii) sometimes true, or (iii) never true. For any statements that are (ii) sometimes true, explain when the statement is true.

   a. A bill of lading is required in the acquisition/payment process.

   b. A data flow diagram of the acquisition/payment process has six numbered circles.

   c. A vendor invoice triggers a cash disbursement event in a well-organized acquisition/payment process.

   d. Companies without a conflict-of-interest policy have weak internal control over the acquisition/payment process.

   e. Daily bank reconciliations eliminate the need for other forms of internal control over cash.

   f. Most of the documents in the acquisition/payment process are paper-based, rather than electronic.

   g. Purchase orders are binding contracts between a customer and a vendor.

   h. The passage of time triggers events in the acquisition/payment process.

   i. The receiving department should have a blind copy of the purchase order.

   j. When two signatures are required, blank checks should be signed by one person to promote operating efficiency.

14. *Process relationships.* The steps in the sales/collection and acquisition/payment processes are listed below, but they are out of order. Put the statements in the proper order based on how they occur in organizations.

   a. An operating department in the buying organization requests goods and services.

   b. The billing department in the selling organization bills the client.

   c. The buying organization's receiving department receives the goods.

   d. The cash disbursements department in the buying organization disburses cash.

   e. The cash receipts department in the selling organization collects payment.

   f. The credit department in the selling organization approves the customer's credit.

   g. The purchasing department in the buying organization authorizes the purchase.

   h. The sales department in the selling organization takes the customer's order.

   i. The selling organization's shipping department ships the product.

   j. The warehouse in the selling organization fills the order based on approved credit.

15. *Prior material application.*

a. Point your Web browser to www.download.com, and search for inventory management software packages, such as inFlow Inventory Software and Inventoria Stock Manager. Choose two or three such packages, and use the weighted rating technique discussed in Chapter 5 to evaluate them for use in a small business.

b. Point your Web browser to www.acfe.com, the Web site for the Association of Certified Fraud Examiners. Look for the June 2001 article by Joseph T. Wells titled "Ghost Goods: How to Spot Phantom Inventory." Use expectancy theory to analyze what might motivate someone to commit inventory fraud.

c. Visit my AIS blog (http://bobhurtais.blogspot.com/) and access the entry titled XBRL posted on 16 April 2011. Use the link there to go to the taxonomy viewer for the Commercial and Industrial taxonomy. What tags are used for the following items associated with the acquisition/payment process: inventory, accounts payable, cost of goods sold, gross profit.

Chapter **Fourteen**

Other Business Processes

AIS in the Business World

Richie's Diner

In the "AIS in the Business World" for Chapter 1, I wrote a bit about Richie's Diner (www.richiesdiner.com). Now that you know a bit about business processes, I'm coming back to that same organization to illustrate one of the three processes discussed in this chapter: the conversion process.

When a customer orders a meal from a table server, the conversion process begins. The table server records the order and takes it back to the kitchen where the cooks begin preparing it from basic ingredients. As you may recall from cost/management accounting, creating a finished product typically requires three components of cost: raw material, direct labor, and manufacturing overhead.

In the case of Richie's, as with most restaurants, the ingredients are the raw materials: eggs, pancake batter, biscuits, bacon, and a host of others. The wages of the kitchen staff are direct labor; they are the workers who actually prepare the food, often referred to as the "touch labor," because they touch the finished product.

All other costs associated with preparing the food are manufacturing overhead: utilities, supervisory salaries, indirect materials, and depreciation on the kitchen equipment. Whereas the costs of direct material and direct labor in a meal can be easily and cheaply measured, overhead costs are more problematic. They have to be allocated because they are either too difficult or too expensive to measure in a direct way.

In addition to the conversion process, we'll also examine two other important business processes in this chapter: human resources and financing.

Discussion Questions

1. Which activities in Porter's value chain are associated with the various business processes discussed in this chapter?
2. Why is it more challenging to talk about the "steps" in the conversion, human resources, and financing processes in a generic way, as we did with sales/ collection and acquisition/payment?
3. How are the five generic parts of the AIS discussed in Chapter 1 applied/ exemplified within the context of the various business processes discussed in this chapter?

In the last two chapters, we've examined business processes that are very similar even in diverse organizations. In this last chapter on business processes, we turn our attention to three others that can vary greatly in their detail, depending on the kind of organization you're considering: conversion, financing, and human resources.

When you finish studying this chapter, you should be able to complete the following tasks for each process listed above:

1. Explain its role and purpose.
2. Explain how the generic structure of most AIS applies.
3. Identify and process common transactions.
4. Design and critique internal controls based on common risk exposures.
5. Develop and interpret process-related systems documentation.

We'll be taking a "big picture" look at each process in the next few pages—not because these processes are less important or less interesting than those we've already examined, but because it's more difficult to talk about them in a generic way. The end-of-chapter exercises will give you plenty of opportunity to apply the concepts in specific situations.

CONVERSION PROCESS

Your study of cost accounting elsewhere in your accounting curriculum will discuss the conversion process in much greater depth.

Organizations can be classified in several ways in today's economy; one such way is by the basic nature of their operations: service, merchandising/retail, and manufacturing. The **conversion process** is typically associated with manufacturing enterprises; its basic purpose is to convert direct material, direct labor, and manufacturing overhead into a finished product. Collectively, direct material, direct labor, and manufacturing overhead are often referred to as "factors of production." Direct material refers to the major kinds of materials in a product—those you can easily "see" when you look at it. Direct labor refers to the salaries, wages, and benefits of assembly-line workers—people who are directly involved in the manufacture of the product. Manufacturing overhead, sometimes referred to as factory overhead, comprises everything else in the production operation. Items such as factory equipment depreciation, salaries of factory supervisors, factory utilities, and custodial costs are typically included in manufacturing overhead.

Manufacturing companies typically organize their conversion processes in one of three major ways: job costing, process costing, or a hybrid system that combines elements from both. Understanding the kind of production system a manufacturing firm uses is important because it helps us design the right kind of AIS.

In **job costing,** units of product are differentiated from one another; that is, you can tell them apart simply by looking at them. Custom-built homes or commissioned works of art fall into that category.

Process costing systems produced undifferentiated goods; in other words, you cannot tell them apart simply by looking at them. Think about mass-produced furniture, like the chairs in a university classroom, or office supplies, like three-ring binders, as examples of process costing.

Hybrid systems combine some elements of both job and process costing systems. They often take a base product (accounted for in a process costing model) and customize it (accounted for in a job costing model). A computer manufacturer, for example, might produce a base unit that can be customized with additional memory, different kinds of ports, and optical drives.

Give examples of two products that would be accounted for in a job costing system. Also give two examples for a process costing system.

AIS Elements

Although the specifics of every conversion process are different, certain tasks are common in nearly every one. And, as with the other business processes we've considered, we use conversion process documents as inputs and outputs of the AIS to track and report on those common activities. Consider Table 14.1, which summarizes some of the input and output documents for the conversion process.

As you can imagine, the processes associated with conversion can be radically different, depending on the finished product. Nevertheless, there are some common conversion process journal entries needed in the accounting information system. In a job costing system, those include:

- Purchasing raw materials
  - Debit raw material inventory
  - Credit accounts payable
- Accumulating costs by job
  - Debit "job account" (e.g., Job 123A)
  - Credit raw materials inventory
  - Credit wages payable (for direct labor costs)
  - Credit manufacturing overhead (for applied overhead)
- Selling finished goods
  - Debit accounts receivable
  - Debit cost of goods sold
  - Credit sales
  - Credit "job account"

In a process costing system, things are a bit more complex. Costs have to be moved from one process to another; they also have to be transferred to finish goods when units are completed and awaiting sale.

TABLE 14.1   Conversion Process Documents

Form Name	Purpose	Originator	Recipient
Materials requisition	Requests raw material from the warehouse for production	Production	Warehouse
Job cost sheet	Summarizes the material, labor, and overhead costs in a job costing system	Production	Accounting
Labor time ticket	Accumulates labor data (time, pay rate, total labor cost)	Production	Accounting
Production cost report	Summarizes cost and quantity information in a process costing system	Production	Accounting
Materials move ticket	Documents the movement of materials from the warehouse into production	Warehouse	Production

- Transferring costs from Process A to Process B
  - Debit Work in Process—Process B
  - Credit Work in Process—Process A
- Transferring costs of completed units to finished goods
  - Debit Finished Goods
  - Credit Work in Process—Process B

Data from the conversion process can be stored electronically or with paper. You would use file structures similar to those we examined in Chapters 12 and 13 for that purpose.

What risks need to be addressed in the conversion process? And what internal controls could organizations use to address them? Consider Table 14.2 as a starting point.

Consider the process of writing a textbook like this one. Authors and publishers typically go through a set of steps such as those listed below:

1. *Author:* Develop a textbook proposal. The proposal includes a general overview of the book and a sample first chapter. The author sends the materials to the publisher for review.
2. *Publisher:* Accept or reject the proposal. If accepted, prepare standard contracts governing the development and publication process.
3. *Author:* Write chapter drafts based on the proposal. Submit the drafts to the publisher in batches.
4. *Publisher:* Solicit professors in the field to review the chapters as they are submitted. Reviews consist of responses to a common set of questions.
5. *Publisher:* Summarize and analyze the reviewers' responses. Send them to the author.
6. *Author:* Revise chapters as necessary based on reviewer feedback. Submit revised chapters to publisher.
7. *Publisher:* Publish and print the text.

Figure 14.1 shows a flowchart depicting those steps.

Misek (2004) discussed the conversion process for Purcell Productions, "a full-service digital video production studio located in Alta Loma, California." Purcell follows a job costing system, as each job is unique. The steps in the company's conversion process include

1. Assemble a video crew for the job.
2. Two days before the event, clean, label, and pack all the cameras and tapes for transport to the job site. The company typically employs at least half a dozen cameras for a single job, thus increasing the chance of getting important parts of the event on film.

TABLE 14.2
Risks and controls in the conversion process

Risk	Control
Damage to raw materials	Special storage conditions Backup power supplies for heating and cooling
Loss / theft of raw materials	Secured storage areas Adequate documentation Separation of duties
Worker injuries	Workers' compensation insurance Safety training Protective clothing

FIGURE 14.1 **Conversion Process Flowchart**

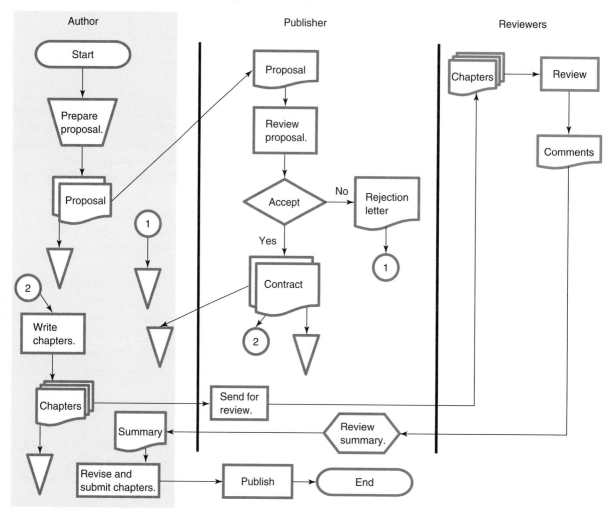

3. One day before the event, put all the cameras in place.

4. Shoot the event.

5. Use computer software to synchronize the views from the various cameras.

6. Edit the synchronized views according to client length specifications (e.g., roughly an hour for an automobile race or other motor sports event).

7. Output the edited film to a master camera and make copies according to the client's formatting needs (e.g., DVD, VHS, MP3).

Purcell would likely use a database to maintain names and contact information for video crew candidates. Naturally, the steps in this company's conversion process are significantly different than what you'd expect to find in, for example, an agricultural company or heavy-equipment manufacturer. The key in understanding the conversion process is to understand the company's operations. AIS designers and auditors can gather data via direct observation, interview, and/or survey, then prepare a flowchart to ensure that they understand the process thoroughly.

Draw a flowchart to depict the conversion process at Purcell Productions. What information would you want to capture in the "video crew" database? What other databases are indicated by the narrative? (You may find it helpful to read the Misek article.)

The risks managers confront in the conversion cycle are as unique as the steps in the cycle itself. In the Purcell Productions case, risks and controls that may help address them include

Risk	Control
Stolen equipment	Engraved identification Recorded serial numbers
Unreliable staff	Fidelity bonding Regular performance evaluations
Malfunctioning equipment	Backup equipment Regular periodic testing
Bad weather contributing to poor output	Production insurance Extra lighting for cloudy days
Software malfunction	Backup software

As you learned in our previous discussion of internal controls, the idea in risk assessment and internal control design is to understand the overall operation. Then, you can think of the most likely problems and create controls to mitigate those problems.

FINANCING PROCESS

Role and Purpose

Courses in intermediate accounting cover the technical aspects of these transactions, while finance courses explore them from a conceptual perspective with discussions of optimal capital structure and weighted average cost of capital.

In our discussion of the acquisition/payment process, we looked at how an organization acquires and pays for many of the physical assets it needs for operations, with a particular emphasis on inventory. But, organizations also need money to operate. While some money comes from the successful operation of the business, some funds have to come from outside; that's where the financing process comes into play.

In general, organizations have two choices about acquiring external financing: debt or equity. As you may recall from your introductory financial accounting course, debt financing has the following characteristics:

- Amounts borrowed must be repaid, usually with interest.
- Interest is, in most cases, a tax deduction.
- It does not dilute ownership of the business, but can throw a firm into bankruptcy if not repaid on time.

Treasury shares can be accounted for at par, but most organizations use the cost method.

You'll commonly see debt financing in the long-term liabilities section of a balance sheet.

Equity financing, on the other hand, is seen in the equity section of the balance sheet. Its characteristics include:

- Amounts do not have to be repaid.
- Dividends are optional, but are not a tax-deductible expense in most cases.
- Equity investors become owners of the organization.

Which is better, you might ask. The answer: it depends. The "best mix" of debt and equity financing is sometimes called the "optimal capital structure." You'll learn more about that topic in an introductory finance course.

AIS Elements

The input and output documents associated with the financing process include shares of capital stock, various forms of notes payable (including mortgages and bonds), and checks (for paying dividends, interest, and principal). Under certain circumstances, the SEC also requires registration forms before a publicly traded corporation can sell its securities in U.S. capital markets.

The process of issuing debt and/or equity securities is highly regulated and very detailed. So, we won't go into a lot of depth on it here. The very first time a corporation offers its stock for sale is called an initial public offering (IPO). The steps in an IPO are:

1. Choose an investment bank, an accounting firm, and a lawyer.
2. Develop a prospectus.
3. File the prospectus with the SEC and wait for approval.
4. Do a "road show" to solicit investors.
5. Distribute a final prospectus.
6. Determine the initial offering price and size of the IPO.
7. Sell the shares of stock.

In the accounting information system, we have to be concerned about how to record various **financing process transactions.** Some of those transactions include issuance of capital stock, purchase of treasury shares, issuance and repayment of long-term debt, and dividend distributions.

An initial public offering (IPO), as the name implies, marks the first time a company offers its securities for sale on a recognized stock exchange. The recordkeeping is more involved in an IPO than in subsequent securities transactions; for more information, point your Web browser to www.entrepreneur.com or do a Google search.

Reflection and Self-Assessment   14.3

Issuance of capital stock is recorded in the AIS by debiting cash for the total market price, crediting capital stock for the par value, and crediting additional paid-in capital for the difference. How are the other transactions listed above recorded?

Storing information about financing process transactions is particularly important. If a company misses a principal or interest payment or if it fails to issue a dividend check to the right stockholder, the consequences can be severe. The AIS therefore needs to capture at least the following information for financing process transactions:

- Equity financing transactions
  - Number of shares
  - Par value per share
  - Market value per share
  - Shareholder identification data
  - Dividend type
  - Dividend per share
  - Dividend dates

- Debt financing transactions
  - Principal
  - Coupon interest rate
  - Market interest rate
  - Issue date
  - Time to repayment
  - Frequency of payments
  - Lender identification data

In August 2005, Federated Department Stores (www.fds.com) completed an acquisition of the May Department Stores Company. Federated's Web site described the financial arrangements for stockholders associated with the merger: "Under terms of the merger agreement, May Company shareholders as of the time of merger on August 30, 2005, will receive $17.75 in cash and 0.3115 shares of Federated common stock for each share of May Company common stock." Consider the data flow diagram in Figure 14.2 illustrating the steps involved in fulfilling that agreement.

Clearly, the biggest risk associated with the financing business process is the misappropriation of cash, either through skimming or larceny. The internal controls over cash discussed in the previous chapters are at least as applicable to the financing business process: separation of duties, bank reconciliations, and adequate documentation, to name a few. Other risks here include missing payment deadlines and insufficient cash to repay principal. Missing payment deadlines can be addressed via automatic electronic funds transfers or simple scheduling software installed on accounting department computers. A sinking fund can be used to mitigate the risk of insufficient cash to repay principal. As you may know, a sinking fund is a pool of money restricted to just one purpose: debt repayment. Because of the time value of money, a borrower can put small amounts of cash into a

FIGURE 14.2   Stock Conversion Data Flow Diagram

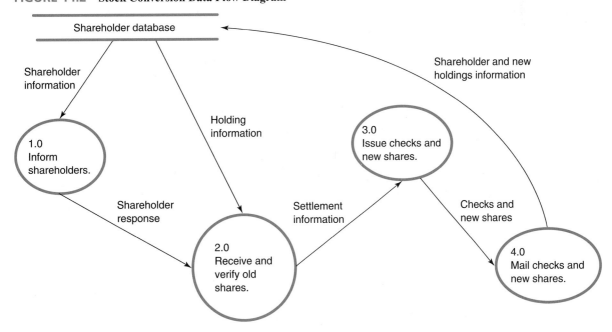

sinking fund throughout the life of the debt; when it matures, then, the sinking fund has sufficient cash to handle the transaction. Finally, a lender also may institute a debt covenant as an internal control. Debt covenants may restrict the borrower's ability to pay dividends to shareholders, specify a minimum current ratio level throughout the life of the debt, or hold the borrowing organization accountable for its overall financial leverage.

HUMAN RESOURCE PROCESS

Role and Purpose

The **human resource process** may be the most complex of all business processes today. Whole textbooks, courses, and fields of study have been devoted to its objectives, which include

- Hiring employees.
- Paying them.
- Coordinating employee benefits (insurance, pensions, and the like).
- Evaluating their performance.
- Managing their departures from the firm via termination, quitting, or retirement.

The Web site of the Professionals in Human Resources Association (www.pihra.org) lists many similar organizations involved in virtually all facets of the human resource process.

Consider the data flow diagram in Figure 14.3, which illustrates the preceding steps in the human resource process.

Because of its complexity and legal implications, many organizations outsource their human resource functions to organizations such as ADP.

FIGURE 14.3   Human Resource Process Data Flow Diagram

AIS Elements

From an AIS point of view, a main concern of the human resource process is the payroll function. It must be managed carefully and diligently to ensure accuracy and integrity. The **payroll forms** listed in Table 14.3 are commonly used as input and output documents in the payroll function.

Non-payroll forms associated with the human resource process would include completed job applications, interview notes, written performance reviews, and termination documents. As you can imagine, each of those can vary radically among firms.

Reflection and Self-Assessment   14.4

For each of the four documents mentioned in the preceding paragraph, suggest two or three information items you would want to include on it.

The risks associated with the human resource process fall into two major groups: financial and human. Financially, managers must ensure that they have sufficient cash on hand to meet payroll obligations; for that reason, companies often maintain a payroll checking account separate from their regular operating accounts. In addition, companies that pay employees by the hour typically need a way of tracking hours worked; Internet time-tracking systems or

TABLE 14.3   Payroll Forms

Form Name	Purpose	Data Included
Form W-4	Establishes payroll withholding status	Employee identification data Withholding status Number of withholding allowances
Form W-2	Reports year-end information for tax purposes	Employee identification data Employer identification data Gross pay and tax withholdings 401(k) contributions
Payroll register	Computes payroll data for all employees for a given pay period	Employee identification data Hours worked Pay rate Total gross pay Tax and benefit withholdings Net pay
Employee earnings record	Summarizes payroll data for a single employee for multiple pay periods	Virtually the same as the payroll register
Form 1099	Reports amounts paid to an independent contractor (I.C.)	I.C. identification data Payer's identification data Total amount paid
Form 940	Reports employer's federal unemployment taxes	Company name Amount paid
Form 941	Reports amounts withheld by employer to IRS	Company name Employee identification data Amounts withheld

Visit the Web site of the Internal Revenue Service (www .irs.gov) and find examples of all the preceding forms except the payroll register and employee earnings record. (The design of those two forms can vary significantly from organization to organization.)

even simple time clocks mitigate the risk that hours will be recorded and reported inaccurately. When employees depart the company, whether through quitting, termination, or retirement, their access to organizational information systems (e.g., intranet accounts, passwords) should be eliminated to mitigate the risks of hacking, sabotage, and other forms of fraud.

Human risks in this business process are equally significant; some might say the human risks are weightier than the financial risks because of their long-term nature and potential for costly litigation. Human risks associated with the HR business process include hiring unqualified workers, failing to follow applicable laws (such as the Americans with Disabilities Act), engaging in acts of sexual harassment, and illegal or inappropriate employee terminations. Perhaps the best internal control for all those risks is a well-informed, educated human resources staff. Seeking the advice of legal counsel also may be appropriate in some cases; adequate documentation of human resource processes is essential, regardless of the type of organization under consideration.

Fraud is also a significant risk associated with employees. Internal controls that can help prevent and detect fraud include

- *Thorough background checks.* Several years ago, one of my students applied for a job with the federal government. The agency sent a representative to my home to ask me about the student, who had listed me as a reference.
- *Forced vacations.* You may be thinking, "Why would anyone need to be forced to take a vacation?" Consider the case of accounts receivable lapping. A/R lapping occurs when a clerk steals money sent by one client, then uses money from another client to cover up the theft. For example, a clerk might steal money from Smith; then, when Jones pays her bill, the clerk would credit Jones's cash to Smith's account. Maintaining a lapping system requires an ongoing fraud; so, if an employee is forced to take a vacation, there's a greater chance of detecting the fraud than if vacations are not mandatory.
- *Adequate training and supervision.* We've looked at this control in connection with other business processes, but it's worth repeating here. Training can help promote effective and efficient operations, while adequate supervision can help safeguard assets.

While those controls will not prevent problems completely, they will be very effective in limiting opportunities to commit fraud.

CRITICAL THINKING

On January 1 of every year, the Tournament of Roses Parade winds its way down Colorado Boulevard in Pasadena, California. And, later that day, two football teams square off for the Rose Bowl. Check out www.tournamentofroses.com for information about both events.

As part of the Rose Parade, organizations from all over the world prepare floats; in recent years, the list included the City of Anaheim, Jack in the Box, and the National Association of Realtors. The two polytechnic universities in the California State University system (Cal Poly Pomona and Cal Poly San Luis Obispo) have a unique way of creating a float for the parade. The schools solicit design ideas from their students; after selecting a winner, each university builds half of the float. The two halves are joined in Pasadena, where the float is finished.

The tournament's Web site, referenced above, describes the float-building process like this:

> Float construction begins shortly after the previous year's Parade is over. The process starts with a specially built chassis, upon which is built a framework of steel and chicken wire. In a process called "cocooning," the frame is sprayed with a polyvinyl material, which is then painted in the colors of the flowers to be applied later. Every inch of the float must be covered with flowers or other natural materials, such as leaves, seeds, or bark. Volunteer workers swarm over the floats in the days after Christmas, their hands and clothes covered with glue and petals. The most delicate flowers are placed in individual vials of water, which are set into the float one by one.

Creating a Rose Parade float is an application of the conversion process because the factors of production (material, labor, and overhead) are combined into a finished product. Figure 14.4 presents a flowchart of how the float creation process works for the Cal Poly universities. The processes depicted in the flowchart (solicit ideas, submit proposals, choose design, and build float) would be represented with numbered circles in a leveled set of data flow diagrams. The "build float" process would probably be decomposed at least one level based on the steps described above.

At Cal Poly Pomona, many student organizations, such as Beta Alpha Psi, work on the Rose Parade float as part of their community service efforts. Thus, the system would need a database for tracking volunteer participation. One good way to organize that database would be with three tables. A "task table" would list the various tasks available to volunteers (build chassis, cocoon float, place materials), while a "volunteer table" would provide details for each volunteer (volunteer ID, last name, first name, organizational affiliation, e-mail, phone number). Because each volunteer can complete many tasks and each task can be completed by many volunteers, a "task/volunteer" junction table also would be required. Each record in the junction table would need fields for the date, number of hours worked (or starting and finishing times), task name, and volunteer ID.

FIGURE 14.4
Systems Flowchart of Rose Parade Float Conversion Process

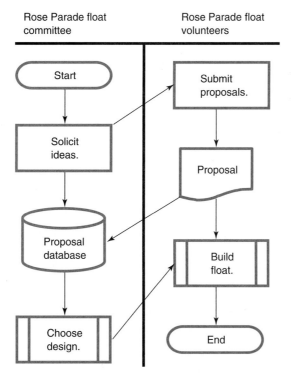

PROCESS RELATIONSHIPS

This chapter concludes our examination of business processes. In total, we've looked at five: sales/collection, acquisition/payment, conversion, financing, and human resources. We studied the business processes separately to focus attention on the issues for each one, but, in real organizations, the processes are interrelated and highly dependent on one another.

Organizations typically need three kinds of resources to function effectively: people, money, and other assets (such as supplies, inventory, and equipment). The *human resource* process is concerned with people—how do organizations find them, train them, compensate them, and manage their separation from the company (e.g., through retirement or termination)? The *financing* process is associated with money—in particular, funds obtained from outside the company. Those funds typically come in the form of debt and equity financing. The *acquisition/payment* process is concerned with other kinds of assets: inventory, office equipment, factory machinery, supplies, and furniture, for example. The *conversion* process is particularly applicable to manufacturers, but also has implications for other types of organizations. In the conversion process, manufacturing companies combine raw material, direct labor, and manufacturing overhead to create a finished product. Finally, then, the company sells its product (or service) through the *sales/collection* process.

Summary

This chapter concludes our discussion of business processes. We've looked at the conversion, financing, and human resource processes, briefly examining the same issues we considered for sales/collection and acquisition/payment. Table 14.4 summarizes the chapter's important points for each of the three processes.

TABLE 14.4
Chapter Summary

	Conversion	Financing	Human Resource
Role and purpose	Transform material, labor, and overhead into finished products	Obtain external funding from debt and equity securities	Manage employees from initial hiring to termination, including payroll and performance evaluation
AIS structure			
Input and output forms	Materials requisition, job cost sheet, labor time ticket, production cost report, materials move ticket	Shares of capital stock, various forms of notes payable, checks, SEC forms	W-2, W-4, 1099, 940, 941, payroll register, employee earnings record
Common transactions	Purchasing raw materials, accumulating and transferring costs, selling finished goods	Capital stock issuance, treasury shares purchase, dividend distributions, issuance and repayment of debt	Wage payments, tax deposits
Storage	Raw material data and transactions, cost accumulation data, and transactions	Capital stock files, shareholder data files, debtholder data files	Applicant database, employee database, payroll database
Internal controls	Adequate raw material storage, procedures manuals, separation of duties, insurance, training	Separation of duties, electronic funds transfers, sinking funds, debt covenants	Separate payroll checking account, time clocks, employee database update procedures, adequate training, background checks

Key Terms	conversion process, *251*	human resource process, *258*	payroll forms, *259*
	financing process, *255*	job costing, *251*	process costing, *251*
	financing process transactions, *256*		

Chapter Reference

Misek, M. 2004. "Home Is Where the Art Is." *Emedia,* August, pp. 36–38.

End-of-Chapter Activities

1. *Reading review questions.*

   a. What is the basic purpose of each business process discussed in this chapter (conversion, financing, human resources)?

   b. What are the similarities and differences between job costing and process costing systems? How is each system reflected in the organization of the accounting information system?

   c. What are the four common transactions associated with the financing business process? What information must be tracked for each transaction?

   d. What forms are commonly used in processing payroll transactions?

   e. How are the purposes of internal control fulfilled in each business process discussed in the chapter?

   f. Respond to the questions for this chapter's "AIS in the Business World."

2. *Reading review problem.* Dr. Mohamed Ali is an internal medicine physician in Upland, California; his office employs two nurses and a physician's assistant. Dr. Ali offers a variety of services, including smoking cessation and weight loss programs, in addition to his regular medical practice. In response to a trend that started as early as 2004, Dr. Ali maintains his patients' medical records electronically using software from Cerner Corporation (www.cerner.com).

   Consider the following comments about electronic medical records (EMR) technology:

   > [A study discussed in the *Journal of the American College of Surgeons*] reported that in just 16 months the University of Rochester (N.Y.) Medical Center recouped its initial $485,000 cost for an EMR system serving five outpatient offices and 28 doctors. The study compared actual before- and -after EMR costs of activities such as pulling and filing charts, creating new charts, and transcription. The savings with electronic medical records added up to $394,000 a year, meaning annual savings of $280,000 after operating costs, the study said.

   Advantages of EMR include labor cost savings, improved records accessibility, and the ability to query databases of patient information. Although security and privacy issues create some concern, information security techniques like encryption can help address them.

   Source: R. Roberts, "Electronic Records Provide Good Return on Investment," *Kansas City Business Journal*, June 8–14, 2007, www.cerner.com/public/Cerner_2.asp?id _ 26328 (January 22, 2009).

   a. How is the EMR system related to one or more of the business processes discussed in the chapter?

   b. Why is it important for accounting professionals to understand organizations in a comprehensive way?

   c. How does the EMR software and process relate to the five generic AIS elements?

3. *Multiple choice review.*

   1. In which type of costing system are goods undifferentiated?

      a. Job order

      b. Process

    c. Both a and b

    d. Neither a nor b

2. Which type of costing system combines characteristics from both job order and process systems?

    a. Activity-based costing

    b. Value chain costing

    c. Hybrid costing

    d. Just-in-time costing

3. Which of the following steps in an IPO typically occurs first?

    a. Determine the initial offering price.

    b. Develop a prospectus.

    c. Determine the size of the IPO.

    d. Sell shares of stock.

4. All of the following are typical database files in a human resource process except:

    a. Applicant.

    b. Employee.

    c. Payroll.

    d. Performance evaluation.

5. Which of the following payroll forms is most closely associated with independent contractors?

    a. Form W-2

    b. Form W-4

    c. Form 940

    d. Form 1099

4. *Making choices and exercising judgment.*

    a. In the last three chapters, you've learned about five different business processes: sales/collection, acquisition/payment, conversion, financing, and human resources. Draw a diagram or write a paper that explains the connections between the five.

    b. Phil and Lil are the owners of Planters for All, a company that makes small decorative planters for homes and offices. Their planters come in various shapes, including a well with a bucket, a telephone, a wheelbarrow, and others. Each shape can be made in two sizes: large and small. If you were advising Phil and Lil about setting up their production process, would you recommend a job costing system or a process costing system? Why?

    c. PKT Corporation has annual sales of $1,600,000 and a profit margin averaging 8 percent. The corporation employs 40 people and currently does its payroll processing internally. Typically, the two accounting staff spend one day every two weeks calculating and processing payroll; each accounting staff member's annual salary is $48,000. The president of PKT has asked your advice regarding outsourcing payroll processing. List and discuss at least three factors you would tell the president to consider in making this decision. Based on the data provided, should PKT outsource its payroll or keep doing it internally?

5. *Field exercises.*

    a. Look online or in your local Yellow Pages for a company that manufactures a product. Arrange an interview with a member of the company's accounting staff and a tour of its production facilities. Prepare a brief presentation or paper discussing the results of your research.

    b. Contact a local human resources professional or an attorney that specializes in labor law. Ask about legislation that impacts the human resource function in organizations, such as the Americans with Disabilities Act, the Family and Medical Leave Act, the Occupational Safety and Health Act, or the Immigration Reform and Control Act, or about the company's policies with regard to sexual harassment, substance abuse testing, or use of information technology. Prepare a brief presentation or paper discussing the results of your research.

6. *Costing systems.* Indicate whether each of the following types of businesses would be more likely to use a job or process costing system. Justify your choices.

   a. Architect

   b. Attorney

   c. Dentist

   d. Heavy-equipment manufacturer

   e. House painter

   f. Landscaper

   g. Magazine publisher

   h. Management consultant

   i. Pet groomer

   j. Tax preparer

7. *Transaction and business processes.* Which business process (conversion, financing, or human resources) is most closely associated with each transaction listed below?

   a. Payroll taxes expense
        Cash
   b. Manufacturing overhead
        Accumulated depreciation
   c. Treasury stock
        Cash
   d. Cash
        Capital stock
        Additional paid-in capital
   e. Payroll expense
        Wages payable
        Withholding taxes payable

   f. Retained earnings
        Capital stock
   g. Work in process
        Manufacturing overhead
   h. Interest expense
        Premium on bonds payable
        Interest payable
   i. Cash
        Discount on bonds payable
        Bonds payable
   j. Cost of goods sold
        Finished goods

8. *Transaction explanations.* Explain what is happening in each transaction presented in the previous exercise. For example, in transaction (*a*), the company is paying its share of payroll taxes.

9. *Payroll computations and analysis.* Eric is the president and chief executive officer of his own management consulting firm. He has five employees: Jon Jones, Lupe Bana, Austin Pei, Diane Driscoll, and Yu Chung Wright. Selected information for each employee is listed in the table below:

	Marital Status	Withholding Allowances	Hourly Wage	Hours Worked
Jon	Single	0	$50	80
Lupe	Single	1	65	85
Austin	Married	3	60	81
Diane	Married	3	55	90
Yu Chung	Married	4	40	75

Employees have three kinds of taxes withheld from their wages: federal income, state income, and Social Security. Social Security is withheld from all employees at 9.75 percent of their gross pay. Single employees have federal income tax withheld at a base rate of $200 plus $50 for each withholding allowance; married employees' federal tax withholding is $150 plus $25 for each withholding allowance. State income tax is withheld at 30 percent of the federal amount for each employee. Employees are paid every two weeks and receive 1.5 times their regular hourly wage for any hours in excess of 80. In addition, Jon and Austin contribute $50 each pay period to an employee pension fund; Lupe and Diane contribute $75 each pay period for group health insurance.

Using Access or Excel, prepare a payroll register based on the preceding data. Then, prepare a report for Eric that shows the average gross pay and the average hourly wage for all five employees. Finally, prepare a pie-chart graph for each employee showing the breakdown of gross pay into each amount withheld and net pay. (An example for Jon is shown below.)

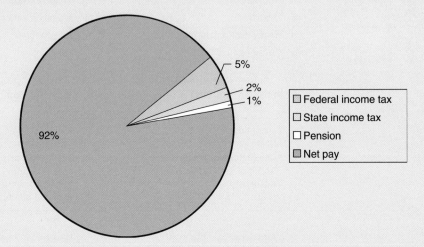

10. *Payroll forms data.* Several data items that might be included on a payroll form are listed below on the left. The standard payroll forms discussed in the chapter are listed below on the right. For each data item, indicate the form(s) on which you'd find it.

a. Address of employee	1. Form 940
b. Employee name	2. Form 941
c. Employer identification number	3. Form 1099
d. Federal income tax withheld	4. Form W-2
e. Location of employer	5. Form W-4
f. Marital status	
g. Number of withholding allowances	
h. Social Security number	
i. State income tax withheld	
j. Unemployment tax paid—federal	

11. *Risk analysis and internal controls.* In each independent situation below, identify and describe at least three risks. For each risk, suggest two internal controls to address it.

a. (CMA adapted, June 1992) Midwest Electronics Corp. manufactures computers. Recently, its products have met stiff competition from lower-priced imports, and the firm is seeking ways to improve its workers' productivity in order to maintain its market share. Over lunch in the company cafeteria, Alice Kumar (manager of the Accounting Department) and Greg Mossman (manager of the Sales Department) recently discussed a presentation made to the management of Midwest by a consultant on employee motivation. In the course of the conversation, Kumar recalled what happened at Spokane Computer Associates, her former employer. A national labor union had sought repeatedly to unionize the workers at the plant but had never succeeded. There was very little turnover among the workers, and the plant was considered a safe and pleasant place to work. Salaries were relatively high, and workers earned not only a base salary but incentive bonuses based on their individual output and company profits.

b. (CMA adapted, June 1992) Alaire Corporation manufactures several different types of printed circuit boards; however, two of the boards account for the majority of the company's sales. The first of these boards, a television circuit board, has been a standard in the industry for several years. The market for this type of board is competitive and, therefore, price sensitive. Alaire plans to sell 65,000 television circuit boards next year at a price of $150 each. The second high-volume product, a personal computer circuit board, is a recent addition to the company's product line. Because it incorporates the latest technology, it can be sold at a premium price; next year's budget calls for the sale of 40,000 personal computer boards at a price of $300 each.

c. (CMA adapted, December 1991) Microtronics Inc. is a private company involved in genetic engineering. The company was started several years ago by Joseph Graham, a scientist, and is financed by a group of venture capitalists. Microtronics has had some successful research, and one of its products recently received approval from the Federal Drug Administration (FDA). Two other products have been submitted to the FDA and are awaiting approval. Because of these successes, the investors believe the time is right for preparing the company for a public stock offering.

d. (CMA adapted, December 1991) Princess Corporation grows, processes, packages, and sells three apple products: sliced apples used in frozen pies, applesauce, and apple juice. The outside skin of the apple, which is removed in the Cutting Department and processed as animal feed, is treated as a by-product. In the company's conversion process, the Cutting Department washes the apples and removes the outside skin. The apples are then cored and trimmed for slicing; the three main products and the by-product are recognizable after processing in the Cutting Department. Each product is then transferred to a separate department for final processing. The trimmed apples are forwarded to the Slicing Department, where they are sliced and frozen. Any juice generated during the slicing operation is frozen with the slices. The pieces of apple trimmed from the fruit are processed into applesauce in the Crushing Department. Again, the juice generated during this operation is used in the applesauce. The core and any surplus apple generated from the Cutting Department are pulverized into a liquid in the Juicing Department. The outside skin is chopped into animal feed and packaged in the Feed Department.

e. (CMA adapted, June 1994) Damian Information Inc. is a four-year-old information processing and software development company serving a number of small clients in the midwestern United States. As its customer base has grown, DII has increased its staff to 30 employees. The company has been considering an arrangement whereby they would lease employees. Currently, there are in excess of 400 employee leasing companies in the United States representing nearly one million workers. The major users of this service are companies that need fewer than 100 workers. If DII were to enter into an employee-leasing arrangement, all of DII's current employees would become employees of the leasing company and then leased back to DII.

f. (CMA adapted, June 1994) Richmond Inc. operates a chain of department stores located in the northwest. The first store began operations in 1965 and the company has steadily grown to its present size of 44 stores. Two years ago, the board of directors of Richmond approved a large-scale remodeling of its stores to attract a more upscale clientele. Before finalizing these plans, two stores were remodeled as a test. Linda Perlman, assistant controller, was asked to oversee the financial reporting for these test stores, and she and other management personnel were offered bonuses based on the sales growth and profitability of these stores. Based on the apparent success of the test (sales growth for the two stores was reported at 11 percent and profitability showed a 14 percent increase), the board is now considering two alternatives for financing the balance of the remodeling effort. Alternative one involves pure debt financing. The company would make a public offering of bonds with a face value of $30 million and a stated interest rate of 11 percent. Alternative two is a combination alternative. It would involve $12 million in 9 percent bonds, common stock of $14.5 million, and retained earnings of $4.5 million. The current market value of Richmond's common stock is $30 per share; the dividends per share have held steady at $3.00 per share for the last year, but investors are expecting growth of 6 percent in the dividend.

12. *Systems documentation.* In each of the following independent cases, document the system using whatever technique(s) your instructor specifies.

   a. Dreambox Creations (www.dreamboxcreations.com/) in Diamond Bar, California, partners with Automatic Data Processing Inc. (ADP) for its payroll processing. Dreambox employs Internet-based time tracking. Employees log in and out based on the client for whom they're working; in that way, the company can track billable hours, which feed into the sales/collection process. (The concept of billable hours is also important in other professional organizations such as law firms and CPA firms.) Dan, in charge of operations and information technology, summarizes each employee's hours on a biweekly basis. He transmits them to ADP electronically or via telephone; ADP then processes the payroll, including all tax withholdings and deposits. ADP also handles Dreambox's year-end reporting via W-2 forms. Dreambox maintains a payroll account separate from its regular operating cash account for internal control purposes. ADP sends paper checks drawn on the payroll account back to Dan, who distributes them to the employees. The checks lag the pay period by one week; for example, checks for the pay period January 10 to January 21 are distributed on January 28.

   b. Point your Web browser to www.sba.gov, the Web site for the Small Business Administration. The SBA is a federal organization that helps entrepreneurs start and manage businesses. Click the link for "Financing Your Business." Browse the topics under "Financing Eligibility Topics" as the basis for documenting the system.

   c. Hiring new faculty is one of the most important human resource processes for universities. The department chair requests funding for a new full-time position and sends it to the dean, who approves or rejects the request. If approved, the department selects a faculty hiring committee. Their first task is to prepare a position description, which must be approved by the university's human resource office. The position description is submitted by the search committee to various Web sites, professional organizations, and periodicals; candidates submit required documentation for consideration. The committee reviews the required documentation and selects a small number of candidates for phone interviews. Based on the phone interviews, a few candidates (perhaps three to five) are invited to an on-campus interview. Based on feedback from references and on-campus interviews, the hiring committee forwards names to the dean, who makes the final selection. The dean's office sends out offer letters, which are either accepted or rejected by the applicant.

   d. Geoff is a Registered Tax Preparer in the State of California. Each year, he renews his registration on the Web site of the California Tax Education Council (www.ctec.org/). Geoff then makes his advertising plans for the year, which usually include direct mail flyers and classified ads in local newspapers. He also sends out appointment cards to his clients from the previous year; about 80 percent of them hire Geoff again. Clients call Geoff to make an appointment; Geoff maintains his appointment schedule in his personal digital assistant (PDA). He uses commercial software to prepare and e-file each client's return.

   e. Corporations that want to prepare for an initial public offering (IPO) generally follow a seven-step process for doing so. (1) Hire an investment bank. (2) Work with the investment bank to prepare an underwriting agreement—a contract that governs the IPO. (3) File a registration statement with the Securities and Exchange Commission. (4) Wait for SEC staff to verify the information in the registration statement—this step is often referred to as a "cooling off period." (5) Issue a preliminary prospectus. (6) Conduct one or more due diligence meetings with accountants, lawyers, and company management. (7) Issue the final prospectus.

13. *Database design.*

   a. Consider the May Company/Federated Department Stores data flow diagram presented in Figure 14.2. What information would you want to capture in the shareholder database to facilitate the conversion transaction?

   b. Consider the generic human resource process data flow diagram presented in Figure 14.3. What information would you want to capture in the employee database and/or payroll database to facilitate the indicated processes?

c. Consider one or more of the diagrams you prepared in Activity 12 above. Create the specifications for any database tables, included in those diagrams.

14. *Terminology.* Please match each item on the left with the most appropriate item on the right.

1. Custom-made bicycles	a.	Associated with dividend payments
2. Date of record	b.	Human resource process internal control
3. Direct material	c.	Internal control for missed payments
4. Electronic funds transfer	d.	Job costing product
5. Factory supplies	e.	Method for gathering data
6. Number of interest payments	f.	Needed for stock issuance transaction
7. Observation	g.	Overhead
8. Par value of a share	h.	Process costing product
9. Pencils	i.	Required data for long-term debt transactions
10. Time clock	j.	Steel, for an automobile

15. *Multiple choice questions.*

1. A company that reproduces fine works of art, such as the Mona Lisa, would most likely use what kind of production process?
   a. Hybrid
   b. Conversion
   c. Job
   d. Process

2. A journal entry in a company's accounting information system debited retained earnings. The purpose of the journal entry is most likely
   a. To record the declaration of a cash dividend.
   b. To account for the sale of finished goods inventory.
   c. To apply manufacturing overhead.
   d. To account for an employee leasing arrangement.

3. TRN Corporation produces a product that is highly perishable. Which of the following internal controls is the best alternative for controlling the risk of product spoilage?
   a. Separation of duties
   b. Adequate documentation
   c. Employee training
   d. Specialized storage containers

4. In a DFD of the human resources business process, "evaluate employees" would be represented with a
   a. Line.
   b. Circle.
   c. Rectangle.
   d. Triangle.

5. RKH Corporation maintains its job costing system using a relational database. Which of the following pieces of information would not be stored in a table in their system?
   a. Total cost of Job A244
   b. Manufacturing employee names
   c. Department affiliations of each employee
   d. Location of manufacturing equipment

16. *Statement evaluation.* Indicate whether each statement below is (i) always true, (ii) sometimes true, or (iii) never true. For statements that are (ii) sometimes true, explain when the statement is true.

   a. All five business processes discussed in the text are required to create value for stakeholders.

   b. Companies with long-term debt establish sinking funds.

   c. Conversion process forms are paper-based.

   d. Individual units of product in a process costing system are homogeneous.

   e. Information technology eliminates the problem of accounts receivable lapping.

   f. Separation of duties can be applied to fixed assets used in the conversion process.

   g. The "date of record" determines who receives dividends on capital stock.

   h. The par value of a share of capital stock is determined by the stock market.

   i. The total cost of a batch of units should be calculated and stored in a relational database table.

   j. With respect to long-term debt, the "coupon interest rate" and the "market interest rate" are two ways of referring to the same thing.

17. *Prior material application.*

   a. You read a bit about Porter's value chain at the beginning of Chapter 12. The value chain links together most, if not all, of the business processes we've examined in the last three chapters. To illustrate how, point your Web browser to www.heatercraft.com, a small manufacturer of marine accessories and other products in northern Idaho. List the primary and support activities in Porter's value chain, and give an example of each activity for Heater Craft. For example, the Web site itself is an example of "marketing and sales" in the value chain.

   b. Use COSO's enterprise risk management framework to develop a risk management plan for Heater Craft (or some other organization that focuses on one of the business processes discussed in the chapter).

   c. Most of today's college and university students have never known a world without information technology; MP3 players, digital video recorders, and laptop computers are commonplace tools in the twenty-first century. Work with a group of students to "invent" some new IT tool that will improve one or more of the business processes discussed in this chapter; for example, a voice-activated system for accessing employees' human resource records. Then, use the systems development life cycle to explain how you would develop and implement your idea.

Part Five

Other Topics in AIS

This last section of the book comprises three chapters:

The chapters in this section build on what you already know; they also connect AIS to other areas of accounting and business. In Chapter 15, you'll learn about Steps for Better Thinking, a structured way to make decisions. You'll also learn about knowledge management, another application of relational database technology.

Chapter 16 considers the critically important topic of ethics. Historic and recent ethics scandals (such as Enron and Bernie Madoff) have rocked the accounting profession, calling into question the ethics and professionalism of accountants in virtually every employment sector. In this chapter, you'll learn what it means to be "a professional." You'll also be exposed to fundamental ideas about ethics and the ethics codes of several professional organizations. The chapter ends by offering some suggestions for planning your career in accounting.

The last chapter of the text provides an introduction to auditing. It discusses various kinds of audits you're likely to encounter in your career and focuses on the financial statement audit. You'll likely have at least one course in financial statement auditing as part of your accounting degree; this chapter will show you how that important area of practice is related to all you've learned about AIS.

Chapter **Fifteen**

Decision-Making Models and Knowledge Management

AIS in the Business World

Knowledge Management in CPA Firms

If studying the previous chapters in this book has taught you anything, I hope they've impressed on you the complexity of practicing accounting in today's global business community. As in most industries, younger professionals have a lot to learn from more experienced professionals; that's where one of our topics for this chapter (knowledge management) comes into play.

Consider the following comments by Kepczyk:

> The AICPA has stated that in the next decade, a significant number of CPAs will leave the profession . . . If the information these CPAs have is not captured in some format by the firm, it will be lost forever. Firms are also aware that there are personnel in their own or peer firms that have figured out procedural best practices that make certain individuals measurably more efficient than others performing the same tasks. If these best practices are not identified and standardized in a formal process, it is highly unlikely that this efficiency will be shared with other users in the firm.

An effective knowledge management system can go a long way in addressing the issues Kepczyk raised.

Discussion Questions

1. Why are knowledge management and decision-making processes important in the study of accounting information systems?
2. What is a knowledge management system?
3. What other kinds of decision contexts do practicing accountants confront? How can they make decisions effectively and efficiently?

Source: R. H. Kepczyk, "Key Concepts in CPA Knowledge Management," *CPA Practice Management Forum* (July 2010).

Accounting is all about decision making—whether you're making decisions about the design and implementation of an accounting information system or using accounting information as the basis for decision making or in some other context. But, at the same time, the information available to business professionals for those decisions is increasing exponentially. So, how do accounting professionals manage all that information? And how do they make decisions based on it? We'll explore those two questions in this chapter.

When you've finished studying it, you should be able to:

1. Discuss and give examples of the concept of information overload, including causes, symptoms, and countermeasures.
2. Explain the nature of decision models and knowledge management.
3. Explain why those two topics are important in the study of accounting information systems.
4. Describe and apply Wolcott and Lynch's Steps for Better Thinking.
5. Develop a personal strategy for making decisions and managing knowledge, including available information technology and other resources.

The principles and ideas we'll discuss in this chapter have broad application across a wide range of business and nonbusiness disciplines. We'll keep our focus, though, on their application and meaning in the context of accounting information systems.

INFORMATION OVERLOAD AND OTHER BARRIERS TO GOOD DECISIONS

Even Albert Einstein is often credited with acknowledging that he couldn't deal with more than seven variables simultaneously—surely a sign that even he was susceptible to information overload!

The idea that managers can be receiving "too much information" goes back to at least the 1960s, according to Eppler and Mengis (2004). They provide several definitions of **information overload,** including (p. 328):

> The decision maker is considered to have experienced information overload at the point where the amount of information actually integrated into the decision begins to decline. Beyond this point, the individual's decisions reflect a lesser utilization of the available information.

> Information overload occurs when the volume of the information supply exceeds the limited human information processing capacity. Dysfunctional effects such as stress and confusion are the result.

> Information overload occurs when the information-processing requirements (information needed to complete a task) exceed the information-processing capacity (the quantity of information one can integrate into the decision-making process).

> Information overload occurs when the decision maker estimates he or she has to handle more information than he or she can efficiently use.

Notice what all those definitions have in common: our brains have a limited capacity for processing information. When too much information starts coming in, or information comes in faster than we can process it, information overload is the result.

So what are the **causes of information overload?** Eppler and Mengis distilled the writing of more than a dozen authors spanning over 30 years of research in this area. They suggest five fundamental causes of information overload (2004, p. 332), as shown in Figure 15.1.

Personal factors refer to everyone's individual limitations to process information. For example, I process information much better in the afternoon and evening than I do in the morning—something my own students can easily verify! If you've ever stayed up all night finishing a school project, you may have noticed your own ability to process information erodes. But, on the positive side, you can probably process more information today than you could 10 years ago, simply because you have more life experience and skills to help you manage information.

FIGURE 15.1

**Causes of
Information
Overload**

Source: Eppler and Mengis,
2004, p. 332.

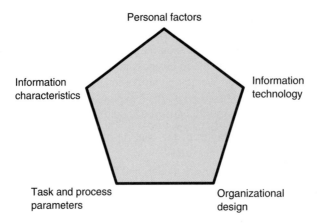

Personal factors

Information
characteristics

Information
technology

Task and process
parameters

Organizational
design

Readability indexes, such as the Gunning Fog index, can give an objective measure of a text's difficulty. A Web search on readability indexes or the Gunning Fog index will return a lot of information, including how to calculate a readability level.

Information characteristics also play an important part in triggering information overload. Information can be uncertain, ambiguous, complex, and intense—all of which create a greater opportunity for decision makers to become overloaded. Consider, for example, the complexity of information you read in an accounting text compared to the information complexity in a newspaper or novel. Newspapers and novels are likely to be much easier to "digest" than an accounting book, simply because of the nature of the information they contain.

Task and process parameters are the third cause of information overload identified by Eppler and Mengis. Have you ever had to make a decision under significant time pressure? If you're like most accounting students, the answer is a resounding "Yes!" Time pressure is one process parameter than can contribute to information overload. If you've taken any intermediate accounting courses, or perhaps a course or two in taxation, you may have found the rules and standards in one or both areas both numerous and incredibly detailed. Other causes of information overload in this area include nonroutine tasks, task complexity and interdependencies, and interruptions.

Fourth, Eppler and Mengis discuss *organizational design.* You've probably experienced this cause of information overload if you've ever worked on a group project in school or in practice. People in groups have differing ideas and approaches for problem solving and decision making; integrating all those different points of view can easily lead to information overload.

The final cause of information overload, according to Eppler and Mengis, is *information technology.* Think of all the ways IT provides you with information: e-mail, instant messaging, cell phones, the Internet, increased numbers of television channels. Every day, people are bombarded with information—much more so than in the past. Having all that information coming at you virtually all the time is bound to create some information overload.

Reflection and Self-Assessment   15.1

Think of a recent experience you had with information overload. What caused it? Can you classify the causes according to the five items in Figure 15.1? For example, as I started to write this chapter, I did a quick online library search for articles dealing with information overload—the search returned over 500 separate sources! My information overload came from three of the five sources: information characteristics, task and process parameters, and information technology.

Since you've probably experienced information overload at one time or another, you probably have at least some idea of its symptoms and effects. Eppler and Mengis grouped the symptoms and effects into four categories and provided several examples of each (2004, p. 333):

- Limited information search and retrieval strategies (information overload causes people to be less effective when looking for information).
  - Less systematic searching.
  - Increased problems differentiating relevant and irrelevant information.
- Arbitrary information analysis and organization (too much information coming in too fast impairs a person's ability to organize and classify information).
  - Overlapping and inconsistent categories.
  - Difficulty seeing "the big picture."
- Suboptimal decisions (decision making is weakened, producing poor results).
  - Inefficient work.
  - Reduced quality and accuracy of decisions.
- Strenuous personal situations (information overload takes its toll on people physically, psychologically, mentally, and spiritually).
  - Stress, confusion, and cognitive strain.
  - Overconfidence.

Are you experiencing information overload right now? Can you describe how it is impacting you?

Of course, the examples given above are but a few of many ways people respond to information overload.

So, since information overload is such a widespread problem, and since its impacts can be diverse and severe, how can managers deal with it? Returning to the five-part framework suggested in Figure 15.1, Eppler and Mengis examined the literature and noted the following **countermeasures** for information overload (2004, pp. 335–36):

- Allow more time to complete important tasks.
- Compress, aggregate, categorize, and structure information.
- Create small, self-contained tasks rather than trying to do everything at once.
- Define decision models and rules for common decision contexts.
- Focus on creating value-added information.
- Formalize the language used to describe information.
- Handle information as it comes to you—don't put it off!
- Improve personal information management.
- Improve personal time management skills and techniques.
- Use graphs and other visual aids.

The list could go on for another page or two, but I don't want you to experience information overload from reading it!

Reflection and Self-Assessment   15.2

Classify the countermeasures noted above using the five categories in Figure 15.1. For each category, suggest at least one other strategy you could use to combat information overload.

Simon (1997) talked about two additional reasons people don't always make the "best" decisions: **satisficing** and **bounded rationality.** *Satisficing* refers to people's tendency to stop looking for solutions to a problem when they find a solution that works—whether that decision is the "best" or not. For example, an accountant trying to choose a piece of general ledger software might "settle" for the first package that came along, rather than continuing to search for software that might meet his or her needs even better.

Bounded rationality is a separate, but related, idea; it means that people will inherently avoid uncertainty and rely on proven "rules" for problem solving whenever they can. Suppose your friend rides with you to school one day and later tells you that there's a better route to take than the way you usually go. The concept of bounded rationality would predict that you'll keep going the same way as always, avoiding the uncertain (and perhaps better) alternative. In our example above, bounded rationality might cause a decision maker to reject hiring a consultant if he or she has had poor experience with consultants in the past.

Betsch et al. (2004) talked about the idea of **relapse errors** in decision making. Their research revealed that people will follow a familiar routine, even if the routine is ineffective and even if they have a positive intention to change. Perhaps you know a student who spends most weekends partying instead of studying. That student may say to him/herself: "I really need to stop partying so much on the weekends. It's starting to impact my grades, and I don't like that." The idea of relapse errors indicates that, even with the positive intention to change, the student is likely to continue repeating the same behavior over and over again. And, in the AIS example, relapse errors might cause a decision maker just to adopt a newer version of an old piece of software, without considering a broad range of choices.

Do the ideas of satisficing, bounded rationality, and relapse errors mean that people are doomed to make bad decisions? Of course not! But it takes tremendous effort to change ineffective decision-making processes, and being aware of those three important ideas may help.

Reflection and Self-Assessment   15.3

Kathy has just started her own business after graduating from college. She is a management consultant, specializing in the development of business plans. She comes to you, a recent accounting graduate, for help in setting up her accounting information system. How would the ideas of satisficing and bounded rationality affect your advice to Kathy?

If you'd like to know more about the ideas in this section of the chapter, use your school's library to locate and read the Eppler and Mengis article. They do an excellent job of distilling and synthesizing the work of many other authors on this important topic.

DECISION MODELS AND KNOWLEDGE MANAGEMENT

One of the ways to combat information overload is to apply effective models for making decisions and managing knowledge. A "model" in this context refers to a generalized set of processes employed to accomplish a specific task. For example, you may have a model for how you get ready to go to school; it is probably significantly different from the model you use when you get ready to go out with friends.

Within the context of an organization, the generalized set of processes people use to gather, organize, and retain information has become known as *knowledge management,* defined as "the organization of intellectual resources and information systems within a business environment" (MSN Encarta dictionary). Santosus and Surmacz (2005) defined **knowledge management** as "the process through which organizations generate value from their intellectual and knowledge-based assets. Most often, generating value from such assets involves sharing them among employees, departments and even with other companies in an effort to devise best practices. It's important to note that the definition says nothing about technology; while [knowledge management] is often facilitated by IT, technology by itself is not [knowledge management]." In today's world, knowledge is power. Organizations no longer derive most of their wealth from physical assets such as cash in the bank or property, plant, and equipment. Information drives the 21st-century economy, and business professionals need strategies for capturing and organizing information, as well as for using that information for making decisions.

Rowley (1999) identified four objectives of knowledge management:

1. *To create knowledge repositories.* Think of this objective as developing a "library" for your organization. Knowledge here can refer to information on the competitive landscape, results of internal research, and the experiences of others in the organization.

2. *To improve knowledge access.* Here, we're talking about making knowledge more available throughout an organization. The most competitive organizations today share knowledge among individuals and responsibility centers. In fact, Drucker (1993) pointed out that knowledge may be the only genuinely sustainable economic resource in the modern economy.

3. *To enhance the knowledge environment.* This objective means stakeholders have a responsibility to create conditions that facilitate knowledge creation and sharing. Techniques that fall into this category include participative management, 360-degree performance evaluation, and decentralized management structures. Fundamentally, creating an environment of knowledge sharing is an issue of organizational culture.

4. *To manage knowledge as an asset.* The strict accounting definition of an asset is a probable future economic benefit obtained or controlled by a particular entity as a result of past transactions or events. While "knowledge" probably falls within that definition, we simply don't know how to measure its economic value for financial-reporting purposes. But, even though you won't see "knowledge" listed as an asset on organizational balance sheets, it must be managed for organizational benefit.

Call (2005) pointed out that "effective knowledge management changes the way organizations and individuals function." Building on the ideas of Nesbitt (2002), Call advocated seven **steps to create a knowledge management system.** Those steps are listed below; the text that follows each step provides an example of how it might "work" in practice.

For more information on organizational culture and its importance, consult the writings of Edgar Schein and/or Vijay Sathe.

1. *Create an organizational culture that supports the ideas of knowledge sharing and development.* In 2010, I worked on a research project at a firm in northern Idaho: Heatercraft Inc. (www.heatercraft.com/). Heatercraft is a well-run organization with a culture that supports the ideas of knowledge sharing and development. The managers I met through the research talked about how their recently implemented ERP system had really helped the firm become more cohesive by providing information that linked together its separate departments and product lines.

2. *Define the business goals the knowledge management system will address.* Heatercraft operates in a highly specialized market; therefore, the goal of a knowledge management system might be to increase the efficiency and effectiveness of production processes, leading to lower costs and higher margins.

3. *Perform a knowledge audit to identify any duplication, gaps, and overlaps in an organization's knowledge base.* A knowledge audit could be as simple as a series of staff meetings or as complex as a formal research project. Although every organization will have its own approach to a knowledge audit, one good approach would involve Heatercraft personnel asking questions such as: What steps are involved in creating and selling our products? Which staff have ideas for improving those steps? How do their ideas interact/contradict one another?

4. *Create a visual map that describes units of knowledge and the relationships between them.* If critical areas of knowledge at Heatercraft include technical, communications, financial, and marketing, a visual map might look like Figure 15.2.

5. *Develop a knowledge management strategy based on the content management, integration, search mechanisms, information delivery, and collaboration.* A strategy refers to a consistent set of processes, policies, and procedures designed to achieve a specific purpose. Heatercraft's knowledge management strategy might include periodic the company's meetings, and client surveys to determine the company's strengths and weaknesses.

FIGURE 15.2
Sample Knowledge Map

6. *Purchase or build appropriate tools for capturing, analyzing, categorizing, and distributing knowledge.* Heatercraft might employ an Access database for this purpose; it might also use its enterprise resource planning system. Tables could be organized around the four themes in the visual map; each table might contain fields for comment number (auto-generated), contributor (employee name), product line/department involved, and "lesson learned" (perhaps a "memo" field). Queries and reports could be based on any of those fields; for example, what lessons were learned from doing business with XYZ Corporation.

7. *Periodically reassess the value of the knowledge management system and make necessary adjustments.* Knowledge is not static; therefore, knowledge management systems cannot be static either. The staff at Heatercraft could review the system annually to determine any needed changes in organizational culture, visual map categories, database layout, and other aspects of the system.

Of those seven tasks, the first one is probably the most daunting. A detailed analysis of how to change organizational culture is far beyond the scope of this text, but you probably have run across the idea of organizational culture in management and/or organizational behavior courses.

Reflection and Self-Assessment 15.4

You might think of the FASB pronouncements that govern financial reporting as a form of knowledge management—although some would say those pronouncements are becoming too extensive and complex to do the job effectively. Suggest at least one other way we organize information in accounting; draw your example from your prior study of any area of accounting (financial, managerial, taxation, etc.).

The idea that accounting involves complex, open-ended problems may come as a surprise to you. In many accounting texts, the focus is on presenting problems with single correct responses. They form the foundation of the Steps for Better Thinking process but are not completely representative of the kinds of problems you'll have to solve in practice.

Business problems today require creative, critical thinking—bringing us to a discussion of Wolcott and Lynch's Steps for Better Thinking (2005). **Steps for Better Thinking** (SBT) is a developmental problem-solving and decision-making process. It is especially relevant to the kinds of problems we face in business today—complex and open-ended, without single, "correct," deterministic responses.

SBT starts with a foundation level, and proceeds through four problem-solving processes. Each process is more complex than the one before it. Wolcott (2005) presented the steps as shown in Figure 15.3.

Developing the skills in SBT is a lifelong process. It takes deliberate, intensive practice to ingrain the steps into your everyday decision-making process. Consider the reading review problem at the end of this chapter. Here's how an analysis of the decision might look using SBT.

1. *Identifying.*

   a. Problem: The problem investigated by Vera-Muñoz, Ho, and Chow was how to improve knowledge sharing in CPA firms. We're going to look at this problem from the point of view of a CPA trying to improve knowledge sharing in his/her own firm—an issue you're highly likely to encounter in your own professional career.

FIGURE 15.3
Steps for Better Thinking

Source: Adapted with permission; Copyright 2005 by Susan K. Wolcott. Steps for Better Thinking and related materials can be accessed at www.wolcottlynch.com.

Step 4: *Envisioning*—deal with limitations to solution and use information to inform future decisions.

Step 3: *Prioritizing*—prioritize factors to consider, choose, and implement solution(s).

Step 2: *Exploring*—interpret and organize the information.

Step 1: *Identifying*—identify the problem, relevant information, and uncertainties.

Foundation: *Knowing*—acquire background knowledge and skills.

The steps are presented in a very linear way in this example. In "real life," decision makers might move back and forth between the steps as new information comes to light.

 b. Relevant information: As background, a decision maker would have to acknowledge the legal and regulatory requirements, such as SOX and the PCAOB, that increase the need for knowledge sharing. In addition, particularly in the current economy, organizations are trying to control costs as much as they can; knowledge sharing may help reduce costs since people won't have to "reinvent the wheel" every time an issue arises.

 c. Uncertainties: As with most decisions, there are plenty of uncertainties here! Are people in the organization willing to share knowledge? Do they know how to do so efficiently and effectively? What information technology tools, if any, will be needed to promote knowledge sharing?

2. *Exploring.*

 a. Biases: While some people are very open to sharing knowledge, others are likely to be resistant (biased against it). The second of the researchers' three recommendations acknowledges this idea.

 b. Assumptions: Knowledge sharing is a good idea. The recommendations offered are practical and legitimate.

 c. Qualitative interpretation from various points of view:

  i. Inexperienced CPAs may feel they don't have much knowledge to share, so they may be less willing to express an opinion or offer suggestions.

  ii. Experienced CPAs may believe they don't have much to learn from others.

  iii. Some clients may be in favor of knowledge sharing as a way to reduce the cost of an audit; on the other hand, clients that have something to hide may not want CPAs to share knowledge.

 d. Information organization: A professional trying to decide whether (and how) to implement knowledge sharing could develop a simple list of costs and benefits, based on reading, self-reflection, and conversation with others. To the extent that those costs and benefits can be quantified reliably, a projected overall cost–benefit of knowledge sharing could be estimated.

3. *Prioritizing.*

   a. Ranked list of factors to consider (note that this ranking is still highly subjective and might differ between decision makers):

     i. Human factors.

     ii. Required information technology knowledge and tools.

     iii. Financial costs and benefits.

   b. Conclusion: Develop a limited knowledge-sharing program on a pilot basis—perhaps within one department or with a subset of clients. The pilot project would help the CPA firm work out some problems before the system was more widely disseminated.

4. *Envisioning.*

   a. Limitations of endorsed solution (decision makers would monitor and report on these over time, using them to inform later decisions):

     i. Knowledge sharing requires a change in organizational culture—seldom an easy thing to accomplish.

     ii. Pilot testing in a subset of the organization may lead to rumors and later bias against knowledge sharing.

   b. Skills integration: Once the pilot test was done, decision makers could use the information to spread the knowledge-sharing project throughout the firm. The program should be monitored and assessed periodically; that is, people should ask whether the program is working. In that way, any needed changes can be implemented.

Reflection and Self-Assessment   15.5

Consider the case of Kathy presented in Reflection and Self-Assessment 15.3. Use the Steps for Better Thinking model to prepare your advice to Kathy.

As you can see, using the Steps for Better Thinking to reach a decision is a detailed process. As noted above, the ability to use the steps must be deliberately, consistently, and continually developed over time; a decision maker's comfort level with the steps will increase with practice, though, and careful application of SBT will typically result in high-quality decisions.

CRITICAL THINKING

In this chapter, we've looked at three important topics: information overload, knowledge management systems, and Steps for Better Thinking. Let's look at a comprehensive example that connects all three topics.

Consider the following situation:

Ricardo, Erika, Stephen, Travis, and Qian all work in the Accounting Department of CHL Corporation; they all have undergraduate degrees in accounting and professional licenses/certifications (CPA, CMA, and the like). Erika is the vice president and corporate controller; the other four are associate vice presidents for specific functions. CHL was getting ready to expand its operations into Brazil, and the five accountants were on a team charged with finding out more about Brazil in anticipation of the expansion. They were supposed to prepare a report with the following sections: country background (history, language, geography), environmental factors (national culture, legal and political systems, business environment), financial matters (currency, exchange rates, taxation), accounting standards (local GAAP, International Financial Reporting Standards), and conclusions/recommendations. Their boss had given them two weeks to complete the task; during that time, they would be relieved of some (but not all) of their usual responsibilities.

What sources of information overload is the team likely to experience? And how should they deal with them? Here are some thoughts on those two questions:

Information Overload Source	Strategy for Managing
Personal factors	Set aside specific times for working on the project and for team meetings to discuss progress.
Information characteristics	Develop a detailed outline of the topics to include in each section of the report.
Task and process parameters	Create a schedule that will allow them to complete the project on time. Ask for additional time if necessary.
Organizational design	Estimate the amount of time each section of the report will take; divide up the responsibility as evenly as possible.

With so much information to synthesize, the team might decide to create a knowledge management system (KMS) as an organizational aid. The report will have five sections, so the KMS could be organized in that way. Each section will have multiple pieces of information; suppose (for the sake of simplicity) that each piece of information applies to only one section. The team could create a database table with the following fields: record number, report section, date, contributor, information source, summary. "Record number" would be the primary key, and could be set up as an "auto-number" field. The team could develop a data input form that would incorporate drop-down lists (i.e., combo boxes) for the "report section" and "contributor" fields. "Information source" should provide a complete reference for accessing the information after its initial input; the field could include (for example) Web addresses, book and article citations, and interview details. The team could set up queries based on report sections and/or other criteria; reports based on those queries would be useful in preparing the report.

The team's task would fit into the Steps for Better Thinking model like this:

1. *Knowing:* The team members would have acquired the skills they need to complete the research as part of their educational experience; the research itself would give them the background knowledge they need about Brazil.

2. *Identifying:* The problem and relevant information are defined by the nature of the task. The team might be uncertain about where to find the information they need and how long the task will take.

3. *Exploring:* Designing the knowledge management system would be part of this step. A properly designed database (or some other way of managing the information they collect) would assist in organizing the information. Team discussions would be useful in interpreting it.

4. *Prioritizing:* The team's basic task is to develop a report that will inform the expansion decision. Once the research is complete, they will have to prioritize the information they've collected, choose what to include in the report, and write the report.

5. *Envisioning:* With such a short time to prepare such a comprehensive and important report, it is almost certain to have some limitations. After the project is complete, the team should meet to discuss those limitations and identify ways to overcome them in similar future situations.

I hope this example has improved your understanding of this chapter's main topics, and that you'll be able to apply them in your own professional career.

Summary

Here's a brief synopsis of this chapter's main points:

1. *Discuss and give examples of the concept of information overload, including causes, symptoms, and countermeasures.* Information overload occurs when people have information coming in faster than they can process that information. Information technology has definitely contributed to information overload in modern organizations; other factors include human, task, process, and information characteristics. Symptoms and responses include suboptimal decisions and arbitrary analysis. Managers can effectively combat information overload with good time management, personal discipline, and knowledge management systems.

2. *Explain the nature of decision models and knowledge management.* A model is a generalized framework for completing a task. Knowledge management systems achieve four important objectives: create knowledge repositories, improve knowledge access, enhance the knowledge environment, and manage knowledge as an asset.

3. *Explain why those two topics are important in the study of accounting information systems.* The essence of accounting is decision making. As accountants, we need to collect information that is relevant and helpful in specific decision contexts.

4. *Describe and apply Wolcott and Lynch's Steps for Better Thinking.* The Steps for Better Thinking is an example of a decision-making model; it involves four levels of increasing complexity: identifying, exploring, prioritizing, and envisioning.

5. *Develop a personal strategy for making decisions and managing knowledge, including available information technology and other resources.* Practice using the models and strategies presented in this chapter will help you become a more effective decision maker. The ideas discussed here can be molded and adapted to a decision style that suits you as an individual—once again reinforcing the idea of "art" over "science."

You make personal and professional decisions every day. Some of them are more mundane (what to wear to school, what to eat for lunch), while others are of vital long-term importance (how to allocate your time, which job offer to accept at graduation). The information presented in this chapter will assist you in developing your own decision-making style and process.

Key Terms

bounded rationality, *276*
causes of information overload, *273*
countermeasures, *275*

information overload, *273*
knowledge management, *277*
relapse errors, *276*
satisficing, *276*

Steps for Better Thinking, *279*
steps to create a knowledge management system, *277*

Chapter
References

Betsch, T., S. Haberstroh, B. Molter, and A. Glockner. 2004. "Oops, I Did It Again—Relapse Errors in Routinized Decision Making." *Organizational Behavior and Human Decision Processes* 93, no. 1, pp. 62–74.

Call, D. 2005. "Knowledge Management—Not Rocket Science." *Journal of Knowledge Management* 9, no. 2, pp. 19–30.

Drucker, P. 1993. *Post-Capitalist Society.* New York: Harper Row Publishing.

Eppler, M., and J. Mengis. 2004. "The Concept of Information Overload: A Review of Literature from Organization Science, Accounting, Marketing, MIS and Related Disciplines." *Information Society,* pp. 325–44.

Nesbitt, K. 2002, February 8. "Designing a Knowledge Management System." http://academic .edu.2081/products/faulknerlibrary/00018382.htm (May 2, 2005).

Rowley, J. 1999. "What Is Knowledge Management?" *Library Management,* pp. 416–19.

Santosus, M., and J. Surmacz. 2005. "The ABCs of Knowledge Management." www.cio.com (April 28).

Simon, H. 1997. *Administrative Behavior.* 4th ed. New York: Free Press.

Wolcott, S., and C. Lynch. 2005. "Steps for Better Thinking." www.wolcottlynch.com (April 29).

End-of-
Chapter
Activities

1. *Reading review questions.*

   a. What is information overload? What causes it? What are its effects? How can decision makers deal with information overload in their professional lives?

   b. Explain the idea of knowledge management. Why is it important? What are some techniques you can use to manage knowledge now and in the future?

   c. Summarize the ideas and steps associated with Wolcott and Lynch's Steps for Better Thinking.

   d. Prepare a response to the questions for this chapter's "AIS in the Business World."

2. *Reading review problem.* To build an effective knowledge management system, people in organizations must first be willing to share knowledge. Vera-Muñoz, Ho, and Chow (2006) studied the idea of knowledge sharing in CPA firms. They point out that CPA firms should improve knowledge sharing due to increased regulation of the accounting profession, pressures to improve the audit process, and the need to leverage knowledge across an entire firm. They offer three recommendations (pp. 134–35) for increasing knowledge sharing:

   • Recommendation 1: While the emergence and proliferation of new information technologies increase the ability of CPA firms to share knowledge, effective knowledge sharing requires more than a technological solution. Successful knowledge sharing further demands an organizational solution that includes the firm's employees, their practices, and their know-how.

   • Recommendation 2: To encourage knowledge sharing, CPA firms need to develop and nurture a culture that simultaneously rewards knowledge sharing and discourages knowledge hoarding as a source of power or job security.

   • Recommendation 3: To enhance the prospects of knowledge sharing in team-based settings, CPA firms should seek synergistic ways of combining extrinsic motivation with intrinsic motivation.

Although their study focused on public accounting firms, the recommendations apply to virtually any accounting context.

   a. How would a knowledge management system facilitate knowledge sharing?

   b. What sources of information overload are accountants likely to experience? What strategies would you recommend for addressing them?

   c. Use Steps for Better Thinking to develop a plan for implementing one of the three recommendations.

3. *Multiple choice* review.

   1. When a decision maker estimates he or she has to handle more information than he or she can efficiently use, the decision maker is experiencing:

      a. Knowledge mismanagement.

      b. Information overload.

      c. Satisficing.

      d. Bounded rationality.

   2. All of the following are objectives of knowledge management except:

      a. Recording knowledge as an asset in the AIS.

      b. Creating knowledge repositories.

      c. Enhancing the knowledge environment.

      d. Improving knowledge access.

   3. In Steps for Better Thinking, which step is concerned with interpreting and organizing information?

      a. Identifying

      b. Exploring

      c. Prioritizing

      d. Interpreting

   4. In the first of the Steps for Better Thinking, decision makers should identify: (i) the problem, (ii) relevant information, (iii) limitations.

      a. i and ii only

      b. ii and iii only

      c. i and iii only

      d. i, ii, and iii

   5. Which of the following steps for creating a knowledge management system should occur first?

      a. Adopt Steps for Better Thinking.

      b. Normalize database tables.

      c. Define business goals the system should address.

      d. Build appropriate tools.

4. *Making choices and exercising judgment.* Betsy and Mark are bookkeepers for CTC Corporation; both have been employed by CTC for over 20 years. They currently use a paper-based accounting information system to complete the steps in the accounting cycle, but the company president (Raj) wants to move to a more automated environment. Use Steps for Better Thinking to analyze the choice of staying with the current paper-based system or moving to an automated system. (Note: This problem is not asking you to evaluate technology alternatives for the AIS. Rather, you are to compare the idea of staying with a paper-based system with the concept of using information technology to complete the steps in the accounting cycle.)

5. *Field work.*

   a. Use your university's library to locate and read "Knowledge Management in Three Financial Organisations: A Case Study" by Martie M. Squier and Retha Snyman. What conclusions do they reach regarding knowledge management?

   b. Talk with other students at your university about their decision-making processes. Compare and contrast the decision-making processes based on at least two of the following factors: age, year in school, major, GPA.

c. Interview a practicing accountant in an area of the profession that interests you. Ask about a recent major decision your interviewee has made and the process he or she used to make it. Write a short paper that summarizes the accountant's decision process. Analyze the decision process through the lens of Steps for Better Thinking as well.

6. *Analyzing current issues in accounting.* Consider the list of current and classic issues in accounting presented below (or others specified by your instructor). With your instructor's help and guidance, form a team of students to investigate one of the issues. Use the Steps for Better Thinking to analyze the issue and prepare a short oral report for the class.

   a. What are the obstacles associated with adopting International Financial Reporting Standards?
   b. Should the provisions of the Sarbanes-Oxley Act be extended to nonpublic corporations?
   c. Will principles-based accounting become the norm for U.S. GAAP?
   d. Has the 150-hour requirement for becoming a CPA been a success?
   e. What systems documentation techniques should be taught in AIS courses?
   f. Has the conceptual framework of accounting fulfilled its purpose?
   g. What issues should managers consider with regard to corporate governance?
   h. Should social and environmental reporting be mandatory?
   i. How, if at all, should fair-value accounting be implemented?

7. *Software acquisition decision using SBT.*

   a. Critter Sitters (www.stlouiscrittersitters.com/) is an in-home pet care company based in St. Louis, Missouri. Their Web site lists several services available to pet owners, including mid-day dog walking, puppy care, and in-home dog training. Suppose Critter Sitters is considering three general ledger packages for its accounting information system: ePeachtree, Quickbooks, and Great Plains Dynamics. Use the Steps for Better Thinking to help the company's president make a choice.

   b. According to its Web site (www.40debts.org/counseling/default.asp), Harbour Credit Management "provides credit management services to families and individuals experiencing financial stress." Suppose the firm is searching for software that will help manage spam on its information system. Point your Web browser to www.download.com, and investigate three different software packages that fulfill that purpose. Make a recommendation to Harbour's management using the Steps for Better Thinking to inform your decision.

   c. Katy is the owner of Active Bodyworks and Wellness in Ontario, California. She has been taking appointments, maintaining her accounting information system, and managing client information using a paper-based system for the last several years but now wants to move to a more computerized environment. She's heard about voice recognition systems and comes to you for a recommendation between three specific packages: Dragon Naturally Speaking, Realize Voice Lite, and e-Speaking. Point your Web browser to www.download.com, and investigate each package. Use the Steps for Better Thinking to make a recommendation to Katy.

8. *Knowledge management tools.* Point your Web browser once again to www.download.com. Search for knowledge management software; choose one example and prepare a short oral report for the class on its capabilities and cost.

9. *Creating knowledge management systems.*

   a. Viola completed her accounting degree in 2000; she has had three professional positions since that time. She summarized information about each position as indicated below. Organize the information into a knowledge management system.

   Dewey, Cheatam and Howe, CPAs (2000 to 2001)

   Responsibilities: Small-business auditing

   Salary: $40,000 annually

   Comments: I like working with small-business clients, but it's tough getting to know them.

ENZ Corporation (2001 to 2003)

Responsibilities: AIS design, accounts receivable management

Salary: $45,000 annually

Comments: More stable hours, interesting work—but not really diverse.

FNN Corporation (2003 to present)

Responsibilities: Divisional controller

Salary: $50,000 annually

Comments: Plenty of responsibility; interesting corporate culture.

b. Most university accounting curricula cover a fairly standard range of topics: financial accounting, cost accounting, taxation, systems, and auditing. Think about the classes you've taken so far within your accounting program; develop a list of at least five topics for each class. Also, develop a list of other abilities (like writing, speaking, and use of information technology) that cut across the accounting classes you've had. Using a software tool of your choice (or one specified by your instructor), develop a system to organize and manage the items in the lists.

c. Sebastian is a self-employed AIS consultant. He has several books on the subject in his library, as shown in Table 15.1, covering a variety of topics. Develop a knowledge management system based on the information provided. (Your instructor may ask you to use a relational database such as Microsoft Access to complete this task.)

10. *Personal decision making and knowledge management system.* Based on what you've learned in this chapter, prepare a brief written report that summarizes your personal plan for making better decisions and managing knowledge. Use a specific example of a recent past or upcoming decision to illustrate your decision-making model.

TABLE 15.1 **Table of Books for Activity 9(c)**

	Books					
Title	*Accounting Information Systems*	*Adventures in AIS*	*Basic AIS Concepts*	*Auditing AIS*	*The Role of AIS in Organizations*	*Safeguarding the AIS*
Author	Brady	Legault	Ogan	Barbagallo	James	Burkett
Publisher	Prentice Hall	Thomson	McGraw-Hill	Thomson	McGraw-Hill	McGraw-Hill
Copyright	2005	2007	2008	2008	2010	2011
Strengths	Easy to read; lots of illustrations	Real-world examples	Real-world examples; Sarbanes-Oxley	Topic breadth; checklists	End-of-chapter materials; independent organization	Small-business focus; easy to read
Weaknesses	Cost	Difficult to read	End-of-chapter materials	Sarbanes-Oxley	Difficult to read	Web materials
Number of Pages	300	150	275	300	185	210
Topics	• Information technology • Internal controls • Data modeling	• Accounting cycle • Fraud detection • Information technology • Data modeling	• Accounting cycle • Internal controls • Data modeling • Information technology	• Fraud detection • Internal controls • Accounting cycle • Data modeling • Information technology	• Information technology • Internal controls	• Internal controls • Fraud detection • Information technology

11. *Terminology.* Please match each item on the left with the most appropriate item on the right.

1.	Wolcott and Lynch	a.	A system for creating value from intellectual assets
2.	Satisficing	b.	Software that can be used to implement a KMS
3.	Relapse errors	c.	Human tendency to rely on rules for making decisions
4.	Prioritizing	d.	Looking at information from multiple points of view
5.	Knowledge management	e.	SBT step that involves identifying personal bias
6.	Identifying	f.	Simon's notion that people will accept the first reasonable solution for a problem
7.	Exploring		
8.	Envisioning	g.	Starting place for Steps for Better Thinking
9.	Bounded rationality	h.	Tendency to make the same mistakes repeatedly
10.	Database	i.	The creator(s) of Steps for Better Thinking
		j.	The last step in SBT

12. *Multiple choice.* Please refer to the following short case as you answer these questions:

After earning both her accounting degree and her CPA license, Barb opened her own public accounting practice. One of her clients was looking for a way to make transaction processing more efficient; Barb immediately knew the client needed to invest in general ledger software. She assumed price and ease of use were the most important factors, so she identified three software packages that were both inexpensive and easy to use. The client chose one of the three for installation; a few months later, Barb conducted a follow-up interview to determine how the software was working.

1. "Identifying" is one of the levels in Steps for Better Thinking. Which element of "identifying" did Barb neglect most seriously?
   a. The problem.
   b. Relevant information.
   c. Uncertainties.
   d. Barb did not neglect any element of "identifying."

2. Gathering information on cost and ease of use for each software package is an element of ___ in Steps for Better Thinking.
   a. Identifying
   b. Exploring
   c. Prioritizing
   d. Envisioning

3. "Prioritizing" is one of the levels in Steps for Better Thinking. Who participated in the prioritizing process?
   a. Barb only.
   b. The client only.
   c. Neither Barb nor the client.
   d. Both Barb and the client.

4. Which of the following phrases is most indicative of the "foundation" level of Steps for Better Thinking?
   a. After earning both her accounting degree and her CPA license.
   b. Barb opened her own public accounting practice.
   c. The client needed to invest in general ledger software.
   d. Make transaction processing more efficient.

5. The follow-up interview is most directly associated with the ___ process in Steps for Better Thinking.

   a. Identifying
   b. Exploring
   c. Prioritizing
   d. Envisioning

13. *Statement evaluation.* Indicate whether each of the following statements is (i) always true, (ii) sometimes true, or (iii) never true. For those that are (ii) sometimes true, explain when the statement is true.

   a. A supportive organizational culture is an important step in knowledge management.
   b. Bounded rationality prevents people from making good decisions.
   c. Breaking up a complex job into smaller tasks can help combat information overload.
   d. Even the smartest human beings have a limited capacity for processing information.
   e. Information characteristics can contribute to information overload.
   f. Information technology is a cause of information overload.
   g. Information technology is a solution for information overload.
   h. Knowledge management systems involve relational database software.
   i. The levels of Steps for Better Thinking involve increasingly complex tasks.
   j. Visual maps resemble data flow diagrams.

14. *Prior material application.*

   a. This chapter outlined seven steps for creating a knowledge management system, using Heater-craft as an example. Think about the steps in the broader context of a functionally organized corporation; who should complete each of the steps for creating the system? In a format specified by your instructor, document the steps based on the parties you believe should complete them.
   b. TRG Corporation is preparing its initial public offering; the corporation's management knows it will have to file documents with the SEC using XBRL. Use Steps for Better Thinking to reach a decision about what tagging software TRG should employ.
   c. This chapter suggested five major causes of information overload. Think about one of the business processes discussed in Part Four. For the business process you choose, suggest one specific example for each major cause of information overload.
   d. When an organization incurs a cost, it has two basic choices for how to record it in the AIS: capitalizing or expensing. Suppose a corporation develops its own knowledge management system using a standard relational database like Access. How should it account for the development cost? Justify your response.

Chapter **Sixteen**

Professionalism, Ethics, and Career Planning

AIS in the Business World

Helen Kanell

Have you ever confronted a situation like this (Mintz and Morris, 2011)?

> Helen Kanell has a 4.0 grade point average and is in her last semester of college at Empire State University. Helen has already accepted a position to join the accounting firm of Big & Apple LLC. Still, she is determined to complete her [education] and graduate with at least a 3.90. However, she has a B average in all five courses going into the final exam. Helen was distracted from her studies the last semester because she agreed to be the president of Beta Alpha Psi, the accounting student honor society, and it has required a great deal more work than anticipated. Helen . . . knows she must get an A grade in at least one course to [achieve her goal].
>
> Prior to the final exam in [one of her accounting courses], Helen is approached by her best friend who . . . had an opportunity to take a copy of the final exam from the professor's mailbox. She gives it to Helen and says, "You can thank me later."

As I often tell my students: The ability to make ethical decisions doesn't descend on you magically when you walk across the stage and get your diploma. Ethics are developed over time—and the time to begin developing the habit of behaving ethically is always *now*.

Discussion Questions

1. Why is it important that accountants behave ethically?
2. What principles and standards guide ethical decision making in the accounting profession?
3. How do ethics interact with your sense of professionalism and plan for your career?

Source: S. M. Mintz and R. E. Morris. *Ethical Obligations and Decision Making in Accounting: Text and Cases*. McGraw-Hill/Irwin, 2011.

Most accounting majors, arguably, are studying the subject because they intend to pursue a career in the accounting profession. In this chapter, we'll take a look at three topics closely related to that goal: professionalism, ethics, and career planning.

Professionalism and ethics are not skills that magically descend upon you once you earn your accounting degree; furthermore, planning your career is something that needs to begin now—not when you're ready to graduate. Indeed, developing a sense of professionalism, the habit of behaving ethically, and a plan for your career is at least as important as learning software applications, FASB pronouncements, and other technical areas of accounting. In this chapter, we'll consider what it means to be a professional, specifically within the context of accounting.

When you complete your study of this chapter, you should be able to:

1. List and discuss characteristics of a professional.
2. Explain how those characteristics apply to the accounting profession.
3. Define *ethics.*
4. Discuss various models/schools of ethical decision making.
5. Explain how to resolve ethical dilemmas.

Although this chapter may mark your first exposure to these issues, it almost certainly will not constitute your last.

PROFESSIONALISM

You probably have heard many people talk about the "accounting profession." And you've probably noticed that people consistently refer to some careers as "professional," but not others. Have you considered what constitutes a "profession"? What is it about accounting that qualifies it as a profession, whereas other valuable and important careers are not labeled as such?

Dr. Nancy Bell (2004) suggests seven **characteristics of a professional.** Although her list is given in the context of insurance and risk management, its elements can be applied equally to accounting. In Dr. Bell's view, a professional

* Communicates effectively.
* Thinks rationally, logically, and coherently.
* Appropriately uses technical knowledge.
* Integrates knowledge from many disciplines.
* Exhibits ethical professional behavior.
* Recognizes the influence of political, social, economic, legal, and regulatory forces.
* Actively seeks additional knowledge.

Consider the idea that a professional communicates effectively. Good communication skills are fundamental in accounting. Our profession uses specialized, technical vocabulary that is not shared by the general population. For example, to the average person on the street, *depreciation* refers to an asset's loss in value over time. In accounting, however, *depreciation* is the periodic allocation of an asset's cost to the periods that benefit from its use—accounting depreciation is unrelated to changes in market value. So, as professionals, part of our job is to explain the differences between accounting depreciation and economic depreciation to those who are outside our profession. The same could be said for a variety of other terms: stock, capital, revenue, expense, and others.

As another example, think about the second characteristic in Dr. Bell's list: a professional thinks rationally, logically, and coherently. I often tell my students that the purpose of earning an accounting degree isn't to prepare to take the CPA exam—or any other accounting professional exam. Rather, the purpose of earning an accounting degree is to teach you how to think like an accountant: rationally, logically, and coherently. One of the most important skills you'll bring to your career is that ability. Being able to think that way develops over time and with practice, through a process of questioning and dialogue. I know some of my students are sometimes reticent to share their thoughts and opinions, out of concern that they'll say something "wrong." But I always try to challenge and encourage them so they can develop their thinking skills. I'm sure your AIS and other accounting professors feel the same way.

Reflection and Self-Assessment   16.1

Choose three of the remaining characteristics in Dr. Bell's list. For each one, give a specific example of how an accounting professional might display it.

McDonald (2001) identified four criteria to be considered a professional:

- *Specialized knowledge base.* Accounting certainly has a specialized knowledge base. Whether we're talking about financial reporting rules, standards for conducting audits, tax research and planning skills, or activity-based accounting processes, the knowledge we share is not part of society's general body of knowledge.
- *Complex skills.* Accounting also involves complex skills. It requires the use of judgment, and also relies on fairly complex computations in some areas (such as pension accounting). Although some accounting software is straightforward and easy to use, some of our IT tools are reasonably sophisticated as well.
- *Autonomy of practice.* Autonomy refers to independence or self-sufficiency. As you'll learn in your later study of auditing, "independence of mind" is an important characteristic for accounting professionals. Historically, the accounting profession was almost completely independent and self-regulating. But ethical scandals, such as Enron, led to the creation of the Public Companies Accounting Oversight Board. The PCAOB "is a private-sector, non-profit corporation, created by the Sarbanes-Oxley Act of 2002, to oversee the auditors of public companies in order to protect the interests of investors and further the public interest in the preparation of informative, fair, and independent audit reports." Although the PCAOB has given less autonomy to auditors, the profession as a whole remains relatively self-sufficient.
- *Adherence to a code of ethical behavior.* Accountants also adhere to codes of ethical behavior. In the exercises at the end of this chapter, you'll have the opportunity to examine the ethical codes of three important organizations: the American Institute of Certified Public Accountants, the Institute of Management Accountants, and the Association of Certified Fraud Examiners.

You can find more information about the PCAOB at www.pcaobus.org/.

Notice how McDonald's four characteristics connect to the list of seven provided by Dr. Bell. For example, both lists include a component regarding ethical behavior.

One common element in almost all definitions of professionalism is the emphasis on professional ethics. Next, we'll turn our attention to that important topic.

You have just read about the ideas of Bell and McDonald regarding professions, professionals, and professionalism. How are the ideas of those authors connected to one another? Develop your own list of the top five character-istics you want to exhibit as a professional accountant based on those ideas and your own original thinking.

ETHICS

In this section, we'll consider five main topics: definitions of ethics, models of ethical decision making, codes of professional ethics in accounting, processes for resolving ethical dilemmas, and ethics cases in accounting. Although our main focus will be on ethical behavior in the accounting profession, I'm sure you've realized that behaving ethically begins long before you enter that portion of your career. As a student, you make choices about your behavior regularly; consider the following questions as examples:

1. Have you ever presented others' ideas as your own?
2. Have you ever collaborated on an assignment when told specifically to complete it individually?
3. Have you inappropriately accessed homework solutions for your accounting or other courses?
4. Have you, implicitly or explicitly, ignored unethical behavior from your fellow students?

Within the context of accounting information systems, ethical issues include

1. Making realistic, unbiased estimates.
2. Using AIS data appropriately.
3. Maintaining strong internal control over cash and other liquid assets.
4. Paying for software and other forms of information technology.

Consider those questions and issues, and others you may think of for yourself, in the broad context of our further discussion of ethics in the following paragraphs.

What is ethics? The Internet Encyclopedia of Philosophy (2004) says:

> The field of ethics, also called moral philosophy, involves systematizing, defending, and recommending concepts of right and wrong behavior. Philosophers today usually divide ethical theories into three general subject areas: metaethics, normative ethics, and applied ethics. *Metaethics* investigates where our ethical principles come from, and what they mean. *Normative ethics* takes on a more practical task, which is to arrive at moral standards that regulate right and wrong conduct. This may involve articulating the good habits that we should acquire, the duties that we should follow, or the consequences of our behavior on others. Finally, *applied ethics* involves examining specific controversial issues.

Dictionary.com (2004) offers several other **definitions of ethics,** including "rules or standards governing the conduct of a person or the members of a profession."

In accounting, we are perhaps most concerned with **normative ethics.** What are the rules and standards, whether personal or professional, that guide our professional decision making?

Ethics information abounds on the Internet. Consult www.ethics .org, www.business-ethics.com/, and www .usoge.gov/ for more information.

One rule/standard that guides ethical decision making in accounting is objectivity. As professional accountants, we have the responsibility to present information as fairly and objectively as possible. Suggest two other rules or standards accountants should observe as part of making ethical decisions.

Merchant and Van der Stede (2003) articulated four basic paradigms for ethical decision making. *Utilitarianism* says that "the end justifies the means." In other words, someone following the **utilitarian model of ethics** would say that as long as you have a successful/ favorable outcome, any method of achieving it is justified. Consider, for example, the goal of increasing a company's stock price. No one really knows what causes changes in stock prices, but accounting numbers do have a significant impact. So, a utilitarian ethical model would say it's okay to increase a company's stock price, even if you have to engage in profit manipulation via accounting policy changes.

The **rights and duties** school of ethical thinking feels that all individuals have certain rights; others have the duty not to interfere with those rights. You might think of this model as an "every person for himself/herself" way of thinking. If, for example, a manager has the right to earn a bonus every year, others have the duty not to interfere with that process. The manager may act in ethical or unethical ways to earn the bonus, but, according to this school of ethical thought, others should not impede the managers' actions. At the same time, the manager has a duty not to interfere with the rights of colleagues to earn a bonus.

Decision makers who follow the **justice model** of ethics feel that all people should be given what they deserve. Of course, the tougher question becomes "What do people deserve?" The justice model weighs a person's actions against the results of those actions. For example, an accountant who has worked hard for several years in a CPA firm would likely deserve to be made a partner. On the other hand, a manager who has slacked off, been difficult to work with, and exhibited unprofessional behavior would probably not be deserving of a promotion under the justice school of ethics.

Finally, Merchant and Van der Stede discussed the **virtues model** of ethical behavior. According to this way of thinking, people should do what is right, moral, and virtuous. The virtues model asks managers to look inwardly to determine the rightness of their actions. Although some managers might make distinctions between moral behavior and ethical behavior, those who subscribe to this way of thinking often do not separate the two. So, a manager who adheres to this definition of ethical behavior might have no difficulty in misappropriating assets to help someone in need, since helping someone in need is a moral act.

Of course, those four models of ethical decision making are not the only ones in existence. And few accountants would be likely to know the names of them if asked. They would only know their personal beliefs regarding ethics and ethical decision making. As professional accountants, we also are subject to the ethical codes of the profession and the professional organizations of which we may be a part..

You'll face countless ethical dilemmas in your professional career, from major choices such as how aggressive accounting practices should be to minor ones such as using office supplies for personal purposes. How do accountants resolve ethical dilemmas? The standards of conduct and ethics codes presented above are more about the "content" of ethical behavior and less about the "process." Next, let's consider the steps you might take to resolve an ethical dilemma in your professional life.

Langenderfer and Rockness (1989) proposed an **eight-step model** for dealing with ethical dilemmas:

1. Identify the facts.
2. Identify the ethics issues and the stakeholders involved.
3. Define the norms, principles, and values related to the situation.
4. Identify the alternative courses of action.
5. Evaluate the consequences of each possible course of action.
6. Decide the best course of action consistent with the norms, principles, and values.
7. If appropriate, discuss the alternative with a trusted person to help gain greater perspective regarding the alternatives.
8. Reach a decision as to the appropriate course of action.

Many companies will have an established practice for resolving ethical issues. They might include discussions with a neutral party (such as an ombuds or ethics officer) or reporting ethical violations anonymously. If a company you work for has an established policy for resolving ethical dilemmas, you should generally follow that policy first. As with many issues in accounting practice, there is no "one right way" to resolve an ethical problem.

If, though, your company has no established policy for dealing with ethics issues, try talking to your supervisor. If your supervisor is involved in unethical conduct, talk to his/her supervisor. After talking with your supervisor, the issue may be resolved. If not, though, take the problem to the next highest level of authority in the organization—with your supervisor's full knowledge. Don't do an "end run" around your boss, unless you suspect his/her involvement in the problem. Continue up the organizational hierarchy until the problem is resolved. In extreme cases, you may need to consider resigning your position with the organization if the issue is egregious and cannot be resolved internally.

Unfortunately, the unethical and unprofessional actions of a small group of accountants have tarnished the profession's reputation in the eyes of the public. To conclude this chapter, let's take a look at a few "infamous" cases of unethical behavior in the profession.

The cases discussed here, along with many others, are available to members of the Association of Certified Fraud Examiners on their Web site (www.cfenet.com).

In the early 20th century, **Charles Ponzi** committed a multimillion-dollar fraud with international postal reply coupons. Ponzi collected money from investors but never purchased the international postal reply coupons. Basically, he was using new investors' money to pay off old investors. This practice has continued to the present day; you may have heard frauds like this one referred to as "pyramid" or "multilevel marketing" schemes. When such a fraud involves the use of securities or financial instruments, we often refer to it as a Ponzi scheme. Ponzi eventually was sentenced to five years in federal prison for mail fraud, followed by an additional seven-to-nine-year sentence in Massachusetts.

In 1952, John Rigas purchased a Pennsylvania cable company for $300. Twenty years later, he and his brother, Gus, created the **Adelphia Communications Corporation.** Adelphia was a family-run business; indeed, *Adelphia* is Greek for "brothers." In the late 1990s, Adelphia purchased Century Communications for $5.2 billion, making it the sixth largest cable company in the United States. John loved the limelight and was quite the philanthropist. But he also had a huge ego. For example, he bought homes for people and also was known to fly people on private planes for medical treatment; at the same time, he personally had to approve every business transaction for Adelphia. Adelphia's fraud was multifaceted. The company funded more than $2 billion in personal loans to the Rigas family. Adelphia management engaged in deceptive accounting practices to meet analysts' expectations for profitability; the company also commingled its assets with the Rigas family's personal assets. Ultimately, Adelphia filed for bankruptcy in June 2002 and was delisted from NASDAQ.

The **Enron/Arthur Andersen** debacle may be the best-known accounting fraud in recent history. Enron filed for bankruptcy in December 2001; at that time, it was the largest bankruptcy filing ever. Enron was created in 1985 from the merger of two other companies in the natural gas and pipeline industries. After a few years, though, Enron found itself with mounting liabilities and loss of exclusive control over its pipelines. Based on the recommendation of consultant Jeffrey Skilling, Enron embarked on a new business strategy by creating a "bank" to buy and sell gas. In 1990, Enron created a financial subsidiary and hired Skilling to run it. The financial subsidiary hired the "best and brightest" but subjected them to a brutal performance evaluation system. Eventually, most of Enron's business came from its financial division, rather than from its original gas pipeline activities. Earnings, but not cash flows, continued increasing, and its stock price went up as well for 20 quarters in a row. Meanwhile, Enron's employees continued making deals of increasing risk, unbeknownst to Enron's investors. The company's accounting information system became rife with earnings management, off balance-sheet debt, and related-party transactions. The company also failed to disclose key facts in the notes to its financial statements. Ultimately, Enron's ethical breaches led to its bankruptcy filing; the downfall of Arthur Andersen, one of the then "Big Five" CPA firms, also was closely related to its activities in auditing Enron.

The preceding cases are just three among many in the accounting profession. By applying the principles of professionalism and ethics discussed in this chapter, you will hopefully be able to avoid such situations and help our profession become more respected in the business world.

CAREER PLANNING

Believe it or not, you've already started planning your career. You may not have been consciously aware of that fact up until now, but making the choice to pursue a degree in accounting is an important first step. In this section, we'll take a look at some additional things you should do to think more concretely about your career.

While your **career plan** will almost certainly change as your career progresses, consider the steps listed here as you develop your initial ideas:

1. *Determine your strengths, aptitudes, and abilities.* You can complete this important step in many ways, one of which is with assessment tools likely available in your campus career center. The Discover Inventory (http://webapps01.act.org/eDISCOVER/) will give you a three-letter code that denotes the kinds of working environments in which you're most comfortable. The code is based on Holland's Hexagon (www.learning4liferesources.com/holland_codes.html), which classifies working environments into six broad categories: enterprising, conventional, realistic, social, artistic, and investigative. Another good instrument for completing this step is the Gallup Organization's StrengthsFinder (www.strengthsquest.com/). StrengthsFinder identifies your five top "themes" based on your responses to a series of objective questions. The themes were developed from extensive research and statistical analyses of hundreds of individuals and can be used to help you find a career that builds on those innate abilities.

2. *Create a career mission statement.* You may have run across the idea of organizational mission statements in your management coursework. Basically, an organizational mission statement explains its reason for being—the way(s) it expects to achieve a competitive advantage in its markets. Your career mission statement can work the same way. It gives you a goal to work toward—one that will not absolutely dictate your educational and professional choices, but will provide some direction as you enter the accounting profession.

3. *Research employment opportunities related to the first two items.* This research might involve conducting informational interviews with practicing accountants, attending student organization events related to career opportunities on your campus, or finding an internship in an environment where you think you might eventually like to work. The earlier you can start that research, the better off you'll be; that way, if you discover you don't have the interest, aptitude, or ability to sustain a particular career, you can change your career plan accordingly. In a very fundamental sense, your career planning process began the day you started college; too many students wait until the year they expect to graduate to think about their career. I encourage you to start the process early, so you can make more informed choices when you graduate.

4. *Build your résumé.* Your campus career center can give you clear, specific guidance about how to create a strong résumé. Too many students wait until they're ready to graduate to visit the career center. I encourage you to visit it early in your academic career. You'll find your job search process goes a lot more smoothly if you take advantage of the career center's services regularly.

5. *Practice your interviewing skills.* Most career centers offer practice (mock) interviews; if your school has an accounting society, an IMA student chapter, and/or a chapter of Beta Alpha Psi, they also may host mock interview events throughout the year. Practicing your interviewing skills in those settings will make you a lot more comfortable when you're ready for the "real thing." While you'll always be somewhat nervous during an interview situation, practicing in advance can significantly reduce those feelings, allowing you to put your best foot forward with potential employers.

These five steps certainly aren't the sum total of career planning efforts, but they are a good beginning. The earlier you begin developing a plan, the more time you'll have to explore it.

CRITICAL THINKING

Earlier in the chapter, you read about some classic ethics cases in accounting practice: Charles Ponzi, Adelphia Communications, and Enron. A more recent case you may have heard about involved Bernie Madoff. Basically, Madoff engaged in an elaborate Ponzi scheme that was eventually discovered by Harry Markopolos, a certified fraud examiner and certified financial analyst. In an interview published in *Fraud Magazine* (Carozza, May/June 2009), Markopolos made the following comments about how he discovered the fraud:

> In late 1999, I was a portfolio manager for a multibillion-dollar equity derivatives asset management firm in Boston's financial district. Frank Casey, a marketing senior vice president for the firm, returned from New York with marketing materials for a high-performing, derivatives-based hedge fund managed by Bernard Madoff. In early 2000, the firm's partners asked me to reverse-engineer the strategy so that we could offer this successful product to our firm's customers. After I modeled the strategy, I determined that the returns could only be coming from illegal front-running of the Madoff broker/dealer arm's client orders or from fictional returns that were the result of a Ponzi scheme. I went to the firm's partners and jokingly asked if they really wanted to get into that business. They hastily replied, "No way, if that's what he's doing then we don't want to compete in that space."

Although Markopolos repeatedly submitted evidence to the SEC over a period of nine years, it wasn't until 2008 that anyone took action against Madoff. Clearly, Markopolos had an ethical dilemma on his hands. The Langenderfer and Rockness model for making ethical decisions presented earlier in this chapter is one good choice for making ethical decisions, but it definitely isn't the only one available. Mintz and Morris (2011, pp. 57–58) suggest a 10-step process for accomplishing that goal. Let's take a look at their recommendations, applying them to the Madoff case:

1. *Frame the ethical issue.* For Markopolos, the ethical issue was fairly straightforward: should he continue warning the SEC about Madoff's Ponzi scheme, or simply let the matter drop?

2. *Gather all the facts.* As Markopolos stated in the quotation above, he was confident Madoff was committing fraud after his initial analysis. The only thing he wasn't sure about was the form of the fraud: illegal front-running or a Ponzi scheme.

3. *Identify the stakeholders and obligations.* This case has many stakeholders, including Madoff, his "investors," and the SEC.

4. *Identify the relevant accounting ethics standards involved in the situation.* Markopolos holds the certified fraud examiner (CFE) credential. The Association of Certified Fraud Examiners (www.acfe.com) has an eight-point code of ethics that includes such statements as: "A Certified Fraud Examiner shall, at all times, demonstrate a commitment to professionalism and diligence in the performance of his or her duties." And "A Certified Fraud Examiner shall, at all times, exhibit the highest level of integrity in the performance of all professional assignments and will accept only assignments for which there is reasonable expectation that the assignment will be completed with professional competence."

5. *Identify the operational issues.* At the time he discovered the Madoff fraud, Markopolos worked for Rampart Investment Management, a Boston-based options trading firm (www.rimco.com/). Using this model, Markopolos would have considered Rampart's organizational culture in considering how to proceed.

6. *Identify the accounting and auditing issues.* Madoff's fraud was a classic Ponzi scheme. The financial reports Madoff's funds were producing, then, could not have been fair and reliable.

7. *List all the possible alternatives you can or cannot do.* Markopolos had two basic choices: continue warning the SEC or let the matter drop.

8. *Compare and weigh the alternatives.* Although letting the matter drop would have been much easier for Markopolos, it would also have called into question his professional ethics.

9. *Decide on a course of action.* In Markopolos' mind, the choice was clear: he had to continue warning the SEC about Madoff's actions.

10. *Reflect on your decision.* Markopolos has clearly reflected on his decision, especially in his book (*No One Would Listen: A True Financial Thriller*, Wiley, 2011).

Markopolos clearly demonstrated all of Bell's and McDonald's characteristics of a professional with his persistence in the Madoff case. His pivotal role also launched a new chapter in his career.

Summary

Here is a summary of the chapter's main points based on its learning outcomes:

1. *List and discuss characteristics of a professional.* A professional communicates effectively; thinks rationally, logically, and coherently; appropriately uses technical knowledge; integrates knowledge from many disciplines; exhibits ethical professional behavior; recognizes the influence of political, social, economic, legal, and regulatory forces; and actively seeks additional knowledge.

2. *Explain how those characteristics apply to the accounting profession.* As professionals, accountants have a responsibility to exhibit all seven of the preceding characteristics. Failing to do so violates the public trust.

3. *Define ethics.* The field of ethics has been subdivided into three parts: metaethics, normative ethics, and applied ethics. Each part concerns the ways people make choices between "right" and "wrong."

4. *Discuss various models/schools of ethical decision making.* The chapter outlined Merchant's thoughts in this area. He identified four broad systems for making ethical decisions: utiliarianism, rights and duties, justice, and virtue.

5. *Explain how to resolve ethical dilemmas.* If a company policy on resolving ethical dilemmas exists, accountants should follow it. However, if no such guidelines are in place, one good model, proposed by Langenderfer and Rockness, for making ethical decisions involves eight steps: identify the facts; identify the ethics issues and the stakeholders involved; define the norms, principles, and values related to the situation; identify the alternative courses of action; evaluate the consequences of each possible course of action; decide the best course of action consistent with the norms, principles, and values; if appropriate, discuss the alternative with a trusted person to help gain greater perspective regarding the alternatives; and reach a decision as to the appropriate course of action. The chapter's Critical Thinking application also outlined a 10-step process suggested by Mintz and Morris.

Although this chapter comes near the end of the text, I hope you now recognize the importance of its three topics.

Key Terms			
	Adelphia Communications Corporation, *295*	Charles Ponzi, *295*	justice model, *294*
	career plan, *296*	definitions of ethics, *293*	normative ethics, *293*
	characteristics of a professional, *291*	eight-step model, *295*	rights and duties, *294*
		Enron/Arthur Andersen, *296*	utilitarian model of ethics, *294*
			virtues model, *294*

Chapter References

Bell, N. 2004. "Characteristics of a Risk Management and Insurance Professional." www.wsu.edu/belln/ (October 4, 2004).

Dictionary.com. 2004. "Ethics." http://dictionary.reference.com/search?q=ethics (October 4).

Internet Encyclopedia of Philosophy. 2004. "Ethics." www.utm.edu/research/iep/e/ethics.htm (October 4).

Langenderfer, H., and J. Rockness. 1989. "Integrating Ethics into the Accounting Curriculum: Issues, Problems, and Solutions." *Journal of Accounting Education,* Spring, pp. 58–69.

McDonald, C. 2001. "A Review of Continuing Professional Education." *Journal of Continuing Higher Education,* Winter, pp. 29–40.

Merchant, K., and W. Van der Stede. 2003. *Management Control Systems.* Upper Saddle River, NJ: Prentice Hall.

End-of-Chapter Activities

1. *Reading review questions.*

   a. List and discuss at least five characteristics of a professional and/or professional behavior. Where possible, include a specific example of each characteristic from your own experience as a student.

   b. Define *ethics.* Explain why ethics is so important in the accounting profession.

   c. What basic schools of thought exist regarding ethical behavior? What are the strengths and weaknesses of each one?

   d. Explain the basic facts of fraud schemes associated with Ponzi, Adelphia, and Enron.

   e. In a manner specified by your instructor, respond to the questions for this chapter's "AIS in the Business World."

2. *Reading review problem.* Consider the following story:

It was a Saturday afternoon, and the two men at the window table in the club lounge were relaxing over drinks, talking football and a little politics, and cooling down after an hour of tennis. "You're getting the hang of it," Fred Smith joked to Jim Cunningham, who, as he often did, had edged out his longtime friend. "Practice, practice, practice," Jim replied with a laugh. Fred and Jim had been playing tennis together for almost as many years as they had worked at Summitt Manufacturing. Fred is vice president for human resources; Jim is one of the company's accountants. They try to keep Summitt out of the conversation when they get together, but this particular day they broke their own rule by getting into some shop talk. That's when Jim dropped a surprise on Fred. "I don't know if I should tell you this," he said, "but there's something going on at work and you should know about it." Jim then told Fred—in strict confidence—that the company's chief financial officer was planning to have Summitt take an aggressive stance on sales revenue reporting that, in Jim's view, would stretch the boundaries of acceptable accounting practices. Jim's accounting expertise and core responsibilities at Summitt center on the company's real estate holdings; he doesn't deal with sales revenue. But he has a pretty good understanding of what's happening in other areas of the company's financial activities, and he was clearly concerned with what he had picked up about what the CFO wanted to do. If the CFO were to prevail, his accounting method would burnish Summitt's earnings outlook and probably help its stock price. "But it could be risky," Jim told Fred. "It could raise questions" about the firm's methods and even its integrity. What's more, Jim said he wasn't sure the company's top executives understood the nuances of the CFO's approach. "They might get talked into going along with something they're not up to speed on," Jim said.

Source: Brenda Franklin, "Spinning the Numbers," *HR Magazine,* no. 47 (November 2002), pp. 64–69.

a. Is Jim acting professionally? Explain your response.

b. Which of the four schools of ethical thought does Jim follow? Explain your response.

c. Is the CFO's proposed action ethical?

3. *Multiple choice review.*

1. A professional:
   a. Communicates effectively.
   b. Minimizes the use of technical knowledge.
   c. Relies solely on professional associations for influence.
   d. All of the above.

2. Arriving at moral standards that regulate right and wrong conduct is called:
   a. Applied ethics.
   b. Business ethics.
   c. Normative ethics.
   d. Professional ethics.

3. Which school of ethical thought has as its central tenet the idea that all people should be given what they deserve?
   a. Utilitarian
   b. Rights and duties
   c. Justice
   d. Virtues

4. Which of the following names is most commonly associated with pyramid schemes?
   a. Ponzi
   b. Enron
   c. Arthur Andersen
   d. John Rigas

5. The output of the Discover Inventory is a three-digit code based on Holland's Hexagon. All of the following are elements of Holland's Hexagon except:

   a. Artistic.

   b. Investigative.

   c. Mathematical.

   d. Social.

4. *Making choices and exercising judgment.* Econo-lube (taken from the ACFE educator documents at www.cfenet.com).

   While living in St. George, Jeff received a coupon in the mail for an oil change for $9.95 at a local Econo-lube. He thought $9.95 was a good deal so he decided to give Econo-lube a try. When Jeff arrived at Econo-lube, the waiting room had approximately five people obviously waiting for their cars to be serviced. He went to the service counter and was greeted by the owner.

   Jeff explained to the owner that he would like to use his coupon for the $9.95 oil change. The owner acted very friendly and told him that the price of $9.95 did not actually include a $3.00 oil disposal fee. Also, the coupon was only good for cars that required four quarts of oil so Jeff would have to purchase one more quart to meet the requirements of his car. So the price would be $14.90. Next, Jeff asked for Valvoline 30wt oil because that was what his uncle, who repairs his own work vehicles, recommended he use in this car. The owner immediately told Jeff that 30wt was not right and proceeded to tell Jeff all about his high performance Porsche that he never runs 30wt oil in. Jeff's 1989 Honda was definitely not a Porsche so he persisted. The owner finally agreed to use 30wt oil on the condition that Jeff signs a liability waiver. Jeff also had to pay an extra dollar for each quart of Valvoline brand oil because Econo-lube used a different brand. The $9.95 oil change was now up to $18.90.

   Jeff sat down next to a young looking man named Rick who told him he was also in for the great deal on an oil change. As they talked, Jeff learned that this man was recently married and was planning to start college in the fall.

   The owner called Rick's name and invited him into the shop to review the "free diagnostic check" details Econo-lube had performed on his car. Rick was with the owner about 5 minutes and came back ghostly white. Jeff asked him what was wrong. He explained that his car was in bad shape. In fact, he felt lucky it had not broken down yet. He was sick that the amount of his estimate was now over $300. When Jeff asked if he was going to let the owner do the work he replied: "Do I really have a choice? My car is in bad shape." He had already given the OK.

   After a while the owner called Jeff's name. He greeted Jeff gravely, asked him to come with him into his shop, and told him that his Honda needed some help. He then proceeded through a detailed checklist and showed Jeff everything that was wrong. Apparently, Jeff was lucky not to be dead because his brakes were on the brink of failing. Also, Jeff was told his transmission fluid needed to be drained and the filter replaced—for added effect the mechanic showed how he had opened the plug and saw that the fluid was black. There were also a lot of small "preventative maintenance items." The final item the owner discussed with Jeff was that the O2 sensor needed to be replaced. Of course, Jeff did not know what an O2 sensor was so the owner explained it to him in great detail. In the end Jeff's bill for the oil change was going to be over $400! The good news was that he could have it all done in a couple of hours.

   Jeff was tempted to have the charges done, but politely declined and asked for the basic $9.95 oil change (which cost $18.90). Later, Jeff drove the car to an uncle's house and went through a copy of the same checklist with him. About half of the small preventive maintenance items were legitimate things that the uncle recommended. The total of these items cost Jeff no more than $50. The expensive items listed (brakes, transmission filter replacement, O2 sensor) were in good shape and did not need to be replaced at all. In fact, because Jeff's car was a standard transmission, it did not even have a transmission filter.

Jeff and his uncle checked the transmission fluid themselves and found it to be clean and clear. Jeff was upset that the owner of the shop would try to take advantage of him so badly but did not pursue the issue any farther.

Did the owner of the Econo-lube in St. George commit fraud? What precautions or controls can consumers use to prevent them from being taken advantage of in a situation like this? Were there any symptoms or indications of fraud present in this case?

5. *Field exercises.*

a. Research one or more of the following accounting frauds. Report the results of your research in a two- to three-page paper and/or an oral presentation to the class.
   - Tenet Healthcare
   - Tyco International
   - Worldcom
   - Bernie Madoff

b. Through interviews or other research, find a company's code of ethics. Summarize it and discuss how it is similar to and different from one of the codes of ethics discussed in the chapter.

c. Point your Web browser to www.cfenet.com. Click the "local chapters" link and find a CFE chapter near you. Attend a meeting, interview a member, or, in cooperation with your instructor, ask a CFE to come and speak to your class.

d. Visit your campus career center; talk with a career counselor about your future career plans. Take an aptitude or interest assessment, such as the Discover Inventory or StrengthsQuest; what does the assessment tell you about yourself?

6. Describe your personal philosophy for making ethical decisions. Your philosophy may be based on one or more of the schools of thought discussed in the chapter; it also may be completely original. Meet with a group of your classmates to discuss your ethical philosophies. Describe a time when you had to make a personal ethical choice; explain the choice you made and its consequences. If confronted with the same decision again, would you make the same choice? Why, or why not?

7. Which school of ethical thought is described in each of the following independent scenarios? Justify your choices.

a. Julie and Bart were talking over their progress in the accounting program at Big State University. Julie was annoyed at the number of students who cheated on exams and class projects in the program. She told Bart: "If prospective employers find out that cheating is so prevalent here, it will hurt my chances of getting a good job when I graduate—even if I don't cheat!"

b. Maria is a certified fraud examiner. She is interviewing Rehan about missing inventory. When Maria asked what should be done to the person who stole the inventory, Rehan replied: "They should be locked up and pay a hefty fine."

c. Anita recently discovered that her co-worker Vicki was engaging in fraudulent activities that harmed their company. She went to her priest for guidance about what to do.

d. Gil is a financial analyst on Wall Street with an accounting and finance degree from Big State University. In an interview for a popular magazine, he said "Everyone 'cheats' a little when they forecast their financial statements. In the end, it's probably okay because everybody's financial results are a little distorted that way."

8. *Professional certification and licensure.* In my view, the purpose of an accounting degree is not to prepare you to take any particular certification/license exam; the purpose of an accounting degree is to teach you to think like an accountant. But, many accounting professionals enjoy both the challenge and recognition associated with obtaining a professional license or certification. Many such certifications are available, including Certified Public Accountant, Certified Management Accountant,

Certified Fraud Examiner, Certified Internal Auditor, Certified Information Systems Auditor, Enrolled Agent, Certified Government Financial Manager. In consultation with your AIS professor, choose one or more of those credentials; respond to the following questions about it.

a. Is the credential a license or a certificate?

b. What are the steps associated with obtaining the credential?

c. What topics are included in the credential's professional exam? How do those topics align with your university studies?

d. What organization sponsors/offers the credential?

e. Does the sponsoring organization have a local chapter in your area? If so, arrange to attend one of its meetings.

f. Summarize the sponsoring organization's code of ethics, if it has one.

g. Look online or in a newspaper for job listings that seem related to the credential. Make a list of the companies, job titles, responsibilities, and (if available) salaries for each position you locate.

9. *Terminology.* Please match each item on the left with the most appropriate item on the right.

1. Autonomy of practice	a. A goal to work toward professionally
2. Career mission statement	b. Another name for ethics
3. Jeff Skilling	c. Associated with the Enron fraud
4. Knowledge integration	d. Characteristic of a professional
5. Metaethics	e. Every person for him- or herself
6. Mintz and Morris	f. Investigation of where ethics come from
7. Moral philosophy	g. People should do what is moral
8. Rights and duties	h. Suggested a 10-step process for resolving ethical dilemmas
9. Utilitarianism	i. The end justifies the means
10. Virtues	j. Was reduced by SOX

10. *Multiple choice questions.*

1. Explaining a person's ethics by analyzing the ethics of his ancestors is an example of:
   a. Metaethics.
   b. Normative ethics.
   c. Applied ethics.
   d. Situational ethics.

2. "People shouldn't cheat" is an example of:
   a. Metaethics.
   b. Normative ethics.
   c. Applied ethics.
   d. Situational ethics.

3. Debating the ethics of insider trading best describes:
   a. Metaethics.
   b. Normative ethics.
   c. Applied ethics.
   d. Situational ethics.

4. As part of his commitment to professionalism, John used the Langenderfer and Rockness model to resolve an ethical dilemma. His action is an example of:

   a. Thinking rationally, logically, and coherently.

   b. Recognizing the influence of legal forces.

   c. Recognizing the influence of social forces.

   d. Recognizing the influence of economic forces.

5. In connection with the Enron bankruptcy, Skilling was most likely following which school of ethical thought?

   a. Virtues.

   b. Utilitarianism.

   c. Normative ethics.

   d. Justice.

11. *Statement evaluation.* Please indicate whether each of the following statements is (i) always true, (ii) sometimes true, or (iii) never true. For those that are (ii) sometimes true, explain when the statement is true.

   a. Legal behavior is the same as ethical behavior.

   b. Metaethics and applied ethics are important in the accounting profession.

   c. The habit of ethical decision making begins once you have your first professional job.

   d. Any response to an ethical dilemma is acceptable, provided the decision maker can justify it.

   e. Pyramid schemes are, by definition, both illegal and unethical.

   f. Effective communication is an important part of professional behavior.

   g. To be considered professional, an accountant must have a CPA license.

   h. A subordinate can bypass his/her supervisor in reporting an ethical dilemma.

   i. Violations of professional codes of ethics can lead to fines, prison, and/or losing your professional license/certification.

   j. The best ethical decision makers in accounting follow the utilitarianism school of ethical thought.

12. *Prior material application.*

   a. Check out the post titled "AIS coverage in professional exams" on my AIS blog (http://bobhurtais.blogspot.com/). It spells out the topics you've studied in your AIS course relative to the CPA exam. Choose another professional certification exam, such as the CMA or CFE. Map the content of the exam to your AIS study, similar to what you'll find in the blog post.

   b. One of Bell's seven characteristics of a professional is integrating knowledge from many disciplines. Look back over the topics we've examined in earlier parts of the book; explain how they fulfill that characteristic. For example, business process management (Chapter 4) is a topic commonly associated with operations management.

   c. McDonald's four criteria for being a professional include a specialized knowledge base and complex skills. Consider the topics you've studied in AIS this quarter; which of them constitute specialized knowledge? Which involve complex skills?

   d. Ethics issues can arise in virtually any business process. Consider the steps in either the sales/collection or acquisition/payment process; suggest an ethical dilemma that could arise in one or more of those steps. For example, in the sales/collection process, an employee could knowingly ship extra units of product in an effort to boost company revenue.

   e. Explain how each school of ethical thought discussed in this chapter would respond to the ethical dilemma you identified in part (d) of this problem. For example, the virtues school of ethics might consider shipping extra units of product unethical because it is not moral/virtuous.

Chapter **Seventeen**

Auditing and Evaluating the AIS

AIS in the Business World

City of Bell

The university where I work, Cal Poly Pomona (www.csupomona.edu), is just outside Los Angeles. Not far from our campus lies the City of Bell (www.cityofbell.org); you may have heard that it has recently been rocked by a scandal involving extremely high salaries for many city officials.

The California State Controller's office shows the following maximum salaries for some Bell city officials in 2009 (http://lgcr.sco.ca.gov/Default.aspx):

- Chief administrative officer, $703,248
- Chief of police, $457,002
- Assistant chief administrative officer, $342,989
- Director of general services, $231,168

To put those figures in perspective, consider that the president of the United States earns an annual salary of $400,000.

The City of Bell, like most governments, is subject to annual audits. And, a lot of people have wondered what role auditors should play in a situation like that.

Discussion Questions

1. What is an audit? What kinds of audits do accountants perform?
2. Do auditors have a responsibility to speak out in situations like the one described here?
3. What is the relationship between auditing and accounting information systems?

Auditing is the area of accounting associated with AIS evaluation. The corporate scandals of the late 20th and early 21st centuries such as Parmalat, Global Crossing, and Enron point to the need for regular, thorough AIS evaluation as part of accountants' professional responsibility and fiduciary duties to shareholders and the public.

When you finish studying this chapter, you should be able to:

1. Describe the various kinds of audits you might encounter in your accounting career.
2. Explain the AICPA's 10 generally accepted auditing standards (GAAS).
3. Discuss the basic steps associated with a financial statement audit.
4. Explain the connection between auditing and accounting information systems.

Your accounting curriculum probably includes at least one course in auditing, so this chapter certainly will not make you an expert in the field, but it will give you an introduction to this important area of professional practice.

TYPES OF AUDITS

Dictionary.com lists several definitions for *audit,* but the one that seems most appropriate here is "a methodical examination or review of a condition or situation." There are seven basic kinds of audits you might be involved in as your career progresses:

1. *Financial audit.* A financial audit involves the examination of a company's accounting information system and financial statements. Auditors express one of four types of opinions on the company's financial statements. An *unqualified* opinion (also known as a *clean* opinion) says that the company's statements are prepared in accordance with generally accepted accounting principles (GAAP). Auditors issue a *qualified* opinion when one or more items don't conform to GAAP—but not so many items as to compromise the overall fairness of the statements. An *adverse* opinion means the statements are not prepared in accordance with GAAP, while a *disclaimer* of opinion denotes that the auditors could not tell if they were. Adverse and disclaimers of opinion are hard to find—most companies would change auditors (or the auditors would resign) before such an opinion was issued.

2. *Operational audit.* In an operational audit, auditors examine a company's rules and procedures for conducting business. They're asking if a company's rules make sense, and if they're followed. Systems documentation techniques such as flowcharting are particularly important in operational audits; for example, a flowchart of the purchasing process would give the operational auditor a standard for comparison against a company's actual practice in the same area. Internal auditors often are involved in operational auditing.

3. *Systems audit.* As we've discussed before, information technology is an integral part of most accounting information systems today. A systems audit determines whether the various forms of information technology in an AIS are producing expected results. It also examines the issue of systems security very closely, making sure the data are safe within the system. Basically, a systems audit looks "inside the box," rather than treating the computer as an unknown quantity in an audit. One important issue in systems auditing is the *service organization* audit discussed in Statement of Auditing Standards 70. Many organizations outsource certain duties and responsibilities to external parties; for example, a corporation might hire ADP to do its payroll processing. Auditors need to know that those service organizations are maintaining adequate internal controls for

their client; SAS 70 speaks to that knowledge. According to www.sas70.com, "SAS No. 70 is the authoritative guidance that allows service organizations to disclose their control activities and processes to their customers and their customers' auditors in a uniform reporting format. A SAS 70 examination signifies that a service organization has had its control objectives and control activities examined by an independent accounting and auditing firm. A formal report including the auditor's opinion ('Service Auditor's Report') is issued to the service organization at the conclusion of a SAS 70 examination."

4. *Compliance audit.* Governmental and not-for-profit organizations (GNFPs) are subject to compliance audits. Although almost every audit involves some sort of judgment on the part of the auditor, compliance audits are virtually devoid of judgment. GNFPs are subject to very strict government rules and regulations, many of which are contained in the **Yellow Book** published by the Government Accountability Office (GAO). You can learn a lot more about the Yellow Book and compliance auditing on the GAO's Web site: www.gao.gov. A compliance audit determines whether or not a GNFP is following the rules and regulations in the Yellow Book.

5. *Management audit.* Of all the kinds of auditing discussed here, the management audit may involve the greatest degree of judgment. A management audit determines the degree to which the assumptions underlying decisions are valid; it also examines the ways in which management decisions are supported. In the chapter on decision-making models, you read about the Steps for Better Thinking; a management audit would be looking for that type of support for major decisions.

6. *Investigative audit.* Also known as a *fraud audit,* it is associated with the broader field of forensic accounting. The recent ethics scandals at Enron, WorldCom, Global Crossing, and other firms have raised awareness of the costs of occupational fraud and abuse in organizations. An investigative audit, which may be conducted by a Certified Fraud Examiner, may be triggered by observation of unusual behavior or discrepancies in the accounting information system. Figure 17.1 lays out a common order for gathering evidence in an investigative audit (www.cfenet.com).

Most investigative audits start with reviewing pertinent *documents;* for example, the auditor might examine physical or electronic copies of checks in cases where

FIGURE 17.1
Investigative Audit Tools

Source: Wells, 2004.

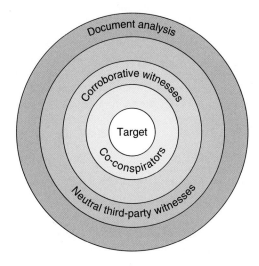

embezzlement is suspected. Interviews of *neutral third-party witnesses* often come next. For example, an employee might have observed a co-worker taking computer equipment out of the office; the employee might have assumed a perfectly innocent, legitimate reason/motivation, even if fraud was involved. *Corroborative witnesses* can lend additional information to the investigation by (for example) confirming information collected in the first two stages—or even in subsequent stages. *Co-conspirators* are involved in the fraud, but often not as deeply or as seriously as the target of the investigation. For example, a purchasing agent might collude with a receiving department employee to steal merchandise; the receiving department employee would be considered a co-conspirator. Finally, the investigative auditor interviews the *target.* By that time, the auditor has a clear idea of how the fraud occurred—an idea supported by evidence from the other steps.

7. *International audit.* This type of audit is really a "basket" of the other types. It can be conducted in a U.S.-based firm with international operations or a non-U.S.-based firm. International auditing is exceptionally challenging. It requires the auditor to understand the accounting rules in another country, but it also necessitates an intimate understanding of national culture, laws, religion, and other nonaccounting issues.

While the degree, role, and type of **professional judgment** vary among the seven types of audits discussed here, all of them incorporate judgment to some degree. Other commonalities between the seven types of audits include

- Checking existing conditions against some predetermined standard.
- Questioning, firmly but professionally, managers and employees of the organization being audited.
- Maintaining an independent attitude and appropriate professional "distance" from the client.

Reflection and Self-Assessment   17.1

What type of audit is indicated by each of the following descriptions? Justify your choices, particularly if more than one type of audit seems applicable.

1. Ray and Gary, partners in a psychotherapy practice, hire Rob to determine if their secretary has been embezzling cash.

2. An internal auditor works with managers in the purchasing department to determine a more efficient way to handle inventory transactions.

3. An audit client uses Peachtree for transaction processing. An auditor examines the system to ensure that the software is processing the transactions correctly.

4. A German-based organization hires a U.S. firm to check out its accounting information system. The overall objective is enabling the German firm to list its securities on the NYSE.

5. A CPA firm conducts its annual evaluation of CHC Corporation's accounting information system. After the evaluation, the CPA firm issues an unqualified opinion.

Financial audits are further guided by 10 generally accepted auditing standards (GAAS), discussed in the next section.

GENERALLY ACCEPTED AUDITING STANDARDS

The Auditing Standards Board (ASB) of the American Institute of Certified Public Accountants (AICPA) identified 10 **auditing standards** that govern external audits by CPAs (Whittington and Pany, 2004, pp. 31–56). See Figure 17.2. Of course, the 10 standards aren't the only guidelines for conducting an audit. We're discussing them here because they represent the foundation of the rest; you'll explore the standards and related issues in significantly greater depth in your auditing course.

The three *general standards* focus on the auditor's background and approach to the audit. First and foremost, an auditor must be well-trained in auditing before an engagement commences. Generalized knowledge of accounting principles and information systems is important, but specific *training* related to auditing is essential. Auditing is an important element of professional practice in accounting; without good auditing, decision makers cannot rely on the financial statements to be fair. *Independence* speaks to the auditor's mental attitude; that is, the auditor must always remain independent from the client. While some have questioned how independent an auditor can be from the organization signing his or her paychecks, maintaining a professional distance and appropriate professional skepticism are key to the conduct of a successful audit. Finally (in this group), the auditor must exercise due *professional care* in preparing for and completing the audit. The engagement must be properly planned in terms of personnel on the audit team and specific audit procedures. The duty of professional care also extends to preparing the audit report.

The second group of standards focuses on *field work;* in other words, they set out important ideas for conducting the audit itself. The audit is to be properly planned, and all staff members must be adequately *supervised.* Most audit teams comprise professionals at

FIGURE 17.2
Generally Accepted
Auditing Standards

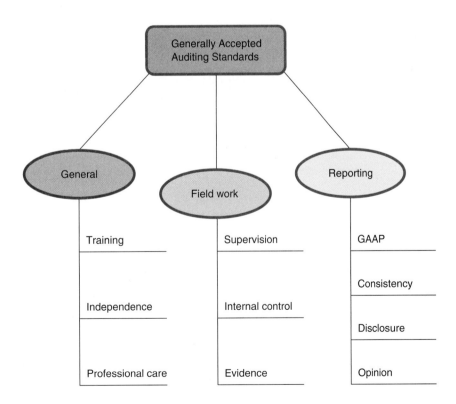

various stages of their careers, with varying levels of experience in auditing. As a team member's experience increases, the need for supervision may decrease. A thorough assessment of *internal controls* is a critical step early in the audit process. While such an assessment has always been critical, the Sarbanes-Oxley Act of 2002 has placed even greater emphasis on internal control issues. Auditors must assess an organization's risk exposures and determine the degree to which the organization's internal controls ameliorate those risks. The *evidence* standard speaks to the importance of having an objective, reasonable basis for expressing an opinion on the company's financial statements. Evidence can be obtained in many different ways, including observing organizational processes, inspecting documents, and obtaining external confirmations of account balances.

GAAS also contains four *reporting standards,* which speak to the ultimate opinion the auditors express on the financial statements. First, the opinion must state whether or not the statements are presented in accordance with *generally accepted accounting principles* (GAAP). The language of an audit opinion is very specific; unqualified opinions always include such a statement. You may recall that *consistency* is one of the qualitative characteristics of accounting information in the conceptual framework; it is also one of the reporting standards. The audit report must explain any inconsistencies between the current period's application of GAAP and the prior period's application. Full *disclosure* is another commonality between GAAS and the conceptual framework. Financial statement users can assume the disclosures in the financial statements are appropriate unless the audit opinion specifically states they are not. Finally, the audit report must clearly state the auditor's *opinion* on the financial statements (unqualified, qualified, disclaimer, or adverse). The auditor also must explain the reason(s) for the opinion.

Whittington and Pany (2004, p. 32) offer these summary comments on the 10 standards:

> The 10 standards set forth by the American Institute of Certified Public Accountants include such subjective terms of measurement as "*adequate* planning," "*sufficient* understanding of internal control," and "*adequate* disclosure." To decide under the circumstances of each audit engagement what is adequate, sufficient and competent requires the exercise of *professional judgment.* Auditing cannot be reduced to rote; the exercise of judgment by the auditor is vital at numerous points in every engagement. However, the formulation and publication of carefully worded auditing standards are of immense aid in raising the quality of audit work, even though these standards require professional judgment in their application.

That professional judgment must be developed deliberately and consistently over time, starting with your formal undergraduate education as an accountant. Critical thinking and interpersonal communication skills are important keys in developing and honing them.

GENERIC AUDIT STEPS

Although professional judgment is an important aspect of auditing, auditors commonly follow a generalized set of steps when conducting an audit. Figure 17.3 outlines the generic steps often involved in a financial statement audit.

Ultimately, and particularly since Sarbanes-Oxley, management is responsible for the content of the organization's financial statements. So, assessing management's integrity is a necessary first step in the audit process. Dictionary.com defines "integrity" as "steadfast adherence to a strict moral or ethical code." Managers have a **fiduciary duty** to their employees and stockholders to act in the best interests of the organization—even when those interests may conflict with their own. COSO's *Internal Control—Integrated Framework*

FIGURE 17.3
Audit Steps

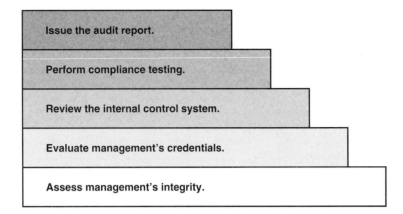

Issue the audit report.

Perform compliance testing.

Review the internal control system.

Evaluate management's credentials.

Assess management's integrity.

(Committee of Sponsoring Organizations, 2002) alludes to this step in its discussion of an organization's control environment:

> The control environment sets the tone of an organization, influencing the control consciousness of its people. It is the foundation for all other components of internal control, providing discipline and structure. Control environment factors include the integrity, ethical values and competence of the entity's people; management's philosophy and operating style; the way management assigns authority and responsibility, and organizes and develops its people; and the attention and direction provided by the board of directors.

Management must set the example by demonstrating integrity and ethical behavior; otherwise, employees throughout the organization are likely to feel justified in engaging in unethical actions.

Reflection and Self-Assessment   17.2

What tools and techniques would you use to assess management's integrity?

After evaluating management's integrity, the auditor should consider management's credentials. This evaluation focuses on two questions: (*a*) Is management technically competent? (*b*) Is management financially competent? Notice that the evaluation of management's competence comes *after* the evaluation of integrity. Managers can understand the organization at a deep and fundamental level; they can even comprehend clearly the role, purpose, and importance of accounting as a reporting mechanism. But those credentials mean very little without a generalized disposition toward ethical behavior. Managers can develop technical and financial competence via formal education and/or experience.

The next step is evaluating the organization's internal control system. The auditor must assess the organization's risk exposures and then determine whether the controls are in place to address those risks successfully. Remember: the goal is not to eliminate risk— that's impossible anyway. Rather, the goal is to address, manage, and/or reduce risk. Common controls you'd expect to find include

- Adequate documentation of business processes.
- Background checks for prospective employees.
- Comprehensive employee training.

- Document matching.
- Multiple signatures for checks over a specified threshold.
- Physical safeguards for assets.
- Regular bank reconciliations.
- Separation of duties.

Computerized AIS environments often require unique internal controls. Louwers et al. (2005, p. 732) listed the following examples:

Administrative Controls	Physical Controls	Technical Controls
Security checks on personnel	Controlled access	Data encryption
Segregation of duties	Computer room entry log record	Access control software and passwords
Program testing after modification	Data backup storage	Transaction logging reports
Rotation of computer duties	Preprinted limits on documents (e.g., checks)	Range and reasonableness checks on transaction amounts
Transaction limit amounts	Inconspicuous location	Control totals

Control Objectives for Information and Related Technology (CoBIT) were discussed in the chapter on computer crime. Those standards also examine internal control issues within the context of computerized information systems.

The auditor's confidence in an organization's internal control system dictates the extent and character of compliance testing conducted in the next phase. Compliance testing involves examining a sample of transactions and verifying that they have been recorded in accordance with GAAP, thus leading to fair account balances on the financial statements. For example, an auditor might conduct a physical count of the inventory. Independent verification of major accounts receivable and accounts payable balances are also common compliance tests at this stage of an audit.

A company's financial statements implicitly involve several assertions by management that must be evaluated as part of auditing. Those assertions are commonly organized into five groups (Louwers et al., 2005, p. 9):

- *Existence or occurrence.* Did the recorded sales transactions really occur? Do the assets listed on the balance sheet really exist?
- *Rights and obligations.* Does the company really own the assets? Are related legal responsibilities identified?
- *Valuation and allocation.* Are the accounts valued correctly? Are expenses allocated to the period(s) benefited?
- *Completeness.* Are the financial statements (including footnotes) complete? Were all the transactions recorded in the right period?
- *Presentation and disclosure.* Were all the transactions recorded in the correct accounts? Are the disclosures understandable to users?

You may recall that a risk-control matrix can include an area for these assertions.

Note that the questions listed above are illustrative, not comprehensive. A well-designed accounting information system that incorporates strong internal controls and appropriate forms of information technology can assist auditors in verifying the five assertions related to financial statements.

The audit culminates with the issuance of the audit report, or opinion. As stated earlier, audit opinions fall into four broad categories: unqualified, qualified, disclaimer, or adverse. Each opinion has very specific language; the audit opinion expressed by KPMG on the financial statements of Home Depot Inc. appears in Figure 17.4.

The Sarbanes-Oxley Act has increased the role of judgment and the responsibility of management for financial statements. In addition, SOX requires its own compliance audit,

FIGURE 17.4   KPMG's Audit Opinion on Home Depot's Financial Statements

We have audited management's assessment, included in the accompanying Management's Report on Internal Control over Financial Reporting, that The Home Depot, Inc. and subsidiaries maintained effective internal control over financial reporting as of January 30, 2005, based on criteria established in *Internal Control-Integrated Framework* issued by the Committee of Sponsoring Organizations of the Treadway Commission (COSO). The Company's management is responsible for maintaining effective internal control over financial reporting and for its assessment of the effectiveness of internal control over financial reporting. Our responsibility is to express an opinion on management's assessment and an opinion on the effectiveness of the Company's internal control over financial reporting based on our audit.

We conducted our audit in accordance with the standards of the Public Company Accounting Oversight Board (United States). Those standards require that we plan and perform the audit to obtain reasonable assurance about whether effective internal control over financial reporting was maintained in all material respects. Our audit included obtaining an understanding of internal control over financial reporting, evaluating management's assessment, testing and evaluating the design and operating effectiveness of internal control and performing such other procedures as we considered necessary in the circumstances. We believe that our audit provides a reasonable basis for our opinion.

A company's internal control over financial reporting is a process designed to provide reasonable assurance regarding the reliability of financial reporting and the preparation of financial statements for external purposes in accordance with generally accepted accounting principles. A company's internal control over financial reporting includes those policies and procedures that (1) pertain to the maintenance of records that, in reasonable detail, accurately and fairly reflect the transactions and dispositions of the assets of the company; (2) provide reasonable assurance that transactions are recorded as necessary to permit preparation of financial statements in accordance with generally accepted accounting principles, and that receipts and expenditures of the company are being made only in accordance with authorizations of management and directors of the company; and (3) provide reasonable assurance regarding prevention or timely detection of unauthorized acquisition, use, or disposition of the company's assets that could have a material effect on the financial statements.

Because of its inherent limitations, internal control over financial reporting may not prevent or detect misstatements. Also, projections of any evaluation of effectiveness to future periods are subject to the risk that controls may become inadequate because of changes in conditions, or that the degree of compliance with the policies or procedures may deteriorate.

In our opinion, management's assessment that The Home Depot, Inc. and subsidiaries maintained effective internal control over financial reporting as of January 30, 2005, is fairly stated, in all material respects, based on criteria established in *Internal Control-Integrated Framework* issued by the Committee of Sponsoring Organizations of the Treadway Commission (COSO). Also, in our opinion, The Home Depot, Inc. and subsidiaries maintained, in all material respects, effective internal control over financial reporting as of January 30, 2005, based on criteria established in *Internal Control-Integrated Framework* issued by the Committee of Sponsoring Organizations of the Treadway Commission (COSO).

We also have audited, in accordance with the standards of the Public Company Accounting Oversight Board (United States), the Consolidated Balance Sheets of The Home Depot, Inc. and subsidiaries as of January 30, 2005 and February 1, 2004, and the related Consolidated Statements of Earnings, Stockholders' Equity and Comprehensive Income, and Cash Flows for each of the fiscal years in the three-year period ended January 30, 2005, and our report dated March 11, 2005 expressed an unqualified opinion on those consolidated financial statements.

conducted by a different firm, in addition to the financial audit. SOX is divided into 11 titles (similar to chapters in a book), which are further subdivided into sections. Some of the most important sections that relate to auditing and the accounting information system include

- *Section 302.* This section relates to the evaluation of internal controls in an audit. Specifically, it obligates the chief executive officer and chief financial officer to attest that they have personally reviewed internal controls within the preceding 90 days.

The CEO and CFO also acknowledge that they are responsible for the financial statements and the internal controls that promote their reliability and integrity. The responsibilities outlined in this section of SOX cannot be delegated, even via power of attorney.

- *Section 401.* This section is titled "Disclosures in Periodic Reports." The financial statements must be "accurate and presented in a manner that does not contain incorrect statements or admit to state material information. These financial statements shall also include all material off-balance-sheet liabilities, obligations or transactions" (www .soxlaw.com). If you've made any study of the Enron debacle in this or another course, you may recall that off-balance-sheet transactions were one of the corporation's primary problems. Enron accountants structured transactions to conform to the "letter" of accounting rules and regulations while disregarding the "spirit" of those regulations.

- *Section 404.* Entitled "Management Assessment of Internal Controls," this section re-emphasizes the importance of a sound internal control system as part of maintaining AIS integrity and reliability. As part of their annual reports, SOX-compliant organizations must discuss the scope and adequacy of internal controls. Independent auditors also must comment on the opinion expressed by the organization's management. In practice, you may hear this practice referred to as a "404 audit."

- *Section 409.* Real-time reporting is the primary issue in this section. If an organization experiences a material change in its financial condition or operations, it is required to disclose that change "on an urgent basis." In other words, the company cannot wait until its quarterly or annual SEC filings to communicate the change; it must be disclosed as quickly as possible. Additionally, section 409 requires that the disclosure be made in nontechnical, easy-to-understand terms. The disclosures should be supported by qualitative information as well.

- *Section 802.* This section spells out the penalties for noncompliance with the Sarbanes-Oxley Act. According to www.soxlaw.com, "This section imposes penalties of fines and/or up to 20 years imprisonment for altering, destroying, mutilating, concealing, falsifying records, documents or tangible objects with the intent to obstruct, impede or influence a legal investigation. This section also imposes penalties of fines and/or imprisonment up to 10 years on any accountant who knowingly and willfully violates the requirements of maintenance of all audit or review papers for a period of 5 years."

With my own students, I've often referred to SOX as the "full employment act for accountants." So long as SOX remains in effect, accountants will have jobs because of the responsibilities the act imposes on organizations.

ACCOUNTING INFORMATION SYSTEMS AND AUDITING

So how does this discussion of auditing relate to your study of accounting information systems? Many of the topics we've discussed in this text, as well as many of the skills you have developed in your study of AIS, have direct relevance when it comes to auditing.

First, this text has emphasized the importance of critical thinking in the design and implementation of accounting information systems. Developing and exercising your professional judgment have been consistent themes in this book—whether they relate to selecting information technology tools, evaluating internal controls, documenting accounting information systems with flowcharts, or making recommendations for improving business processes. Decision-making models such as Wolcott and Lynch's Steps for Better

Thinking (www.wolcottlynch.com) provide a rational, systematic approach for making complex decisions. Professional judgment is critically important in the auditing process. It is an integral component of the general standards of independence and professional care; critical thinking also comes into play in maintaining appropriate levels of professional skepticism in the audit process.

Second, the discussion of internal controls throughout the text has an important relationship to auditing. Understanding the four broad purposes of internal control, the risk exposures for a specific organization, and the types of controls that can reduce those risk exposures are key elements of the third step in an audit: reviewing internal controls. Because no two organizations are likely to have identical sets of risk exposures and internal controls, accounting professionals must consistently return to the bedrock principles and ideas of this important area in their examination and evaluation of accounting information systems.

Third, in our examination of business processes, we talked about the importance of understanding an organization's environment as part of understanding its accounting information system. Understanding the organization's internal and external environment is also an important skill for the auditor. Specialization in specific industries is therefore a somewhat common practice among auditing firms. For example, Vicenti, Lloyd and Stutzman (www.vlsllp.com) in southern California maintains a strong practice in the government and not-for-profit sector.

Finally, information technology skills link accounting information systems and auditing in very important ways. Familiarity and skill with common forms of IT, such as spreadsheets and databases, can enable an auditor to examine the accounting information system much more effectively and efficiently. Auditors with backgrounds in both accounting and information systems may conduct information technology audits. As more and more large organizations move to enterprise systems and the utilization of enterprise resource planning software, this connection will only become more important.

CRITICAL THINKING

I'm using the fraud audit as an example in this section because most of my students find discussions of fraud and forensic accounting really interesting. Also, as a certified fraud examiner, I like to use any opportunity I can to educate people about fraud detection and prevention.

Like accounting information systems, auditing is a multidisciplinary field. Of course, it requires an in-depth knowledge of accounting; but auditors also need to master various aspects of information technology, business law, and human behavior. Let's look at how each of those topics might impact one of the seven types of audits listed at the beginning of this chapter: the fraud audit.

Information technology can certainly be used to commit fraud; the good news is, information technology also can be used to detect fraud. IT allows auditors to examine transaction databases quickly and efficiently; here are some tasks auditors can complete more easily using information technology when conducting a fraud audit:

- *Graphical trend analysis.* Consider the data below, which shows total cash disbursements by week for two years:

Week	20x2	20x1
1	$2,245	$2,720
2	1,557	1,886
3	3,710	4,494
4	4,792	2,441
5	1,657	2,008

If you were looking for anomalies between the two years, a graphical representation of the data would be a lot easier to evaluate than a table of numbers. Here's that same data in graphic form:

- *Statistical tests.* You've probably completed at least one statistics course by this time in your education. You may recall some of the tests that can be used to analyze differences between two samples, such as a *t*-test. While *t*-tests can be performed without the use of information technology, they are much easier and quicker when IT is used—whether the IT is a simple spreadsheet or some more complex statistics software like SPSS.

- *Database queries.* A "find unmatched" query could be used to generate a list of unpaid purchase invoices or uncollected receivables. If a fraud auditor finds significant numbers of those transactions associated with a particular manager, department, or location, additional investigation is probably a good idea. A "just under limit" query can be used to locate suspicious amounts. For example, if an organization requires two signatures on purchase orders over $10,000, a "just under limit" query could identify purchase orders that are more than $9,000 but less than the $10,000 limit. Too many of those transactions may indicate that someone is trying to circumvent internal controls.

We've talked a lot about the Sarbanes-Oxley Act and its impact on accounting and auditing, but forensic auditors need to be aware of many other laws and legal issues, too. The Bank Secrecy Act, for example, requires banks to file a Currency Transaction Report for cash transactions that exceed $10,000 in a single day—whether from a single transaction or a series of transactions. The act also requires banks to keep a Monetary Instrument Log that records cash purchases between $3,000 and $10,000 of money orders, cashier's checks, traveler's checks, and other monetary instruments; finally, banks must file a Suspicious Activity Report for any transaction where it seems the customer is trying to avoid other reporting requirements, launder money, or engage in other potentially illegal activity.

While no single behavior provides conclusive evidence of fraud, there are some behavioral indications that a person may be lying or otherwise distorting the truth during a fraud audit. Some of them include nervous gestures (like tapping a pencil on the table), answering a question with a question ("What possible motivation would I have for stealing money?"), trying to cast suspicion on someone else in the organization, or an employee obviously living beyond his/her means (e.g., an employee who makes $20,000 a year driving an expensive new sports car to work).

If you'd like to know more about fraud auditing, check out *Managing the Business Risk of Fraud: A Practical Guide,* published by the Institute of Internal Auditors, the American Institute of CPAs, and the Association of Certified Fraud Examiners. According to its introduction (pp. 5–6):

> This guide recommends ways in which boards, senior management, and internal auditors can fight fraud in their organization. Specifically, it provides credible guidance from leading professional organizations that defines principles and theories for fraud risk management and describes how organizations of various sizes and types can establish their own fraud risk management program. The guide includes examples of key program components and resources that organizations can use as a starting place to develop a fraud risk management program effectively and efficiently. Each organization needs to assess the degree of emphasis to place on fraud risk management based on its size and circumstances.

You can download the guide free from the Web site of any one of the three organizations: www.theiia.org, www.aicpa.org, or www.acfe.com.

Summary

In this chapter, then, you've had the briefest introduction to auditing—the evaluation of an accounting information system. Here is a summary of the chapter in terms of its learning objectives:

1. *Describe the various kinds of audits you might encounter in your accounting career.*
   a. Financial
   b. Operational
   c. Systems
   d. Compliance
   e. Management
   f. Investigative
   g. International

2. *Explain the AICPA's 10 generally accepted auditing standards (GAAS).*
   a. General standards: training, independence, and professional care.
   b. Field work standards: supervision, internal control, and evidence.
   c. Reporting standards: GAAP, consistency, disclosure, and opinion.

3. *Discuss the basic steps associated with a financial statement audit.*
   a. Assess management's integrity.
   b. Evaluate management's credentials.
   c. Review the internal control system.
   d. Perform compliance testing.
   e. Issue the audit report.

4. *Explain the connection between auditing and accounting information systems.* Auditing and AIS are linked via at least four important skill areas: critical thinking, internal controls analysis, understanding of business processes, and effective use of information technology.

Recent financial scandals have shaken public confidence in financial reporting and the accounting profession in general. Therefore, conducting audits with diligence and integrity is even more important today than in the past.

Key Terms

auditing, *306*
auditing standards, *309*

fiduciary duty, *310*
professional judgment, *308*

Yellow Book, *307*

Chapter References

Committee of Sponsoring Organizations of the Treadway Commission. 2002. *Internal Control— Integrated Framework.* New York: AICPA.

Louwers, T., R. Ramsay, D. Sinason, and J. Strawser. 2005. *Auditing and Assurance Services.* 1st ed. New York: McGraw-Hill/Irwin.

Wells, J. 2004. *Principles of Fraud Examination.* 1st ed. New York: John Wiley & Sons.

Whittington, R., and K. Pany. 2004. *Principles of Auditing and Other Assurance Services.* 14th ed. New York: McGraw-Hill/Irwin.

End-of-Chapter Activities

1. *Reading review questions.*
   a. List and discuss the seven types of audits described in the chapter.
   b. Explain the 10 generally accepted auditing standards that guide financial audits.
   c. Describe the common steps associated with an audit.
   d. Prepare a response to the questions for this chapter's "AIS in the Business World."

2. *Reading review problem.* Nolan pointed out that internal auditing is at a crossroads. Many large corporations pumped significant money into internal auditing departments when the Sarbanes-Oxley Act of 2002 passed; in today's stressed economy, those same corporations are trying to trim those budgets back. At the same time, organizations face many significant business issues and risks, such as fraud, systems, corporate social responsibility, corporate governance, privacy, and liquidity. Internal auditors need a broad skill set to address those risks and create value for organizations. Nolan's article advocates outsourcing parts of the internal auditing function to promote good cost control.

   Source: M. Nolan, "Internal Audit at the Crossroads," *Risk Management,* November 2008.

   a. In addition to internal audits, what other kinds of audits do accounting professionals commonly perform?
   b. How are the various types of audits similar to one another? How are they different?
   c. What concepts and standards guide financial statement audits?
   d. How is auditing related to your study of AIS?

3. *Multiple choice review.*
   1. When a financial statement auditor cannot determine if financial statements were prepared according to GAAP, the auditor issues a(n):
      a. Qualified opinion.
      b. Adverse opinion.
      c. Disclaimer of opinion.
      d. Exception report.

   2. A SAS 70 audit is otherwise known as a(n):
      a. Service organization audit.
      b. Auxiliary audit.
      c. Qualified audit.
      d. Operational audit.

3. Generally accepted auditing standards are divided into three groups. Which of the following correctly pairs a group with a standard?

   a. General, supervision
   b. Field work, independence
   c. Reporting, disclosure
   d. All of the above.

4. Which of the following steps in a financial statement audit normally occurs first?

   a. Assess management's integrity.
   b. Review the internal control system.
   c. Perform compliance testing.
   d. Evaluate management's credentials.

5. A company's financial statements implicitly involve several assertions by management that must be evaluated as part of auditing. Those assertions include: (i) existence or occurrence, (ii) completeness, (iii) ethical preparation.

   a. i and ii only
   b. i and iii only
   c. ii and iii only
   d. i, ii, and iii

4. *Making choices and exercising judgment.* Barb is an auditor for Vicenti, Lloyd and Stutzman (VLS), a regional CPA firm; she earned her CPA license three years ago and is supervising the audit team for CDR Corporation, a company that manufactures blank CDs. Last year's audit resulted in a qualified opinion, and both Barb and CDR's management are highly motivated to achieve a clean opinion this year. The audit team comprises four individuals (including Barb):

   - Richard has been with VLS a little over two years. He has passed three parts of the CPA exam and is currently working on the fourth part. He graduated with a 3.8 GPA from a prestigious local university and is working on CDR's audit for the first time. In previous audits, Richard has been in charge of inventory observation and bank reconciliations.

   - Laura joined VLS at the same time as Barb. She was licensed as a CPA one year ago. Laura has a master's degree in accounting from a local university and is an experienced auditor. In previous audits, she has taken the lead in evaluating internal controls and discussing audit matters with company management. This audit is her first for CDR Corporation.

   - Albert came to work for VLS from one of the Big Four CPA firms about six months before the CDR audit started. He is an experienced CPA and made the move to get better working hours and a better chance at becoming a partner. The CDR audit will be Albert's first for VLS.

What responsibilities should Barb assign to each member of the audit team for the CDR audit? Explain your choices.

5. *Field work.*

   a. Contact an experienced auditor in your area for an interview about common audit procedures. Compare the process with the generic one presented in Figure 17.3. Prepare a short report or presentation comparing and contrasting the two.

   b. Reviewing internal controls is an important part of any AIS evaluation. Visit a local business such as a restaurant, movie theater, bank, or amusement park; observe one or more common transactions and assess the strength of internal control over those transactions. Classify the internal controls as preventive, detective, or corrective. If you wanted to circumvent the internal control system, how would you do it?

   c. Using your work in (*b*) above as a basis, create a flowchart/data flow diagram/REA model of the transaction process.

d. Point your Web browser to www.soxtoolkit.com. Review and summarize the tools available for accountants and managers seeking to comply with the Sarbanes-Oxley Act of 2002.

e. Use your school's library to find Greg Rogers, "Environmental Transparency: Five Areas for Concern," *Financial Executive,* June 2004. Summarize the article and suggest at least three ways an auditor would discover undisclosed environmental liabilities.

6. *Audit types.* What type of audit is indicated in each of the following situations?

a. Checking internal controls over the sales/collection process.

b. Determining how an employee embezzled cash.

c. Establishing whether an audit conformed to all provisions of Sarbanes-Oxley.

d. Evaluating the accounting policy choices management made for conformity with GAAP.

e. Expressing an opinion on the fairness of a company's financial statements.

f. Inputting sample transactions and verifying the output from Peachtree.

g. Observing internal controls over inventory to improve process effectiveness.

h. Performing a comprehensive analysis of an Italian firm's accounting information system.

i. Using test data to determine how QuickBooks processes transactions.

j. Validating the assumptions made for a major capital investment.

7. *Generally accepted auditing standards.* Figure 17.2 presents a diagram of the 10 standards that govern financial audits. Prepare a similar, but original, diagram that illustrates the same concepts.

8. *Violations of GAAS.* Which of the 10 standards is violated in each of the following independent situations? Some situations may violate more than one.

a. A team of auditors, each with varying levels of experience, divided up the audit tasks and completed them independently before expressing an opinion on the statements.

b. An audit client changed its inventory cost flow assumption from LIFO to FIFO in the last year. The audit opinion makes no mention of the change.

c. Auditors relied solely on the client's assertions in evaluating account balances.

d. Austin supervised the audit team for a company in which he has an investment.

e. Chip relied solely on the client's assessment of its AIS integrity in determining compliance tests for an audit.

f. Sebastian conducted his first audit during his last semester of college. He audited the accounting information system of a nonprofit organization where he volunteers.

9. *Investigative audit.* For each independent case presented below, use Figure 17.1 as a guide in explaining the steps you would take to uncover fraud. Also suggest at least two internal controls that could have prevented the fraud described.

a. KC Group is basically a high-integrity company with sound approaches to financial reporting. Associates involved in financial reporting are of high competence and ethical values. KC Group has grown in recent years. There are new systems, sometimes administered by those who do not fully understand them. KC Group is performance driven, and managers are under tremendous pressure to make their goals. KC Group has acquired several new companies. Some of the associates in the acquired companies do not share certain values inherent in the KG culture. Consequently, reporting and integrity in some of these subsidiaries have proven to be a problem. At an acquired subsidiary, certain executives who never traveled had traditionally been allowed $2,000 to $25,000 in travel advances. These permanent travel advances were essentially noninterest-bearing loans. The subsidiary had been told to stop the practice. Instead, the subsidiary's controller obtained repayment checks from the executives and credited the travel advance account. Rather than actually depositing the checks at the bank before year-end, he held them until after the end of the year. He then issued company checks to the executives to replace the travel advances purportedly repaid.

The executives thus could cover their own checks by depositing company checks before their checks cleared. The controller back-dated the deposit slip reflecting the repayments from the executives and a fictitious deposit in transit. Although the amount was minor, the controller was knowingly and intentionally making false entries in the company records. (Source: C. Thompson, "The Reporting Challenge,"*Internal Auditor,* December 2002.)

b. During a routine audit of your client, you discover the price the company pays for widgets has doubled in the past year. Moreover, you notice all of the business is going to a new vendor. You check further and find the price of widgets on the open market is half what your client is currently paying. Maybe there is a legitimate reason for this anomaly. Or maybe it's a fraud. (Source: J. Wells, "Sherlock Holmes, CPA—Part 1," *Journal of Accountancy,* August 2003.)

10. *Terminology.* Please match each item on the left with the most appropriate item on the right.

1. Bank reconciliation	a. A "clean" opinion
2. Compliance	b. Field work standard
3. Disclosure	c. General standard
4. Flowcharting	d. Important in international audits
5. GAAP	e. Internal control example
6. Independence	f. Reporting standard
7. Internal control	g. Standard associated with financial statement audits
8. Laws and religion	h. Systems documentation technique often used in operational audits
9. Target	i. Type of audit most closely associated with governmental entities
10. Unqualified	j. Ultimate subject of an investigative audit

11. *Multiple choice.* Please select the best answer for each of the following questions.

1. An ERP system could be associated with ___ audits.

   a. Systems
   b. Financial
   c. Investigative
   d. All of the above.

2. In an investigative audit, co-conspirators are interviewed before the target

   a. Because the information they can provide is more important.
   b. So the investigative auditor will be certain to get a confession from the target.
   c. Because they can be offered a "deal" that will help prove the fraud.
   d. Because they are younger.

3. Which type of audit opinion ensures that financial statements are true and correct?

   a. Unqualified
   b. Qualified
   c. Both of the above.
   d. None of the above.

4. An auditor is dating an accounting manager in a firm he is auditing. His behavior is most likely in violation of a ___ standard.

   a. General
   b. Field work
   c. Reporting
   d. Forensic

5. A client refuses to let a financial statement auditor examine certain documents. The auditor is most likely to issue a(n) ____ opinion.

   a. Unqualified
   b. Qualified
   c. Disclaimer
   d. Adverse

12. *Statement evaluation.* Determine whether each of the following statements is (i) always true, (ii) sometimes true, or (iii) never true. For those that are (ii) sometimes true, explain when the statement is true.

   a. A disclaimed audit opinion means the financial statements contain errors.
   b. Audits focus on a company's financial statements.
   c. Field work standards contain guidelines for conducting an audit.
   d. Financial statement audits result in an unqualified opinion.
   e. Following the provisions of Sarbanes-Oxley, CEOs can delegate their responsibility to examine internal controls.
   f. In an investigative audit, the target should be interviewed first.
   g. Independent auditors in the United States help determine whether financial statements are true.
   h. Investigative audits examine five main assertions about financial statements.
   i. U.S. companies need to undergo annual financial statement audits.
   j. Weak internal controls lead to qualified audit opinions.

13. *Prior material application.*

   a. Consider the five generic AIS elements discussed in Chapter 1. A financial statement auditor might examine input documents like purchase orders for mathematical accuracy, complete information, and proper recording in the AIS. How might a financial statement auditor examine the other four generic elements of the AIS?
   b. Many organizations process thousands of transactions every year. An auditor, therefore, cannot possibly examine all of them in the course of an investigative audit. How would an investigative auditor determine which transactions to examine more closely?
   c. WHM Corporation recently established an internal audit function. The chief internal auditor has developed a plan for conducting operational audits throughout the organization but has not shared the plan with anyone else at WHM. How would you classify the plan based on the capability maturity model? Suggest some signs that would indicate the internal audit plan is moving up the model's hierarchy.
   d. All publicly traded corporations must now file their SEC documents using XBRL. How would the use of XBRL affect a financial statement audit? A systems audit?
   e. Your accounting degree opens up a broad array of career opportunities, one of which is auditing. Use Steps for Better Thinking to develop a plan for determining if you want to pursue auditing as a career. (Note that this question is not asking you to make the determination; rather, it's asking you to create a plan that will enable you to make an informed choice.)

Answers for Multiple Choice Review Questions

	Part One				
	Chapter 1	**Chapter 2**	**Chapter 3**	**Chapter 4**	**Chapter 5**
Question 1	A	A	D	A	B
Question 2	D	C	A	C	A
Question 3	C	A	B	D	C
Question 4	B	C	D	D	B
Question 5	B	D	A	C	D

	Part Two		
	Chapter 6	**Chapter 7**	**Chapter 8**
Question 1	B	B	A
Question 2	D	A	D
Question 3	A	D	B
Question 4	C	C	C
Question 5	D	A	C

	Part Three		
	Chapter 9	**Chapter 10**	**Chapter 11**
Question 1	B	D	B
Question 2	C	C	A
Question 3	C	B	D
Question 4	A	A	C
Question 5	D	A	A

	Part Four		
	Chapter 12	**Chapter 13**	**Chapter 14**
Question 1	B	D	B
Question 2	A	B	C
Question 3	C	B	B
Question 4	B	A	D
Question 5	D	C	D

	Part Five		
	Chapter 15	**Chapter 16**	**Chapter 17**
Question 1	B	A	C
Question 2	A	C	A
Question 3	B	C	C
Question 4	A	A	A
Question 5	C	C	A

Glossary

A

accounting   Accounting is the process of identifying, measuring, and communicating economic information to permit informed judgments and decisions by users of the information. (Ch. 2)

accounting cycle   The set of repetitive activities used to prepare general purpose financial statements. Although many parts of the accounting cycle can be completed more easily with information technology, some parts require significant human judgment and decision making. (Ch. 2)

accounting information system   A collection of interrelated processes, technologies, and documents designed to capture primarily financial data and process them into information for making decisions. (Ch. 1)

accounting information system (AIS) structure   Most accounting information systems comprise five parts: inputs (such as source documents), processing tools (such as general ledger software), outputs (such as the general purpose financial statements), storage (such as computer disks), and internal controls (such as separation of duties). (Ch. 1)

Adelphia Communications Corporation   Well-known fraud case involving a cable company. Key figure was John Rigas. (Ch. 16)

adjusting entries   Journal entries made at the end of an accounting period to account for timing differences between cash flow and accrual basis revenues and expenses. Types include accrued revenue, accrued expense, deferred revenue, prepaid assets, uncollectible receivables, and depreciation. (Ch. 2)

administrative security controls   One of three internal control types necessary to protect data integrity in a computerized information system. (Ch. 11)

agents   One element of a REA model. Agents can be internal (such as a sales clerk) or external (such as a customer). In laying out a REA model, agents should be in the third column from the left. (Ch. 8)

application service providers   Companies that deliver software on an as-needed basis to their clients. (Ch. 10)

auditing   A systematic review of an organization's accounting information system, often for the purpose of expressing an opinion on the financial statements. (Ch. 17)

auditing standards   The rules auditors use to promote integrity and consistency in the audit process. Often referred to collectively as GAAS (generally accepted auditing standards). (Ch. 17)

B

balanced   Characteristic of a set of data flow diagrams. Balanced diagrams do not allow symbols to disappear between levels. (Ch. 7)

basic principles of business process management   The text discusses seven principles suggested by Eppele. The seven principles focus on the relationship between BPM and strategy, attitude toward change, top management support, focusing on people, external consultants, task definition, and communication. (Ch. 4)

basic principles of information security   Confidentiality, availability, and data integrity are the three basic principles of information security. They are often referred to as the C-I-A triad. (Ch. 11)

benefits of XBRL   XBRL facilitates information exchange regardless of hardware or software platform. In addition, XBRL is flexible, allowing users to create their own tags when the need arises. (Ch. 9)

bookkeeping   The process of recording transactions in a journal, posting them to ledger accounts, and preparing basic financial statements. Though often confused with accounting, bookkeeping is distinct; it focuses on the mechanical aspects and rules of accounting and often can be completed more easily with the aid of information technology. (Ch. 2)

bounded rationality   The idea that most decision makers will avoid uncertainty; rather, they will depend on a set of rules for making decisions. (Ch. 15)

Brown's taxonomy of risk   A way of looking at and categorizing risk. Four broad categories include financial, operational, strategic, and hazard. (Ch. 3)

business process   The set of steps associated with an activity; one way an organization creates value. The processes discussed in the text include sales/collection, acquisition/payment, conversion, financing, and human resources. (Ch. 12)

business process management   Analyzing business processes with a view toward making them more efficient and/or effective. (Ch. 4)

C

capability maturity model   A five-stage model developed by Humphrey, used to categorize and improve business processes. (Ch. 5)

cardinalities   Relationships between elements of a REA model. Cardinalities are set up in pairs, with each element of the pair having a minimum value and a maximum value. Proper design of cardinalities facilitates the development of a relational database. (Ch. 8)

career plan   The plans an accountant makes for his/her career in the profession. (Ch. 16)

causes of ERP implementation failure   ERP systems most often fail because of poor planning and lack of strategic vision. The chapter discusses other causes of ERP failure. (Ch. 10)

causes of information overload   As discussed in the chapter, at least five things can cause information overload: personal factors, information technology, information characteristics, organizational design, and task and process parameters. (Ch. 15)

characteristics of a professional   Bell's list includes seven components: communicates effectively; thinks rationally, logically, and coherently; appropriately uses technical knowledge; integrates knowledge from many disciplines; exhibits ethical professional behavior; recognizes the influence of political, social, economic, legal, and regulatory forces; and actively seeks additional knowledge. (Ch. 16)

Charles Ponzi   Originator of the fraud, now labeled a "Ponzi scheme," that involves paying off old investors with money from new investors, rather than money generated by an investment itself. (Ch. 16)

CoBIT accountability framework   The accountability framework shows the relationships between six groups of people as part of that process: stakeholders, board of directors, audit committee, IT and information security management, internal audit, and external audit. (Ch. 11)

CoBIT framework   The CoBIT framework (Control Objectives for Information and Related Technology) was developed by the Information Systems Audit and Control Association (ISACA) to provide guidance for information systems internal controls. (Ch. 11)

CoBIT information criteria   The ideal characteristics for information. They include effectiveness, efficiency, confidentiality, integrity, availability, compliance, and reliability. (Ch. 11)

common files   AIS include three major types of files: master, transaction, and junction. Every business process has specific examples of them. (Chs. 12, 13)

computer networks   The defining feature of e-commerce. Computers can be networked via hardware or software, in the same physical location or different physical locations. (Ch. 10)

conceptual framework of accounting   A document produced by the Financial Accounting Standards Board in 1977, intended to guide the development of future accounting principles. Parts include objective of financial reporting, elements of financial statements, qualitative characteristics of accounting information, assumptions, principles, and constraints. (Ch. 1)

conditions for a successful ERP implementation   Conditions include organizational commitment, clearly communicated strategic goals for the project, and involvement of the entire organization. (Ch. 10)

context diagram   Highest-level data flow diagram. Contains the least detail. Depicts a business process in a single circle, showing its interaction with external entities. (Ch. 7)

conversion process   The process of combining raw material, labor, and overhead in the production of finished goods. (Ch. 14)

Cost-benefit analysis   The process of analyzing an alternatives costs and benefits, not all of which are expressed in dollar terms. Should be utilized when designing internal controls and other elements of the AIS to ensure that benefits outweigh costs. (Ch. 4)

COSO   Committee of Sponsoring Organizations of the Treadway Commission. Includes five organizations: the Institute of Management Accountants, the American Institute of Certified Public Accountants, the American Accounting Association, the Institute of Internal Auditors, and the Financial Executives Institute. Created two important documents (integrated frameworks) related to internal control and risk management. (Ch. 3)

countermeasures   Actions people can take to avoid, or reduce the effects of, information overload. Examples include allowing additional time to complete important tasks and using graphs or other visual aids. (Ch. 15)

D

data flow   One of four elements of a data flow diagram. Depicted with an arrow. Always contains a noun phrase as a label, such as "purchase order information." (Ch. 7)

data store   One of four elements of a data flow diagram. Depicted with two parallel lines containing a noun phrase label, such as "employee database." (Ch. 7)

database tables   Primary organizational element of a relational database. Composed of fields and records. Each record must contain a primary key that uniquely identifies it. (Ch. 7)

definitions of ethics   Rules or standards governing the conduct of a person or the members of a profession (www.dictionary.com). Others are presented in the chapter as well. (Ch. 16)

document flowcharts   One of four flowchart types discussed in the chapter. Follows the flow of one or more documents through an information system. (Ch. 6)

documents   Hard copy or electronic forms, often used as the basis for data entry in an accounting information system. For the sales/collection process, they may include remittance advices and customer invoices; in the acquisition/payment process, they may include purchase orders and receiving reports. (Chs. 12, 13)

E

e-business categories Most taxonomies in this area identify five categories: business-to-business, business-to-consumer, government-to-consumer, government-to-business, and consumer-to-consumer. (Ch. 10)

e-commerce The process of conducting business using computer networks. (Ch. 10)

eight-step model Generic process for responding to ethical problems developed by Langenderfer and Rockness. (Ch. 16)

Enron/Arthur Andersen At the time, the largest bankruptcy in U.S. history. Issues of organizational culture and reward systems contributed to financial statement fraud through the use of special-purpose entities and non-GAAP revenue recognition policies. Andersen served as Enron's independent auditor; the scandal led to the demise of both firms. (Ch. 16)

enterprise resource planning system A very large relational database, designed to capture data for use in decision making. Most ERP systems are organized into modules such as human resource management and supply chain management. (Ch. 10)

Enterprise Risk Management: Integrated Framework
One of two COSO documents. Contains eight elements to help professionals think about managing risk: internal environment, objective setting, event identification, risk assessment, risk response, control activities, information and communication, and monitoring. (Ch. 4)

events One element of a REA model. Events typically fall into one of three categories: operating, information, and decision/management. Only strategically significant operating events appear in a REA model; examples include selling services to a client or paying employees. Information events, such as updating ledger account balances, focus on recording and maintaining data, as well as reporting information. Decision/management events involve human decision making, such as changing compensation packages. (Ch. 8)

expectancy theory Motivation = Expectancy × Instrumentality × Valence. Suggested by Vroom. (Ch. 4)

external entity One of four elements of a data flow diagram. Depicted with a rectangle. Represents an entity outside the boundary of an information system, such as a vendor. (Ch. 7)

external transactions Transactions that involve parties external to the organization. Typically do not require adjusting entries at the end of a period. Examples include selling inventory, purchasing plant assets, and paying vendors. (Ch. 2)

F

fiduciary duty The responsibility of an accountant to act in the best interests of others, such as stockholders. (Ch. 17)

financing process The process of acquiring external funding, most commonly through debt or equity. (Ch. 14)

financing process transactions Issuance of capital stock, purchase of treasury shares, issuance and repayment of long-term debt, and dividend distributions. (Ch. 14)

Foreign Corrupt Practices Act One of the earliest laws focused on business ethics. Passed in 1977. Prohibits conduct that would be considered illegal in the United States, even if that conduct is acceptable in foreign countries. (Ch. 3)

foreign keys A field in a database table that is a primary key in another table. For example, a customer identification number would be a primary key in the customer table and a foreign key in a sales transaction table. (Ch. 7)

freight terms Terms that govern when title to merchandise passes from the seller to the buyer (destination or shipping point) and who is responsible for the cost of freight (collect or prepaid). (Ch. 12)

G

general purpose financial statements Collective term referring to the balance sheet, income statement, statement of changes in equity, and statement of cash flows. Must be prepared in accordance with generally accepted accounting principles. (Ch. 2)

generalized model of BPM Seven generic steps associated with many business process management initiatives. (Ch. 4)

H

hardware flowcharts One of four flowchart types discussed in the chapter. Depicts the hardware layout of an information system. (Ch. 6)

human judgment A critical element of accounting and accounting information systems. For example, accountants exercise judgment in deciding which transactions are recordable in the AIS and in making decisions based on financial information. (Ch. 2)

human resource process Associated with personnel activities in an organization, from the time of hiring to the time of discharge via retirement, termination, or quitting. (Ch. 14)

I

information competence The ability to formulate research questions, locate the information to answer the questions, evaluate information quality, and use it for decision making. (Ch. 1)

information overload One factor that negatively impacts decision making. Symptoms and effects include limited information retrieval strategies, increased stress, arbitrary analysis, and suboptimal decisions. (Ch. 15)

information technology   Computer hardware and software, often employed in accounting information systems to make routine tasks more efficient. Examples include general ledger packages and enterprise resource planning software. (Ch. 2)

instance document   As applied in XBRL, an instance document refers to properly tagged information. For example, a balance sheet with XBRL tags would be an instance document. (Ch. 9)

internal control   One element of an accounting information system. Policies and procedures designed to achieve four objectives: safeguarding assets, ensuring financial statement reliability, promoting operational efficiency, and encouraging compliance with management's directives. (Chs. 3, 12, 13)

Internal Control: Integrated Framework   One of two COSO documents. Contains five elements to help professionals think about internal control: control environment, risk assessment, control activities, information and communications, and monitoring. (Ch. 3)

internal transactions   Transactions that do not involve parties external to the organization. Typically require adjusting entries at the end of an accounting period. Examples include depreciation of fixed assets and the use of prepaid assets such as supplies. (Ch. 2)

iterative   In the context of accounting information systems, iterative refers to the idea that steps don't always proceed in a linear fashion and/or that the development of systems documentation, internal controls, and other AIS elements is rarely accomplished in a single attempt. (Ch. 5)

J

job costing   A production operation typically associated with unique, customized, or made-to-order goods. Examples include consulting assignments and custom-built homes. (Ch. 14)

junction table   Type of relational database table used to capture cardinalities where the maximum is many on both ends. For example, consider this cardinality: Sales (0,*)—(1,*) Inventory. That cardinality indicates that each sale involves one to many items of inventory; each item of inventory can be included in zero to many sales transactions. A junction table would be required in this situation. It would capture data such as the sales transaction number and inventory item numbers for each transaction. (Ch. 8)

justice model   One of four schools of ethical thought discussed in the chapter. Relies on the idea that people should get what they deserve. (Ch. 16)

K

knowledge management   The way(s) managers and other decision makers organize knowledge to facilitate decision making. (Ch. 15)

L

Level Zero diagram   One element of a leveled set of data flow diagrams. The next level down from a context diagram. Shows the processes, data flows, data stores, and external entities of an information system at a high level, but with more detail than a context diagram. (Ch. 7)

leveled sets   Applied to data flow diagrams. Refers to the idea that business processes are decomposed into greater levels of detail until they cannot be decomposed any more. Leveled sets of data flow diagrams must be balanced. (Ch. 7)

M

macro-level issues   The "big picture" issues to be considered in adopting a specific form of information technology. The chapter discusses need, strategic fit, personnel involvement, and financing. (Ch. 5)

McCarthy   Professor credited with the development of REA modeling techniques and their application to accounting information systems. (Ch. 8)

micro-level issues   The more focused issues to be considered in adopting a specific form of information technology. The chapter discusses cost, adaptability, training, and vendor reliability. (Ch. 5)

Microsoft Visio   Software that can be used to create flowcharts and other forms of systems documentation. (Ch. 6)

N

namespace   Related to XBRL. A place on the Internet that defines tags used for coding. Users can use an existing namespace and/or create one of their own. (Ch. 9)

normalization   The rules for creating an efficient, effective relational database. Although six normal forms exist, most organizations use only the first three as a practical matter. The rules are summarized at **www.datamodel.org/ NormalizationRules.html**. (Ch. 8)

normative ethics   Statements about what is right and what is wrong. For example, "people shouldn't cheat" or "lying is wrong." (Ch. 16)

P

payroll forms   The forms commonly used to process payroll transactions. Examples include Form W-4, Form W-2, payroll register, employee earnings record, Form 1099, Form 940, and Form 941. (Ch. 14)

perpetrators   People who commit crimes, specifically involving information systems. (Ch. 11)

physical security controls   One of three internal control types necessary to protect data integrity in a computerized information system. (Ch. 11)

popular/practitioner information   One of three information types used in accounting information systems. This type of information has often been through some review and editing process but may not rely on strict research protocols. Examples include *Strategic Finance, Fraud Magazine,* and the *Journal of Accountancy.* (Ch. 1)

primary key   The field in a database table that uniquely identifies each record in the table. For example, a product identification code in an inventory table. (Ch. 7)

primitive   The lowest level of decomposition for processes in a data flow diagram. Systems analysts and designers use judgment in selecting/establishing primitive processes. (Ch. 7)

principles of debit and credit   The rules used to record transactions in a journal. Assets and expenses increase with debits and decrease with credits; liabilities, equity, and revenue follow the opposite rules. (Ch. 2)

process   Any set of procedures an organization uses to gather data, change the data into information, or report the information to system users. Depicted in data flow diagrams with circles, each of which has both a number and a name. (Ch. 7)

process costing   A production operation typically associated with mass-produced, undifferentiated goods such as flash drives. (Ch. 14)

professional judgment   A key element of the audit process and accounting information systems design and implementation. (Ch. 17)

program flowcharts   One of four flowchart types discussed in the chapter. Illustrates the logic of a computer program and the steps required to complete it. (Ch. 6)

Q

queries   One object in relational databases. Allow the user to ask questions of the database based on specific conditions. For example, what are the names of all customers with credit limits exceeding $10,000? (Ch. 7)

R

relapse errors   The human tendency to make the same mistakes repeatedly, even when determined not to. (Ch. 15)

relational database   A type of software that allows users to enter data, ask questions about the data, and create reports in response to those questions. Microsoft Access is an example of relational database software, which forms the basis for event-driven accounting systems. Enterprise resource planning systems are a sophisticated form of relational databases. (Ch. 8)

resources   One element of a REA model. Resources refer to items such as inventory, cash, and supplies, which are required to carry out the events in a REA model. In

a properly constructed REA model, all resources appear in the leftmost column. (Ch. 8)

rights and duties   One of four schools of ethical thought discussed in the chapter. Relies on the idea that people have specific rights that should not be compromised by others. (Ch. 16)

risks and threats   Potential hazards for information systems. The development of internal controls often begins by identifying risks and threats. (Ch. 11)

rules/conventions   The rules associated with creating data flow diagrams. (Ch. 7)

S

Sarbanes-Oxley Act of 2002   Federal legislative response to the corporate scandals of the late 20th century. Imposes specific duties on managers and auditors for the review of internal controls, disclosures, and related issues. Specifies fines and penalties for noncompliance. (Ch. 3)

satisficing   The idea that decision makers will not necessarily look for the best solution to a problem—just a solution that solves the problem. (Ch. 15)

scholarly information   One of three information types used in accounting information systems. This type of information is intended primarily for an academic audience and has been through a rigorous review process before publication. Typically follows strict research protocols. Examples include *Accounting, Behavior and Organizations* and the *Journal of Accounting Research.* (Ch. 1)

six-step process   The steps AIS designers take to develop a REA model. (Ch. 8)

SmartDraw   Software that can be used to create flowcharts and other forms of systems documentation. www.smartdraw .com. (Ch. 6)

source documents   Paper-based or electronic documents often used as the basis for journal entries in an accounting information system. Examples include remittance advices, purchase orders, and check stubs. (Ch. 2)

specification   A specific example of a larger group. For example, "California" is a specification of "U.S. states." XBRL is a specification of a larger family of languages called XML (eXtensible Markup Language). (Ch. 9)

sponsored/commercial information   One of three information types used in accounting information systems. This type of information may be less objective than the other two forms but can be useful in researching specific products or gaining a company's point of view on an issue. Examples include www. peoplesoft.com and www.findaccountingsoftware.com. (Ch. 1)

steps   The common activities associated with a business process. Although the steps may vary slightly for some processes between organizations, certain common elements are nearly always present. (Chs. 12, 13)

Steps for Better Thinking A decision-making model developed by Wolcott and Lynch. The model is organized in five levels: knowing, identifying, exploring, prioritizing, and envisioning. (Ch. 15)

steps to create a knowledge management system The seven-step process for creating a knowledge management system (recommended by Call) begins with developing an organizational culture that supports knowledge sharing and concludes with periodically reevaluating the system's value and making needed adjustments. (Ch. 15)

strategically significant operating activities The subset of operating activities depicted in a REA model. AIS designers use judgment to identify strategically significant operating activities, which may include things such as purchasing inventory and paying vendors. (Ch. 8)

symbols Elements of a flowchart and other forms of systems documentation. (Ch. 6)

systems development life cycle Generic set of steps used to develop, implement, and maintain information systems. Four iterative phases include analysis, logical design, physical design, and implementation and maintenance. (Ch. 5)

systems flowcharts One of four flowchart types discussed in the chapter. Shows the components of an information system. Of the four types, this one is used most often in accounting information systems work. (Ch. 6)

T

taxonomies In general, a taxonomy is a way of organizing knowledge. In XBRL, a taxonomy refers to a specific set of tags, most often associated with an industry group. For example, XBRL contains government accounting taxonomies and manufacturing industry taxonomies. (Ch. 9)

taxonomy for computer crime A classification system for computer crime. Carter's taxonomy has four parts: target, instrumentality, incidental, and associated. (Ch. 11)

technical security controls One of three internal control types necessary to protect data integrity in a computerized information system. (Ch. 11)

three-stage process Framework proposed by Sylla and Wen regarding the adoption of information technology. Stages include intangible benefits evaluation, IT investment risk analysis, and tangible benefits evaluation. (Ch. 5)

U

unstructured problems Frequently encountered in the study of accounting information systems and the practice of accounting. Refers to problems without single, correct responses/solutions that require creativity and judgment. Unstructured problems may have more than one acceptable answer, although some responses to them may clearly be incorrect or inappropriate. (Ch. 1)

utilitarian model of ethics One of four schools of ethical thought discussed in the chapter. Relies on the idea that the "end justifies the means." (Ch. 16)

V

value chain Model suggested by Porter that describes how organizations create value. Activities are in two groups: primary and support. (Ch. 12)

virtues model One of four schools of ethical thought discussed in the chapter. Relies on the idea that people should do what is right/moral/virtuous. (Ch. 16)

W

Watts Humphrey First suggested the capability maturity model. (Ch. 5)

weighted-rating technique System for comparing specific software packages. The user selects a list of criteria, such as cost and ease of use, and assigns each criterion a weight. Then, each software package is rated on each criterion. The rating is multiplied by the weighting to arrive at an overall weighted score, which informs (but does not dictate) the choice. (Ch. 5)

X

XBRL The eXtensible Business Reporting Language. A software- and hardware-independent way of coding financial data. According to **www.xbrl.org**, it is "a language for the electronic communication of business and financial data which is set to revolutionize business reporting around the world." (Ch. 9)

Y

Yellow Book A document published by the Government Accountability Office (GAO) that explains the rules for conducting a compliance audit. (Ch. 17)

Comprehensive Chapter References

ASPNews.com. 2002. "ASPNews Glossary." www .aspnews.com/strategies/asp_basics/article.php/759691 (January 11).

Association of Certified Fraud Examiners. 2010. *Report to the Nations on Occupational Fraud and Abuse.* Downloaded 31 January 2011 from www.acfe.com.

Barker, T., and M. Frolick. 2003. "ERP Implementation Failure: A Case Study." *Information Systems Management,* Fall, pp. 43–49.

Bell, N. 2004. "Characteristics of a Risk Management and Insurance Professional." www.wsu.edu/~belln/ (October 4, 2004).

Betsch, T. S. Haberstroh, B. Molter, and A. Glockner. 2004. "Oops, I Did It Again—Relapse Errors in Routinized Decision Making." *Organizational Behavior and Human Decision Processes* 93, no. 1, pp. 62–74.

Bradford, M., S. Richtermeyer, and D. Roberts. 2007. "System Diagramming Techniques: An Analysis of Methods Used in Accounting Education and Practice." *Journal of Information Systems,* Spring, pp. 173–212.

Brown, B. 2001. "Step-by-Step Enterprise Risk Management." *Risk Management,* September, pp. 43–49.

Call, D. 2005. "Knowledge Management—Not Rocket Science." *Journal of Knowledge Management* 9, no. 2, pp. 19–30.

Carter, D. 1995. "Computer Crime Categories." *FBI Law Enforcement Bulletin,* pp. 21–28.

Committee of Sponsoring Organizations of the Treadway Commission. 1985. *Internal Control: Integrated Framework.* New York: Committee of Sponsoring Organizations of the Treadway Commission.

Committee of Sponsoring Organizations of the Treadway Commission. 2002. *Internal Control: Integrated Framework.* New York: AICPA.

Committee of Sponsoring Organizations of the Treadway Commission. 2004. *Enterprise Risk Management: Integrated Framework.* New York: Committee of Sponsoring Organizations of the Treadway Commission.

Committee of Sponsoring Organizations of the Treadway Commission. 2006. *Internal Control over Financial Reporting—Guidance for Smaller Public Companies.* New York: Committee of Sponsoring Organizations of the Treadway Commission.

Curzon, S. 1995. *Information Competence in the CSU.* www.calstate.edu/LS/Archive/info_comp_report.shtml (May 25, 2005).

Debreceny, R., and S. White. 2005, June. *XBRL Working Paper.*

DeMarco, T. 1979. *Structured Analysis and Systems Specifications.* Englewood Cliffs, NJ: Prentice Hall.

Dictionary.com. 2004. "Ethics." http://dictionary. reference.com/search?q=ethics (October 4).

Drucker, P. 1993. *Post-Capitalist Society.* New York: Harper Row Publishing.

Egerdahl, R. 1995. "A Risk Matrix Approach to Data Processing Facility Audits." *Internal Auditor,* June, pp. 34–40.

Eppler, M., and J. Mengis. 2004. "The Concept of Information Overload: A Review of Literature from Organization Science, Accounting, Marketing, MIS and Related Disciplines." *Information Society,* pp. 325–44.

Halbert, J. 2003. "Mining Back Office Operations May Bolster the Bottom Line." *Los Angeles Business Journal,* April 14. www.findarticles.com (last visited November 4, 2004).

Harmon, P., and C. Wolf. 2008. *The State of Business Process Management.* San Francisco: Business Process Trends.

Hoffner, J., J. George, and J. Valacich. 1996. *Modern Systems Analysis and Design.* Reading, MA: Benjamin/ Cummings.

Hollander, A. S., E. L. Denna, and J. O. Cherrington. 2000. *Accounting, Information Technology, and Business Solutions.* 2nd ed. New York: McGraw-Hill/Irwin.

Hurst, J. 2007. *The Capability Maturity Model and Its Applications.* www.giac.org/resources/whitepaper/ application/242.php (September 15, 2008).

Hurt, R. 1994. "Wholelife Counseling Center." *Journal of Accounting Case Research,* pp. 97–98.

Internet Encyclopedia of Philosophy. 2004. "Ethics." www.utm.edu/research/iep/e/ethics.htm (October 4).

Johnston, R. 2003. "A Strategy for Finding the Right Accounting Software." *Journal of Accountancy,* September, pp. 39–46.

Jonietz, E. 2001. "Wireless Stockroom." *Technology Review,* July/August, p. 32.

Kishel, G., and P. Kishel. 1993. "Safeguarding Your Business." *Black Enterprise,* July, pp. 98–104.

Langenderfer, H., and J. Rockness. 1989. "Integrating Ethics into the Accounting Curriculum: Issues, Problems, and Solutions." *Journal of Accounting Education,* Spring, pp. 58–69.

Lemos, Robert. 2006. "Gangland Web Attacks: How Not to Get Whacked by the Botnet Mafia." *PC Magazine* 25, no. 13 (August), p. 116. ABI/INFORM Trade & Industry database (Document ID: 1107044611, February 1, 2009).

Louwers, T., R. Ramsay, D. Sinason, and J. Strawser. 2005. *Auditing and Assurance Services.* 1st ed. New York: McGraw-Hill/Irwin.

McCarthy, W. E. 1982. "The REAL Accounting Model: A Generalized Framework for Accounting Systems in a Shared Data Environment." *Accounting Review,* July, pp. 554–77.

McDonald, C. 2001. "A Review of Continuing Professional Education." *Journal of Continuing Higher Education,* Winter, pp. 29–40.

Merchant, K., and W. Van der Stede. 2003. *Management Control Systems.* Upper Saddle River, NJ: Prentice Hall.

Misek, M. 2004. "Home Is Where the Art Is." *Emedia,* August, pp. 36–38.

Nesbitt, K. 2002, February 8. "Designing a Knowledge Management System." http://academic.edu.2081/products/faulknerlibrary/00018382.htm (May 2, 2005).

Poole, V. 2006. "Why Information Security Governance Is Critical to Wider Corporate Governance Demands— A European Perspective." *Information Systems Control Journal* 1, pp. 23–25.

Porter, M. 1985. *Competitive Advantage: Creating and Sustaining Superior Performance.* New York: Free Press.

Ricciardi, S. 1994 . "Database Design: Redundancy and Normalization." *PC Magazine,* January 25, pp. 285–89.

Rowley, J. 1999. "What Is Knowledge Management?" *Library Management,* pp. 416–19.

Santosus, M., and J. Surmacz. 2005. "The ABCs of Knowledge Management." www.cio.com (April 28).

Seppanen, M., S. Kumar, and C. Chandra. 2005. *Process Analysis and Improvement: Tools and Techniques.* 1st ed. New York: McGraw-Hill/Irwin.

Simon, H. 1997. *Administrative Behavior.* 4th ed. New York: Free Press.

SmartDraw.com. 2008. "Standard and Methodologies." www.smartdraw.com/tutorials/bpm/methodologies.htm (August 27).

Spiceland, J. D., J. Sepe, M. W. Nelson, and L. A. Tomassini 2009. *Intermediate Accounting.* 5th ed. New York: McGraw-Hill/Irwin.

Stapleton, G., and C. Rezak. 2004. "Change Management Underpins a Successful ERP Implementation at Marathon Oil." *Journal of Organizational Excellence,* Autumn, pp. 15–21.

Sylla, C., and H. J. Wen. 2002. "A Conceptual Framework for Evaluation of Information Technology Investments." *International Journal of Technology Management,* pp. 236–61.

Thorp, J. A. 1991. "European Uniform Chart of Accounts." *Management Accounting,* July/August, pp. 20–23.

Trites, G. D. 2002. *Audit and Control Implications of XBRL.* Toronto, Ontario: Canadian Institute of Chartered Accountants.

Umble, E., and M. Umble. 2002. "Avoiding ERP Implementation Failure." *Industrial Management,* January/February, pp. 25–34.

Vroom, V. H. 1964. *Work and Motivation.* San Francisco: Jossey-Bass.

Walker, K. B., and E. Denna. 1997. "Arrivederci, Pacioli? A New Accounting System Is Emerging." *Management Accounting,* July, pp. 22–30.

Wells, J. 2004. *Principles of Fraud Examination.* 1st ed. New York: John Wiley & Sons.

Whittington, R., and K. Pany. 2004. *Principles of Auditing and Other Assurance Services.* 14th ed. New York: McGraw-Hill/Irwin.

Williamson, D. 2006. "Coding Systems for Accountants: An Introduction." www.duncanwil.co.ukcu.de.htm (June 10, 2006).

Wolcott, S., and C. Lynch. 2005. "Steps for Better Thinking." www.wolcottlynch.com (April 29).

XBRL International. www.xbrl.org.

Index

Bold page numbers indicate glossary definitions.